Legal Notice

All content in this book is the original and exclusive work of Dr. Steve Warner

This book is copyright 2018 with all rights reserved. It is illegal to copy, distribute, or create derivative works from this book in whole or in part or to contribute to the copying, distribution, or creating of derivative works of this book.

For information on bulk purchases and licensing agreements, please email

support@SATMathPrep.com

SAT® is a trademark registered by the College Board, which is not affiliated with, and does not endorse this publication.

BOOKS FROM THE GET 800 COLLECTION FOR COLLEGE BOUND STUDENTS

28 SAT Math Lessons to Improve Your Score in One Month
    Beginner Course
    Intermediate Course
    Advanced Course
New SAT Math Problems arranged by Topic and Difficulty Level
320 SAT Math Problems arranged by Topic and Difficulty Level
500 SAT Math Problems arranged by Topic and Difficulty Level
SAT Verbal Prep Book for Reading and Writing Mastery
320 SAT Math Subject Test Problems
    Level 1 Test
    Level 2 Test
320 SAT Chemistry Subject Test Problems
Vocabulary Builder
28 ACT Math Lessons to Improve Your Score in One Month
    Beginner Course
    Intermediate Course
    Advanced Course
320 ACT Math Problems arranged by Topic and Difficulty Level
320 GRE Math Problems arranged by Topic and Difficulty Level
320 AP Calculus AB Problems
320 AP Calculus BC Problems
Physics Mastery for Advanced High School Students
400 SAT Physics Subject Test and AP Physics Problems
SHSAT Verbal Prep Book to Improve Your Score in Two Months
555 Math IQ Questions for Middle School Students
555 Advanced Math Problems for Middle School Students
555 Geometry Problems for High School Students
Algebra Handbook for Gifted Middle School Students
1000 Logic and Reasoning Questions for Gifted and Talented
    Elementary School Students

CONNECT WITH DR. STEVE WARNER

www.facebook.com/SATPrepGet800

www.youtube.com/TheSATMathPrep

www.twitter.com/SATPrepGet800

www.linkedin.com/in/DrSteveWarner

www.pinterest.com/SATPrepGet800

plus.google.com/+SteveWarnerPhD

48 New SAT Math Lessons to Improve Your Score in 48 Days

For the Revised SAT March 2016 and Beyond

Dr. Steve Warner

© 2018, All Rights Reserved

Table of Contents

Actions to Complete Before You Read This Book — vi

Introduction: The Proper Way to Prepare — 7
    1. Using this book effectively — 7
    2. Calculator use — 9
    3. Tips for taking the SAT — 10

Lesson 1 – Heart of Algebra: Solving Linear Equations — 13
Lesson 2 – Passport to Advanced Math: Factoring — 21
Lesson 3 – Problem Solving: Ratios — 31
Lesson 4 – Geometry: Lines and Angles — 37
Lesson 5 – Heart of Algebra: Solving Linear Inequalities — 46
Lesson 6 – Passport to Advanced Math: Functions — 53
Lesson 7 – Problem Solving: Tables — 59
Lesson 8 – Geometry: Triangles — 66
Lesson 9 – Heart of Algebra: Setting Up Linear Expressions — 73
Lesson 10 – Passport to Advanced Math: Graphs of Functions — 80
Lesson 11 – Problem Solving: Graphs — 91
Lesson 12 – Geometry: Circles — 98
Lesson 13 – Heart of Algebra: Additional Practice 1 — 106
Lesson 14 – Passport to Advanced Math: Additional Practice 1 — 109
Lesson 15 – Problem Solving: Additional Practice 1 — 112
Lesson 16 – Geometry: Additional Practice 1 — 117
Lesson 17 – Heart of Algebra: Equations of Lines and Their Graphs — 120
Lesson 18 – Passport to Advanced Math: Operations on Polynomials — 128
Lesson 19 – Problem Solving: Statistics — 135
Lesson 20 – Geometry: Solid Geometry — 143
Lesson 21 – Heart of Algebra: Interpreting Linear Expressions — 149
Lesson 22 – Passport to Advanced Math: Exponents and Roots — 156
Lesson 23 – Problem Solving: Data Analysis — 162
Lesson 24 – Geometry: Parallel Lines and Symmetry — 170
Lesson 25 – Heart of Algebra: Manipulating Linear Expressions — 179
Lesson 26 – Passport to Advanced Math: Manipulating Nonlinear Expressions — 184
Lesson 27 – Problem Solving: Scatterplots — 191
Lesson 28 – Complex Numbers: Operations — 198
Lesson 29 – Heart of Algebra: Additional Practice 2 — 203
Lesson 30 – Passport to Advanced Math: Additional Practice 2 — 206
Lesson 31 – Problem Solving: Additional Practice 2 — 209
Lesson 32 – Geometry and Complex Numbers: Additional Practice 2 — 213
Lesson 33 – Heart of Algebra: Solving Linear Systems of Equations — 216
Lesson 34 – Passport to Advanced Math: Solving Quadratic Equations — 224
Lesson 35 – Problem Solving: Percents — 234
Lesson 36 – Trigonometry: Right Triangle Trigonometry — 239

Lesson 37 – Heart of Algebra: Setting Up Linear Systems	246
Lesson 38 – Passport to Advanced Math: Nonlinear Systems of Equations	252
Lesson 39 – Problem Solving: Probability	258
Lesson 40 – Geometry: Polygons	263
Lesson 41 – Heart of Algebra: Advanced Linear Systems	271
Lesson 42 – Passport to Advanced Math: Graphs of Parabolas	279
Lesson 43 – Problem Solving: Growth	288
Lesson 44 – Coordinate Geometry: Graphs of Circles	294
Lesson 45 – Heart of Algebra: Additional Practice 3	301
Lesson 46 – Passport to Advanced Math: Additional Practice 3	304
Lesson 47 – Problem Solving: Additional Practice 3	307
Lesson 48 – Geometry and Complex Numbers: Additional Practice 3	311
Actions to Complete After You Have Read This Book	**314**
About the Author	*315*
Books by Dr. Steve Warner	**316**

ACTIONS TO COMPLETE BEFORE YOU READ THIS BOOK

1. Purchase a TI-84 or equivalent calculator

It is recommended that you use a TI-84 or comparable calculator for the SAT. Answer explanations in this book will always assume you are using such a calculator.

2. Take a practice SAT to get your preliminary SAT math score

You can use your last PSAT/SAT math score or an official College Board practice SAT for this. Use this score to help you determine the problems you should be focusing on (see page 8 for details).

3. Claim your FREE bonuses

See page 314 for a link that will give you access to solutions to all the supplemental problems in this book.

4. 'Like' my Facebook page

This page is updated regularly with SAT prep advice, tips, tricks, strategies, and practice problems. Visit the following webpage and click the 'like' button.

www.facebook.com/SATPrepGet800

INTRODUCTION
THE PROPER WAY TO PREPARE

There are many ways that a student can prepare for the SAT. But not all preparation is created equal. I always teach my students the methods that will give them the maximum result with the minimum amount of effort.

The book you are about to read is a self-contained math guide for the SAT. Each lesson was carefully created to ensure that you are making the most effective use of your time while preparing for the test. Problems in this book are indistinguishable from actual SAT math questions and all concepts and strategies that you need to know will be covered here.

There are two math sections on the SAT: one where a calculator is allowed and one where it is not. I therefore recommend trying to solve as many problems as possible both with and without a calculator. If a calculator is required for a specific problem, it will be marked with an asterisk (*).

Note: "Problem Solving" questions appear only on the calculator section. So, if you wish, you can allow yourself to always use a calculator for these questions. However, it's never a bad idea to practice without a calculator whenever it is possible to do so. Once again, any problem that is not marked with an asterisk (*) does not need a calculator to be solved.

1. Using this book effectively
- Begin studying at least three months before the SAT.
- Practice SAT math problems twenty minutes each day.
- Choose a consistent study time and location.

You will retain much more of what you study if you study in short bursts rather than if you try to tackle everything at once. So, try to choose about a twenty-minute block of time that you will dedicate to SAT math each day. Make it a habit. The results are well worth this small time commitment.

- Every time you get a question wrong, **mark it off, no matter what your mistake**.
- Begin each study session by first redoing problems from previous study sessions that you have marked off.
- If you get a problem wrong again, **keep it marked off**.

Note that this book often emphasizes solving each problem in more than one way. Please listen to this advice. The same question is not generally repeated on any SAT, so the important thing is for you to learn as many techniques as possible.

Being able to solve any specific problem is of minimal importance. The more ways you have to solve a single problem the more prepared you will be to tackle a problem you have never seen before, and the quicker you will be able to solve that problem. Also, if you have multiple methods for solving a single problem, then on the actual SAT when you "check over" your work you will be able to redo each problem in a different way. This will eliminate all "careless" errors on the actual exam. Note that in this book the quickest solution to any problem will always be marked with an asterisk (*).

Practice problems of the appropriate level: If you are a student currently scoring at least 600 in SAT math, then you can go through the 48 lessons, solve each problem in order, and vastly improve your score. These lessons can even take you right up to a perfect score. If you don't have much time before your SAT, you can skip many of the Level 1 and 2 problems, and focus on Levels 3, 4, and 5. If you are already scoring above 700, then you should focus on the Level 4 and 5 problems.

If you are scoring less than 600, then this book can still get you close to a perfect score, but you need to be a little more careful about how you use it. Doing every problem in order is not in your best interest. You need to focus on the problems that will contribute to raising your score.

For example, if you are currently scoring between 400 and 500 on practice tests, then you should be focusing primarily on Level 1, 2, and 3 problems. You can easily raise your score 100 points without having to practice a single hard problem. So please, skip all the Level 4 and 5 problems. You can come back to some of the harder questions after you go through the book once.

If you are currently scoring between 500 and 600 on practice tests, then your primary focus should be Level 2 and 3, but you should also do some Level 1 and 4 problems.

If you really want to refine your studying, then you should keep track of your ability level in each of the four major categories of problems:

- **Heart of Algebra**
- **Passport to Advanced Math**
- **Problem Solving**
- **Geometry and Complex Numbers**

For example, many students have trouble with easier Passport to Advanced Math problems, even though they can do difficult Heart of Algebra problems. This type of student may want to focus on Level 1, 2, and 3 Passport to Advanced Math questions, but Level 3 and 4 Heart of Algebra questions.

Practice in small amounts over a long period of time: Ideally you want to practice doing SAT math problems for about twenty minutes each day beginning at least 3 months before the exam. You will retain much more of what you study if you study in short bursts than if you try to tackle everything at once.

The only exception is on a day you do a practice test. You should do at least four practice tests before you take the SAT. Ideally you should do your practice tests on a Saturday or Sunday morning. At first you can do just the math sections. The last one or two times you take a practice test you should do the whole test in one sitting. As tedious as this is, it will prepare you for the amount of endurance that it will take to get through this exam.

2. Calculator use

- Use a TI-84 or comparable calculator if possible when practicing and during the SAT.
- Make sure that your calculator has fresh batteries on test day.
- You may have to switch between DEGREE and RADIAN modes during the test. If you are using a TI-84 (or equivalent) calculator press the MODE button and scroll down to the third line when necessary to switch between modes.

Below are the most important things you should practice on your graphing calculator.

- Practice entering complicated computations in a single step.
- Know when to insert parentheses:
  - Around numerators of fractions
  - Around denominators of fractions
  - Around exponents
  - Whenever you actually see parentheses in the expression

Examples:

We will substitute a 5 in for x in each of the following examples.

Expression	Calculator computation
$\frac{7x+3}{2x-11}$	$(7*5+3)/(2*5-11)$
$(3x-8)^{2x-9}$	$(3*5-8)\wedge(2*5-9)$

- Clear the screen before using it in a new problem. The big screen allows you to check over your computations easily.
- Press the **ANS** button (**2ND (-)**) to use your last answer in the next computation.
- Press **2ND ENTER** to bring up your last computation for editing. This is especially useful when you are plugging in answer choices, or guessing and checking.
- You can press **2ND ENTER** over and over again to cycle backwards through all the computations you have ever done.
- Know where the $\sqrt{}$, π, and ^ buttons are so you can reach them quickly.
- Change a decimal to a fraction by pressing **MATH ENTER ENTER**.
- Press the **MATH** button - in the first menu, you can take cube roots and nth roots for any n.
- Know how to use the **SIN, COS,** and **TAN** buttons as well as **SIN⁻¹, COS⁻¹,** and **TAN⁻¹**.

You may find the following graphing tools useful.

- Press the **Y=** button to enter a function, and then hit **ZOOM 6** to graph it in a standard window.
- Practice using the **WINDOW** button to adjust the viewing window of your graph.
- Practice using the **TRACE** button to move along the graph and look at some of the points plotted.
- Pressing **2ND TRACE** (which is really **CALC**) will bring up a menu of useful items. For example, selecting **ZERO** will tell you where the graph hits the x-axis, or equivalently where the function is zero. Selecting **MINIMUM** or **MAXIMUM** can find the vertex of a parabola. Selecting **INTERSECT** will find the point of intersection of 2 graphs.

3. Tips for taking the SAT

Each of the following tips should be used whenever you take a practice SAT as well as on the actual exam.

Check your answers properly: When you go back to check your earlier answers for careless errors *do not* simply look over your work to try to catch a mistake. This is usually a waste of time.

- When "checking over" problems you have already done, **always redo the problem from the beginning** without looking at your earlier work.
- If possible, use a different method than you used the first time.

For example, if you solved the problem by picking numbers the first time, try to solve it algebraically the second time, or at the very least pick different numbers. If you do not know, or are not comfortable with a different method, then use the same method, but do the problem from the beginning and do not look at your original solution. If your two answers do not match up, then you know that this is a problem you need to spend a little more time on to figure out where your error is.

This may seem time consuming, but that is okay. It is better to spend more time checking over a few problems, than to rush through a lot of problems and repeat the same mistakes.

Take a guess whenever you cannot solve a problem: There is no guessing penalty on the SAT. Whenever you do not know how to solve a problem take a guess. Ideally you should eliminate as many answer choices as possible before taking your guess, but if you have no idea whatsoever, do not waste time overthinking. Simply put down an answer and move on. You should certainly mark it off and come back to it later if you have time.

Pace yourself: Do not waste your time on a question that is too hard or will take too long. After you've been working on a question for about 30 to 45 seconds you need to make a decision. If you understand the question and think that you can get the answer in another 30 seconds or so, continue to work on the problem. If you still do not know how to do the problem or you are using a technique that is going to take a long time, mark it off and come back to it later if you have time.

If you do not know the correct answer, eliminate as many answer choices as you can and take a guess. But you still want to leave open the possibility of coming back to it later. Remember that every problem is worth the same amount. Do not sacrifice problems that you may be able to do by getting hung up on a problem that is too hard for you.

Attempt the right number of questions: Many students make the mistake of thinking that they have to attempt every single SAT math question when they are taking the test. There is no such rule. In fact, many students will increase their SAT score by *reducing* the number of questions they attempt.

There are two math sections on the SAT—one where a calculator is allowed and one where a calculator is not allowed. The calculator section has 30 multiple choice (mc) questions and 8 free response (grid in) questions. The non-calculator section has 15 multiple choice (mc) questions and 5 free response (grid in) questions.

You should first make sure that you know what you got on your last SAT practice test, actual SAT, or actual PSAT (whichever you took last). What follows is a general goal you should go for when taking the exam.

Score	MC (Calculator Allowed)	Grid In (Calculator Allowed)	MC (Calculator Not Allowed)	Grid In (Calculator Not Allowed)
< 330	10/30	3/8	4/15	1/5
330 – 370	15/30	4/8	6/15	2/5
380 – 430	18/30	5/8	8/15	2/5
440 – 490	21/30	6/8	9/15	3/5
500 – 550	24/30	6/8	11/15	4/5
560 – 620	27/30	7/8	13/15	4/5
630 – 800	30/30	8/8	15/15	5/5

For example, a student with a current score of 570 should attempt 27 multiple choice questions and 7 grid ins from the section where a calculator is allowed, and 13 multiple choice questions and 4 grid in questions from the section where a calculator is not allowed.

This is *just* a general guideline. Of course, it can be fine-tuned. As a simple example, if you are particularly strong at Heart of Algebra problems, but very weak at Passport to Advanced Math problems, then you may want to try every Heart of Algebra problem no matter where it appears, and you may want to reduce the number of Passport to Advanced Math problems you attempt.

Remember that there is no guessing penalty on the SAT, so you should *not* leave any questions blank. This *does not* mean you should attempt every question. It means that if you are running out of time make sure you fill in answers for all the questions you did not have time to attempt.

Grid your answers correctly: The computer grades only what you have marked in the bubbles. The space above the bubbles is just for your convenience, and to help you do your bubbling correctly.

Never mark more than one circle in a column or the problem will automatically be marked wrong. You do not need to use all four columns. If you do not use a column just leave it blank.

The symbols that you can grid in are the digits 0 through 9, a decimal point, and a division symbol for fractions. Note that there is no negative symbol. So, answers to grid-ins *cannot* be negative. Also, there are only four slots, so you cannot get an answer such as 52,326.

Sometimes there is more than one correct answer to a grid-in question. Simply choose one of them to grid-in. *Never* try to fit more than one answer into the grid.

If your answer is a whole number such as 2451 or a decimal that requires four or less slots such as 2.36, then simply enter the number starting at any column. The two examples just written must be started in the first column, but the number 16 can be entered starting in column 1, 2, or 3.

Note that there is no zero in column 1, so if your answer is 0 it must be gridded into column 2, 3, or 4.

Fractions can be gridded in any form as long as there are enough slots. The fraction $\frac{2}{100}$ must be reduced to $\frac{1}{50}$ simply because the first representation will not fit in the grid.

Fractions can also be converted to decimals before being gridded in. If a decimal cannot fit in the grid, then you can simply *truncate* it to fit. But you must use every slot in this case. For example, the decimal .167777777... can be gridded as .167, but .16 or .17 would both be marked wrong.

Instead of truncating decimals you can also *round* them. For example, the decimal above could be gridded as .168. Truncating is preferred because there is no thinking involved and you are less likely to make a careless error.

Here are three ways to grid in the number $\frac{8}{9}$.

Never grid-in mixed numerals. If your answer is $2\frac{1}{4}$, and you grid in the mixed numeral $2\frac{1}{4}$, then this will be read as $\frac{21}{4}$ and will be marked wrong. You must either grid in the decimal 2.25 or the improper fraction $\frac{9}{4}$.

Here are two ways to grid in the mixed numeral $1\frac{1}{2}$ correctly.

LESSON 1 – HEART OF ALGEBRA
SOLVING LINEAR EQUATIONS

Must We Always Be So Formal?

Suppose we are asked to solve for x in the following equation:

$$x - 2 = 7$$

In other words, we are being asked for a number such that when we subtract 2 from that number we get 7. It is not too hard to see that $9 - 2 = 7$, so that $x = 9$.

I call the technique above solving this equation **informally**. In other words, when we solve algebraic equations informally we are solving for the variable very quickly in our heads.

We can also solve for x **formally** by adding 2 to each side of the equation:

$$\begin{aligned} x - 2 &= 7 \\ +2 &+2 \\ x &= 9 \end{aligned}$$

In other words, when we solve an algebraic equation formally we are writing out all the steps—just as we would do it on a test in school.

To save time on the SAT you should practice solving equations informally as much as possible. And you should also practice solving equations formally – this will increase your mathematical skill level.

Let's try another:

$$7x = 42$$

Informally, 7 times 6 is 42, so we see that $x = 6$.

Formally, we can divide each side of the equation by 7:

$$\begin{aligned} \frac{7x}{7} &= \frac{42}{7} \\ x &= 6 \end{aligned}$$

Now let's get a little harder:

$$8x + 3 = 59$$

We can still do this informally. First, let's figure out what number plus 3 is 59. Well, 56 plus 3 is 59. So, $8x$ is 56. Therefore, x must be 7.

Here is the formal solution:

$$\begin{aligned} 8x + 3 &= 59 \\ -3 &-3 \\ \frac{8x}{8} &= \frac{56}{8} \\ x &= 7 \end{aligned}$$

On the SAT, a combination of formal and informal algebra often works best. Let's look at an example.

LEVEL 1: HEART OF ALGEBRA – SOLVING LINEAR EQUATIONS

1. If $5 + x + x = 1 + x + x + x$, what is the value of x ?

    A) 1
    B) 2
    C) 3
    D) 4

Algebraic solution: Here is a quick algebraic solution to the problem.

$$5 + x + x = 1 + x + x + x$$
$$5 + 2x = 1 + 3x$$
$$5 = 1 + x$$
$$4 = x$$

Thus, the answer is choice **D**.

Notes: (1) For the first step, we **combined like terms**. On the left, we have $x + x = 2x$ and on the right, we have $x + x + x = 3x$.

(2) For the second step, we *formally* subtracted $2x$ from each side of the equation. Here are the details.

$$\begin{array}{r} 5 + 2x = 1 + 3x \\ -2x \quad\ \ - 2x \\ \hline 5 \quad\ \ = 1 + x \end{array}$$

(3) The last step is best done *informally*. To solve $5 = 1 + x$, we are asking "5 is 1 plus what number?" Well the number is 4.

A Balancing Act

In this problem, we can use a little "balancing" trick to get to the answer faster. If the same quantity appears on each side of an equation, we can simply *strike it off from each side*.

* **Striking off x's:** We strike off two x's from each side of the equation to get

$$5 = 1 + x.$$

This becomes $4 = x$, choice **D**.

Notes: (1) You can physically use your pencil to strike off those x's. The marked-up problem would look as follows.

$$5 + \cancel{x} + \cancel{x} = 1 + x + \cancel{x} + \cancel{x}$$

(2) As in the previous solution, the equation $5 = 1 + x$ is best solved *informally* to save the most time.

Plug It In!

In lots of SAT math problems, you can get the answer simply by trying each of the answer choices until you find the one that works. Unless you have some intuition as to what the correct answer might be, starting in the middle with **B** or **C** is best (although there are some exceptions to this rule that we will see later). The reason for this is simple. Answers are usually given in increasing or decreasing order. If choice B or C fails, you can often eliminate one or two of the other choices as well.

Solution by starting with choice C: We start with choice C and substitute 3 in for x on each side of the equation.

$$5 + 3 + 3 = 1 + 3 + 3 + 3$$
$$11 = 10$$

Since this is false, we can eliminate choice C. A little thought should allow you to eliminate choices A and B as well (don't worry if you don't see this – just take another guess). Let's try choice D next.

$$5 + 4 + 4 = 1 + 4 + 4 + 4$$
$$13 = 13$$

Thus, the answer is choice **D**.

Notes: (1) We can begin with an algebraic solution, and then switch to plugging in later. For example, in this problem, we can write $5 + 2x = 1 + 3x$, and then start substituting in the answer choices from here.

(2) The method of "plugging it in" illustrated here is usually *not* the most efficient method for solving math problems on the SAT. However, it is a *reliable* method that can be used to solve many types of multiple choice questions of varying difficulties. Keep this as a *fallback* method for when you get stuck.

Time to Practice

LEVEL 1: HEART OF ALGEBRA – SOLVING LINEAR EQUATIONS

$$x + x + 6x - 6 = 5 + 4 + 2x + x + x + x$$

2. In the equation above, what is the value of x ?

   A) 5
   B) $\frac{15}{4}$
   C) $-\frac{2}{3}$
   D) -5

3. If $2j = \frac{x-4}{3}$ and $j = 6$, what is the value of x?

   A) 10
   B) 20
   C) 30
   D) 40

4. For what value of x is $\frac{5x}{2} - 7 = 23$?

$$\frac{3}{7}x = \frac{4}{3}$$

5. What value of x is the solution of the equation above?

   A) $\frac{4}{7}$
   B) $\frac{9}{7}$
   C) $\frac{28}{9}$
   D) $\frac{28}{3}$

LEVEL 2: HEART OF ALGEBRA – SOLVING LINEAR EQUATIONS

$$L = 11 + 1.6M$$

6. One end of an elastic band is taped to the bottom of a ceiling fan. When an object of mass M kilograms is attached to the other end of the elastic band, the band stretches to a length of L centimeters as shown in the equation above. What is M when $L = 13$?

7. If $4x - 5 = 53$, what is the value of $12x - 2$?

LEVEL 3: HEART OF ALGEBRA – SOLVING LINEAR EQUATIONS

8. If $15x = 73$, what is the value of $3(x + \frac{4}{5})$?

   A) 17
   B) 15
   C) $\frac{73}{15}$
   D) $\frac{77}{15}$

9. On Sunday, Janice studied 3 more hours than Chris. If they studied for a combined total of 13 hours, how many hours did Chris study for on Sunday?

   A) 5
   B) 6
   C) 7
   D) 8

LEVEL 4: HEART OF ALGEBRA – SOLVING LINEAR EQUATIONS

10. A gymnast's final score is determined by the sum of the difficulty score and execution score, less any deductions for neutral errors. Jackie had a difficulty score of p points and an execution score of q points. Assuming that Jackie lost $\frac{1}{8}$ of a point for each of her 20 neutral errors and had a final score of 6.5, what is the value of $p + q$?

Answers

1. D   2. A   3. D   4. 12   5. C   6. 5/4, 1.25   7. 172   8. A   9. A   10. 9

Full Solutions

2.

* Algebraic solution: Let's start by striking off two x's from each side of the equation to get

$$6x - 6 = 5 + 4 + 2x + x$$

We now combine like terms on the right to get $6x - 6 = 9 + 3x$. We then add 6 to each side of the equation and subtract $3x$ from each side of the equation to get $3x = 15$. Finally, we divide each side of this last equation by 3 to get $x = \frac{15}{3} = 5$, choice **A**.

Notes: (1) We can use any of the three methods of solution from problem 1 above, or a combination of those methods to solve this problem.

(2) Observe how the solution above uses a combination of the techniques that we saw after problem 1 to get to the answer as quickly as possible. We started by *striking off x's*. We then *combined like terms*. And then we finished with some *formal algebra*.

(3) It would be slightly more efficient to solve the last equation $3x = 15$ informally.

3.

* Algebraic solution: Since $j = 6$, we have $2j = 2 \cdot 6 = 12$, and so, $\frac{x-4}{3} = 12$. After multiplying each side of this equation by 3, we see that $x - 4 = 3 \cdot 12 = 36$. So, $x = 36 + 4 = 40$, choice **D**.

Note: Once we have $\frac{x-4}{3} = 12$, we can solve the equation informally in two steps. Since 36 divided by 3 is 12, we have $x - 4 = 36$. Finally, $40 - 4 = 36$, and so $x = 40$.

Solution by starting with choice C: Since $j = 6$, we have that $2j = 2 \cdot 6 = 12$, and so $\frac{x-4}{3} = 12$.

Let's start with choice C and guess that $x = 30$. We then have $\frac{x-4}{3} = \frac{30-4}{3} = \frac{26}{3} \approx 8.67$. This is a bit too small and so, the answer must be choice **D**.

Note: Let's just verify that choice D is correct. We replace x by 40 to get $\frac{x-4}{3} = \frac{40-4}{3} = \frac{36}{3} = 12$. This is correct, and so, the answer is in fact choice D.

4.

* **Algebraic solution:** We add 7 to each side of the equation to get $\frac{5x}{2} = 23 + 7 = 30$. Multiplying each side of this equation by $\frac{2}{5}$ gives $x = 30 \cdot \frac{2}{5} = \frac{30}{5} \cdot 2 = 6 \cdot 2 = \mathbf{12}$.

Notes: (1) We begin by keeping all terms with an x on the left-hand side of the equation, and moving any terms without an x to the right-hand side. To do this we add 7 to each side of the equation.

(2) The **reciprocal** of $\frac{5}{2}$ is $\frac{2}{5}$. The product of reciprocals is 1. In this case, $\frac{2}{5} \cdot \frac{5}{2} = 1$.

It follows that we can solve the equation $\frac{5x}{2} = 30$ for x formally by multiplying each side of the equation by $\frac{2}{5}$.

5.

* **Algebraic solution:** We multiply each side of the equation by $\frac{7}{3}$ to get $x = \frac{4}{3} \cdot \frac{7}{3} = \frac{28}{9}$, choice **C**.

Note: See the solution to problem 4 above for more information about using reciprocals to solve equations.

Solution by starting with choice C: Let's start with choice C and substitute $\frac{28}{9}$ in for x on the left-hand side of the equation. We then have $\frac{3}{7} \cdot \frac{28}{9} = \frac{3}{9} \cdot \frac{28}{7} = \frac{1}{3} \cdot \frac{4}{1} = \frac{4}{3}$. Since this is equal to the right-hand side, the answer is choice **C**.

6.

* **Algebraic solution:** We let $L = 13$ and solve for M.

$$13 = 11 + 1.6M$$
$$2 = 1.6M$$
$$M = \frac{2}{1.6} = \frac{20}{16} = \mathbf{5/4} \text{ or } \mathbf{1.25}.$$

Note: There are lots of words in this problem that are completely unnecessary. The question could have simply been asked as follows:

If $L = 11 + 1.6M$, what is M when $L = 13$?

The SAT often likes to artificially create a "real world" context which is not needed when solving the problem.

7.

* Algebraic solution: We add 5 to each side of the given equation to get $4x = 53 + 5 = 58$. We now multiply each side of this last equation by 3 to get $12x = 174$. Finally, we subtract 2 from each side of this last equation to get $12x - 2 = 174 - 2 = \mathbf{172}$.

Notes: (1) We did *not* need to find x to solve this problem. Since the expression we are trying to find has $12x$ as one of its terms, it is more efficient to multiply $4x$ by 3, than it is to solve the original equation for x and then multiply by 12.

(2) If you didn't notice that you could change $4x$ into $12x$ by multiplying by 3, then it's not too big of a deal. The problem could still be solved easily by solving for x first. Once we have $4x = 58$, we can divide each side of the equation by 4 to get $x = \frac{58}{4}$. We then have

$$12x - 2 = 12 \cdot \frac{58}{4} - 2 = \frac{12}{4} \cdot 58 - 2 = 3 \cdot 58 - 2 = 174 - 2 = 172.$$

8.

Algebraic solution: We divide each side of the given equation by 15 to get $x = \frac{73}{15}$. It follows that $3\left(x + \frac{4}{5}\right) = 3\left(\frac{73}{15} + \frac{4}{5}\right) = 17$, choice **A**.

Notes: (1) If a calculator is allowed for this problem we can simply type the following in our calculator to get the answer:

$$3(73/15 + 4/5) \text{ ENTER}$$

(2) If a calculator is not allowed, then we would begin by rewriting $\frac{4}{5}$ as $\frac{4}{5} \cdot \frac{3}{3} = \frac{12}{15}$. We then have $\frac{73}{15} + \frac{4}{5} = \frac{73}{15} + \frac{12}{15} = \frac{(73+12)}{15} = \frac{85}{15}$. Then $3\left(\frac{73}{15} + \frac{4}{5}\right) = 3\left(\frac{85}{15}\right) = \left(\frac{3}{15}\right)(85) = \left(\frac{1}{5}\right)(85) = 17$.

* Quicker algebraic solution: We divide each side of the given equation by 5 to get $3x = \frac{73}{5}$. We then have

$$3\left(x + \frac{4}{5}\right) = 3x + 3 \cdot \frac{4}{5} = 3x + \frac{12}{5} = \frac{73}{5} + \frac{12}{5} = \frac{73 + 12}{5} = \frac{85}{5} = 17.$$

This is choice **A**.

Notes: (1) The **distributive property** says that for all real numbers a, b, and c,

$$a(b + c) = ab + ac$$

More specifically, this property says that the operation of multiplication distributes over addition.

(2) We used the distributive property in the first step of this solution. In this problem, we have $a = 3$, $b = x$, and $c = \frac{4}{5}$. Thus, we have $3\left(x + \frac{4}{5}\right) = 3x + 3 \cdot \frac{4}{5}$.

(3) See Lesson 2 for more on the distributive property.

9.

* Algebraic solution: Let x be the number of hours Chris studied. Then Janice studied $x + 3$ hours, and we have $x + (x + 3) = 13$. Therefore, $2x + 3 = 13$, and so $2x = 13 - 3 = 10$. So, the number of hours that Chris studied is $x = \frac{10}{2} = 5$, choice **A.**

Note: This problem can also be solved by plugging in the answer choices (start with choice B or C). I leave the details of this solution to the reader.

10.

* Algebraic solution: We have $p + q - \frac{1}{8} \cdot 20 = 6.5$. So, $p + q = 6.5 + \frac{1}{8} \cdot 20 = 6.5 + 2.5 = \textbf{9}$.

Notes: (1) Since Jackie's difficulty score was p and her execution score was q, it follows that the *sum* of her difficulty score and execution score was $p + q$.

(2) Jackie had 20 neutral errors and she lost $\frac{1}{8}$ of a point for each one. It follows that she lost a *total* of $d = \frac{1}{8} \cdot 20 = \frac{20}{8} = 2.5$ points due to neutral errors.

(3) Jackie's final score, F, is determined by $F = p + q - d$, where p is Jackie's difficulty score, q is Jackie's execution score, and d is Jackie's total deductions due to neutral errors.

We were given that $F = 6.5$ in the question, and we found that $d = 2.5$ in Note (2). It follows that $6.5 = p + q - 2.5$. Adding 2.5 to each side of this last equation gives us $p + q = 6.5 + 2.5 = 9$.

LESSON 2 – PASSPORT TO ADVANCED MATH
FACTORING

Distributing Properly

The **distributive property** says that for all real numbers a, b, and c,

$$a(b + c) = ab + ac$$

More specifically, this property says that the operation of multiplication distributes over addition. The distributive property is very important, as it allows us to multiply and factor algebraic expressions.

Numeric example: Show that $2(3 + 4) = 2 \cdot 3 + 2 \cdot 4$

Solution: $2(3 + 4) = 2 \cdot 7 = 14$ and $2 \cdot 3 + 2 \cdot 4 = 6 + 8 = 14$.

Geometric Justification: The following picture gives a physical representation of the distributive property for this example.

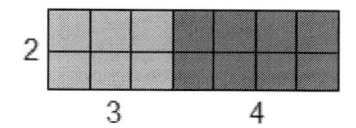

Note that the area of the light grey rectangle is $2 \cdot 3$, the area of the dark grey rectangle is $2 \cdot 4$, and the area of the whole rectangle is $2(3 + 4)$.

Algebraic examples: Use the distributive property to write each algebraic expression in an equivalent form.

(1) $3(x + 5)$ (2) $x(y - 2)$ (3) $-(x - y)$

Solutions: (1) $3(x + 5) = 3x + 15$

(2) $x(y - 2) = xy - 2x$

(3) $-(x - y) = -x + y$

Distribution Errors

When you try to expand the expression $-(x + 2)$, do you get $-x + 2$ or $-x - 2$?

The answer is in fact $\boldsymbol{-x - 2}$.

When negating an expression with two terms, many students forget to distribute the minus sign correctly. In this case, both terms need to be negated.

If it helps you, you can rewrite $-(x + 2)$ as $(-1)(x + 2)$. Then we get $(-1)x + (-1)2 = \boldsymbol{-x - 2}$.

As another example, try to simplify this expression: $(x - 3) - (x - 5)$

Let's begin by removing the parentheses and distributing the subtraction symbol in the middle correctly: $x - 3 - x + 5$

Finally, we combine like terms to get $x - x - 3 + 5 = \boldsymbol{2}$.

A Factor in the Rough

When we use the distributive property in the opposite direction, we usually call it **factoring**.

Examples: $3x + 6y = 3(x + 2y)$ $2x + 7xy = x(2 + 7y)$ $8xy + 12yz = 4y(2x + 3z)$

As a Matter of Fact(or)

The Difference of Two Squares: $a^2 - b^2 = (a - b)(a + b)$

Examples: $x^2 - 16 = (x - 4)(x + 4)$ $9x^2 - 49y^2 = (3x - 7y)(3x + 7y)$

Trinomial Factoring: $x^2 - (a + b)x + ab = (x - a)(x - b)$

Examples: $x^2 - 3x + 2 = (x - 1)(x - 2)$
$x^2 + 2x - 15 = (x - 3)(x + 5)$
$x^2 + 12x + 35 = (x + 5)(x + 7)$

Let's try an example.

LEVEL 1: PASSPORT TO ADVANCED MATH – FACTORING

1. Which of the following is equivalent to the expression $35b + 40bk$?

    A) $(7 + 8k)b$
    B) $(35 + 40k)b$
    C) $75(b + 2k)$
    D) $75b^2k$

* **Solution by factoring:** Since $35b$ and $40bk$ each have b as a factor, we can write

$$35b + 40bk = b(35 + 40k)$$

This is equivalent to answer choice **B**.

Notes: (1) $b(35 + 40k)$ is *not* completely factored. Since 35 and 40 are both divisible by 5, we can factor further as $5b(7 + 8k)$. However, this is not an answer choice.

(2) The **commutative property** for multiplication says that for all real numbers c and d, $cd = dc$.

For this problem, if we let $c = b$ and $d = 35 + 40k$, we see that $b(35 + 40k) = (35 + 40k)b$. This clarifies why choice B is the answer.

Pick Some Numbers

A problem may become much easier to understand and to solve by substituting specific numbers in for the unknown quantities.

Solution by picking numbers: Let's choose values for b and k, say $b = 2$ and $k = 3$. The given expression then becomes $35b + 40bk = 35 \cdot 2 + 40 \cdot 2 \cdot 3 = 70 + 240 =$ **310**.

Put a nice big, dark circle around this number so that you can find it easily later. We now substitute the numbers that we chose into each answer choice.

A) $(7 + 8k)b = (7 + 8 \cdot 3)(2) = (7 + 24)(2) = 31 \cdot 2 = 62$
B) $(35 + 40k)b = (35 + 40 \cdot 3)(2) = (35 + 120)(2) = 155 \cdot 2 = 310$
C) $75(b + 2k) = 75(2 + 2 \cdot 3) = 75(2 + 6) = 75 \cdot 8 = 600$
D) $75b^2k = 75(2)^2(3) = 75 \cdot 4 \cdot 3 = 900$

Since A, C, and D are incorrect we can eliminate them. Therefore, the answer is choice **B**.

Notes: (1) D is **not** the correct answer simply because it is equal to 310. It is correct because all 3 of the other choices are **not** 310.

The strategy of "picking numbers" can usually be used only to eliminate answer choices. Make sure that you check every answer choice, even if one of the answers comes out correct. If more than one choice comes out correct, you must pick new numbers, and use them in the remaining choices.

(2) When picking numbers, I often (but not always) avoid numbers as simple as 0 or 1 because more than one choice often comes out correct when these numbers are chosen. For example, if we were to choose $b = 0$ in this problem, then the expression becomes 0 and choices A, B, and D also become 0. So, we would need to pick new numbers anyway to eliminate more choices.

(3) This method is usually *not* the most efficient method for solving math problems on the SAT, but like the strategy of "plugging in," it is a *reliable* method that can be used to solve many types of problems of varying difficulties. Keep this strategy around as a *fallback* method for when you cannot solve a problem another way.

Time to Practice

LEVEL 1: PASSPORT TO ADVANCED MATH – FACTORING

$$7x(y + 4z)$$

2. Which of the following is equivalent to the expression above?

A) $xy + 11xz$
B) $7xy + 11xz$
C) $7xy + 4z$
D) $7xy + 28xz$

LEVEL 2: PASSPORT TO ADVANCED MATH – FACTORING

$$3x^2 - 7 = (ax + b)(ax - b)$$

3. In the equation above, a and b are constants. Which of the following could be the value of a ?

A) 1.5
B) $\sqrt{3}$
C) 3
D) 9

4. The length of a rectangular garden is k meters, and the width of the garden is 10 meters longer than its length. Which of the following expresses the area, in meters, of the garden in terms of k ?

   A) $2k + 10$
   B) $4k + 20$
   C) $k^2 + 10$
   D) $k^2 + 10k$

LEVEL 3: PASSPORT TO ADVANCED MATH – FACTORING

$$4x^4 + 16x^2y^2 + 16y^4$$

5. Which of the following is equivalent to the expression shown above?

   A) $(2x + 4y)^4$
   B) $(2x^2 + 4y^2)^2$
   C) $(4x + 16y)^4$
   D) $(4x^2 + 16y^2)^2$

6. Which of the following is equivalent to the expression $x^3y + x^2y^3 + 3x + 3y^2$?

   A) $x^2y(x + 1) + 3x(x + y^2)$
   B) $(xy + 3)(x^2 + y^2)$
   C) $(x^2y + 3)(x + y^2)$
   D) $x^2y(x + 3 + y)$

$$7(a + b) = 2(b - a)$$

7. If (a, b) is a solution to the equation above and $a \neq 0$, what is the ratio $\frac{b}{a}$?

   A) $-\frac{9}{5}$
   B) $-\frac{8}{5}$
   C) 8
   D) 11

8. Which of the following is equivalent to $\left(\frac{ab}{c}\right)(cb - a)$?

   A) $ab^2 - \frac{b}{c}$
   B) $ab^2 - \frac{a^2b}{c}$
   C) $\frac{ab}{c} - \frac{a^2b}{c}$
   D) $\frac{ab}{c} - a^2bc$

24

LEVEL 4: PASSPORT TO ADVANCED MATH – FACTORING

9. If $x - y = \frac{27}{2}$ and $x + y = \frac{4}{9}$, what is the value of $x^2 - y^2$?

10. Let $m = 2x + 7$ and $k = 2x - 7$, and write $km = cx^2 + d$, where c and d are constants. What is the value of $c - d$?

Answers

1. B   2. D   3. B   4. D   5. B   6. C   7. A   8. B   9. 6   10. 53

Full Solutions

2.

* Solution using the distributive property: $7x(y + 4z) = 7x \cdot y + 7x \cdot 4z = 7xy + 28xz$

So, the answer is choice **D**.

Notes: (1) We used the **distributive property**, $a(b + c) = ab + ac$, with $a = 7x$, $b = y$, and $c = 4z$.
(2) $7x \cdot 4z = 7 \cdot 4 \cdot x \cdot z = 28xz$. Similarly, $7x \cdot y = 7xy$.

Solution by picking numbers: Let's choose values for x, y, and z, say $x = 2$, $y = 3$, and $z = 5$. Then

$$7x(y + 4z) = 7 \cdot 2(3 + 4 \cdot 5) = 14(3 + 20) = 14 \cdot 23 = \boxed{322}$$

Put a nice big, dark circle around this number so that you can find it easily later. We now substitute the numbers that we chose into each answer choice.

- A) $2 \cdot 3 + 11 \cdot 2 \cdot 5 = 6 + 110 = 116$
- B) $7 \cdot 2 \cdot 3 + 11 \cdot 2 \cdot 5 = 42 + 110 = 152$
- C) $7 \cdot 2 \cdot 3 + 4 \cdot 5 = 42 + 20 = 62$
- D) $7 \cdot 2 \cdot 3 + 28 \cdot 2 \cdot 5 = 42 + 280 = 322$

Since A, B, and C are incorrect we can eliminate them. Therefore, the answer is choice **D**.

Notes: (1) D is **not** the correct answer simply because it is equal to 322. It is correct because all 3 of the other choices are **not** 322.

(2) See problem 1 from this lesson for more information on picking numbers.

3.

* Solution using the difference of two squares: $3x^2 - 7 = (\sqrt{3}x + \sqrt{7})(\sqrt{3}x - \sqrt{7})$

So, a could be $\sqrt{3}$, choice **B**.

Notes: (1) When factoring by the difference of two squares, you always take the positive square root of the individual pieces. The positive square root of 3 is $\sqrt{3}$ and the positive square root of 7 is $\sqrt{7}$.

(2) The expressions $(ax + b)$ and $(ax - b)$ are called **binomials** (the prefix "bi" means 2, and a binomial has 2 **terms**). Usually, when multiplying two binomials, we need to do *four* multiplications (many of us like to use the mnemonic FOIL), but for expressions of the form $(ax + b)$ and $(ax - b)$, the *inner* and *outer* products always cancel. So, in this special case, we need to do only 2 multiplications (the *first* terms and the *last* terms).

In this problem, we have $(ax + b)(ax - b) = (ax)(ax) + (b)(-b) = a^2x^2 - b^2$. It follows that $3x^2 - 7 = a^2x^2 - b^2$, and therefore, we must have $a^2 = 3$ and $b^2 = 7$. So, a can be $\sqrt{3}$. This leads us to select choice B.

(3) Although the strategy of picking numbers can be used to solve this problem (by choosing values for x), it is not an easy method to use in this case. Try setting x equal to some simple values and see if you can find a. You might want to try using 0 and 1. I leave the details to the reader.

4.
* Solution using the distributive property: The length of the garden is k meters, and so the width of the garden is $k + 10$ meters. It follows that the area of the garden, in meters, is
$$A = k(k + 10) = k^2 + 10k$$
This is choice **D**.

Notes: (1) The formula for the area of a rectangle is $A = lw$, where l is the length of the rectangle and w is the width of the rectangle. This formula is given at the beginning of each math section of the SAT.

(2) This problem can also be solved by picking numbers. I leave this solution to the reader.

5.
* Solution by starting with choice B: We start with choice B and multiply to get
$$(2x^2 + 4y^2)^2 = (2x^2 + 4y^2)(2x^2 + 4y^2) = 4x^4 + 16x^2y^2 + 16y^4$$
This is correct, so that the answer is choice **B**.

Notes: (1) If you are very comfortable with factoring you can simply factor the original expression.

(2) There is actually no need to factor the whole expression. We can just use part of the expression. For example, we can simply observe that $4x^4 = (2x^2)(2x^2)$ to see that the answer is most likely choice B. It's easy to see that the other three choices will not produce $4x^4$.

(3) To square an expression means to multiply that expression by itself. For example, $2^2 = 2 \cdot 2 = 4$ and $x^2 = x \cdot x$. Similarly, $(2x^2 + 4y^2)^2 = (2x^2 + 4y^2)(2x^2 + 4y^2)$.

A common error that students make is they assume that $(a + b)^2 = a^2 + b^2$. However, this equation is FALSE. For example, if we let $a = 1$ and $b = 1$, then we have $(a + b)^2 = (1 + 1)^2 = 2^2 = 4$, but $a^2 + b^2 = 1^2 + 1^2 = 1 + 1 = 2$. Since $4 \neq 2$, we see that $(a + b)^2 \neq a^2 + b^2$.

In this problem, $(2x^2 + 4y^2)^2 \neq (2x^2)^2 + (4y^2)^2$, or equivalently, $(2x^2 + 4y^2)^2 \neq 4x^4 + 16x^4$.

(4) To expand $(a + b)^2$ correctly requires two applications of the distributive property. We hav
$$(a + b)^2 = (a + b)(a + b) = (a + b)a + (a + b)b$$
$$= a^2 + ba + ab + b^2 = a^2 + 2ab + b^2$$
A little shortcut here is to "FOIL" the expression. The mnemonic FOIL stands for *first, outer, inner, last*. In the expression $(a + b)(a + b)$, the F gives us $a \cdot a = a^2$, the O gives us ab, the I gives us ba, and the L gives us b^2. When we add all these up, we get $a^2 + 2ab + b^2$.

(5) See Lesson 18 for an alternative method of multiplying polynomials and for a special factoring formula that can be used to do the multiplication here quickly.

Solution by picking numbers: If we let $x = y = 1$, then the given expression becomes $4 + 16 + 16 = \boxed{36}$. Put a nice big dark circle around 36 so you can find it easier later. We now substitute $x = 1, y = 1$ into each answer choice:

A) 6^4
B) $6^2 = 36$
C) 20^4
D) 20^2

Since A, C and D each came out incorrect, the answer is choice **B**.

Notes: (1) B is **not** the correct answer simply because it is equal to 36. It is correct because all three of the other choices are **not** 36. **You** must check all four choices!

(2) We did violate one of the guidelines for picking numbers here, namely that 1 shouldn't be used because it is too simple. In this case, however, picking numbers different from 1 will lead to much messier computations.

Also, replacing all the variables by 1 in a polynomial is equivalent to just adding up all the coefficients of the polynomial.

For example, the coefficients of $4x^4 + 16^2y^2 + 16y^4$ are 4, 16, and 16. So, when we set x and y equal to 1, we get $4 + 16 + 16 = 36$.

(3) All the above computations can be done in a single step with your calculator (if a calculator is allowed for this problem).

In this problem, it should be clear that 6^4, 20^4, and 20^2 are all much larger than 36.

6.
* **Solution by factoring:** We use the method of **factoring by grouping**.
$$x^3y + x^2y^3 + 3x + 3y^2$$
$$= x^2y(x + y^2) + 3(x + y^2)$$
$$= (x^2y + 3)(x + y^2)$$

This is choice **C**.

Notes: (1) Notice that the first two terms factor as
$$x^3y + x^2y^3 = x^2y(x + y^2)$$
and the last two terms factor as
$$3x + 3y^2 = 3(x + y^2)$$
So, we have
$$x^3y + x^2y^3 + 3x + 3y^2 = x^2y(x + y^2) + 3(x + y^2)$$

27

(2) The expressions $x^2y(x+y^2)$ and $3(x+y^2)$ have $(x+y^2)$ in common, and we can therefore factor it out of the expression $x^2y(x+y^2) + 3(x+y^2)$ as was done in the solution.

(3) If you have trouble seeing why the last expression is the same as what we started with, try working backwards and multiplying instead of factoring. In other words, we have

$$(x^2y + 3)(x + y^2)$$
$$= (x^2y)(x) + (x^2y)(y^2) + 3(x) + 3(y^2)$$
$$= x^3y + x^2y^3 + 3x + 3y^2$$

I used FOIL here to multiply this out, but you can use the method for multiplying polynomials that you like best (see Lesson 18 for another method).

(4) We can also solve this problem by starting with the answer choices and multiplying (as we did in note (3)) until we get $x^3y + x^2y^3 + 3x + 3y^2$.

(5) This problem can also be solved by picking numbers. I leave this solution to the reader.

7.

* Solution using the distributive property: We begin by distributing the 7 on the left-hand side of the equation and the 2 on the right-hand side of the equation to get

$$7a + 7b = 2b - 2a.$$

We get a to one side of the equation by adding $2a$ to each side, and we get b to the other side by subtracting $7b$ from each side.

$$9a = -5b$$

We can get $\frac{b}{a}$ to one side by performing **cross division.** We do this just like cross multiplication, but we divide instead. Dividing each side of the equation by $-5a$ will do the trick (this way we get rid of a on the left and -5 on the right).

$$\frac{9}{-5} = \frac{b}{a}$$

So, $\frac{b}{a} = -\frac{9}{5}$ and the answer is choice **A**.

Notes: (1) We used the distributive property twice here:

$$7(a + b) = 7a + 7b \qquad 2(b - a) = 2b - 2a$$

(2) As stated earlier in this lesson, many students fail to apply the distributive property correctly. For example, it is common for students to write $7(a + b) = 7a + b$ and $2(b - a) = 2b - a$. Make sure that you are aware that these equations are not correct.

(3) To get from $7a + 7b = 2b - 2a$ to $9a = -5b$ we performed two operations. Let's do it one step at a time. We first add $2a$ to each side of the equation as follows:

$$7a + 7b = 2b - 2a$$
$$\underline{+2a \qquad\qquad + 2a}$$
$$9a + 7b = 2b$$

We now subtract $7b$ from each side of this last equation to get

$$9a = 2b - 7b = -5b.$$

(4) Let's also do the cross division one step at a time. Beginning with $9a = -5b$, we divide each side of the equation by a to get $9 = -\frac{5b}{a}$. We then divide each side of the equation by -5 to get $\frac{9}{-5} = \frac{b}{a}$. So, $\frac{b}{a} = -\frac{9}{5}$.

Solution by picking a number: Let's choose a value for a. Using the answer choices as a guide, let's choose $a = 5$. The equation then becomes

$$7(5 + b) = 2(b - 5).$$

At this point, we can either find b algebraically, similar to what we did in the last solution, or we can use the answer choices to try some educated guesses for b.

For example, if we use choice A as a guide, and guess that $b = -9$, then we have

$$7(5 - 9) = 2(-9 - 5)$$
$$7(-4) = 2(-14)$$
$$-28 = -28$$

Since this last equation is true, we see that the point $(5, -9)$ is a solution to the given equation, and therefore $\frac{b}{a} = -\frac{9}{5}$, choice **A**.

Notes: If we choose to find b algebraically, then the computations look as follows:

$$7(5 + b) = 2(b - 5)$$
$$35 + 7b = 2b - 10$$
$$5b = -45$$
$$b = -\frac{45}{5} = -9$$

8.
* Solution using the distributive property:

$$\left(\frac{ab}{c}\right)(cb - a) = \left(\frac{ab}{c}\right)(cb) - \left(\frac{ab}{c}\right)(a) = \frac{abcb}{c} - \frac{aba}{c} = abb - \frac{aab}{c} = ab^2 - \frac{a^2b}{c}$$

This is choice **B**.

Notes: (1) In the first equality above we used the distributive property.

(2) If a term has no denominator, then this is equivalent to having a denominator of 1. For example, $cb = \frac{cb}{1}$.

(3) We multiply two fractions by multiplying the numerators together and the denominators together. For example, $\left(\frac{ab}{c}\right)(cb) = \left(\frac{ab}{c}\right)\left(\frac{cb}{1}\right) = \frac{abcb}{c}$.

(2) We can always cancel a factor in the numerator with the same factor in the denominator. For example, in the expression $\frac{abcb}{c}$, we can cancel the c in the numerator with the c in the denominator to get abb.

(3) By definition, $bb = b^2$. So, $abb = ab^2$. Similarly, $aba = aab = a^2b$.

Solution by picking numbers: Let's choose values for a, b, and c, say $a = 2$, $b = 3$, $c = 6$. Then $\left(\frac{ab}{c}\right)(cb - a) = 1(18 - 2) =$ **16**

Put a nice big dark circle around **16** so you can find it easier later. We now substitute $a = 2$, $b = 3$, $c = 6$ into each answer choice:

A) $2 \cdot 3^2 - \frac{3}{6} = 18 - \frac{1}{2} = 17.5$

B) $2 \cdot 3^2 - \frac{2^2 \cdot 3}{6} = 18 - 2 = 16$

C) $\frac{2 \cdot 3}{6} - \frac{2^2 \cdot 3}{6} = 1 - 2 = -1$

D) $\frac{2 \cdot 3}{6} - 2^2 \cdot 3 \cdot 6 = 1 - 72 = -71$

Since A, C, and D each came out incorrect, the answer is choice **B**.

Notes: (1) B is **not** the correct answer simply because it is equal to 16. It is correct because all three of the other choices are **not** 16. **You must check all four choices!**

(2) All the above computations can be done in a single step with your calculator (if a calculator is allowed for this problem).

(3) Observe that we picked a different number for each variable. We are less likely to get more than one answer choice to come out to the correct answer this way.

(4) We picked numbers that were simple, but not too simple. The number 2 is usually a good choice to start, if it is allowed. We then also picked 3 and 6 so that the numbers would be distinct (see note (3)). We chose 6 instead of 4 because it makes the fractions come out to whole numbers.

(5) See problem 1 above for more information on picking numbers.

9.

* **Solution using the difference of two squares:** $x^2 - y^2 = (x - y)(x + y) = \frac{27}{2} \cdot \frac{4}{9} = \frac{27}{9} \cdot \frac{4}{2} = 6$.

10.

* **Solution using the difference of two squares:** $km = (2x - 7)(2x + 7) = 4x^2 - 49$. So, we have $4x^2 - 49 = cx^2 + d$. Thus, $c = 4$ and $d = -49$. It follows that $c - d = 4 - (-49) = 4 + 49 = $ **53**.

LESSON 3 – PROBLEM SOLVING
RATIOS

1-2-3-4 Ratios

Here is a foolproof 4-step system for setting up a ratio.

Step 1: Identify two key words and write them down one over the other.

Step 2: Next to each of these key words, write down the numbers, variables, or expressions that correspond to each key word in two columns.

Step 3: Draw in 2 division symbols and an equal sign.

Step 4: Cross multiply and divide.

Let's look at an example.

LEVEL 1: PROBLEM SOLVING – RATIOS

1. At an adoption center, 4 guinea pigs are selected at random from each group of 15. At this rate, how many guinea pigs will be selected in total if the adoption center has 90 guinea pigs?

Solution by setting up a ratio: (Step 1) We identify 2 key words. Let's choose "selected" and "group."

(Step 2) Next to the word "selected" we put the number 4 for the 4 guinea pigs that were selected from 15, followed by x for the unknown number of guinea pigs selected from the entire group of 90. Then, next to the word group, we put 15, followed by 90. Here is how it should look:

$$\begin{array}{lcc} \text{selected} & 4 & x \\ \text{group} & 15 & 90 \end{array}$$

Note that it is important that the 15 goes under the 4 and the 90 goes under the x.

(Step 3) We now draw in 2 division symbols and an equal sign.

$$\frac{4}{15} = \frac{x}{90}$$

(Step 4) Finally, we find x by cross multiplying and then dividing.

$$15x = 4 \cdot 90$$

$$x = \frac{4 \cdot 90}{15} = 4 \cdot \frac{90}{15} = 4 \cdot 6 = \mathbf{24}$$

Notes: (1) There are always four correct ways to set up a ratio. Here are the other three possibilities:

$$\frac{15}{4} = \frac{90}{x} \qquad \frac{x}{4} = \frac{90}{15} \qquad \frac{4}{x} = \frac{15}{90}$$

All four possibilities result in the equation $15x = 4 \cdot 90$ after cross multiplying.

(2) Be careful! Some setups are NOT acceptable. For example, $\frac{4}{15} = \frac{90}{x}$ is incorrect because the "selected" and "group" are mixed and matched.

Ratio Quickies

Once you get the hang of ratios, you may be able to do all four steps at the same time. When practicing, use both the 4-step and 1-step systems until you get very comfortable with the 1-step system.

* Quick ratio: $\frac{90}{15} \cdot 4 = 6 \cdot 4 = \mathbf{24}$.

Notes: (1) There are 90 guinea pigs in total, and there are 15 in each group. So, dividing 90 by 15 gives us the number of groups.

$$\frac{90}{15} = 6 \text{ groups}$$

(2) Since 4 guinea pigs are selected from each group, and there are 6 groups, the total number of guinea pigs selected is $6 \cdot 4 = 24$.

Time to Practice

LEVEL 1: PROBLEM SOLVING – RATIOS

2. * In a random sample of 125 light bulbs, 4 are found to be broken. At this rate, how many of 9,750 light bulbs will be broken?

   A) 250
   B) 268
   C) 300
   D) 312

3. * The sculpture *Winged Victory of Samothrace* stands 5.57 meters high and has an approximate width of 1.524 meters. If a duplicate of the sculpture is made where each dimension is $\frac{1}{7}$ the corresponding original dimension, what is the height of the duplicate to the nearest tenth of a meter?

LEVEL 2: PROBLEM SOLVING – RATIOS

4. * The tallest giraffe on record was a male that stood 19.3 feet tall. Approximately what is the height of the tallest giraffe on record in <u>meters</u>? (1 meter ≈ 3.28 feet)

   A) 0.17
   B) 2.79
   C) 5.88
   D) 63.3

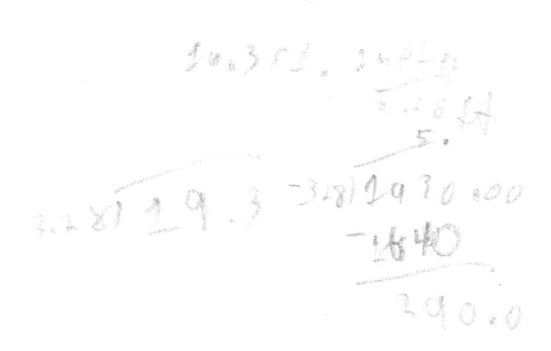

5. If a standard pallet can carry 60 boxes, then how many boxes can p pallets carry?

   A) $p + 60$
   B) $\frac{60}{p}$
   C) $\frac{p}{60}$
   D) $60p$

6. * Running at a constant speed, a race horse traveled 205 meters in 8.2 seconds. At this rate, what is the distance, in meters, the horse will travel in 2 minutes?

LEVEL 3: PROBLEM SOLVING – RATIOS

$$1 \text{ hectometer} = 100 \text{ meters}$$
$$10 \text{ decimeters} = 1 \text{ meter}$$

7. A manager splits his warehouse into equal subdivisions so that each subdivision has a length of 3 hectometers. Based on the information given above, what is the length, in decimeters, of each subdivison of the warehouse?

   A) 30,000
   B) 3,000
   C) 30
   D) 0.003

8. * Dennis completed a 1600 meter race in 145 seconds. What was his average speed, to the nearest meter, in meters per minute?

LEVEL 4: PROBLEM SOLVING – RATIOS

9. Starting from rest, a cat begins chasing a mouse, traveling d feet in t seconds. For the first ten seconds of the chase, the distance d can be estimated by using the formula $d = 9t^2\sqrt{t}$. Which of the following gives the average speed of the cat, in feet per second, over the first t seconds after the cat begins chasing the mouse, where $0 \leq t \leq 10$.

   A) $9t^2$
   B) $\frac{9t}{\sqrt{t}}$
   C) $9t\sqrt{t}$
   D) $3t\sqrt{t}$

10. The formula $E = \frac{1}{2}mv^2$ gives the kinetic energy E, in joules, of an object with mass m, in kilograms, that is moving with velocity v, in meters per second. A scientist uses the formula to find the kinetic energy of an object moving with velocity w and the kinetic energy of the same object moving with velocity $3.5w$. What is the ratio of the kinetic energy of the faster object to the kinetic energy of the slower object?

Answers

1. 24   2. D   3. 4/5, .8   4. C   5. D   6. 3000   7. B   8. 662   9. C   10. 49/4, 12.25

Full Solutions

2.

Solution by setting up a ratio: Key words: "broken" and "total"

$$\begin{array}{ccc} \text{broken} & 4 & x \\ \text{total} & 125 & 9{,}750 \end{array}$$

$$\frac{4}{125} = \frac{x}{9{,}750}$$

$$125x = 4 \cdot 9{,}750$$

$$x = \frac{4 \cdot 9{,}750}{125} = 312$$

This is choice **D**.

* **Quick ratio:** $\frac{4}{125} \cdot 9{,}750 = 312$, choice **D**.

3.

* **Quick solution:** $\frac{1}{7} \cdot 5.57 \approx 0.7957$. To the nearest tenth, this is .**8**.

Notes: (1) The width is not needed here because the question is asking only for the height of the duplicate.

(2) A ratio can also formally be set up as follows:

$$\begin{array}{ccc} \text{duplicate} & 1 & x \\ \text{sculpture} & 7 & 5.57 \end{array}$$

$$\frac{1}{7} = \frac{x}{5.57}$$

$$7x = 1 \cdot 5.57$$

$$x = \frac{5.57}{7} \approx 0.7957$$

4.

Solution by setting up a ratio: Key words: "feet" and "meters"

$$\begin{array}{ccc} \text{feet} & 19.3 & 3.28 \\ \text{meters} & x & 1 \end{array}$$

$$\frac{19.3}{x} = \frac{3.28}{1} \Rightarrow 3.28x = 19.3 \Rightarrow x = \frac{19.3}{3.28} \approx 5.88$$

So, the answer is choice **C**.

Quick ratio: $\frac{19.3}{3.28} \cdot 1 \approx 5.88$, choice **C**.

* **Solution by estimating:** 19.3 is approximately 18 and 3.28 is approximately 3. Since 3 goes into 18 six times, we look for the answer closest to 6. This is choice **C**.

5.

Solution by setting up a ratio: Key words: "pallets" and "boxes"

$$\begin{array}{ccc} \text{pallets} & 1 & p \\ \text{boxes} & 60 & x \end{array}$$

$$\frac{1}{60} = \frac{p}{x} \Rightarrow x = 60p$$

So, the answer is choice **D**.

* **Quick ratio:** $\frac{60}{1} \cdot p = 60p$, choice **D**.

6.

Solution by setting up a ratio: Key words: "meters" and "seconds"

$$\begin{array}{ccc} \text{meters} & 205 & x \\ \text{seconds} & 8.2 & 120 \end{array}$$

$$\frac{205}{8.2} = \frac{x}{120} \Rightarrow 8.2x = 24{,}600 \Rightarrow x = \frac{24{,}600}{8.2} = \mathbf{3000}$$

Notes: (1) We chose to use seconds here (instead of minutes) because it is easier to convert 2 minutes into seconds (2 minutes = 2 · 60 = 120 seconds).

(2) If we did choose to use minutes instead of seconds, we would need to convert 8.2 seconds into minutes. We can do this by setting up yet another ratio. Can you do it the quick way? The computation is $\frac{8.2}{60} \cdot 1 \approx 0.136667$.

We could then use a ratio with keywords "meters" and "minutes" to get $\frac{205}{0.136667} \cdot 2 \approx 3000$.

Observe that if you use the ANS button in your calculator to do this last ratio, you will get the exact answer of 3000. If, however, you type in the number 0.136667 yourself, there will be some roundoff error and you will get a number slightly less than 3000. If you grid in anything other than 3000, you will get the answer wrong!

* **Quick ratio:** $\frac{205}{8.2} \cdot 120 = \mathbf{3000}$.

Solution using $d = rt$: Using $d = r \cdot t$ (distance = rate · time), we have

$$205 = r \cdot 8.2 \Rightarrow r = \frac{205}{8.2} = 25 \text{ meters per second}$$

Using $d = r \cdot t$ again, we have $d = 25 \cdot 120 = \mathbf{3000}$.

7.

* **Quick solution:** 3 hectometers is equivalent to $3 \cdot 100 = 300$ meters, and 300 meters is equivalent to $300 \cdot 10 = 3{,}000$ decimeters, choice **B**.

Solution using ratios: We first set up a ratio to find the number of meters in 3 hectometers. The two things being compared are "meters" and "hectometers."

$$\begin{array}{ccc} \text{meters} & 100 & m \\ \text{hectometers} & 1 & 3 \end{array}$$

$$\frac{100}{1} = \frac{m}{3} \Rightarrow m = 300$$

We next set up a ratio to find the number of decimeters in 300 meters. The two things being compared are "meters" and "decimeters."

$$\begin{array}{ccc} \text{meters} & 1 & 300 \\ \text{decimeters} & 10 & d \end{array}$$

$$\frac{1}{10} = \frac{300}{d} \Rightarrow d = 3{,}000$$

This is choice **B**.

8.

Solution by setting up a ratio: Key words: "meters" and "seconds"

$$\begin{array}{ccc} \text{meters} & 1600 & x \\ \text{seconds} & 145 & 60 \end{array}$$

$$\frac{1600}{145} = \frac{x}{60} \Rightarrow 145x = 96{,}000 \Rightarrow x = \frac{96{,}000}{145} \approx 662.069$$

To the nearest meter, this is **662**.

Note: For an explanation of why we used seconds, and the changes that need to be made to work in minutes, see problem 6.

* **Quick ratio:** $\frac{1600}{145} \cdot 60 \approx \mathbf{662}$.

Solution using $d = rt$: Using $d = r \cdot t$ (distance = rate · time), we have $1600 = r \cdot 145$. So, $r = \frac{1600}{145} \approx 11.03$ meters per second. Using $d = r \cdot t$ again, we have $d = 11.03 \cdot 60 \approx \mathbf{662}$.

9.

* **Solution using** $d = rt$: Using $d = r \cdot t$ (distance = rate · time), we have $9t^2\sqrt{t} = r \cdot t$, and so $r = \frac{9t^2\sqrt{t}}{t} = 9t\sqrt{t}$ feet per second. This is choice **C**.

10.

* The kinetic energy of the slower object is $\frac{1}{2}mw^2$ and the kinetic energy of the faster object is $\frac{1}{2}m(3.5w)^2 = \frac{1}{2}m(3.5)^2w^2 = \frac{1}{2}m(12.25)w^2$. Therefore, the ratio of the kinetic energy of the faster object to the kinetic energy of the slower object is $\frac{\frac{1}{2}m(12.25)w^2}{\frac{1}{2}mw^2} = \mathbf{12.25}$.

LESSON 4 – GEOMETRY
LINES AND ANGLES

What's Your Angle?

A figure formed by two rays with a common endpoint is called an **angle**.

In the three figures below, the angle formed by the **rays** $\overrightarrow{AB}$ and $\overrightarrow{AC}$ is $\angle BAC$. The point A is called the **vertex** of the angle. The vertex letter is always written between the two others.

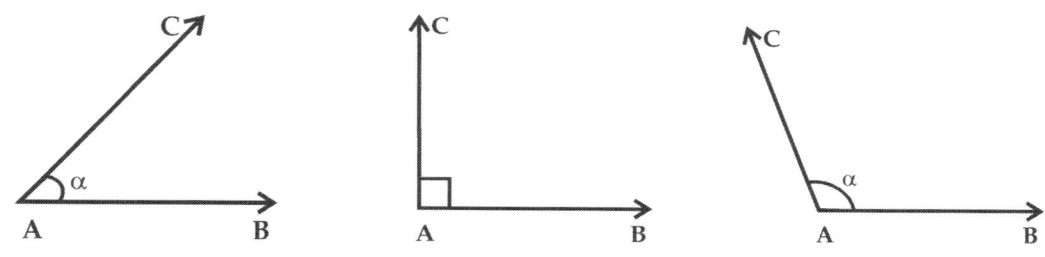

Notes: (1) The angles above can also be written $\angle CAB$, or they can be abbreviated as $\angle A$ since there is only one angle with vertex A. The left and rightmost angles can also be labeled as $\angle \alpha$.

(2) $\overrightarrow{AB}$ and $\overrightarrow{AC}$ in the figure above are called **rays** because they have one endpoint. If they had no endpoints they would be called **lines**, and if they had two endpoints they would be called **line segments**.

The leftmost angle above is an **acute angle** because its measure is between 0° and 90°.

The middle angle is a **right angle** because its measure is 90°.

The rightmost angle is an **obtuse angle** because its measure is between 90° and 180°.

A **straight angle** has a measure of 180°.

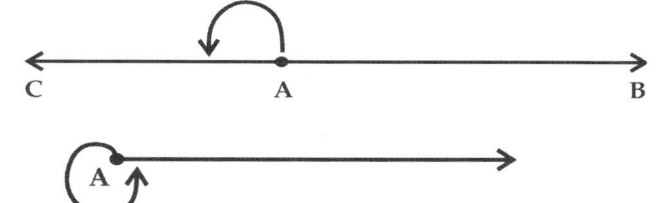

A **full angle** has a measure of 360°.

Two angles that have a common vertex and share one common ray, but do not share a common interior, are called **adjacent angles**. In the figures below, $\angle CAD$ and $\angle DAB$ are adjacent angles.

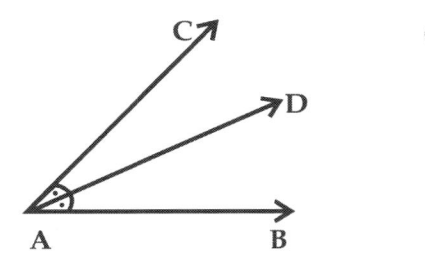

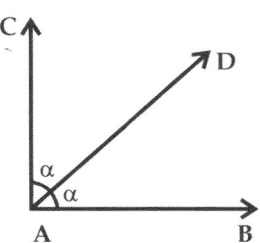

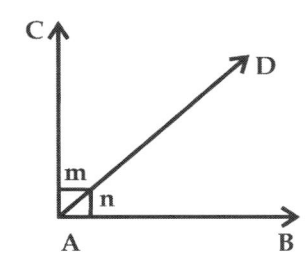

37

A ray that divides an angle into two angles of equal measure is called an **angle bisector**. Ray $\overrightarrow{AD}$ in the middle figure above is an example of an angle bisector.

Two angles whose measures sum to 90° are called **complementary angles**. In the rightmost figure above, ∠CAD and ∠DAB are complementary angles because $m\angle CAD + m\angle DAB = 90°$ ($m\angle CAD$ is read "the measure of angle CAD").

Note: In the rightmost figure above, we could also write ∠CAD as ∠m, and we can write ∠DAB as ∠n.

Two angles whose measures sum to 180° are called **supplementary angles**. In the figure below, ∠n and ∠m are supplementary angles because $m\angle m + m\angle n = 180°$. In this case, we also sometimes say that ∠m and ∠n form a **linear pair**.

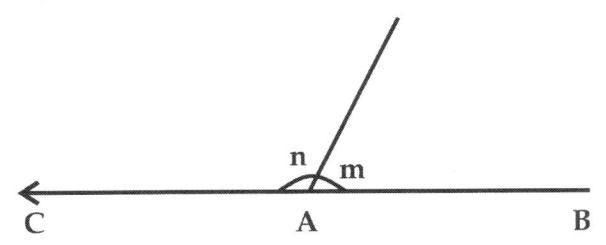

Two non-adjacent angles formed by two intersecting lines are called **vertical angles**. In the figure below, ∠a and ∠c form a pair of vertical angles, and ∠b and ∠d also form a pair of vertical angles.

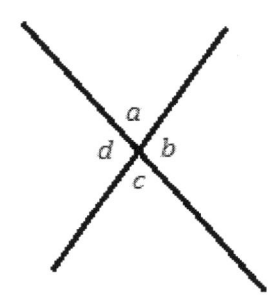

Vertical angles are **congruent**, meaning they have the same measure. For example, $m\angle a = m\angle c$. We can also write $\angle a \cong \angle c$. The symbol "≅" can be read "is congruent to."

Let's try an example.

LEVEL 1: GEOMETRY – LINES AND ANGLES

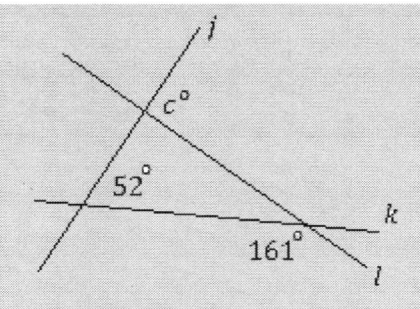

1. Intersecting lines j, k, and l are shown above. What is the value of c ?

38

TRIANGLE FACT 1: The measures of the interior angles of a triangle sum to 180°.

Solution using TRIANGLE FACT 1: The rightmost angle in the triangle is supplementary with the 161° angle, and therefore it has measure $180 - 161 = 19°$ as shown in the figure on the left. The third angle of the triangle has measure $180 - 52 - 19 = 109°$ as shown in the figure on the right.

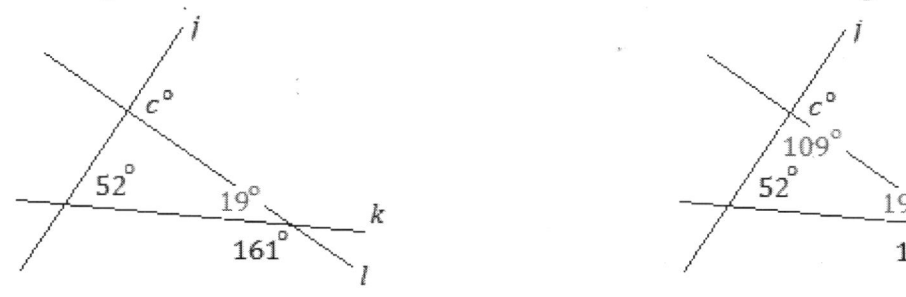

Finally, we have $c = 180 - 109 = \mathbf{71}$.

TRIANGLE FACT 2: The measure of an exterior angle to a triangle is the sum of the measures of the two opposite interior angles of the triangle.

* Solution using TRIANGLE FACT 2: Using the left figure above from the previous solution, we have $c = 52 + 19 = \mathbf{71}$.

Time to Practice

LEVEL 1: GEOMETRY – LINES AND ANGLES

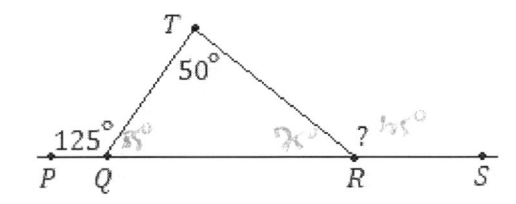

2. In the figure above, vertices Q and R of $\triangle QTR$ lie on $\overline{PS}$, the measure of $\angle PQT$ is 125°, and the measure of $\angle QTR$ is 50°. What is the measure of $\angle TRS$? (Disregard the degree symbol when gridding your answer.)

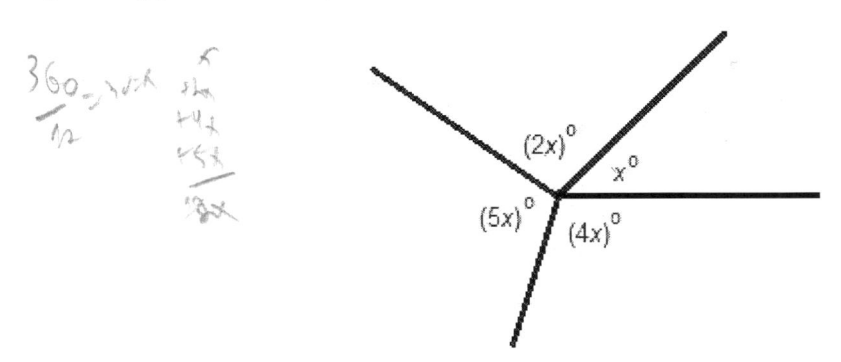

3. In the figure above, four line segments meet at a point to form four angles. What is the value of x?

LEVEL 2: GEOMETRY – LINES AND ANGLES

4. C is the midpoint of line segment $\overline{AB}$, and D and E are the midpoints of $\overline{AC}$ and $\overline{CB}$, respectively. If the length of $\overline{AB}$ is 17, what is the length of $\overline{DE}$?

    A) 4.25
    B) 6.75
    C) 8.5
    D) 17

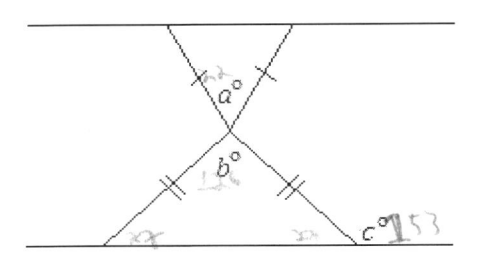

Note: Figure not drawn to scale.

5. In the figure above, the two triangles are isosceles. If $a + c = 175$ and $a = 22$, what is the value of b?

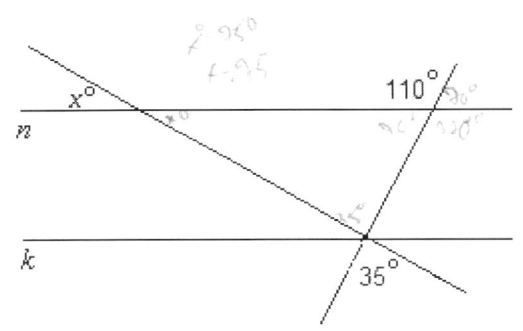

Note: Figure not drawn to scale.

6. In the figure above, what is the value of x?

LEVEL 3: GEOMETRY – LINES AND ANGLES

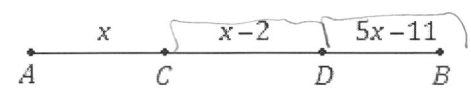

Note: Figure not drawn to scale.

7. On $\overline{AB}$ above, $CD = DB$. What is the length of $\overline{AB}$?

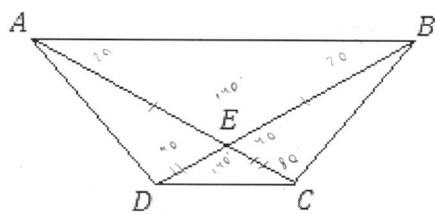

A, B, D, C figure with intersection at E.

Note: Figure not drawn to scale.

8. In the figure above, $\overline{AC}$ and $\overline{BD}$ intersect at E, $AE = BE$, $CE = DE$, $m\angle AED = 40°$, and $m\angle BCE = 80°$. What is the measure, in degrees, of $\angle ABC$? (Disregard the degree symbol when gridding your answer.)

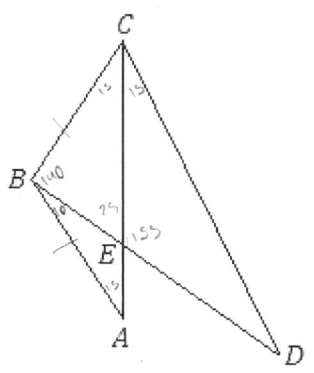

Note: Figure not drawn to scale.

9. In the figure above, $AB = BC$, $m\angle BCA = 15°$, $m\angle ABD = 10°$, and AC bisects $\angle BCD$. What is $m\angle CED$? (Disregard the degree symbol when gridding your answer.)

LEVEL 5: GEOMETRY – LINES AND ANGLES

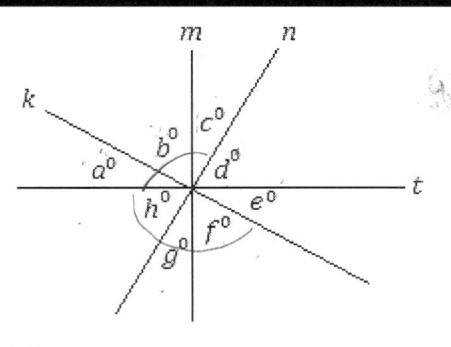

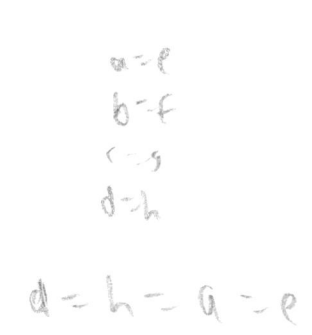

Note: Figure not drawn to scale.

10. In the figure above, lines k, m, n, and t intersect at a point. If $a + b + c = f + g + h$, which of the following must be true?

   I. $d = e$
   II. $a + b = f + h$
   III. $b + c = g + h$

   A) I and II only
   B) I and III only
   C) II and III only
   D) I, II, and III

41

Answers

1. 71   2. 105   3. 30   4. C   5. 126   6. 75   7. 11/4, 2.75   8. 80   9. 155   10. A

Full Solutions

2.
Solution using TRIANGLE FACT 1: Angles PQT and TQR are supplementary, and so $m\angle TQR = 180 - 125 = 55°$ as shown in the figure on the left. Since the angle measures of a triangle sum to $180°$, we have that $m\angle TRQ = 180 - 50 - 55 = 75°$ as shown in the figure on the right.

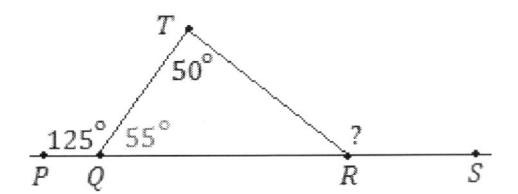

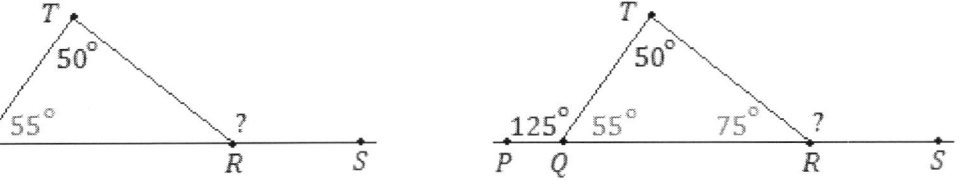

Finally, since angles TRQ and TRS are supplementary, we have $m\angle TRS = 180 - 75 = 105°$. So, we grid in **105**.

* **Solution using TRIANGLE FACT 2:** Using the left figure above from the previous solution, we have $m\angle TRS = 50 + 55 = 105°$. So, we grid in **105**.

3.
* First note that the measures of the four angles must add up to $360°$. It follows that $x + 2x + 4x + 5x = 360$. So, we have $12x = 360$, and therefore $x = \frac{360}{12} = \mathbf{30}$.

4.
* Let's draw a figure.

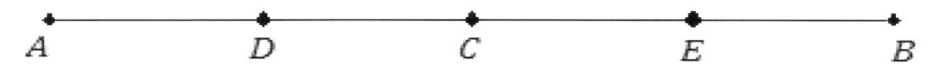

Since the length of AB is 17, it is not hard to see that the length of each of the smaller segments is $\frac{17}{4} = 4.25$. So, $DE = DC + CE = 4.25 + 4.25 = 8.5$, choice **C**.

Note: The **midpoint** of a line segment lies midway between the two endpoints of the segment, and thus it splits the segment in half.

5.
* We have $c = 175 - a = 175 - 22 = 153$. So, the angle inside the triangle adjacent to c measures $180 - 153 = 27°$ (the two angles are supplementary). It follows that $b = 180 - 27 - 27 = \mathbf{126}$.

Note: An **isosceles triangle** has 2 congruent sides. The angles opposite the 2 congruent sides are also congruent.

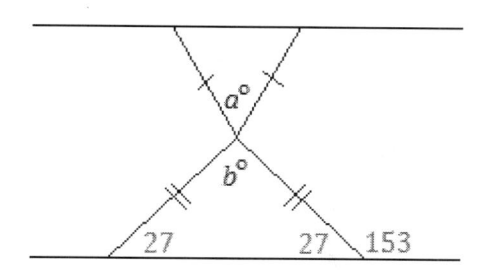

In this problem, as we can see in the figure above, once we find that the angle adjacent to c measures $27°$, we get that the other lower angle in the triangle also measures $27°$.

6.
* Let's use supplementary and vertical angles to add some information to the picture.

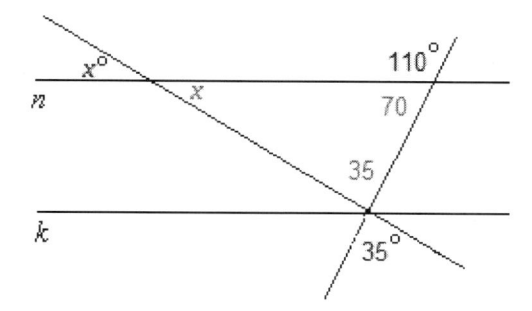

We got the angles marked 35 and x inside the triangle because vertical angles are congruent. The third angle is supplementary with the 110 degree angle, and so its measure is $180 - 110 = 70°$.

Finally, since the sum of the angle measures in a triangle is 180 degrees, $x = 180 - 70 - 35 = \mathbf{75}$.

7.
* Since $CD = DB$, we have $x - 2 = 5x - 11$. So, $9 = 4x$, and therefore $x = \frac{9}{4} = 2.25$.

So, $AB = x + (x - 2) + (5x - 11) = 7x - 13 = 7 \cdot 2.25 - 13 = 15.75 - 13 = \mathbf{2.75}$.

8.
* Since angles AED and AEB are supplementary, $m\angle AEB = 180 - m\angle AED = 180 - 40 = 140$, as shown in the figure on the left. Since the angle measures of a triangle sum to $180°$, we have $m\angle EAB + m\angle EBA = 180 - 140 = 40°$. Since $AE = BE$, $m\angle EAB = m\angle EBA = 20°$. This is also shown in the figure on the left.

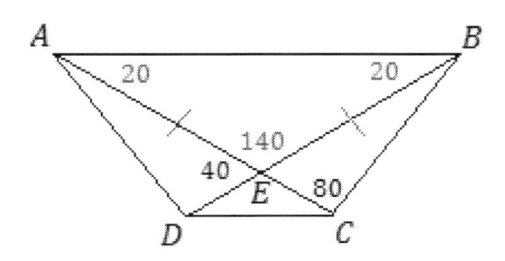

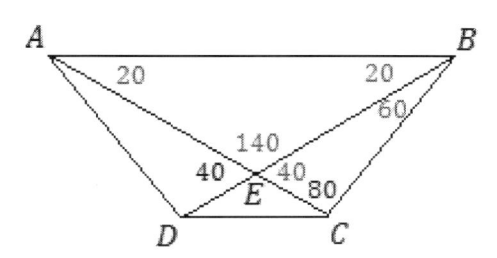

Now, since angles BEC and AED are vertical angles, $m\angle BEC = m\angle AED = 40°$, as shown in the figure on the right. Since the angle measures of a triangle sum to $180°$, we have that $m\angle CBE = 180 - 80 - 40 = 60°$, also shown in the figure on the right.

Finally, we have $m\angle ABC = m\angle EBA + m\angle CBE = 20 + 60 = \mathbf{80}$.

9. In the figure above, $AB = BC$, $m\angle BCA = 15°$, $m\angle ABD = 10°$, and AC bisects $\angle BCD$. What is $m\angle CED$? (Disregard the degree symbol when gridding your answer.)

* Since AC bisects $\angle BCD$, we have $m\angle ACD = m\angle BCA = 15°$, as shown in the figure on the left. Since $AB = BC$, $m\angle CAB = m\angle BCA = 15°$. This is also shown in the figure on the left.

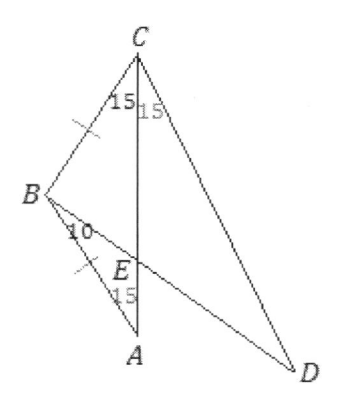

Note: Figure not drawn to scale.

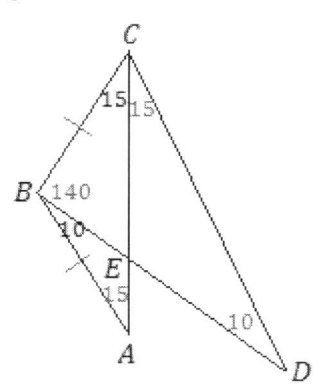

Note: Figure not drawn to scale.

Since the angle measures in a triangle sum to $180°$, $m\angle CBD = 180 - 10 - 15 - 15 = 140°$, as shown in the figure on the right. For the same reason, $m\angle BDC = 180 - 140 - 15 - 15 = 10°$. This is also shown in the figure on the right. Finally, for the same reason once again, $m\angle CED = 180 - 15 - 10 = \mathbf{155}$.

10.
* **Complete geometric solution:** Since t is a straight line, we have both $a + b + c + d = 180$ and $e + f + g + h = 180$. So,
$$a + b + c + d = e + f + g + h$$
Since $a + b + c = f + g + h$, we can substitute:
$$f + g + h + d = e + f + g + h$$
Subtracting $f + g + h$ from each side of this last equation yields $d = e$.

So, I is true, and we can eliminate choice C.

Since the angles with measures c and g are vertical, they have the same measure. So, $c = g$. Therefore, we can substitute c for g in the given equation $a + b + c = f + g + h$ to get $a + b + g = f + g + h$. Subtracting g from each side of this last equation yields $a + b = f + h$. So, II is true, and we can eliminate choice B.

If we let $a = e = 65$, $b = f = 30$, $c = g = 20$, and $d = h = 65$, then we have
$$a + b + c + d = e + f + g + h = 180.$$

We also have
$$a + b + c = f + g + h = 115, b + c = 50, \text{ and } g + h = 85.$$
So, III is false, and the answer is choice **A**.

Notes: (1) In this problem, there are four obvious pairs of vertical angles, leading to the following true equations:
$$a = e, b = f, c = g, d = h$$
There are also other pairs of vertical angles, but we don't need those to solve the problem (as one example, we have $a + b = e + f$).

(2) A straight line consists of 180°. So, for example, since t is a straight line, we must have $a + b + c + d = 180$.

There are four straight lines in the given figure. This leads to eight equations similar to the one we just wrote down. As a simple exercise, you may want to write out these eight equations.

(3) If you are trying to solve this problem by picking numbers (which might prove a little tricky here), be careful to notice that there are several equations that are not explicitly written in the question itself. Altogether, there are seven equations that must be satisfied:
$$a = e, b = f, c = g, d = h$$
$$a + b + c + d = 180$$
$$e + f + g + h = 180$$
$$a + b + c = f + g + h$$

The first four equations follow from note (1), the next two from note (2), and the last one is given in the question.

LESSON 5 – HEART OF ALGEBRA
SOLVING LINEAR INEQUALITIES

More or Less...

$x < y$ means "x is less than y."

For example, $5 < 8$ and $-11 < -3$ are TRUE, whereas $2 < -1$ is FALSE.

$x > y$ means "x is greater than y."

For example, $7 > 2$ and $0 > -6$ are TRUE, whereas $-2 > 2$ is FALSE.

It sometimes helps to remember that for $<$ and $>$, the symbol always points to the smaller number.

Solving inequalities is very similar to solving equations. Let's try a problem. Try to solve it both informally and formally.

LEVEL 1: HEART OF ALGEBRA – SOLVING LINEAR INEQUALITIES

1. What is the greatest integer x that satisfies the inequality $3 + \frac{x}{6} < 8$?

* **Algebraic solution:** We subtract 3 from each side of the given inequality to get $\frac{x}{6} < 5$. We then multiply each side of this inequality by 6 to get $x < 30$. The greatest integer less than 30 is **29**.

Note: The **integers** are the counting numbers together with their negatives.

$$\{\ldots, -4, -3, -2, -1, 0, 1, 2, 3, 4, \ldots\}$$

Time to Practice

LEVEL 1: HEART OF ALGEBRA – SOLVING LINEAR INEQUALITIES

2. If $7t + 11 < 46$, which of the following CANNOT be the value of t ?

   A) 0
   B) 1
   C) 3
   D) 5

Algebraic solution:
$$7t + 11 < 46$$
$$7t < 35$$
$$t < 5$$

Thus, the answer is choice **D**.

Notes: (1) We get from the first inequality to the second inequality by subtracting 11 from each side: $(7t + 11) - 11 = 7t$ and $46 - 11 = 35$

(2) We get from the second inequality to the third inequality by dividing each side by 7: $\frac{7t}{7} = t$ and $\frac{35}{7} = 5$.

"Plug It In" Strikes Again!

In Lesson 1 we discussed the "fallback" strategy of plugging in answer choices. There it was mentioned that it's often best to start with choice B or C as our first guess. In certain cases, however, it is more efficient to start with the least or greatest answer choice. For example, when one of the words "least" or "greatest" appears in the problem, and sometimes when there is an inequality in the problem.

Solution by starting with choice D: We start with choice D and substitute 5 in for t in the given inequality.

$$7t + 11 < 46$$
$$7(5) + 11 < 46$$
$$35 + 11 < 46$$
$$46 < 46$$

Since this is FALSE, the answer is choice **D**.

Note: If we were to try choice C first, then the left-hand side of the inequality gives us $7(3) + 11 = 21 + 11 = 32$. Since $32 < 46$ is true, we see that 3 CAN be a solution. This computation not only allows us to eliminate choice C as an answer, but choices A and B as well.

* Solution with some clever logical reasoning: A moment's thought tells us that we are looking for a number that is too big. So, the largest number given must be the answer. Using this reasoning, we can actually solve this problem without doing a single computation. The answer is choice **D**.

LEVEL 2: HEART OF ALGEBRA – SOLVING LINEAR INEQUALITIES

3. Which of the following ordered pairs (x, y) does not satisfy the inequality $7x - 2y < 3$?

   A) $(1, 4)$
   B) $(2, 10)$
   C) $(3, 11)$
   D) $(4, 12)$

LEVEL 3: HEART OF ALGEBRA – SOLVING LINEAR INEQUALITIES

4. Which of the following numbers is NOT a solution of the inequality $8x - 4 \geq 9x - 2$?

   A) -4
   B) -3
   C) -2
   D) -1

5. * A copacker has a maximum daily budget of $8000. The copacker makes n identical items, each costing $8 to produce. If the daily fixed costs to run the copacker's warehouse are $2300, what is the maximum possible value for n that will keep the combined daily fixed costs and production costs within the copacker's daily budget?

6. When 7 is increased by $5x$, the result is less than 62. What is the greatest possible integer value for x ?

7. Kayleigh plans to go skiing for the day. The ski rental costs $15 per hour, and the lift ticket is $50 for the day. Kaleigh wants to spend less than $130 for the lift ticket and the ski rental. If skis can be rented for only a whole number of hours, what is the maximum number of hours for which Kayleigh can ski?

LEVEL 4: HEART OF ALGEBRA – SOLVING LINEAR INEQUALITIES

8. * Jim makes watches that he sells at his store "Jim's watches." Jim pays $2980 each month in rent to keep his store. Each watch costs Jim $10 to make, and he sells each watch for $90. What is the least number of watches Jim needs to sell each month to cover the cost of his rent?

$$C = 15h + p + 2000$$

9. The formula above gives the weekly cost C, in dollars, of running a local pizza parlor, where h is the total number of hours the store is open and p is the number of pizzas made. If, during a particular week, the pizza parlor was open for at least 40 hours and it cost no more than $2,750 to run the pizza parlor, what is the maximum number of pizzas that could have been made?

LEVEL 5: HEART OF ALGEBRA – SOLVING LINEAR INEQUALITIES

10. * A worker earns $12 per hour for the first 40 hours he works in any given week, and $18 per hour for each hour above 40 that he works each week. If the worker saves 75% of his earnings each week, what is the least number of hours he must work in a week to save at least $441 for the week?

    A) 6
    B) 8
    C) 46
    D) 47

Answers

1. 29   2. D   3. D   4. D   5. 712   6. 10   7. 5   8. 38   9. 150   10. C

Full Solutions

3.

* **Solution by starting with choice C:** We start with choice C and substitute 3 for x and 11 for y into the left-hand side of the inequality. We get $7 \cdot 3 - 2 \cdot 11 = 21 - 22 = -1$. Since $-1 < 3$, we can eliminate choice C.

Let's try choice D next and substitute 4 for x and 12 for y into the left-hand side of the inequality. We get $7 \cdot 4 - 2 \cdot 12 = 28 - 24 = 4$. Since $4 \not\leq 3$, the answer is choice **D**.

4.

* Solution by starting with choice D: We start with choice D since it is the largest answer choice. We have

$$8(-1) - 4 \geq 9(-1) - 2$$
$$-8 - 4 \geq -9 - 2$$
$$-12 \geq -11$$

This is false, and so the answer is choice **D**.

Algebraic solution: We solve the inequality for x:

$$8x - 4 \geq 9x - 2$$
$$-4 \geq x - 2$$
$$-2 \geq x$$
$$x \leq -2$$

Since -1 is NOT less than or equal to -2, the answer is choice **D**.

5.

* Algebraic solution: We need to find the largest integer n for which $8n + 2300 \leq 8000$.

We subtract 2300 from each side of this inequality to get

$$8n \leq 8000 - 2300$$
$$8n \leq 5700$$

We now divide each side of this last inequality by 8 to get

$$n \leq \frac{5700}{8} = 712.5$$

So, we grid in **712**.

Notes: (1) The cost to produce 1 item is 8 dollars. The cost to produce 2 items is $8 \cdot 2 = 16$ dollars. The cost to produce 3 items is $8 \cdot 3 = 24$ dollars. In general, the cost to produce n items is $8n$ dollars.

(2) When we add the daily fixed costs to the cost to produce n items, we get $8n + 2300$ dollars.

(3) Once we get the answer 712, we can substitute this value back into the original inequality to make sure that it works: $8 \cdot 712 + 2300 = 7996$

Since $7996 < 8000$, producing 712 items keeps the costs within the copacker's daily budget.

(4) To be extra safe, let's make sure that 713 fails:

$$8 \cdot 713 + 2300 = 8004$$

Since $8004 > 8000$, 713 items is too many, and we see that the maximum possible acceptable number of items is 712.

Guess What?

Sometimes the answer choices themselves cannot be substituted in for the unknown or unknowns in the problem. But that does not mean that you cannot guess your own numbers. Try to make as reasonable a guess as possible, but do not over think it. Keep trying until you zero in on the correct value.

Solution by guessing: We do not have answer choices to help us out this time, but we can still take some educated guesses. We need to get close to $8000, and we're multiplying by 8, so we'll probably want to start with a pretty large number. Let's try 600. We have $8 \cdot 600 + 2300 = 7100$. That's too small, so we'll have to go bigger. If we try 700, we get $8 \cdot 700 + 2300 = 7900$. We're getting close. Let's try 720: $8 \cdot 720 + 2300 = 8060$. We overshot it. Let's go a little smaller and try 710: $8 \cdot 710 + 2300 = 7980$. Almost there! Let's go with 712: $8 \cdot 712 + 2300 = 7996$. Looks good. Let's just make sure 713 doesn't work: $8 \cdot 713 + 2300 = 8004$. That's too big, so the answer is **712**.

6.

* Algebraic solution: We need to solve the inequality $7 + 5x < 62$. We subtract 7 from each side of the inequality to get $5x < 62 - 7 = 55$. We then divide each side of this last inequality by 5 to get $x < \frac{55}{5} = 11$. So, we are looking for the greatest integer strictly less than 11. The answer is **10**.

Notes: (1) Let's check that $x = 10$ is correct. If $x = 10$, then $5x = 5 \cdot 10 = 50$. So, 7 increased by $5x$ is 7 increased by 50, which is 57. This is in fact less than 62. To ensure that it's the *greatest* possible integer value for x, we need to check that $x = 11$ fails. If $x = 11$, then $5x = 55$ and 7 increased by $5x$ is 7 increased by 55, which is 62. Since 62 is NOT less than 62, 11 fails, and 10 is in fact the answer.

(2) This problem can also be solved by taking guesses. Note (1) shows how to go about it.

7.

* Algebraic solution: We need to find the largest integer t such that $15t + 50 < 130$. We subtract 50 from each side of the inequality to get $15t < 130 - 50 = 80$. We then divide each side of this last inequality by 15 to get $t < \frac{80}{15} = 5\frac{1}{3}$. So, we are looking for the greatest integer strictly less than $5\frac{1}{3}$. So, the answer is **5**.

Notes: (1) The following two computations show that 5 works and 6 does not, verifying that the answer is 5: $15 \cdot 5 + 50 = 75 + 50 = 125$ and $15 \cdot 6 + 50 = 90 + 50 = 140$.

(2) This problem can also be solved by taking guesses.

8.

* Algebraic solution: Let x be the number of watches that Jim sells each month. The amount of money that Jim earns, in dollars, is $80x$. To find the least value of x so that Jim's rent is covered, we need to solve the inequality $80x \geq 2980$. Dividing each side of this inequality by 80 gives us $x \geq \frac{2980}{80} = 37.25$. So, the least number of watches that Jim needs to sell to cover his rent is **38**.

Notes: (1) Since it *costs* Jim $10 to make each watch, and Jim *sells* each watch for $90, the amount that Jim *earns* for selling each watch is $90 - 10 = 80$ dollars.

For selling 2 watches, Jim earns $80 \cdot 2 = 160$ dollars.

For selling 3 watches, Jim earns $80 \cdot 3 = 240$ dollars.

In general, for selling x watches, Jim earns $80x$ dollars.

(2) Once we get the answer 38, we can substitute both 37 and 38 back into the original inequality to make sure that we got the right answer. See notes (3) and (4) from problem 5 for details.

9.

∗ Algebraic solution: We are given that $h \geq 40$ and $C \leq 2750$. So, $-15h \leq -15 \cdot 40 = -600$, and it follows that $C - 15h \leq 2750 - 600 = 2150$. So, $p + 2000 = C - 15h \leq 2150$. Subtracting 2000 from each side of this last inequality yields $p \leq 2150 - 2000 = \mathbf{150}$.

Notes: (1) When we multiply each side of an inequality by a negative number, the inequality reverses. For example, since $h \geq 40$, we have $-15h \leq -15 \cdot 40$, which is equivalent to $-15h \leq -600$.

It's good that this happened because the inequalities for C and $-15h$ are facing the same way. Since $C \leq 2750$ and $-15h \leq -600$, we can add these two inequalities to get $C - 15h \leq 2750 - 600$. Thus, $C - 15h \leq 2150$.

(2) We can subtract $15h$ from each side of the given equation to get $C - 15h = p + 2000$.

(3) It's pretty safe in this problem to forget the inequalities and simply plug in 40 for h and 2750 for C. We then have $2750 = 15 \cdot 40 + p + 2000 = p + 2600$. Subtracting 2600 from each side of this equation gives us $150 = p$.

10.

∗ Informal solution: If \$441 represents 75% of the worker's earnings, then the worker's total earnings is $\frac{441}{0.75} = \$588$.

For the first 40 hours, the worker earns $12 \cdot 40 = 480$ dollars. So, the remaining amount that the worker needs to earn is $588 - 480 = 108$ dollars. So, the number of additional hours above 40 that the worker will work is $\frac{108}{18} = 6$.

The total number of hours that the worker must work is therefore $40 + 6 = 46$, choice **C**.

Notes: (1) We change a percent to a decimal by moving the decimal point to the left 2 places. The number 75 has a "hidden" decimal point at the end of the number ($75 = 75.$ or 75.0). When we move this decimal point to the left two places we get $.75$ or 0.75.

(2) We can find the worker's total earnings formally as follows:

We are given that 441 is 75% of the worker's total earnings. So, we have $441 = 0.75T$, where T is the worker's total earnings. We divide each side of this equation by 0.75 to get $T = \frac{441}{0.75} = 588$.

(3) Be careful that you do not accidentally choose 6 as the answer. 6 is the number of hours above 40 that the worker must work. The question is asking for the total number of hours, which is $40 + 6$.

Algebraic solution 1: Let x be the number of hours that the worker works *above* 40 hours. We need to solve the following inequality for x:

$$0.75(12 \cdot 40 + 18x) \geq 441$$
$$480 + 18x \geq \frac{441}{0.75}$$
$$480 + 18x \geq 588$$
$$18x \geq 108$$
$$x \geq 6$$

So, the least number of hours the worker needs to work is $40 + 6 = 46$, choice **C**.

Notes: (1) For the first 40 hours, the worker earns $12 \cdot 40 = 480$ dollars.

(2) For x hours above 40, the worker earns $18x$ dollars.

(3) Using notes (1) and (2), we see that he worker earns a total of $12 \cdot 40 + 18x = 480 + 18x$ dollars.

(4) We are given that 75% of the total earned must be at least 441. So, $0.75T = 441$, where $T = 12 \cdot 40 + 18x$ (see note (2) in the previous solution).

(5) Remember that we let x represent the number of hours the worker works *above* 40. So, at the end, we need to add 40 to the result.

Algebraic solution 2: This time we let x be the total number of hours that the worker works, where x must be at least 40. We need to solve the following inequality for x:

$$0.75\big(12 \cdot 40 + 18(x - 40)\big) \geq 441$$
$$480 + 18x - 720 \geq \frac{441}{0.75}$$
$$18x - 240 \geq 588$$
$$18x \geq 828$$
$$x \geq 46$$

So, the least number of hours the worker needs to work is 46, choice **C**.

Notes: (1) This time we are letting x represent a number greater than or equal to 40.

If $x = \mathbf{40}$, the total earnings is $12 \cdot 40 + 18 \cdot \mathbf{0}$

If $x = \mathbf{41}$, the total earnings is $12 \cdot 40 + 18 \cdot \mathbf{1}$

If $x = \mathbf{42}$, the total earnings is $12 \cdot 40 + 18 \cdot \mathbf{2}$

Observe the relationship between x and the last number in the expression (both in bold). We subtract 40 from the x-value to get that number.

This shows that the total earnings is $12 \cdot 40 + 18(x - 40)$.

(2) This time, the value that we get for x is the answer to the question.

LESSON 6 – PASSPORT TO ADVANCED MATH
FUNCTIONS

Functions

A function is simply a rule that for each "input" assigns a specific "output." Functions may be given by equations, tables, or graphs.

Orderly Conduct

When evaluating functions, it is important to perform computations in the correct order. The following table reviews the correct **order of operations**.

PEMDAS	
P	Parentheses
E	Exponentiation
M	Multiplication
D	Division
A	Addition
S	Subtraction

Note that multiplication and division have the same priority, and addition and subtraction have the same priority.

Let's try an example.

LEVEL 1: PASSPORT TO ADVANCED MATH - FUNCTIONS

1. For the function $f(x) = 7x^2 - 2x$, what is the value of $f(-5)$?

   A) -175
   B) -165
   C) 165
   D) 185

* $f(-5) = 7(-5)^2 - 2(-5) = 7 \cdot 25 + 10 = 175 + 10 = 185$, choice **D**.

Notes: (1) The variable x is a placeholder. We evaluate the function f at a specific value by substituting that value in for x. In this question, we replaced x by -5.

(2) The exponentiation was done first, followed by the multiplication. Addition was done last. See the table above for more information on order of operations.

(3) To square a number means to multiply it by itself. So,
$$(-5)^2 = (-5)(-5) = 25.$$

Many students get this confused with the computation $-5^2 = (-1)(5)(5) = -25$.

(4) If a calculator is allowed, we can do the whole computation in our calculator in one step. Simply type 7(−5)^2 − 2(−5) ENTER. The output will be 185.

Make sure to use the minus sign and not the subtraction symbol in front of the 5. Otherwise the calculator will give an error.

Time to Practice

LEVEL 1: PASSPORT TO ADVANCED MATH – FUNCTIONS

2. If $g(x) = \frac{x^3 - 2x + 5}{x^2 - 2}$, what is $g(-2)$?

   A) $-\frac{3}{2}$
   B) $-\frac{1}{6}$
   C) $\frac{1}{2}$
   D) $\frac{9}{2}$

3. If $f(x) = 3(x - 1) + 5$, which of the following is equivalent to $f(x)$?

   A) $8 - 3x$
   B) $3x - 8$
   C) $3x + 2$
   D) $3x + 4$

LEVEL 2: PASSPORT TO ADVANCED MATH – FUNCTIONS

$$h(x) = kx^2 - 11$$

4. For the function h defined above, k is a constant and $h(3) = 19$. What is the value of $h(-3)$?

   A) -19
   B) 0
   C) 9
   D) 19

LEVEL 3: PASSPORT TO ADVANCED MATH – FUNCTIONS

5. If $g(x - 5) = 2x + 7$ for all values of x, what is the value of $g(-1)$?

6. A function f satisfies $f(-6) = 1$ and $f(3) = 11$. A function g satisfies $g(-6) = 3$ and $g(1) = 5$. Find the value of $f(g(-6))$.

7. If $f(x) = -7x + 2$, which of the following is equivalent to $f(x + h)$?

   A) $-7x + h + 2$
   B) $-7(x + 7h) + 2$
   C) $-7x - 7h + 2$
   D) $-7x - 5h$

x	$f(x)$	$g(x)$
-1	2	2
3	6	2
5	5	5
8	-2	4

8. The table above shows some values of the functions f and g. For which of the following values of x is $f(x) + g(x) = f(x)g(x)$?

   A) -1
   B) 3
   C) 5
   D) 8

9. If $g(x) = -x^2 + 6x - 4$ and n is an integer greater than 4, what is one possible value of $g(n)$ for which $g(n)$ is positive?

LEVEL 4: PASSPORT TO ADVANCED MATH – FUNCTIONS

$$f(x) = x^2 + 5x - 19$$
$$g(x) = 3 - f(x)$$
$$h(x) = \sqrt{g(x)}$$

10. For the functions f, g, and h defined above, what is the value of $h(1)$?

    A) -13
    B) 0
    C) 4
    D) 16

Answers

1. D   2. C   3. C   4. D   5. 15   6. 11   7. C   8. A   9. 1   10. 4

Full Solutions

2.

* $g(-2) = \frac{(-2)^3 - 2(-2) + 5}{(-2)^2 - 2} = \frac{-8 + 4 + 5}{4 - 2} = \frac{1}{2}$, choice **C**.

Note: $(-2)^3 = (-2)(-2)(-2) = 4(-2) = -8$

Observe that when we raise a negative number to an odd exponent, the result is negative.

3.

* **Solution using the distributive property:** We have

$$3(x - 1) + 5 = 3x - 3 + 5 = 3x + 2$$

So, $f(x) = 3x + 2$, choice **C**.

Notes: (1) Recall from Lesson 2 that the **distributive property** says that if a, b, and c are real numbers, then $a(b + c) = ab + ac$. In this question, $a = 3$, $b = x$, and $c = -1$.

So, we have $3(x - 1) = 3(x + (-1)) = 3x + 3(-1) = 3x - 3$.

(2) A common mistake would be to write $3(x - 1) = 3x - 1$. This would lead to writing $3(x - 1) + 5 = 3x - 1 + 5 = 3x + 4$. This is choice D, which is **wrong!**

Solution by picking a number: Let's choose a value for x, say $x = 2$. It then follows that $f(x) = f(2) = 3(2 - 1) + 5 = 3 \cdot 1 + 5 = $ ⑧ Put a nice, big, dark circle around this number so that you can find it easily later. We now substitute $x = 2$ into each answer choice.

A) $8 - 3x = 8 - 3 \cdot 2 = 8 - 6 = 2$
B) $3x - 8 = 3 \cdot 2 - 8 = 6 - 8 = -2$
C) $3x + 2 = 3 \cdot 2 + 2 = 6 + 2 = 8$
D) $3x + 4 = 3 \cdot 2 + 4 = 6 + 4 = 10$

Since A, B, and D are incorrect we can eliminate them. Therefore, the answer is choice **C**.

Important note: C is **not** the correct answer simply because it is equal to 8. It is correct because all three of the other choices are **not** 8. **You must check all four choices!**

4.

Algebraic solution: Since $h(3) = 19$, we have $19 = h(3) = k(3)^2 - 11 = 9k - 11$.

So, $9k = 19 + 11 = 30$, and therefore, $k = \frac{30}{9} = \frac{10}{3}$.

Thus, $h(x) = \frac{10}{3}x^2 - 11$, and so we have

$$h(-3) = \frac{10}{3}(-3)^2 - 11 = \frac{10}{3} \cdot 9 - 11 = 30 - 11 = 19$$

This is choice **D**.

* **Quick solution:** The function h is an even function. It follows that $h(-3) = h(3) = 19$, choice **D**.

Even Steven or Odd Todd?

A function f with the property that $f(-x) = f(x)$ for all x is called an **even** function. For example, $f(x) = |x|$ is an even function because $f(-x) = |-x| = |x| = f(x)$.

A function f with the property that $f(-x) = -f(x)$ for all x is called an **odd** function. For example, $g(x) = \frac{1}{x}$ is odd because $g(-x) = \frac{1}{-x} = -\frac{1}{x} = -g(x)$.

A **polynomial function** is a function for which each **term** has the form ax^n where a is a real number and n is a positive integer.

Polynomial functions with only even powers of x are even functions. Keep in mind that a constant c is the same as cx^0, and so c is an even power of x. Here are some examples of polynomial functions that are even.

$$f(x) = x^2 \quad g(x) = 4 \quad h(x) = 3x^8 - 2x^6 + 9$$

Polynomial functions with only odd powers of x are odd functions. Keep in mind that x is the same as x^1, and so x is an odd power of x. Here are some examples of polynomial functions that are odd.

$$f(x) = x^3 \quad g(x) = x \quad h(x) = 3x^{11} - 2x^5 + 9x$$

A quick graphical analysis of even and odd functions: The graph of an even function is **symmetrical with respect to the y-axis**. This means that the y-axis acts like a "mirror," and the graph "reflects" across this mirror.

The graph of an odd function is **symmetrical with respect to the origin**. This means that if you rotate the graph 180 degrees (or equivalently, turn it upside down) it will look the same as it did right side up.

So, another way to determine if $f(-x) = f(x)$ is to graph f in your graphing calculator, and see if the y-axis acts like a mirror. Another way to determine if $f(-x) = -f(x)$ is to graph f in your graphing calculator, and see if it looks the same upside down. This technique will work for **all** functions (not just polynomials).

5.
* $g(-1) = g(4 - 5) = 2 \cdot 4 + 7 = 8 + 7 = \mathbf{15}$.

Note: We need to replace x by the number so that $x - 5$ is -1. In other words, we simply need to solve the equation $x - 5 = -1$ to see what to substitute for x. We have $x = -1 + 5 = 4$. So, we substitute 4 in for x in the expression $2x + 7$.

6.
* $f(g(-6)) = f(3) = \mathbf{11}$.

Note: $g(-6)$ is given to be 3. So, we replace $g(-6)$ by 3 in the expression $f(g(-6))$.

Do you see that we have $f(\boxed{\text{something}})$, where $\boxed{\text{something}}$ is $g(-6)$? Since $g(-6)$ is 3, we can replace $\boxed{\text{something}}$ by 3 to get $f(3)$. Finally, $f(3)$ is given to be 11.

7.

* $f(x+h) = -7(x+h) + 2 = -7x - 7h + 2$, choice **C**.

Notes: (1) If you're having trouble understanding how to replace x by $x + h$, try thinking of it this way. We can rewrite $f(\boxed{\text{something}}) = -7(\boxed{\text{something}}) + 2$. Now replace $\boxed{\text{something}}$ by $(x + h)$.

$$f(\boxed{(x+h)}) = -7(\boxed{(x+h)}) + 2$$

(2) See problem 3 to see how to use the distributive property correctly here.

8.

* Take a look at the first row and simply observe that $2 + 2 = 4$ and $2 \cdot 2 = 4$. So, the answer is -1, choice **A**.

Notes: (1) The first row of the table gives us $f(-1) = 2$ and $g(-1) = 2$. So, we have $f(-1) + g(-1) = 2 + 2 = 4$ and $f(-1)g(-1) = 2 \cdot 2 = 4$.

(2) Let's take a look at the second row for comparison. There, we have $f(3) = 6$ and $g(3) = 2$. So, $f(3) + g(3) = 6 + 2 = 8$ and $f(3)g(3) = 6 \cdot 2 = 12$.

9.

* $g(5) = -5^2 + 6 \cdot 5 - 4 = -25 + 30 - 4 = \mathbf{1}$.

Notes: (1) Since we want an integer greater than 4, it's only natural to try $n = 5$ first. Luckily, $n = 5$ leads to a positive answer.

(2) 5 is the only integer greater than 4 that will produce a positive result. For example, we have $g(6) = -6^2 + 6 \cdot 6 - 4 = -36 + 36 - 4 = -4$.

(3) Remember to perform operations in the correct order here: $-5^2 = (-1) \cdot 5^2 = -1 \cdot 25 = -25$.

10. For the functions f, g, and h defined above, what is the value of $h(1)$?

* **Solution 1:** We have $f(1) = 1^2 + 5 \cdot 1 - 19 = 1 + 5 - 19 = -13$.

It follows that $g(1) = 3 - f(1) = 3 - (-13) = 3 + 13 = 16$. So, $h(1) = \sqrt{g(1)} = \sqrt{16} = \mathbf{4}$.

Solution 2: $h(1) = \sqrt{g(1)} = \sqrt{3 - f(1)} = \sqrt{3 - (1^2 + 5 \cdot 1 - 19)} = \sqrt{3 - (1 + 5 - 19)}$
$= \sqrt{3 - (-13)} = \sqrt{3 + 13} = \sqrt{16} = \mathbf{4}$.

Solution 3:

$h(x) = \sqrt{g(x)} = \sqrt{3 - f(x)} = \sqrt{3 - (x^2 + 5x - 19)} = \sqrt{3 - x^2 - 5x + 19} = \sqrt{22 - 5x - x^2}$

So, $h(1) = \sqrt{22 - 5 \cdot 1 - 1^2} = \sqrt{22 - 5 - 1} = \sqrt{16} = \mathbf{4}$.

LESSON 7 – PROBLEM SOLVING
TABLES

Table Manners

Let's jump right into some problems.

LEVEL 1: PROBLEM SOLVING – TABLES

Questions 1 - 4 refer to the following information.

	Microchip	No Microchip	Total
Cats	3	1	4
Dogs	4	3	7
Rabbits	1	4	5
Total	8	8	16

The table above shows the number of animals with and without microchips at an animal shelter.

1. How many of the dogs at the shelter do not have microchips?

2. Of the 16 animals at the shelter, how many are not cats?

3. What is the ratio of the number of dogs in the shelter to the number of animals in the shelter without microchips?

LEVEL 2: PROBLEM SOLVING – TABLES

4. What fraction of the rabbits at the shelter do not have microchips?

   A) $\frac{1}{4}$
   B) $\frac{5}{16}$
   C) $\frac{1}{2}$
   D) $\frac{4}{5}$

Where Did People Hear About Company?	
Source	Percent who responded to survey
Friend or Family	51%
Email	15%
Direct Mailing	5%
Search Engine	18%
Other Source	11%

5. * A company sent out a survey to their clients to try to determine where their clients were hearing about them. The table above shows a summary of the 1800 responses they received. Based on the table, how many of those that responded to the survey found out about the company from a friend, a family member, or a search engine?

   A) 324
   B) 558
   C) 918
   D) 1242

LEVEL 3: PROBLEM SOLVING – TABLES

		Entree	
		Chicken	Fish
Dessert	Ice Cream	34	27
	Cake	20	21

6. The table above shows the entrees and desserts chosen by 102 attendees of a wedding reception. Each attendee chose exactly one entrée and one dessert. Of the attendees who chose fish, what fraction chose ice cream as a desert?

   A) $\frac{27}{102}$
   B) $\frac{19}{46}$
   C) $\frac{23}{50}$
   D) $\frac{27}{48}$

Number of minutes Aki plans to run per day	120
Aki's average heartbeat, in beats per minute, while running	143
Number of steps Aki runs per minute	180
Total number of laps Aki plans to run during training	560
Total number of steps Aki plans to take during training	151,200

7. * Aki is planning to train for a marathon. The table above shows information about Aki's training. If Aki runs at the rates given in the table, which of the following is closest to the number of days it would take Aki to complete his training?

   A) 7
   B) 25
   C) 53
   D) 126

LEVEL 4: PROBLEM SOLVING - TABLES

8. A square lawn measures 8 yards by 8 yards. Eight landscapers each mark off a randomly selected square region with side length 1 yard. There is no overlap between any of the regions. Each landscaper counts the number of weeds in the soil to a depth of 6 inches beneath the surface in each region. The results are shown in the table below.

Region	Number of weeds	Region	Number of weeds
I	30	V	31
II	25	VI	16
III	27	VII	36
IV	22	VIII	18

Which of the following is a reasonable approximation of the number of weeds to a depth of 6 inches beneath the surface on the entire lawn?

   A) 25
   B) 200
   C) 1,600
   D) 12,800

Questions 9 - 10 refer to the following information.

Janet's Sunday Run		
Part of run	Distance (miles)	Average running speed (miles per hour)
From home to park entrance	0.2	8
Each lap around the park	0.5	12
From park entrance to home	1.4	6

Every Sunday, Janet goes for a run. She runs from her home to the park, followed by 3 laps around the park, and then she runs home. The table above shows the distance, in miles, and her typical average running speed, in miles per hour, for each part of her run.

9. One Sunday, Janet completed her entire run in exactly 30 minutes. What was her average speed, in miles per hour, during her run that Sunday?

10. * During one Sunday run, Janet decided to speed up for one of her 3 laps around the park, decreasing her total running time by 10%. Based on the table, how many fewer minutes does Janet take to finish her run than if she ran with her usual average running speed the whole way?

Answers

1. 3   2. 12   3. 7/8, .875   4. D   5. D   6. D   7. A   8. C   9. 31/5, 6.2   10. 2.3

Full Solutions

1.
* We look at the row labeled "Dogs" and the column labeled "No Microchip." The answer is **3**.

Note: The appropriate entry is highlighted in the table below.

	Microchip	No Microchip	Total
Cats	3	1	4
Dogs	4	3	7
Rabbits	1	4	5
Total	8	8	16

2.

* The animals that are not cats are the dogs and the rabbits. There are 7 dogs and 5 rabbits for a total of **12**.

Note: The appropriate entries are highlighted in the table below.

	Microchip	No Microchip	Total
Cats	3	1	4
Dogs	4	3	**7**
Rabbits	1	4	**5**
Total	8	8	16

3.

* There are 7 dogs in the shelter and 8 animals without microchips in the shelter. So, the desired ratio is **7/8** or **.875**.

Note: The appropriate entries are highlighted in the table below.

	Microchip	No Microchip	Total
Cats	3	1	4
Dogs	4	3	**7**
Rabbits	1	4	5
Total	8	**8**	16

4.

* There is a total of 5 rabbits at the shelter and 4 of them do not have microchips. The answer is $\frac{4}{5}$, choice **D**.

Note: The appropriate entries are highlighted in the table below.

	Microchip	No Microchip	Total
Cats	3	1	4
Dogs	4	3	7
Rabbits	1	**4**	**5**
Total	8	8	16

5.

* 51% of the clients that responded found out about the company from a friend or family member and 18% of the clients that responded found out about the company from a search engine. This gives a total of $51 + 18 = 69\%$. Finally, we have that 69% of 1800 is $0.69 \cdot 1800 = 1242$, choice **D**.

6.

* The number of attendees that chose fish is $27 + 21 = 48$, and 27 of those chose ice cream as a dessert. So, the desired fraction is $\frac{27}{48}$, choice **D**.

7.

* Using the third and fifth rows of the table, we see that Aki will run for a total of $\frac{151{,}200}{180} = 840$ minutes during his training. Using this number, together with the first row of the table, we see that the number of days that Aki will train is $\frac{840}{120} = 7$, choice **A**.

Notes: (1) For the first computation, we can formally set up a ratio using the keywords "steps" and "minutes."

$$\begin{array}{ccc} \text{steps} & 180 & 151{,}200 \\ \text{minutes} & 1 & x \end{array}$$

$$\frac{180}{1} = \frac{151{,}200}{x} \Rightarrow 180x = 151{,}200 \Rightarrow x = \frac{151{,}200}{180} = 840$$

(2) Similarly, for the second computation, we can formally set up a ratio using the keywords "minutes" and "days."

$$\begin{array}{ccc} \text{minutes} & 120 & 840 \\ \text{days} & 1 & x \end{array}$$

$$\frac{120}{1} = \frac{840}{x} \Rightarrow 120x = 840 \Rightarrow x = \frac{840}{120} = 7$$

(3) We did not need the second and fourth rows of the table to solve this problem.

8.

* **Solution by estimation:** We add up all the numbers in the table to get 205, which is approximately 200. So, 8 square yards of the lawn contain approximately 200 weeds to a depth of 6 inches beneath the garden's surface.

But the size of the garden is $8 \cdot 8 = 64$ square yards. So, we need to multiply 200 by 8 to get $8 \cdot 200 = 1{,}600$, choice **C**.

Notes: (1) The average of the numbers seems to be somewhere near 25 (some numbers are a bit more than 25 and other numbers are a bit less than 25). It's okay if this estimate is off a bit because the answer choices are so far away from each other.

(2) Using note (1), we can get a quick estimate for the sum of the entries in the table by multiplying 25 by the number of entries 8. We get a sum of $8 \cdot 25 = 200$.

(3) Alternatively, we can use our calculator to actually add up all the numbers to get a more precise answer of 205.

(4) Whether we use 200 or 205, we are still just getting an estimate in the end. The 205 is just the number of weeds in 8 of the 64 square yards. We actually have no idea how many weeds are in the remaining 56 square yards. But $8 \cdot 200$ or $8 \cdot 205$ are both reasonable guesses for a rough estimate.

9.

* Solution using $d = rt$: Janet ran a total distance of $0.2 + 3 \cdot 0.5 + 1.4 = 3.1$ miles.

Using $d = r \cdot t$ (distance = rate · time), and the fact that 30 minutes = $\frac{1}{2}$ hour, we have:

$$3.1 = r \cdot \frac{1}{2}$$
$$r = 3.1 \cdot 2 = \mathbf{6.2}.$$

10.

* Solution using $d = rt$: We use the formula $d = r \cdot t$ three times to compute the time Janet takes to complete each part of her run when she runs at her average running speed as shown in the table. From her home to the park entrance, her running time, in hours, is $t_1 = \frac{0.2}{8}$. For each lap around the park, her running time, in hours, is $t_2 = \frac{0.5}{12}$. From the park entrance to her home, her running time, in hours, is $t_3 = \frac{1.4}{6}$. It follows that her total running time in <u>minutes</u> is $60(t_1 + 3t_2 + t_3) = 23$. Finally, 10% of 23 is $0.1 \cdot 23 = \mathbf{2.3}$.

LESSON 8 – GEOMETRY
TRIANGLES

Acute and Not So Acute Triangles

A **triangle** is a two-dimensional geometric figure with three sides and three angles. The sum of the degree measures of all three angles of a triangle is 180°.

A triangle is **acute** if all three of its angles measure less than 90°.
A triangle is **obtuse** if one angle has a measure greater than 90°.
A triangle is **right** if it has one angle that measures exactly 90°.

Example 1:

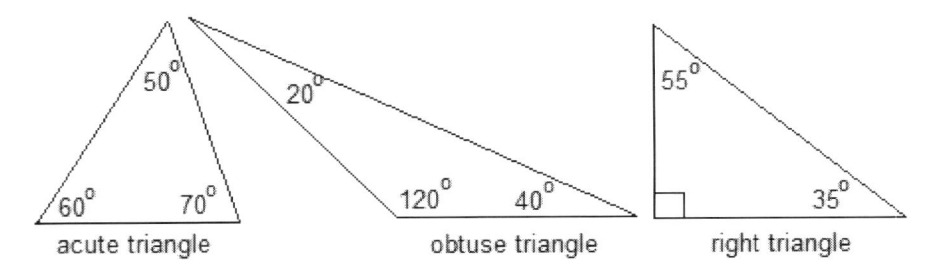

acute triangle (50°, 60°, 70°)   obtuse triangle (20°, 120°, 40°)   right triangle (55°, 35°)

A triangle is **isosceles** if it has two sides of equal length. Equivalently, an isosceles triangle has two angles of equal measure.

A triangle is **equilateral** if all three of its sides have equal length. Equivalently, an equilateral triangle has three angles of equal measure (all three angles measure 60°).

Example 2:

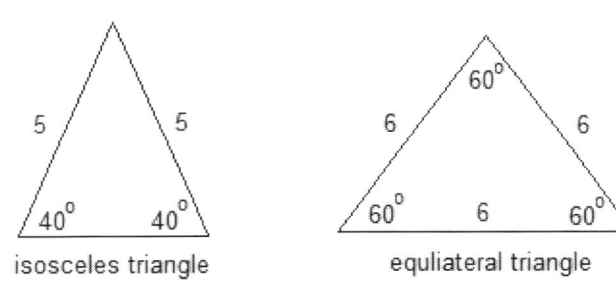

isosceles triangle (sides 5, 5; angles 40°, 40°)   equliateral triangle (sides 6, 6, 6; angles 60°, 60°, 60°)

LEVEL 1: GEOMETRY – TRIANGLES

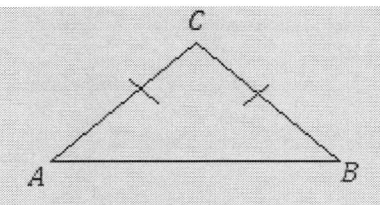

1. In $\triangle ABC$, the measure of $\angle B$ is 40°, and $\overline{AC} \cong \overline{BC}$, as shown in the figure above. What is the measure, in degrees, of $\angle C$? (Disregard the degree symbol when gridding your answer.)

* Since the angle measures of a triangle sum to 180°, we have
$$m\angle A + m\angle B + m\angle C = 180°$$
Since $\overline{AC} \cong \overline{BC}$, the triangle is isosceles, and in fact the two angles opposite these sides have the same measure. So, $m\angle A = m\angle B = 40°$.

Therefore, we have the following.
$$40° + 40° + m\angle C = 180°$$
$$80° + m\angle C = 180°$$
$$m\angle C = 180 - 80 = 100°$$

Therefore, the answer is **100**.

Time to Practice

LEVEL 1: GEOMETRY – TRIANGLES

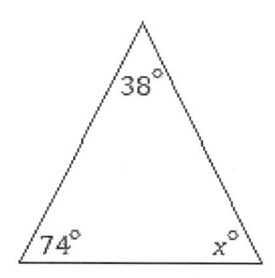

2. In the triangle above, what is the value of x?

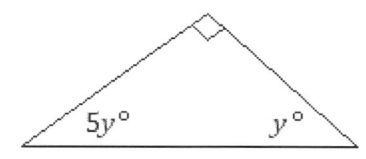

3. In the right triangle above, what is the value of y?

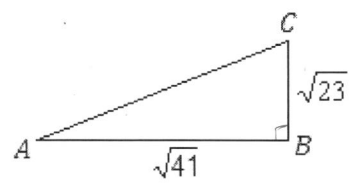

Note: Figure not drawn to scale.

4. In right triangle ABC above, what is the length of side AC?

LEVEL 2: GEOMETRY – TRIANGLES

5. A basketball player runs due west x feet to receive a pass. He catches the basketball and then moves due north 24 feet. If the basketball player winds up 26 feet from his starting point, what is the value of x?

LEVEL 3: GEOMETRY – TRIANGLES

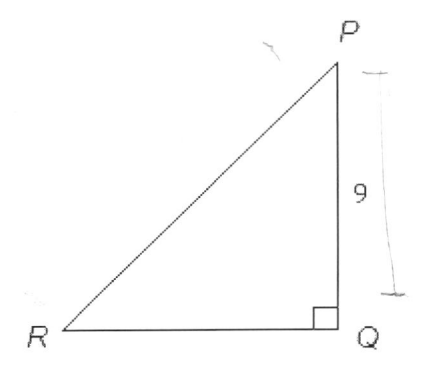

6. In the isosceles right triangle above, $PQ = 9$. What is the length, in inches, of $\overline{PR}$?

   A) $9\sqrt{2}$
   B) $\sqrt{18}$
   C) 18
   D) 9

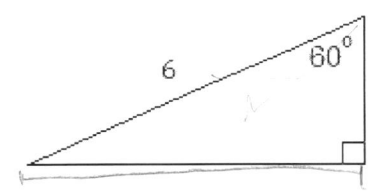

7. The figure above shows a right triangle whose hypotenuse is 6 feet long. How many feet long is the longer leg of this triangle?

   A) 3
   B) 12
   C) $\sqrt{3}$
   D) $3\sqrt{3}$

LEVEL 4: GEOMETRY – TRIANGLES

8. If x is an integer, how many different triangles are there with sides of length 1, 2, and x ?

   A) None
   B) One
   C) Two
   D) Three

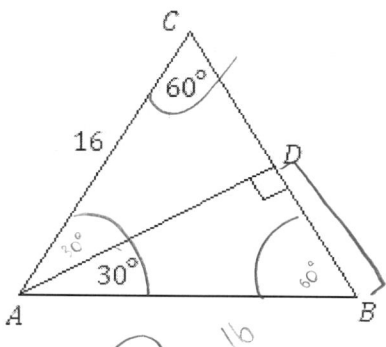

9. In △ABC above, what is the length of $\overline{BD}$?

   A) 4
   B) 8
   C) $8\sqrt{2}$
   D) $8\sqrt{3}$

LEVEL 5: GEOMETRY – TRIANGLES

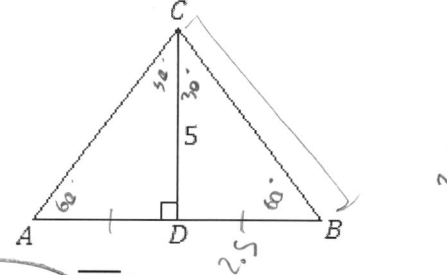

10. △ABC shown above is equilateral, $\overline{CD}$ is an altitude, and $CD = 5$. What is the length of a side of △ABC ?

    A) $\frac{5\sqrt{3}}{3}$
    B) $\frac{10\sqrt{3}}{3}$
    C) $5\sqrt{3}$
    D) $10\sqrt{3}$

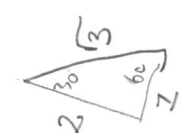

Answers

1. 100 2. 68 3. 15 4. 8 5. 10 6. A 7. D 8. B 9. B 10. B

Full Solutions

2.
* $x = 180 - 74 - 38 = \mathbf{68}$.

Note: More formally, since the sum of the degree measures of all three angles of a triangle is 180°, we have the following.

$$x + 38 + 74 = 180$$
$$x + 112 = 180$$
$$x = 180 - 112 = \mathbf{68}.$$

3.

* Algebraic solution: We must have $5y + y = 90$. So, $6y = 90$, and therefore $y = \frac{90}{6} = \mathbf{15}$.

4.

Solution by the Pythagorean Theorem: $AC^2 = AB^2 + BC^2 = 41 + 23 = 64$. So, $AC = \mathbf{8}$.

Notes: (1) The **Pythagorean Theorem** says that if a right triangle has legs of length a and b, and a hypotenuse of length c, then $c^2 = a^2 + b^2$.

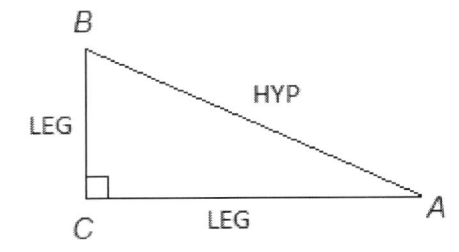

Note that the hypotenuse is always opposite the right angle.

The Pythagorean Theorem is one of the formulas given to you in the beginning of every SAT math section.

(2) The equation $AC^2 = 64$ would normally have two solutions: $c = 8$ and $c = -8$. But the length of a side of a triangle cannot be negative, so we reject -8.

5.

Solution by the Pythagorean Theorem: Let's first draw a picture

By the Pythagorean Theorem, we have $26^2 = x^2 + 24^2$. So, $676 = x^2 + 576$. We subtract 576 from each side of this last equation to get $x^2 = 676 - 576 = 100$. So, $x = \sqrt{100} = \mathbf{10}$.

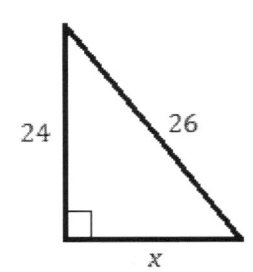

Note: Always remember that the length of the hypotenuse always goes by itself in the Pythagorean Theorem. In this case, 26 goes by itself, and NOT x.

Pythagoras—Pythagoras—Pythagoras

A **Pythagorean triple** is a set of three numbers that satisfy the Pythagorean Theorem. The two that come up most often on the SAT are $3, 4, 5$ and $5, 12, 13$. Note that the largest number is always the length of the hypotenuse of the right triangle (the hypotenuse is ALWAYS longer than both legs).

If you multiply all the numbers in a Pythagorean triple by the same number, then you always get another Pythagorean triple. For example, since $2 \cdot 3 = 6$ and $2 \cdot 4 = 8$, a right triangle with legs of length 6 and 8 has a hypotenuse of length $2 \cdot 5 = 10$.

Two other less common Pythagorean triples that may come up are $8, 15, 17$ and $7, 24, 25$.

* **Solution using a Pythagorean triple:** Since $24 = 2 \cdot 12$ and $26 = 2 \cdot 13$, we have $x = 2 \cdot 5 = \mathbf{10}$.

6.

Solution by the Pythagorean Theorem: Since the triangle is isosceles, $RQ = PQ = 9$. By the Pythagorean Theorem, we have

$$PR^2 = 9^2 + 9^2 = 81 + 81 = 81 \cdot 2.$$

So, $PR = \sqrt{81 \cdot 2} = \sqrt{81} \cdot \sqrt{2} = 9\sqrt{2}$, choice A.

Note: The equation $PR^2 = 81 \cdot 2$ would normally have two solutions: $PR = 9\sqrt{2}$ and $PR = -9\sqrt{2}$. But the length of a side of a triangle cannot be negative, so we reject $-9\sqrt{2}$.

I'd Like You to Meet Two Very Special Triangles

The following two special triangles are given on the SAT:

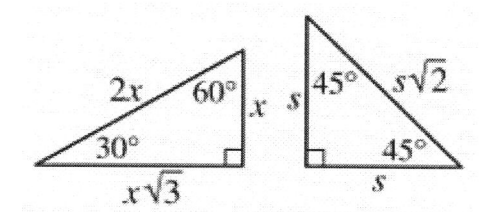

Some students get a bit confused because there are variables in these pictures. We can simplify the pictures if we substitute a 1 in for the variables.

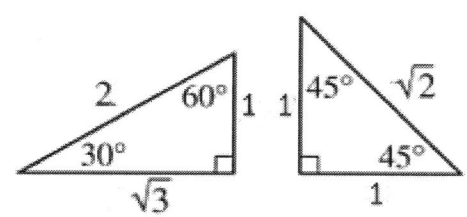

Notice that the sides of the 30, 60, 90 triangle are then 1, 2 and $\sqrt{3}$ and the sides of the 45, 45, 90 triangle are 1, 1 and $\sqrt{2}$. The variables in the first picture above just tell us that if we multiply one of the sides in the second picture by a number, then we have to multiply the other two sides by the same number. For example, instead of 1, 1, and $\sqrt{2}$, we can have 9, 9, and $9\sqrt{2}$ (here $s = 9$), or $\sqrt{2}$, $\sqrt{2}$, and 2 (here $s = \sqrt{2}$).

* **Solution using a 45, 45, 90 triangle:** An isosceles right triangle is the same as a 45, 45, 90 triangle, and so the hypotenuse has length $PR = 9\sqrt{2}$, choice **A**.

7.

* **Solution using a 30, 60, 90 triangle:** Comparing the figure given in the problem to the figure of the 30, 60, 90 triangle above, we see that $2x = 6$. It follows that $x = \frac{6}{2} = 3$, and therefore $x\sqrt{3} = 3\sqrt{3}$, choice **D**.

Note: The longer leg in a 30, 60, 90 triangle is always opposite the 60° angle.

More generally, in any triangle, there is a direct relationship between the sides of a triangle and their opposite angles. For example, the shortest side of a triangle is always opposite the smallest angle.

8.

TRIANGLE FACT 3 (The Triangle Inequality): The length of the third side of a triangle is between the sum and difference of the lengths of the other two sides.

Solution using TRIANGLE FACT 3: By the **Triangle Inequality**, $2 - 1 < x < 2 + 1$, or equivalently, $1 < x < 3$. The only integer between 1 and 3 is 2, and so there is just one triangle, choice **B**.

Notes: (1) In this problem, we are not told that the triangle is a right triangle, and so we CANNOT use the Pythagorean Theorem.

(2) There are infinitely many triangles with sides of length 1, 2, and x. For example, x can be 1.1, 1.73, or 2.006. However, 2 is the only *integer* value that satisfies the triangle inequality.

9.

* **Solution using a 30, 60, 90 triangle:** $\triangle ACD$ and $\triangle ABD$ are both 30, 60, 90 right triangles. Using $\triangle ACD$, we have $CD = 8$, $AD = 8\sqrt{3}$. Now, using $\triangle ABD$, we have $BD = 8$, choice **B**.

Notes: (1) Let's fill in the angle measures in the triangle (see the figure to the right).

Notice that $\triangle ABC$ is equilateral because all angle measures of the triangle are 60°.

(2) An **altitude** of a triangle is perpendicular to the base. A **median** of a triangle splits the base into two equal parts. An **angle bisector** of a triangle splits an angle into two equal parts. In an isosceles triangle (and in particular, an equilateral triangle), the altitude, median, and angle bisector are all equal.

In this problem, $\overline{AD}$ is given to be an altitude (the little square at $\angle ADB$ indicates a right angle). Once we know that the triangle is equilateral, it follows that $\overline{AD}$ is also a median and that $\overline{AD}$ bisects $\angle A$.

10.

* **Solution using a 30, 60, 90 triangle:** $\triangle ACD$ is a 30, 60, 90 triangle. CD is opposite the 60° angle. So, $x\sqrt{3} = 5$, and $x = \frac{5}{\sqrt{3}} = \frac{5}{\sqrt{3}} \cdot \frac{\sqrt{3}}{\sqrt{3}} = \frac{5\sqrt{3}}{3}$. Since $\overline{AC}$ is the hypotenuse of the triangle, $AC = 2x = \frac{10\sqrt{3}}{3}$, choice **B**.

Note: Remember that an equilateral triangle has three 60° angles and an altitude to the base is also a median and angle bisector (see problem 9). To the right is a picture of the triangle with all the angles added.

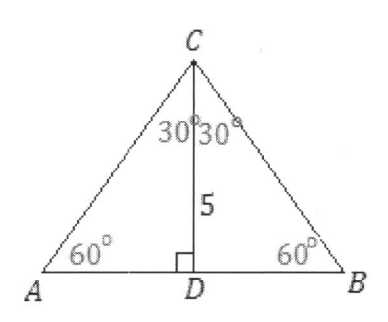

LESSON 9 – HEART OF ALGEBRA
SETTING UP LINEAR EXPRESSIONS

Words Will Never Hurt Me

Let's jump right into some problems.

LEVEL 1: HEART OF ALGEBRA – SETTING UP LINEAR EXPRESSIONS

1. An SAT course is available as a book and as an app. The author of the course earns $5.72 for each book sale and $2.85 for each app download. Which of the following expressions represents the amount, in dollars, that the author of the course earns if b books are sold and a apps are downloaded?

    A) $5.72b + 2.85a$
    B) $5.72b - 2.85a$
    C) $2.85b + 5.72a$
    D) $2.85b - 5.72a$

2. Last Sunday, Samuel ran c errands per hour for 2 hours and Timothy ran d errands per hour for 4 hours. Which of the following represents the total number of errands run by Samuel and Timothy last Sunday?

    A) $2c + 4d$
    B) $2d + 4c$
    C) $6cd$
    D) $8cd$

3. A juggler is hired to perform for 35 children at a birthday party. He will be paid $50 per hour and an additional $75 tip if he stays for the whole party. If the juggler stays for the whole party, which of the following expressions can be used to determine how much the juggler earns, in dollars?

    A) $75x + (50 + 35)$, where x is the number of children
    B) $(50 + 35)x + 75$, where x is the number of children
    C) $75x + 50$, where x is the number of hours
    D) $50x + 75$, where x is the number of hours

4. To stay healthy, it is recommended that one walks 10,000 steps per day. Hootan currently walks 5000 steps per day. He plans to increase his number of steps per day by 220 steps each week. Which of the following represents the number of steps per day that Hootan will be taking w weeks from now?

    A) $220 + 5000w$
    B) $5000 + 220w$
    C) $5000 - 220w$
    D) $10,000 + 220w$

LEVEL 2: HEART OF ALGEBRA – SETTING UP LINEAR EXPRESSIONS

5. A carpenter is building cabinets for a homeowner. The carpenter charges c dollars per hour plus a flat fee of m dollars for lumber. If the carpenter charges $750 for a 3-hour job, which of the following represents the relationship between c and m?

    A) $750 = c - 3m$
    B) $750 = 3m - c$
    C) $750 = 3c + m$
    D) $750 = c + 3m$

6. The number of veterinarians working in an animal hospital between 1970 and 1985 was three times the number of veterinarians working in the same animal hospital between 1985 and 2000. If there were 18 veterinarians working in the animal hospital between 1970 and 1985 and there were n veterinarians working in the animal hospital between 1985 and 2000, which of the following equations is true?

    A) $n + 18 = 3$
    B) $\frac{n}{3} = 18$
    C) $3n = 18$
    D) $18n = 3$

LEVEL 3: HEART OF ALGEBRA – SETTING UP LINEAR EXPRESSIONS

7. In 2012, Timothy had a collection consisting of 123 comic books. Starting in 2013, Timothy has been collecting 15 comic books per year. At this rate, if t is the number of years after 2012, which of the following functions C gives the number of comic books Timothy will have?

    A) $C(t) = 15 + 123t$
    B) $C(t) = 123 + 15t$
    C) $C(t) = 2012 + 123t$
    D) $C(t) = 2012 + 15t$

8. Tammy and Yeeshing went out to lunch. The price of Tammy's meal was m dollars, and the price of Yeeshing's meal was $5 more than the price of Tammy's meal. If Tammy and Yeeshing split the cost of the meals evenly and each paid a 22% tip, which of the following expressions represents the amount, in dollars, each of them paid? (Assume there is no sales tax.)

    A) $2.44m + 6.10$
    B) $1.22m + 6.10$
    C) $1.22m + 3.05$
    D) $0.22m + 0.5$

LEVEL 5: HEART OF ALGEBRA – SETTING UP LINEAR EXPRESSIONS

9. A scientist studying mouse behavior created a maze with an entrance consisting of three different paths. Two of the paths required traveling up an incline, whereas the third path was flat. The scientist wished to test the tendency for a mouse to choose the flat path over the inclined paths. Over the course of a day, 100 mice were placed at the entrance to the maze. Of the first 50 mice, 21 chose to move along the flat path. Among the remaining 50 mice, n mice chose to move along the flat path. Assuming that more than 35% of the 100 mice chose to move along the flat path, which of the following inequalities best describes the possible values of n ?

   A) $n + 21 > 0.35 \cdot 100$, where $n \leq 50$
   B) $n - 21 > 0.35 \cdot 100$, where $n \leq 50$
   C) $n > 0.35(100 - 21)$, where $n \leq 50$
   D) $n > 0.35(100 + 21)$, where $n \leq 50$

10. A publisher spends an average of $12,500 per year in distribution fees. The distributer is offering the option of a one-time fee of $40,000 in exchange for reducing distribution costs to a fixed fee of $3700 per year. Which of the following inequalities can be solved to find t, the number of years after which the savings on distribution costs will exceed the one-time distribution fee?

   A) $40,000 > \frac{12,500}{3700} t$
   B) $40,000 - 12,500 > 3700t$
   C) $40,000 > (12,500 - 3700)t$
   D) $40,000 < (12,500 - 3700)t$

Answers

1. A   2. A   3. D   4. B   5. C   6. C   7. B   8. C   9. A   10. D

Full Solutions

1.

* Algebraic solution: The total amount the author earns from book sales, in dollars, is $5.72b$ and the total amount the author earns in app downloads is $2.85a$. So, all together the total amount that the author earns is $5.72b + 2.85a$, choice **A**.

Notes: (1) If 1 book is sold, the author earns 5.72 dollars.

If 2 books are sold, the author earns $5.72 \cdot 2 = 11.44$ dollars.

If 3 books are sold, the author earns $5.72 \cdot 3 = 17.16$ dollars.

Following this pattern, we see that if b books are sold, the author earns $5.72b$ dollars.

(2) A similar analysis to what was done in Note (1) shows that if a apps are downloaded, the author earns $2.85a$ dollars. Try plugging in different values for a starting at $a = 1$, so that you can see this for yourself.

Solution by picking numbers: Let's suppose that 10 books were sold and the app was downloaded 2 times. Then we have $b = 10$ and $a = 2$.

The total amount the author earns from paperback sales, in dollars, is $5.72 \cdot 10 = 57.20$. The total amount the author earns from app downloads is $2.85 \cdot 2 = 5.70$. So, the total the author earns, in dollars, is $57.20 + 5.70 = $ **62.90**.

Put a nice big dark circle around **62.90** so you can find it easier later. We now substitute $b = 10$ and $a = 2$ into each answer choice:

A) $57.2 + 5.70 = 62.90$
B) $57.2 - 5.70 = 51.50$
C) $28.5 + 11.44 = 39.94$
D) $28.5 - 11.44 = 17.06$

Since B, C and D each came out incorrect, the answer is choice **A**.

Notes: (1) A is **not** the correct answer simply because it is equal to 62.90. It is correct because all three of the other choices are **not** 62.90. **You must check all four choices!**

(2) All the above computations can be done in a single step with your calculator (if a calculator is allowed for this problem).

(3) See Lesson 2 for more information on picking numbers.

2.
* **Algebraic solution:** Samuel ran a total of $2c$ errands and Timothy ran a total of $4d$ errands. So, together Samuel and Timothy ran a total of $2c + 4d$ errands, choice **A**.

Solution by picking numbers: Let's suppose that Samuel ran 3 errands per hour, and timothy ran 5 errands per hour. Then we have $c = 3$ and $d = 5$.

Samuel ran $3 \cdot 2 = 6$ errands and Timothy ran $5 \cdot 4 = 20$ errands. So, the total number of errands run by Samuel and Timothy was $6 + 20 = $ **26**.

Put a nice big dark circle around **26** so you can find it easier later. We now substitute $c = 3$, $d = 5$ into each answer choice:

A) $2 \cdot 3 + 4 \cdot 5 = 6 + 20 = 26$
B) $2 \cdot 5 + 4 \cdot 3 = 10 + 12 = 22$
C) $6 \cdot 3 \cdot 5 = 90$
D) $8 \cdot 3 \cdot 5 = 120$

Since B, C, and D each came out incorrect, the answer is choice **A**.

Notes: (1) A is **not** the correct answer simply because it is equal to 26. It is correct because all three of the other choices are **not** 26. **You must check all four choices!**

(2) See Lesson 2 for more information on picking numbers.

   3.

* Algebraic solution: The juggler is being paid 50 dollars per hour, and he is working an unknown number of hours. So, we let x be the number of hours that the juggler is working. It follows that he makes $50x$ dollars, not including his tip. When we add in the 75 dollar tip, we see that the juggler will have earned a total of $50x + 75$ dollars, where x is the number of hours he worked, choice **D**.

Notes: (1) Disregarding his tip, the juggler makes 50 dollars for 1 hour, $50 \cdot 2 = 100$ dollars for 2 hours, $50 \cdot 3 = 150$ dollars for 3 hours, and so on.

Following this pattern, we see that, in general, the juggler makes $50x$ dollars, where x is the number of hours he works.

(2) Don't forget to add in the tip of 75 dollars at the end to get a total of $50x + 75$ dollars.

(3) The number of children is not relevant in this problem. The juggler is being paid per hour, independent of the number of children at the party.

If instead the juggler was being paid 50 dollars per child, then he would have been paid a fixed amount of $50 \cdot 35 = 1750$ dollars.

Solution by picking a number: Let's choose a value for x, say $x = 2$. This means that the juggler worked for 2 hours. Since he makes \$50 per hour, he will make $50 \cdot 2 = 100$ dollars before receiving his tip. Since the juggler stays the whole party, he gets his tip of \$75. So, the juggler earns a total of $100 + 75 = $ **175** dollars.

Put a nice big dark circle around **175** so you can find it easier later. We now substitute $x = 2$ into each answer choice:

   A) $75 \cdot 2 + (50 + 35) = 150 + 85 = 235$
   B) $(50 + 35) \cdot 2 + 75 = 85 \cdot 2 + 75 = 170 + 75 = 245$
   C) $75 \cdot 2 + 50 = 150 + 50 = 200$
   D) $50 \cdot 2 + 75 = 100 + 75 = 175$

Since A, B, and C each came out incorrect, the answer is choice **D**.

Note: D is **not** the correct answer simply because it is equal to 175. It is correct because all three of the other choices are **not** 175. **You must check all four choices!**

   4.

* Algebraic solution: The number of additional steps per day that Hootan will be taking w weeks from now is $220w$. So, the total number of steps Hootan will be taking w weeks from now is $5000 + 220w$, choice **B**.

Notes: (1) 1 week from now, Hootan's steps per day will be increased by $220 \cdot 1 = 220$.

2 weeks from now, Hootan's steps per day will be increased by $220 \cdot 2 = 440$.

3 weeks from now, Hootan's steps per day will be increased by $220 \cdot 3 = 660$.

Following this pattern, w weeks from now, Hootan's steps per day will be increased by $220w$.

(2) Don't forget to add in the initial number of steps to get $5000 + 220w$.

(3) The number $10,000$ is not needed for the problem. It is just information placed there to confuse you.

(4) This problem can also be solved by picking numbers. I leave the details to the reader.

5.
* **Algebraic solution:** The carpenter is charging c dollars per hour for 3 hours for a total of $3c$ dollars. We need to add in the flat fee of m dollars for lumber and we get a total dollar amount of $3c + m$. We are told that this is equal to 750, and so we have $750 = 3c + m$, choice **C**.

Solution by picking numbers: If we assume that the lumber cost is 0 ($m = 0$), then it follows that the carpenter charges $\frac{750}{3} = 250$ dollars per hour ($c = 250$). So, let's substitute $m = 0$ and $c = 250$ into each answer choice and eliminate any equations that come out false.

- A) $750 = 250$ False
- B) $750 = -250$ False
- C) $750 = 750$ True
- D) $750 = 250$ False

Since choices A, B, and D came out false, the answer is choice **C**.

6.
* **Algebraic solution:** 18 must be three times as large as n. This can be written as $18 = 3n$, or equivalently $3n = 18$, choice **C**.

Solution by finding n: Since there were 18 veterinarians working in the animal hospital between 1970 and 1985, there must have been 6 veterinarians working in the animal hospital between 1985 and 2000. So, $n = 6$. Let's now just eliminate any answer choices that come out false when $n = 6$.

- A) $6 + 18 = 3$ False
- B) $\frac{6}{3} = 18$ False
- C) $3 \cdot 6 = 18$ True
- D) $18 \cdot 6 = 3$ False

Since A, B, and D came out false, we can eliminate them, and the answer is choice **C**.

7.

*** Algebraic solution:** The number of additional comic books Timothy will have t years after 2012 is $15t$. Adding in the initial number of comic books, we see that the total number of comic books Timothy will have t years after 2012 is $123 + 15t$. So, the answer is choice **B**.

Notes: (1) In 2013 (1 year after 2012), Timothy had $123 + 15 \cdot 1 = 138$ comic books.

In 2014 (2 years after 2012), Timothy had $123 + 15 \cdot 2 = 153$ comic books.

In 2015 (3 years after 2012), Timothy had $123 + 15 \cdot 3 = 168$ comic books.

Following this pattern, t years from 2015, Timothy will have $123 + 15t$ comic books.

(2) This problem can also be solved by picking numbers. I leave the details to the reader.

8.

*** Algebraic solution:** Yeeshing's meal was $m + 5$ dollars, and so the total for the two meals was $m + (m + 5) = 2m + 5$ dollars. When we add the 22% tip we get a total price of $1.22(2m + 5)$ dollars. Since they split the cost evenly, they each paid $0.61(2m + 5) = 1.22m + 3.05$ dollars. This is choice **C**.

Notes: (1) 22% of $2m + 5$ is $0.22(2m + 5)$. We need to add this to the original cost of the two meals to get $(2m + 5) + 0.22(2m + 5) = (1 + 0.22)(2m + 5) = 1.22(2m + 5)$.

Notice how we used the distributive property: $x + 0.22x = 1x + 0.22x = (1 + 0.22)x = 1.22x$, where $x = 2m + 5$

(2) This problem can also be solved by picking numbers. I leave the details of this solution to the reader.

9.

*** Algebraic solution:** 21 out of the first 50 mice chose to move along the flat path, and n out of the remaining 50 mice chose to move along the flat path. So, all together, $n + 21$ mice chose to move along the flat path. We are told that more than 35% of the 100 mice chose to move along the flat path. So, $n + 21$ is more than 35% of 100. In other words, $n + 21 > 0.35 \cdot 100$, choice **A**.

10.

*** Algebraic solution:** The savings on distribution costs each year is $12{,}500 - 3700$. So, the total savings on distribution costs for t years is $(12{,}500 - 3700)t$. We want this expression to exceed the one-time distribution fee of \$40,000. So, we need $(12{,}500 - 3700)t > 40{,}000$. This is equivalent to the inequality in choice **D**.

LESSON 10 – PASSPORT TO ADVANCED MATH
GRAPHS OF FUNCTIONS

Get to the POINT!

If f is a function, then

$f(a) = b$ is equivalent to "the point (a, b) lies on the graph of f."

Example 1:

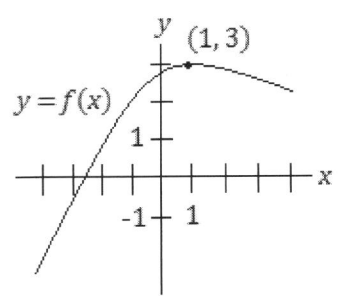

In the figure above, we see that the point $(1,3)$ lies on the graph of the function f. It follows that $f(1) = 3$.

The **y-intercept** of the graph of a function $y = f(x)$ is the point on the graph where $x = 0$ (if it exists). There can be at most one y-intercept for the graph of a function. A y-intercept has the form $(0, b)$ for some real number b. Equivalently, $f(0) = b$. Sometimes we also say that the y-intercept is the number b.

An **x-intercept** of the graph of a function is a point on the graph where $y = 0$. There can be more than one x-intercept for the graph of a function or none at all. An x-intercept has the form $(a, 0)$ for some real number a. Equivalently, $f(a) = 0$. Sometimes we may also say that the x-intercept is the number a.

The **domain** of a function is the set of all the allowed x-values (the "inputs") and the **range** of a function is the set of all the possible y-values (the "outputs").

Example 2:

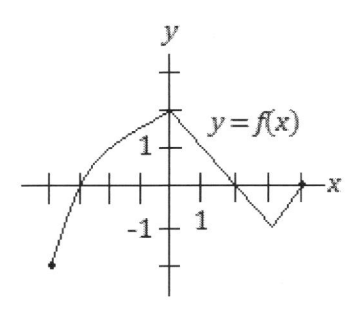

In the figure above, we see that the domain of f is $-4 \leq x \leq 4$, the range of f is $-2 \leq y \leq 2$, and the graph of f has y-intercept $(0, 2)$ and x-intercepts $(-3, 0)$, $(2, 0)$, and $(4, 0)$ (the SAT often likes to say that the y-intercept is 2 and the x-intercepts are -3, 2, and 4).

The numbers -3, 2, and 4 are also called **zeros**, **roots**, or **solutions** of the function.

Note that in example 2 we have $f(-3) = 0$, $f(2) = 0$, and $f(4) = 0$. We also have $f(0) = 2$.

If the graph of $f(x)$ is above the x-axis, then $f(x) > 0$. If the graph of $f(x)$ is below the x-axis, then $f(x) < 0$. If the graph of f is higher than the graph of g, then $f(x) > g(x)$.

In the figure for example 2 above, observe that $f(x) < 0$ for $-4 \leq x < -3$ and $2 < x < 4$. Also, $f(x) > 0$ for $-3 < x < 2$.

The graph of a function always passes the **vertical line test**: any vertical line can hit the graph *at most* once.

For example, a circle is *never* the graph of a function. It always fails the vertical line test as shown in the figure to the right.

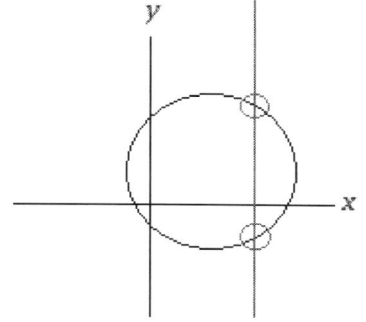

Check Out These Amazing Transformations

Let $y = f(x)$, and $k > 0$. We can move the graph of f around by applying the following basic transformations.

$y = f(x) + k$ shift up k units
$y = f(x) - k$ shift down k units
$y = f(x - k)$ shift right k units
$y = f(x + k)$ shift left k units
$y = -f(x)$ reflect in x-axis
$y = f(-x)$ reflect in y-axis.

Example: Let $f(x) = x^2$. If you move the graph of f right 3 units and down 2 units you get the graph of the function g. What is the definition of g?

Solution: We have $g(x) = (x - 3)^2 - 2$. Here is a picture.

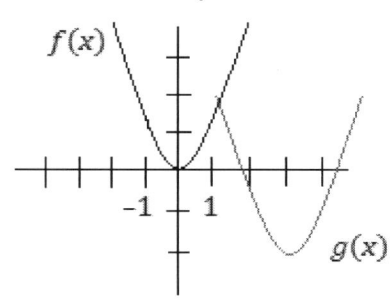

Note: After applying a transformation, you may want to "track a point" to make sure you applied the transformation correctly.

For example, after transforming f into g, the point $(0, 0)$ was moved to the point $(3, -2)$, as can be seen in the figure. In other words, $g(3)$ should be equal to -2. Let's check if this is true by plugging in 3 for x in the equations for g. We have $g(3) = (3 - 3)^2 - 2 = 0^2 - 2 = 0 - 2 = -2$. It's correct, and so it is likely that we applied the transformation correctly.

81

LEVEL 2: PASSPORT TO ADVANCED MATH – GRAPHS OF FUNCTIONS

Questions 1 - 6 refer to the following information.

The entire graph of the function g is shown in the xy-plane below.

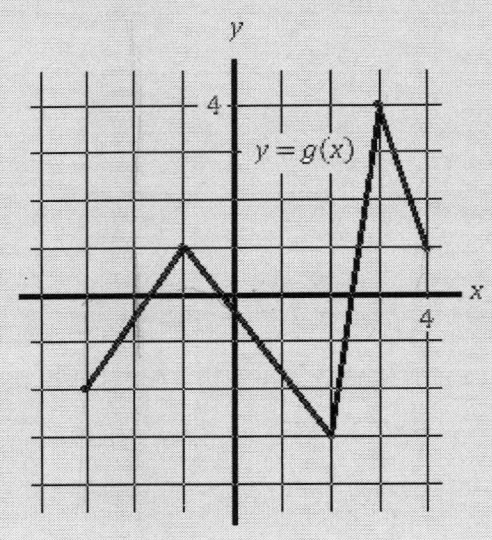

1. What is the value of $g(4) - g(-3)$?

   A) -1
   B) 1
   C) 2
   D) 3

* The points $(4, 1)$ and $(-3, -2)$ are on the graph of g. Therefore, $g(4) = 1$ and $g(-3) = -2$. So, $g(4) - g(-3) = 1 - (-2) = 1 + 2 = 3$, choice **D**.

Note: Let's circle the points $(4, 1)$ and $(-3, -2)$ on the graph for emphasis.

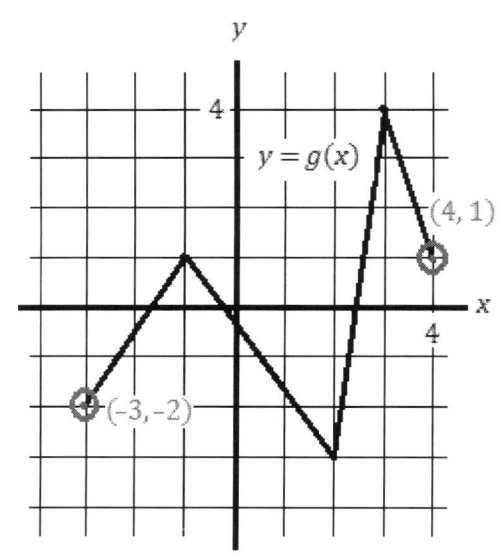

LEVEL 3: PASSPORT TO ADVANCED MATH – GRAPHS OF FUNCTIONS

2. For what value of x is the value of $g(x)$ at its maximum?

   A) -1
   B) 2
   C) 3
   D) 4

3. What is the maximum value of g ?

   A) -1
   B) 1
   C) 3
   D) 4

4. For how many values of x between -3 and 4 does $g(x) = -2.5$?

   A) None
   B) One
   C) Two
   D) More than two

5. If the function h is defined by $h(x) = -g(x)$, which of the following points is on the graph of h ?

   A) $(3, 4)$
   B) $(3, -4)$
   C) $(-3, 4)$
   D) $(-3, -4)$

6. Which of the following expressions does NOT represent the positive difference between the maximum and minimum values of g on the interval $-3 \leq x \leq 4$?

   A) $g(3) - g(2)$
   B) $g(3 - 2)$
   C) $|g(2) - g(3)|$
   D) $4 - (-3)$

7. In the xy-plane, the point $(-3, 7)$ lies on the graph of the function $h(x) = 5x^2 - kx + 1$. What is the value of $|k|$?

8. The range of the polynomial function p is the set of real numbers greater than or equal to -3, and the zeros of p are -2 and 3. Which of the following could be the graph of $y = p(x)$ in the xy-plane?

A)

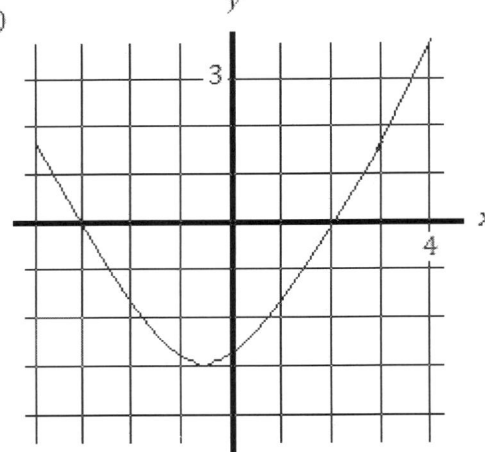

B)

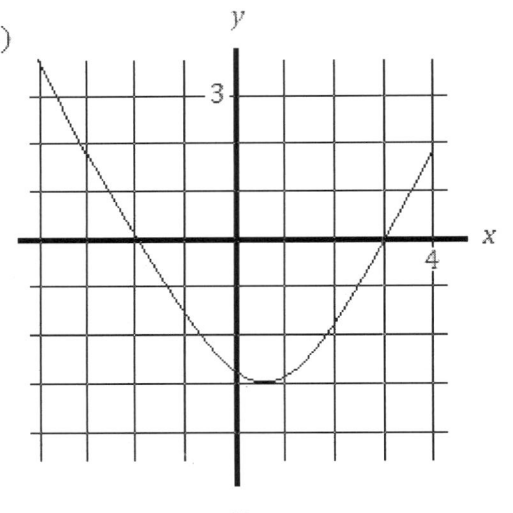

C)

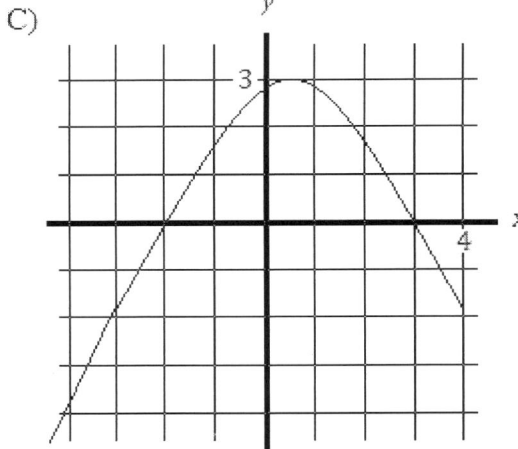

D)

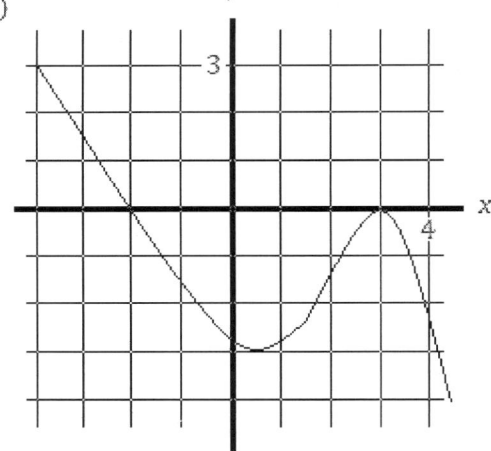

LEVEL 4: PASSPORT TO ADVANCED MATH – GRAPHS OF FUNCTIONS

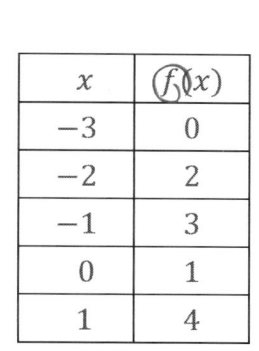

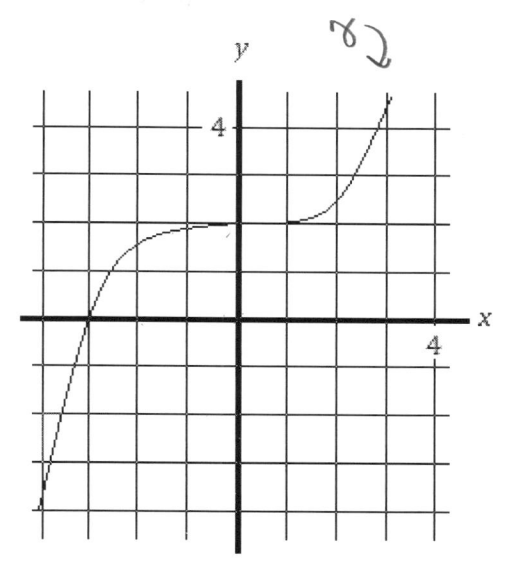

x	$f(x)$
-3	0
-2	2
-1	3
0	1
1	4

9. Selected values for the function f are shown in the table above, and the graph of the function g is shown in the xy-plane above. For which of the following values of x is $f(x) < g(x)$?

   A) -3
   B) -2
   C) -1
   D) 0

LEVEL 5: PASSPORT TO ADVANCED MATH – GRAPHS OF FUNCTIONS

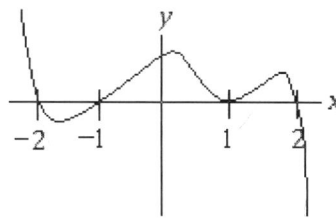

10. Which of the following could be an equation for the graph shown in the xy-plane above?

   A) $y = (x-2)(x-1)(x+1)(x+2)$
   B) $y = (x-2)(x-1)^2(x+1)(x+2)$
   C) $y = (2-x)(x-1)^2(x+1)(x+2)$
   D) $y = (2-x)(x-1)^3(x+1)(x+2)$

Answers

1. D 2. C 3. D 4. C 5. B 6. B 7. 13 8. B 9. D 10. C

85

Full Solutions

2.
* Let's circle the maximum on the graph (drawn to the right) and observe that the maximum occurs at $x = 3$, choice **C**.

3.
* If we look at the graph on the right, we see that the maximum value is $y = 4$, choice **D**.

Note: The maximum is always a y value. In this case, the maximum value is $y = 4$ and the maximum value occurs at $x = 3$.

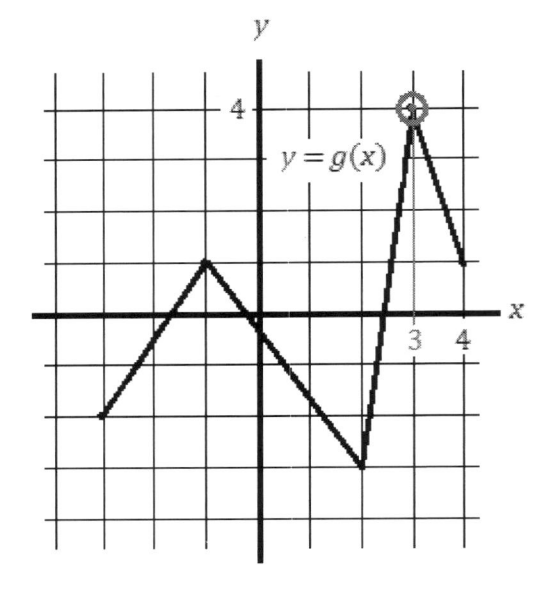

4.
* We draw a horizontal line at a height of -2.5 (see the graph on the right below) and observe that the horizontal line hits the graph twice. So, $g(x) = -2.5$ for 2 values of x, choice **C**.

Note: Each point on the horizontal line has the form $(x, -2.5)$, and each point on the curve has the form $(x, g(x))$. So, if a point is simultaneously on the horizontal line **and** the curve, then $g(x) = -2.5$.

5.
* **Solution by substituting values for x:** Using the answer choices as a guide, we evaluate the function h at $x = 3$ to get $h(3) = -g(3) = -4$. So, the point $(3, -4)$ is on the graph of h, choice **B**.

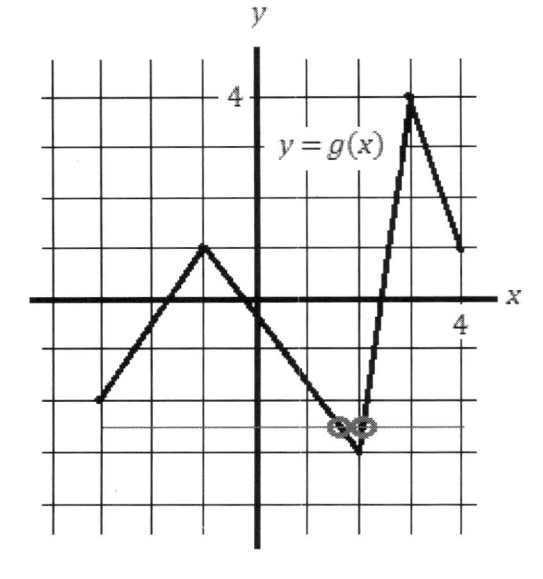

Notes: (1) We evaluated $g(3)$ by looking at the graph of g and observing that the point $(3, 4)$ is on the graph, as shown in the figure below.

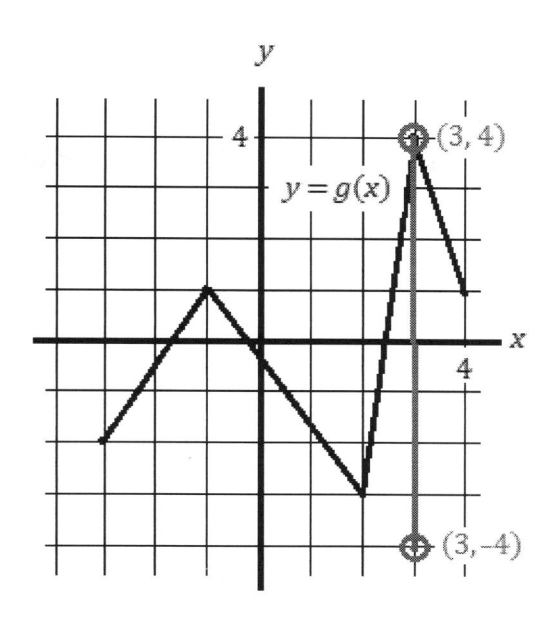

(2) If computing $h(3)$ didn't lead to an answer, we would try evaluating h at -3 next. In this case, we have $h(-3) = -g(-3) = -(-2) = 2$. But observe that $(-3, 2)$ is not an answer choice.

* Solution using a transformation: We get the graph of h by reflecting the graph of g in the x-axis. In particular, the point $(3, 4)$ is reflected across the x-axis to the point $(3, -4)$, choice **B**.

Notes: (1) To answer the question, we can simply "track" where the point $(3, 4)$ goes when we reflect the graph of g in the x-axis. This is shown in the figure above on the previous page.

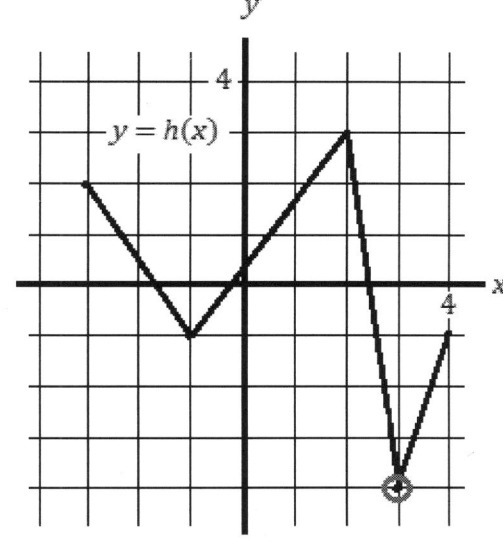

(2) The figure on the right shows the graph of h. Observe how this graph is the graph of g reflected in the x-axis.

6.
* The maximum value of g on the interval is $g(3) = 4$ and the minimum value of g on the interval is $g(2) = -3$. So, the positive difference between the maximum and minimum values of g on the interval is $\boldsymbol{g(3) - g(2) = 4} - (-3) = 4 + 3 = 7$. This shows that choices A and D work, and are therefore not the answer. Since $|g(2) - g(3)| = |g(3) - g(2)| = g(3) - g(2)$, C works as well. So, the answer is choice **B**.

Notes: (1) For completeness, we have $g(3 - 2) = g(1) \approx -1.75 \neq 7$.

(2) $|x|$ is the **absolute value** of x. If x is nonnegative, then $|x| = x$. If x is negative, then $|x| = -x$ (in other words, if x is negative, then taking the absolute value just eliminates the minus sign). For example, $|12| = 12$ and $|-12| = 12$. The absolute value of something is *always* greater than or equal to 0. In answer choice C, the "something" is $g(2) - g(3)$.

(3) In general, $b - a = -(a - b)$. For example, if $a = 4$ and $b = -3$, then $b - a = -3 - 4 = -7$ and $a - b = 4 - (-3) = 4 + 3 = 7$. It follows that $|b - a| = |a - b|$.

7.

* Since the point $(-3, 7)$ lies on the graph of h, we have $h(-3) = 7$. But by direct computation, $h(-3) = 5(-3)^2 - k(-3) + 1 = 5 \cdot 9 + 3k + 1 = 45 + 3k + 1 = 46 + 3k$.

So, $46 + 3k = 7$. Therefore, $3k = 7 - 46 = -39$. Dividing each side of this last equation by 3 gives us $k = -13$. Finally, $|k| = \mathbf{13}$.

8.

* The graphs in choices C and D have the wrong range because some points on the graph have y-coordinates that are less than -3. So, we can eliminate C and D.

The zeros of the graph in choice A are -3 and 2, and so we can eliminate choice A. So, the answer is choice **B**.

Notes: (1) The graph in choice B has a range of $y \geq -3$ and zeros of -2 and 3 as shown to the right.

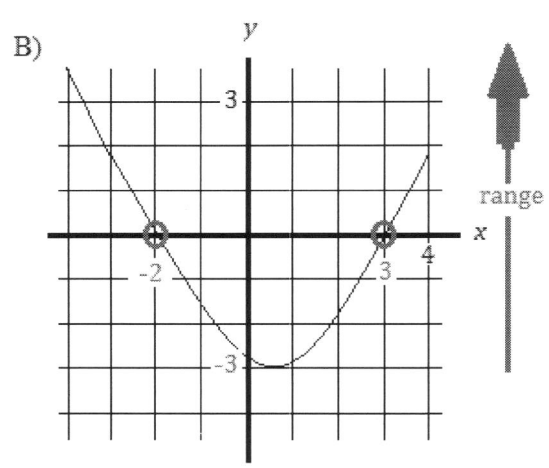

(2) Below we see the graphs in choices C and D with a rectangle around the portion of the graph that violates the requirement on the range.

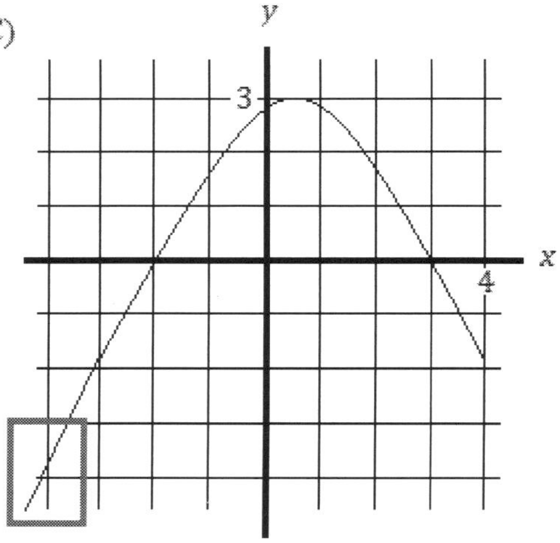

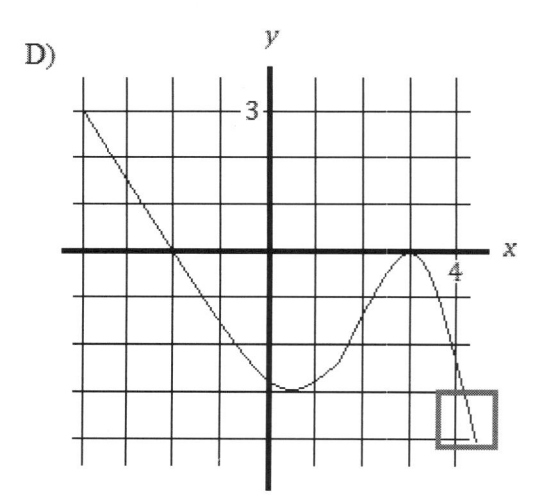

9.
* $f(0) = 1$ and $g(0) = 2$. Since $1 < 2$, we have $f(0) < g(0)$, and the answer is choice **D**.

Note: Let's plot the points that are given to be on the graph of f with the graph of g.

Observe that at -3, f and g have the same value and at -2, -1, and 1, $f(x) > g(x)$. Only at 0 do we have $f(x) < g(x)$.

10.
Solution by process of elimination: The answer choices show us that the answer must be a polynomial.

Since there are 4 turning points, the polynomial must have degree at least 5. We can therefore eliminate choice A (this polynomial has degree 4).

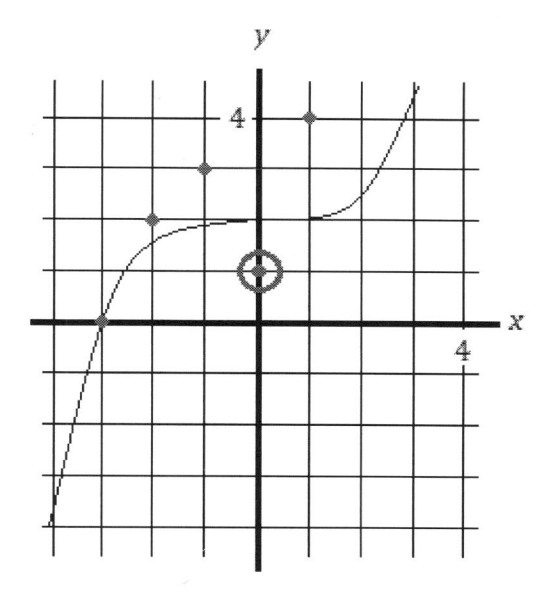

Since both "ends" of the graph go in opposite directions, the polynomial must have odd degree. This eliminates choice D (this polynomial has degree 6). Note that we can also use this same reasoning to eliminate choice A.

We can eliminate choice B by observing that if we plug a very large value of x into $y = (x-2)(x-1)^2(x+1)(x+2)$, we will get a large positive value for y. But according to the graph we should get a negative value for y (since the graph is below the x-axis for large x).

So, the answer is choice **C**.

Notes: (1) A **polynomial** has the form $a_n x^n + a_{n-1} x^{n-1} + \cdots + a_1 x + a_0$, where $a_0, a_1, \ldots, a_n$ are real numbers. For example, $x^2 + 2x - 35$ is a polynomial. The **degree** of the polynomial is n. In other words, it is the highest power that appears in the expanded form of the polynomial.

(2) If a polynomial is in factored form, then we can get the degree of the polynomial by adding the degrees of the factors. For example, the polynomial in choice A has degree $1 + 1 + 1 + 1 = 4$. Similarly, the polynomials in choices B, C, and D have degrees 5, 5, and 6, respectively.

(3) The "end behavior" of the graph of a polynomial can tell you whether the polynomial has even or odd degree. If both ends of the graph head in the same direction (both up to ∞, or both down to $-\infty$), then the polynomial must have even degree. If the ends head in different directions (one up and the other down), then the polynomial must have odd degree. The graph shown in this problem is therefore for an odd degree polynomial.

(4) The degree of a polynomial is at least one more than the number of "turning points" on its graph. Since the graph in this problem has 4 turning points (at $x \approx -1.7$, $x \approx 0.2$, $x = 1$, and $x \approx 1.9$), the degree of the polynomial must be at least 5.

(5) Putting notes (3) and (4) together, we see that the possible degrees for the polynomial whose graph is shown are 5, 7, 9,...

* Quick solution: Since the graph does not pass through the x-axis at the zero $x = 1$, it follows that 1 is a zero with even multiplicity. Equivalently, the factor $(x - 1)$ must appear an even number of times (or equivalently, it must have an even power). This eliminates choices A and D.

As in the previous solution, we can eliminate choice B by observing that if we plug a very large value of x into $y = (x - 2)(x - 1)^2(x + 1)(x + 2)$, we will get a large positive value for y. But according to the graph we should get a negative value for y (since the graph is below the x-axis for large x)

So, the answer is choice **C**.

Notes: (1) c is a **zero** of a polynomial $p(x)$ if $p(c) = 0$. For example, all the polynomials in the answer choices have the same zeros. They are $-2, -1, 1,$ and 2.

(2) $p(c) = 0$ if and only if $x - c$ is a factor of the polynomial $p(x)$.

(3) The multiplicity of the zero c is the degree of the factor $x - c$. For example, in choice D, $-2, -1,$ and 2 have multiplicity 1, and 1 has multiplicity 3.

(4) A zero c of a polynomial has odd multiplicity if and only if the graph of the polynomial passes through the x-axis at $x = c$. From the graph given, we see that $-2, -1,$ and 2 are zeros of the polynomial with odd multiplicity.

(5) A zero c of a polynomial has even multiplicity if and only if the graph of the polynomial touches the x-axis at $x = c$, but does not pass through it. From the graph given, we see that 1 is a zero of the polynomial with even multiplicity.

(6) It might be tempting to try to plug in the zeros to try to eliminate answer choices in this problem. Unfortunately, as we saw in note (1), all the answer choices have polynomials with the same zeros.

LESSON 11 – PROBLEM SOLVING GRAPHS

When in Doubt, Graph it Out

LEVEL 1: PROBLEM SOLVING – GRAPHS

Questions 1 - 5 refer to the following information.

A honeybee scout leaves his swarm for 2 and a half hours to search for a new home. The graph below shows the honeybee's distance from his swarm over the 2-hour period for which he was gone. The honeybee stopped to rest on a leaf for 20 minutes during his search.

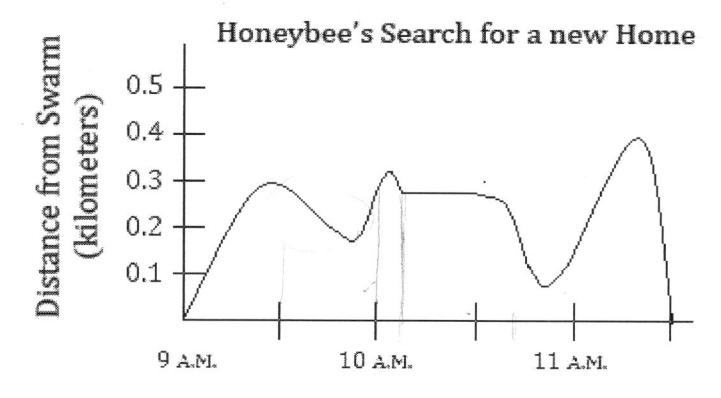

Honeybee's Search for a new Home

1. Based on the graph, which of the following is closest to the time the honeybee landed on the leaf and began resting?

   A) 9:30 A.M.
   B) 9:45 A.M.
   C) 10:10 A.M.
   D) 10:40 A.M.

2. During which of the following time periods was the distance between the honeybee and his swarm strictly decreasing?

   A) Between 9:30 A.M. and 10:00 A.M.
   B) Between 10:00 A.M. and 10:10 A.M.
   C) Between 10:30 A.M. and 10:45 A.M.
   D) Between 11:00 A.M. and 11:30 A.M.

3. During which of the following time periods was the distance between the honeybee and his swarm strictly decreasing, then strictly increasing?

   A) Between 9:30 A.M. and 10:00 A.M.
   B) Between 10:00 A.M. and 10:10 A.M.
   C) Between 10:30 A.M. and 10:45 A.M.
   D) Between 11:00 A.M. and 11:30 A.M.

4. Based on the graph, which of the following is closest to the time the honeybee is farthest from his swarm?

   A) 10:05 A.M.
   B) 10:50 A.M.
   C) 11:20 A.M.
   D) 11:30 A.M.

5. Based on the graph, which statement is true?

   A) The honeybee's maximum distance from the swarm is reached about 1 hour and 15 minutes after he leaves the swarm.
   B) The honeybee's distance from the swarm steadily increases for the first hour after he leaves the swarm.
   C) The honeybee's minimum distance from the swarm during the second hour is approximately 1 kilometer.
   D) The honeybee's minimum distance from the swarm during the second half hour is greater than the honeybee's minimum distance from the swarm during the fourth half hour.

LEVEL 2: PROBLEM SOLVING – GRAPHS

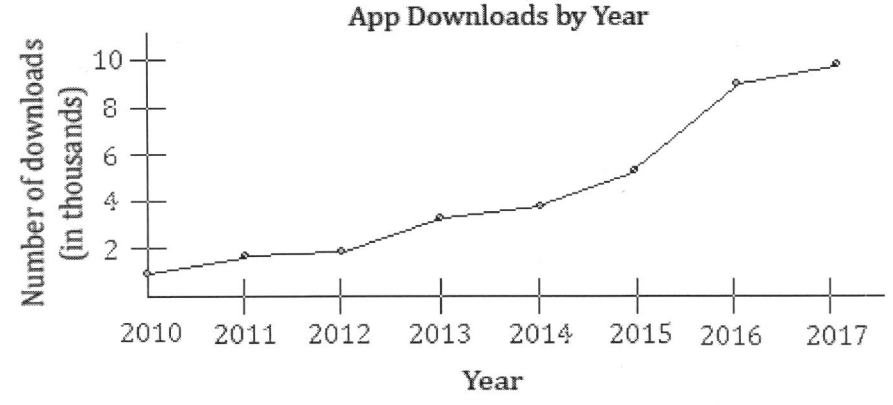

6. A small company released an app in early 2010. The number of downloads each year is shown in the line graph above. According to the graph, between which two consecutive years was there the greatest change in the number of app downloads?

   A) 2010 – 2011
   B) 2014 – 2015
   C) 2015 – 2016
   D) 2016 – 2017

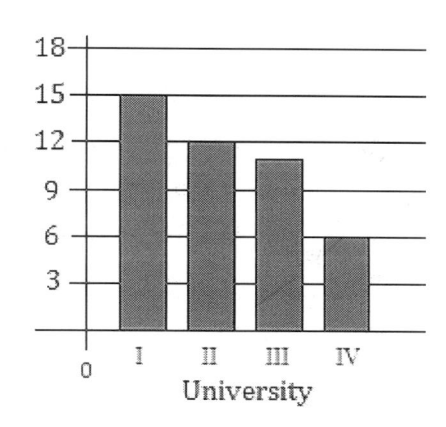

7. The number of students attending 4 universities is shown in the graph above. If the total number of students is 4350, what is an appropriate label for the vertical axis of the graph?

    A) Number of students (in tens)
    B) Number of students (in hundreds)
    C) Number of students (in thousands)
    D) Number of students (in tens of thousands)

LEVEL 3: PROBLEM SOLVING – GRAPHS

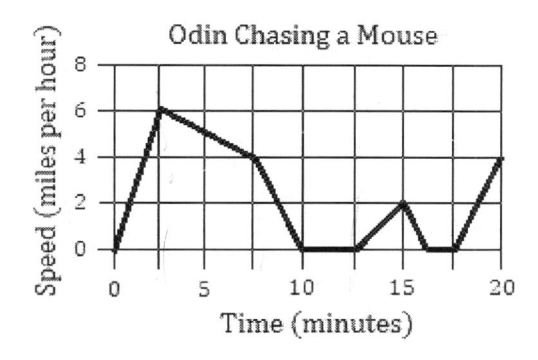

8. Odin the cat chased a mouse for twenty minutes. His time and speed are displayed in the graph above. According to the graph, which of the following statements concerning Odin's chase is true?

    A) Odin's speed decreased at a constant rate for 10 minutes sometime during the chase.
    B) Odin's speed reached its maximum during the last five minutes of the chase.
    C) Odin never stopped during the chase.
    D) While Odin was moving, his speed was never constant.

Questions 9 and 10 refer to the following information.

A bird species called a *garret* is best known for "plunge diving" to catch fish. The graph below shows the height of a garret over a period of 1 minute as it dives for fish.

Height versus Time for a Garret

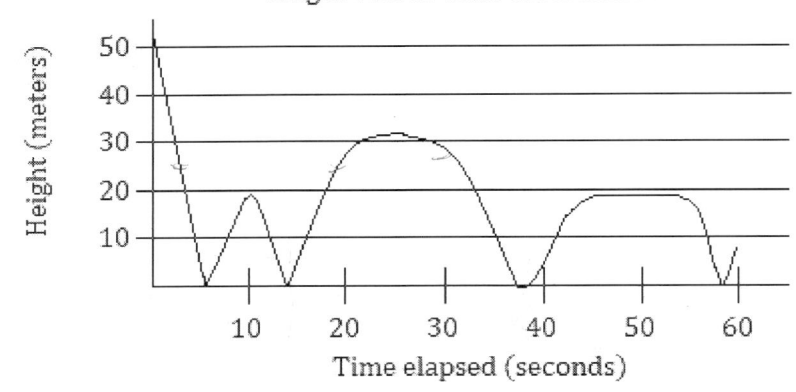

9. During the 1 minute period, how many times was the garret at a height of 25 meters?

    A) One
    B) Two
    C) Three
    D) More than three

10. Of the following, which best approximates the maximum height, in meters, of the garret between the second and third time it hit the water?

    A) 50
    B) 32
    C) 25
    D) 19

Answers

1. C   2. C   3. A   4. C   5. D   6. C   7. B   8. D   9. C   10. B

Full Solutions

1.

* When the honeybee stops, the distance is **constant** (it's not changing). This occurs for about 20 minutes between 10:10 A.M. and 10:30 A.M. So, the answer is choice **C**.

Note: The time period for which the honeybee was resting is highlighted in bold below.

2.

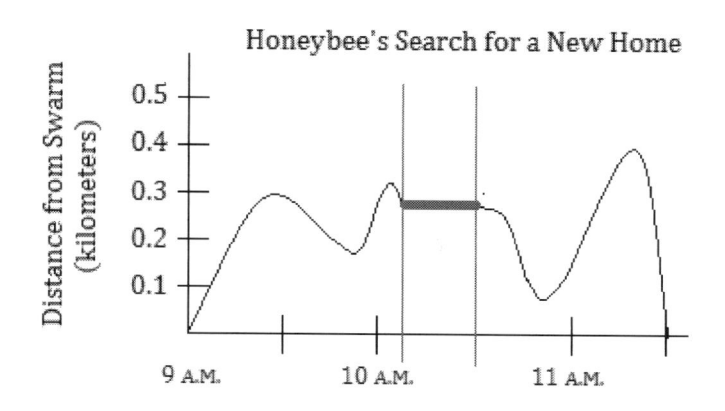

* We are looking for the graph to go down as we move from left to right. This happens between 10: 30 A.M. and 10: 45 A.M., choice **C**.

Notes: (1) Let's isolate the part of the graph between 10: 30 A.M. and 10: 45 A.M.

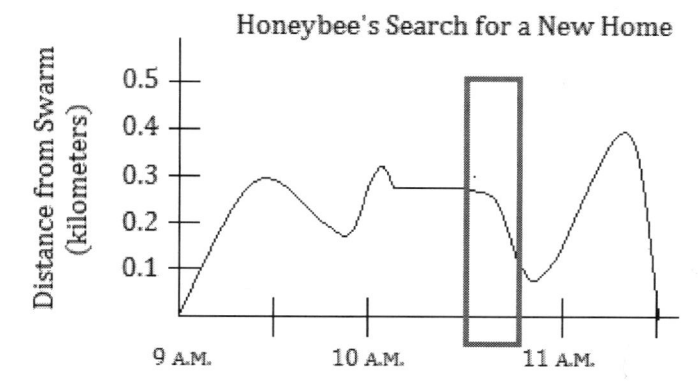

Notice how in the boxed portion, the graph goes down as we move from left to right.

(2) Between 9: 30 A.M. and 10 A.M., the distance is decreasing, then increasing.

(3) Between 10 A.M. and 10: 10 A.M. the distance is increasing, then decreasing.

(4) Between 11 A.M. and 11: 30 A.M. the distance is increasing, then decreasing.

3.

* We are looking for the graph to go down and then up as we move from left to right. This happens between 9: 30 A.M. and 10 A.M., choice **A**.

Note: Let's isolate the part of the graph between 9: 30 A.M. and 10: 00 A.M.

Notice how in the boxed portion, the graph goes down and then up as we move from left to right.

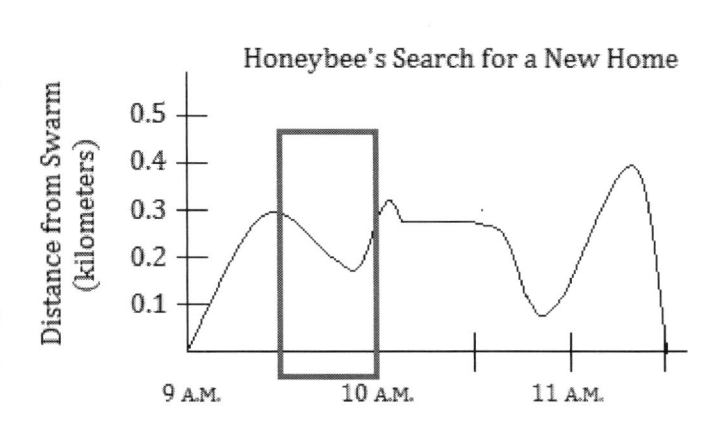

4.

* The farthest the honeybee gets from his swarm is about 0.4 kilometers, and this occurs at approximately 11: 20 A.M., choice **C**.

Note: The farthest distance and the time at which it occurs is highlighted below.

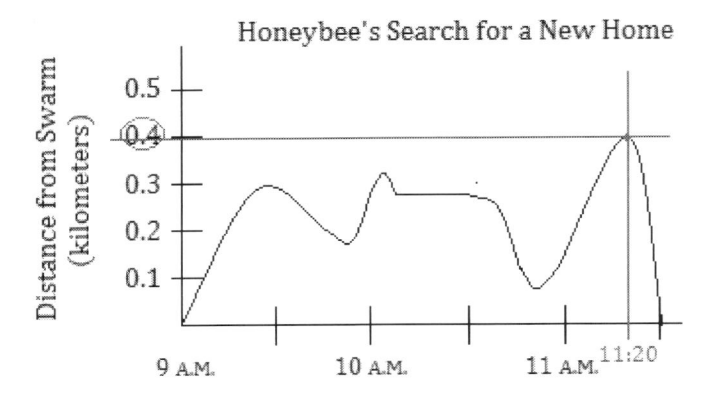

5.

* Let's look at the minimum distances during each of the second and fourth half hours after the honeybee leaves the swarm.

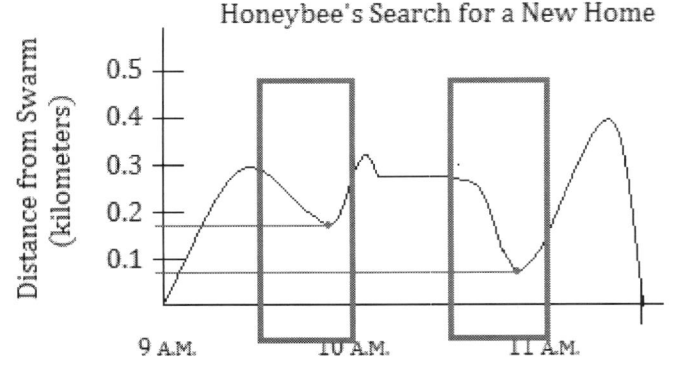

Observe that during the second half hour the minimum is approximately 0.18 and during the fourth half hour the minimum is approximately 0.08. So, the answer is choice **D**.

Notes: (1) In the last problem, we saw that the honeybee's maximum distance from the swarm was reached at approximately 11: 20 A.M. This is 2 hours and 20 minutes after he leaves the swarm. This eliminates choice A.

(2) The honeybee's distance from the swarm increases from 9: 00 to 9: 30, but then begins to decrease. This eliminates choice B.

(4) In the picture above, we see that the honeybee's minimum distance from the swarm during the second hour is approximately 0.08 kilometers, which is much less than 1 kilometer. This eliminates choice C.

6.

* The increase from 2015 to 2016 was the greatest, choice **C**.

Notes: The increase from 2010 to 2011 was approximately $2 - 1 = 1$.

The increase from 2014 to 2015 was approximately $5 - 4 = 1$.

The increase from 2015 to 2016 was approximately $9 - 5 = 4$.

The increase from 2016 to 2017 was approximately $10 - 9 = 1$.

7.

* Using the numbers on the vertical axis, we get a total of

$$15 + 12 + 10.5 + 6 = 43.5.$$

To get to 4350, we multiply 43.5 by 100. So, the answer is choice **B**.

Note: Multiplying a number by 100 is equivalent to moving the decimal point 2 places to the right. In this case, as we move the decimal point to the right in the number 43.5, we have to place an extra 0 at the end.

8.

* **Solution by process of elimination:** Odin's speed decreased at a constant rate twice during the 20 minutes, first between 2.5 and 7.5 minutes, and then again between 15 and approximately 16 minutes. So, the longest amount of time that Odin's speed decreased at a constant rate was $7.5 - 2.5 = 5$ minutes. This eliminates choice A.

Odin reached a maximum speed of 6 miles per hour 2.5 minutes into the chase. This eliminates choice B.

Odin's speed is 0 between 10 and 12.5 minutes and again between about 16 and 17.5 minutes. So, Odin stopped twice during the chase. This eliminates choice C.

Therefore, the answer is choice **D**.

Note: The only two intervals at which Odin's speed is constant are when his speed is 0. So, Odin is not moving during the 2 time intervals when his speed is constant.

9.

* We draw a horizontal line at a height of 25 meters (as shown in the picture on the right).

The horizontal line hits the graph three times, choice **C**.

10.

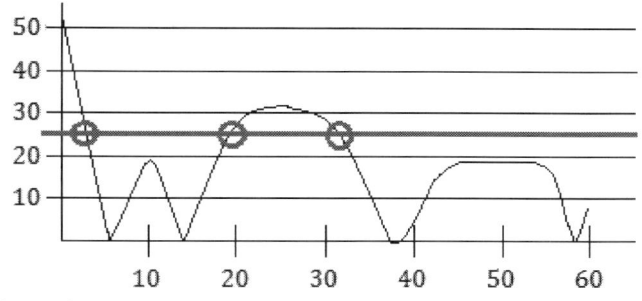

* Let's circle the second and third times the garret hits the water, as well as the maximum between those two values.

It looks like the answer is about 32, choice **B**.

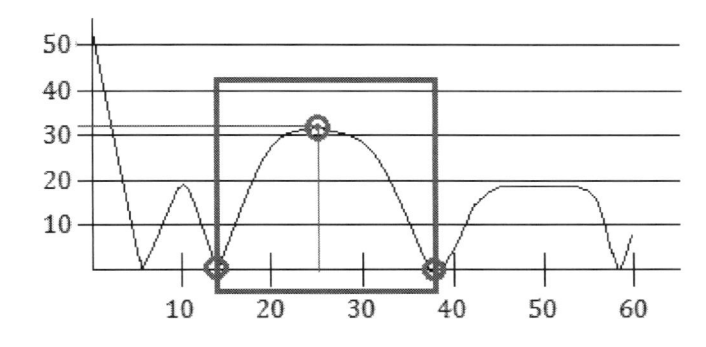

LESSON 12 – GEOMETRY
CIRCLES

A **circle** is a two-dimensional geometric figure formed of a curved line surrounding a center point, every point of the line being an equal distance from the center point. This distance is called the **radius** of the circle. The **diameter** of a circle is the length of any line segment passing through the center of the circle with endpoints on the circle. The diameter is twice the radius.

The perimeter of a circle is called its **circumference** which can be found by using the formula $C = 2\pi r$, where r is the radius of the circle.

The area of a circle can be found using the formula $A = \pi r^2$, where r is the radius of the circle.

Example:

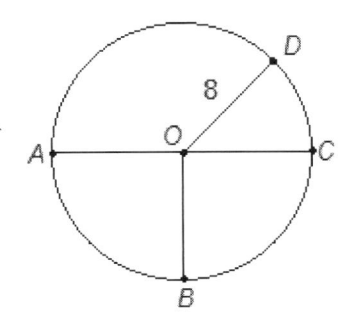

In the figure above, we have a circle with center O and radius $r = 8$. Note that $\overline{OA}$, $\overline{OB}$, $\overline{OC}$, and $\overline{OD}$ are all radii of the circle. Also, $\overline{AC}$ is a diameter of the circle with length 16, the circumference of the circle is $C = 16\pi$, and the area of the circle is $A = 64\pi$.

Angles formed when two radii of a circle meet at the center are called **central angles**.

In the figure above, there are many central angles. For example, $\angle DOC$, $\angle DOB$, and $\angle DOA$ are all central angles.

An **arc** is part of the circumference of a circle. **Minor arcs** are less than half of the circumference of the circle and **major arcs** are greater than half of the circumference of the circle.

In the figure above, minor arc $\widehat{AD}$ is the portion of the circumference of the circle as we move clockwise from A to D, whereas major arc $\widehat{ABD}$ is the portion of the circumference as we move counterclockwise from A to D, passing through point B. $\widehat{AC}$ is a **semicircle**.

One full rotation of a circle is $360°$. All other rotations are in proportion to the full rotation. For example, half of a rotation of a circle is $\frac{360}{2} = 180°$.

In addition to degree measure, another way to measure rotations of a circle is to divide the arc length of the circle by the radius of the circle. This is called **radian** measure. For example, one full rotation of a circle is $\frac{2\pi r}{r} = 2\pi$ radians, and so half of a rotation of a circle is π radians.

So, we just showed that $180° = \pi$ radians.

We can convert between degree measure and radian measure by using the following simple ratio:

$$\frac{\text{degree measure}}{180°} = \frac{\text{radian measure}}{\pi}$$

Let's try an example.

LEVEL 2: GEOMETRY – CIRCLES

1. An angle with a measure of 45° has a measure of x radians, where $0 \leq x < 2\pi$. What is the value of x?

   A) $\frac{1}{4}$

   B) $\frac{1}{2}$

   C) $\frac{\pi}{4}$

   D) $\frac{\pi}{2}$

Solution using a ratio: $\frac{45°}{180°} = \frac{x}{\pi} \Rightarrow x = \frac{45\pi}{180} = \frac{\pi}{4}$ radians, choice **C**.

Shortcut 1: We can convert from degrees to radians by multiplying the given angle by $\frac{\pi}{180}$.

* Quick solution: $45 \cdot \frac{\pi}{180} = \frac{\pi}{4}$, choice **C**.

Notes: (1) Suppose we instead wanted to convert $\frac{\pi}{4}$ radians to degrees. Let's use the appropriate ratio. $\frac{x}{180°} = \frac{\pi/4}{\pi} \Rightarrow \pi x = \frac{180\pi}{4} = 45\pi \Rightarrow x = 45°$.

Shortcut 2: We can convert from radians to degrees by multiplying the given angle by $\frac{180}{\pi}$.

(2) Let's use shortcut 2 to convert $\frac{\pi}{4}$ radians to degrees. We get $\frac{\pi}{4} \cdot \frac{180}{\pi} = \frac{180}{4} = 45°$.

Shortcut 3: When converting from radians to degrees, if the angle has π in the numerator, we can simply replace π by 180.

(3) Let's use shortcut 3 to convert $\frac{\pi}{4}$ radians to degrees. We get $\frac{\pi}{4} = \frac{180}{4} = 45°$.

(4) It's important to understand that we can use shortcut 3 ONLY if π appears in the numerator.

For example, if we want to change $\frac{1}{2}$ radians to degrees, we CANNOT use shortcut 3. We can, however, still use shortcut 2 to get $\frac{1}{2} = \frac{1}{2} \cdot \frac{180}{\pi} = \left(\frac{90}{\pi}\right)°$.

Time to Practice

LEVEL 1: GEOMETRY – CIRCLES

2. What is the diameter of a circle whose area is 36π?

   A) 6
   B) 12
   C) 36
   D) 12π

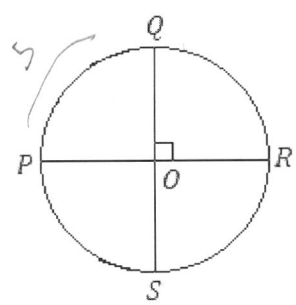

3. In the circle above with center O, the length of minor arc $\widehat{PQ}$ is 5. What is the circumference of the circle?

   A) 10
   B) 20
   C) 25
   D) 30

LEVEL 2: GEOMETRY – CIRCLES

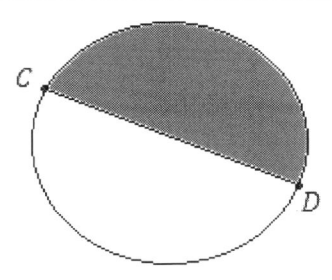

4. In the circle above, segment CD is a diameter. If the area of the shaded region is 32π, what is the length of the diameter of the circle?

   A) 4
   B) 8
   C) 12
   D) 16

LEVEL 3: GEOMETRY – CIRCLES

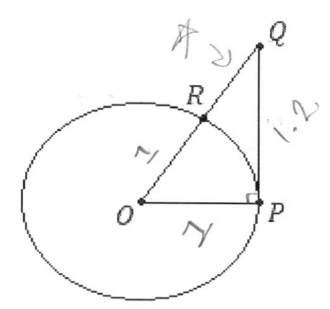

Note: Figure not drawn to scale.

5. In the figure above, the circle has center O and line segment $\overline{PQ}$ is tangent to the circle at point P. If $PQ = 1.2$ and the length of a diameter of the circle is 1, what is the length of $\overline{RQ}$?

LEVEL 4: GEOMETRY – CIRCLES

6. Points P and Q lie on a circle with diameter 4, and arc $\widehat{PQ}$ has length $\frac{\pi}{4}$. What fraction of the circumference of the circle is the length of arc $\widehat{PQ}$?

7. In a circle with center O, central angle POQ has a measure of $\frac{\pi}{3}$ radians. The area of the sector formed by central angle POQ is what fraction of the area of the circle?

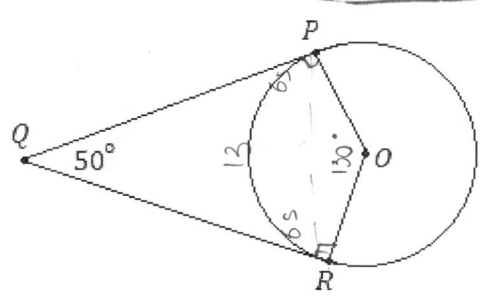

8. In the figure above, O is the center of the circle, line segments PQ and RQ are tangent to the circle at points P and R, respectively. The two segments intersect at point Q as shown. If the length of minor arc $\widehat{PR}$ is 13, what is the circumference of the circle?

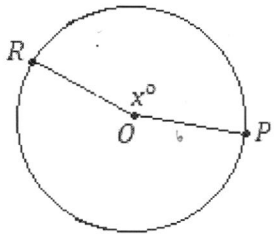

Note: Figure not drawn to scale.

9. * In the figure above, O is the center of the circle, and the radius of the circle is 6. If the length of arc $\widehat{PR}$ is between 16 and 17, what is one possible integer value of x?

Level 5: Geometry – Circles

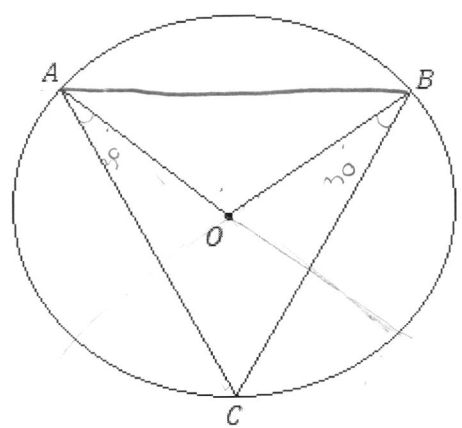

Figure: Circle with center O, triangle ACB inscribed with A and B on top, C on bottom. Angle at A (marked near O) is shown, angle $CBO = 30°$.

Note: Figure not drawn to scale.

10. In the circle above with center O, $m\angle CAO = m\angle CBO = 30°$. What is $m\angle AOB$? (Disregard the degree symbol when gridding your answer.)

Answers

1. C   2. B   3. B   4. D   5. 4/5, .8   6. 1/16, .062, .063   7. 1/6, .166, .167   8. 36   9. 153, 154, 155, 156, 157, 158, 159, 160, 161, 162   10. 120

Full Solutions

2.
Solution by starting with choice C: The area of a circle is $A = \pi r^2$. Let's start with choice C as our first guess. If $d = 36$, then $r = 18$, and so we have $A = \pi \cdot 18^2 = \pi \cdot 324 = 324\pi$. Since this is too big we can eliminate choices C and D.

Let's try choice B next. If $d = 12$, then $r = 6$, and so $A = \pi \cdot 6^2 = 36\pi$. This is correct, and so the answer is choice **B**.

* **Algebraic solution:** We use the area formula $A = \pi r^2$, and substitute 36π in for A.

$$A = \pi r^2$$
$$36\pi = \pi r^2$$
$$36 = r^2$$
$$6 = r$$

Now, the diameter of a circle is twice the radius, and so we have $d = 2r = 2 \cdot 6 = 12$, choice **B**.

Note: The equation $r^2 = 36$ would normally have two solutions: $r = 6$ and $r = -6$. But the radius of a circle must be positive, and so we reject -6.

3.
* Since $\overline{PR}$ and $\overline{QS}$ are diameters of the circle, the length of minor arc $\overset{\frown}{PQ}$ is $\frac{1}{4}$ of the circumference of the circle. So, the circumference is $4 \cdot 5 = 20$, choice **B**.

4.

* A diameter divides a circle into two equal halves. It follows that the area of the circle is $2 \cdot 32\pi = 64\pi$. So, the radius of the circle is 8, and thus, the diameter of the circle is 16, choice **D**.

Notes: (1) Recall that the area of a circle is $A = \pi r^2$. In this problem, we found that the area is 64π. So, we have $64\pi = \pi r^2$. Dividing each side of this equation by π gives us $64 = r^2$. So, $r = \sqrt{64} = 8$.

(2) The equation $64 = r^2$ has the two solutions $r = \pm 8$. Since a radius must be positive, we reject the negative solution.

5.

CIRCLE FACT 1: A radius of a circle is perpendicular to a tangent line at its point of tangency.

* **Solution using CIRCLE FACT 1:** Since the length of a diameter of the circle is 1, the radius $\overline{OP}$ has length 0.5. By CIRCLE FACT 1, $\angle OPQ$ is a right angle. So, by the Pythagorean Theorem, $OQ^2 = OP^2 + PQ^2 = 0.5^2 + 1.2^2 = 0.25 + 1.44 = 1.69$. So, $OQ = \sqrt{1.69} = 1.3$. Finally, we have $RQ = OQ - OR = 1.3 - 0.5 = .\mathbf{8}$ or $\mathbf{4/5}$.

Note: We can use a Pythagorean triple here instead of the Pythagorean Theorem. We have $OP = 0.5 = 0.1 \cdot 5$ and $PQ = 1.2 = 0.1 \cdot 12$. It follows that $OQ = 0.1 \cdot 13 = 1.3$. See Lesson 8 for more information about Pythagorean triples.

6.

* The circumference of the circle is $C = \pi d = 4\pi$, and $\frac{\pi}{4} \div 4\pi = \frac{\pi}{4} \cdot \frac{1}{4\pi} = \mathbf{1/16}$.

Note: We can also grid in $.062$ or $.063$.

7.

* One full rotation is 2π radians, and $\frac{\pi}{3} \div 2\pi = \frac{\pi}{3} \cdot \frac{1}{2\pi} = \mathbf{1/6}$.

Notes: (1) We can also grid in one of the decimals $.166$ or $.167$.

(2) We can also change $\frac{\pi}{3}$ to degrees first. Using shortcut 3 above, we have $\frac{\pi}{3} = \frac{180}{3} = 60°$. We then have $\frac{60}{360} = \mathbf{1/6}$.

8.

CIRCLE FACT 2: A central angle in a circle has the same measure as the arc it intercepts.

* Since PQ is tangent to the circle and OP is a radius of the circle, we have $QP \perp OP$ (by CIRCLE FACT 1). Therefore, $m\angle P = 90°$. Similarly, $m\angle R = 90°$. So, $m\angle O = 360 - 90 - 90 - 50 = 130°$. Since a central angle has the same measure as the arc it intercepts (by CIRCLE FACT 2), minor arc $\widehat{PR}$ measures $130°$ as well. We can now find the circumference of the circle by setting up a ratio:

$$\frac{130}{360} = \frac{13}{C}$$

We cross multiply to get $130C = 13 \cdot 360$. Finally, we divide by 130 to get $C = \frac{13 \cdot 360}{130} = \mathbf{36}$.

Notes: (1) Notice that $\overline{OP}$ and $\overline{OR}$ are both radii of the circle. Therefore, $OP = OR$.

(2) A tangent line to a circle is always perpendicular to the appropriate radius of the circle (CIRCLE FACT 1). We use the symbol $\perp$ to represent "perpendicular."

In this problem $QP \perp OP$ and $QR \perp OR$. Therefore, $m\angle P = m\angle R = 90°$.

(3) $OPQR$ is a quadrilateral. The angle measures of a quadrilateral sum to $360°$. It follows that $m\angle O + m\angle P + m\angle Q + m\angle R = 360°$.

(4) $\angle POR$ is a **central angle** of the circle because its vertex is at the center of the circle. The measure of a central angle is equal to the measure of the arc it intercepts (CIRCLE FACT 2).

9.
Let's use some ratios to figure out the possible values for x. Our key words will be "arc" and "circumference." First let's let the arc length be 16

$$\begin{array}{ccc} \text{arc} & 16 & x \\ \text{circumference} & 12\pi & 360 \end{array}$$

$$\frac{16}{12\pi} = \frac{x}{360} \Rightarrow 12\pi x = 16 \cdot 360 \Rightarrow x = \frac{16 \cdot 360}{12\pi} \approx 152.8$$

Now, let's let the arc length be 17.

$$\begin{array}{ccc} \text{arc} & 17 & x \\ \text{circumference} & 12\pi & 360 \end{array}$$

$$\frac{17}{12\pi} = \frac{x}{360} \Rightarrow 12\pi x = 17 \cdot 360 \Rightarrow x = \frac{17 \cdot 360}{12\pi} \approx 162.3$$

So, we can grid in any integer from **153** through **162**, inclusive.

Note: Since the radius of the circle is 6, the circumference of the circle is $C = 2\pi r = 12\pi$.

* **Alternate solution:** We use the formula $s = r\theta$, where r is the radius of the circle, θ is the angle in radians, and s is the length of the intercepted arc.

Here we are given $r = 6$ and $16 < s < 17$. Since $\theta = \frac{s}{r}$, we have

$$\frac{16}{6} < \theta < \frac{17}{6} \Rightarrow 2.667 < \theta < 2.833$$

Since x is in degrees, and θ is in radians, we have $x = \frac{180\theta}{\pi}$. So,

$$\frac{180 \cdot 2.667}{\pi} < x < \frac{180 \cdot 2.833}{\pi} \Rightarrow 152.8 < x < 162.3$$

So, we can grid in any integer from **153** through **162**, inclusive.

10.

CIRCLE FACT 3: An inscribed angle in a circle has half the measure of the arc it intercepts.

Solution using CIRCLE FACT 3: If we let $x = m\angle ACB$, then by CIRCLE FACT 3, $m\angle AOB = 2x$. Since the angle measures of a quadrilateral sum to $360°$, we have $30 + x + 30 + (360 - 2x) = 360$, or equivalently, $x = 60°$. So, we have $m\angle AOB = 2x = \mathbf{120}$.

Notes: (1) In the picture on the left, we have labeled the four angles. Notice that central angle $\angle AOB$ has twice the measure of inscribed angle $\angle ACB$.

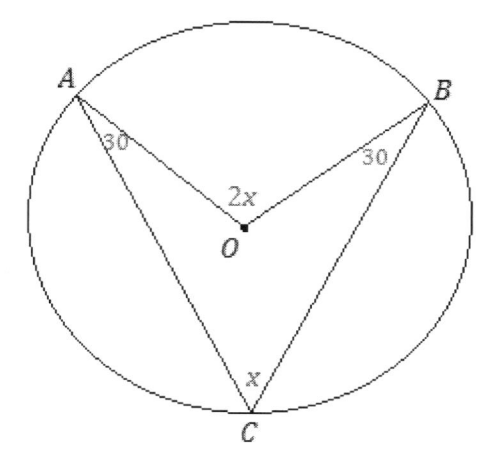

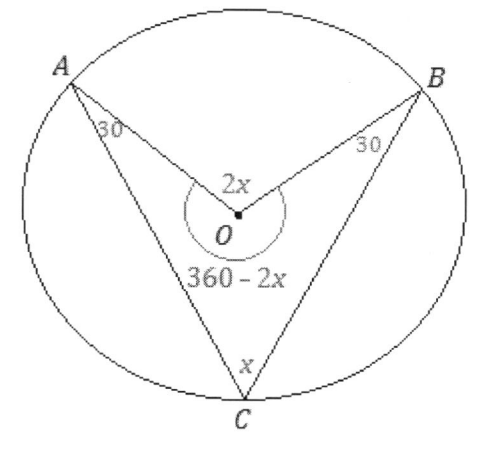

(2) Quadrilateral $AOBC$ is an example of a *concave* quadrilateral. It has an angle that is greater than $180°$. Nonetheless, all four angles of the quadrilateral still add up to $360°$.

(3) Observe that $\angle AOB$ as labeled with $2x$ in the figure on the left is an *exterior* angle to quadrilateral $AOBC$. The corresponding interior angle, displayed with a sweeping arc in the picture on the right, has measure $360 - 2x$.

(4) When we add up the four angle measures in the interior of the quadrilateral, we need to make sure to use $360 - 2x$, and NOT $2x$.

(5) In the end, remember that we are looking for $m\angle AOB$ which is $2x$, and NOT x.

* Solution using two isosceles triangles: We draw radius OC forming two isosceles triangles $\triangle AOC$ and $\triangle BOC$, as shown in the figure on the right.

Since $\overline{OA}$ and $\overline{OC}$ are both radii of the circle, they are congruent, and therefore, so are their opposite angles. So, $m\angle ACO = m\angle CAO = 30°$. Similarly, $m\angle BCO = 30°$.

It follows that $m\angle AOC = m\angle BOC = 180 - 30 - 30 = 120°$.

Finally, $m\angle AOB = 360 - 120 - 120 = \mathbf{120}.$

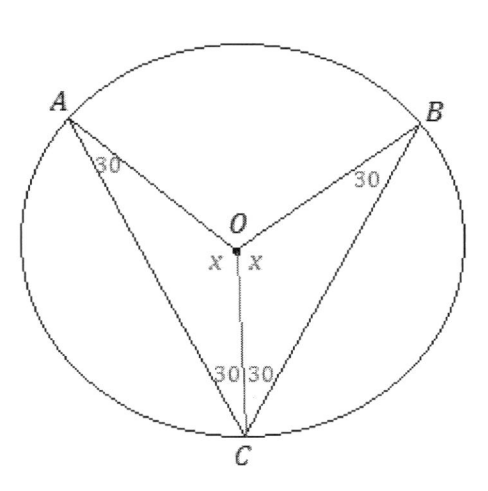

LESSON 13 – HEART OF ALGEBRA
ADDITIONAL PRACTICE 1

Full solutions to these problems are available for free download here:
www.SATPrepGet800.com/48SATy5

LEVEL 1

1. If $5k = 7$, what is the value of $10k + 2$?

   A) $\frac{7}{5}$
   B) 10
   C) 14
   D) 16

2. If $3k - 5 \geq 7$, which of the following CANNOT be the value of k ?

   A) 3
   B) 4
   C) 5
   D) 6

3. A hose is used to fill a swimming pool with water. When the hose is turned on, the pool fills up with water at the rate of 10 gallons per minute. If the pool initially contains 200 gallons of water, which of the following equations can be used to express the amount of water A in the pool, in gallons, t minutes after the hose is turned on?

   A) $A = 10t$
   B) $A = 10t + 200$
   C) $A = 10t - 200$
   D) $A = 200t + 10$

LEVEL 2

4. Which of the following ordered pairs (x, y) satisfies the inequality $2x - 5y \geq -5$?

   A) $(1, 2)$
   B) $(2, 3)$
   C) $(3, 3)$
   D) $(3, 2)$

5. If $\frac{13}{5}x - \frac{6}{5}x = \frac{7}{2} + \frac{7}{6}$, what is the value of x ?

7. A private club is accepting k new members each month. Assuming that there were m members in the club at the beginning of this month, which function best models the total number of members, T, the club plans to have n months from now?

   A) $T = kn + m$
   B) $T = kn - m$
   C) $T = m(k)^n$
   D) $T = k(m)^n$

LEVEL 3

6. Jamie currently has 350 "friends" on a popular social media site. Her goal is to have at least 800 "friends" within the next 15 weeks. What is the minimum number of "friends" per week, on average, she needs to make?

   A) 22
   B) 25
   C) 28
   D) 30

8. What value of x is the solution of the equation $3.4(x - 1) = 2x + 1.6$?

LEVEL 4

9. Brandon needs to get his car repaired. Barry's Auto Repair gives Brandon an estimate of $300 in parts and $5 per minute in labor costs. Sentinel Mechanics gives Brandon an estimate of $200 in parts and $7 per minute in labor costs. Let t represent the number of minutes that it takes to complete the repairs, and assume that the two repair shops will take the same amount of time. What are all values of t for which Barry's Auto Repair's total charge is less than Sentinel Mechanics' total charge?

   A) $t < 20$
   B) $20 \leq t \leq 35$
   C) $35 \leq t \leq 50$
   D) $t > 50$

10. Tanglewood Lumber's revenue decreased from $22 million in 1990 to $17.5 million in 2007. If Tanglewood Lumber's revenue decreased at a constant rate, which of the following linear functions R best models the revenue, in millions of dollars, t years after 1990 ?

    A) $R(t) = \frac{9}{34}t + 22$
    B) $R(t) = -\frac{9}{34}t + 22$
    C) $R(t) = \frac{35}{34}t + 22$
    D) $R(t) = -\frac{35}{34}t + 22$

11. For 7 consecutive even integers, the sum of the first, fourth, and fifth integer is 40 less than 5 times the sixth integer. What is the seventh integer?

LEVEL 5

12. An ornithologist oversees a 400-acre bird sanctuary with only two types of birds: egrets and flamingos. There are currently 150 egrets and 200 flamingos living within the sanctuary. If 75 more egrets are introduced into the sanctuary, how many more flamingos must be introduced so that $\frac{5}{6}$ of the total number of birds in the sanctuary are flamingos?

Answers

1. D   2. A   3. B   4. D   5. 10/3, 3.33   6. D   7. A   8. 25/7, 3.57   9. D   10. B   11. 14   12. 925

LESSON 14 – PASSPORT TO ADVANCED MATH
ADDITIONAL PRACTICE 1

Full solutions to these problems are available for free download here:
www.SATPrepGet800.com/48SATy5

LEVEL 1

$$g(x) = \frac{2x - 5}{3}$$

1. For the function g above, what is the value of $g(-11)$?

   A) -9
   B) -6
   C) -3
   D) $-\frac{5}{3}$

2. If $14xz - 21yz = az(2x - by)$, where a and b are positive real numbers, what is the value of $a + b$?

LEVEL 2

$$f(x) = \frac{2}{5}x + k$$

3. In the function above, k is a constant. If $f(10) = 3$, what is the value of $f(-15)$?

   A) -7
   B) -1
   C) 5
   D) 7

4. Which of the following functions has a graph in the xy-plane for which y is always greater than -5 ?

   A) $f(x) = x^3 - 4$
   B) $f(x) = x^2 - 5$
   C) $f(x) = (x - 2)^2 - 5$
   D) $f(x) = |x - 3| - 4$

LEVEL 3

5. Which of the following is equivalent to the expression $(x-5)^2 - 9$?

   A) $x^2 + 16$
   B) $x^2 - 10x - 9$
   C) $(x-2)(x-8)$
   D) $(x-2)(x+8)$

6. If $f(x) = -5x - 2$, what is $f(-3x)$ equal to?

   A) $15x^2 + 6x$
   B) $15x + 2$
   C) $15x - 2$
   D) $-15x + 2$

7. In the xy-plane, the point $(3, 1)$ lies on the graph of the function g. If $g(x) = a - 2x^2$, where a is a constant, what is the value of a ?

LEVEL 4

$$g(x) = \frac{3x + 6}{5x^2 - 20x + 15}$$

8. For the rational function defined above, which of the following is an equivalent form that displays values that are not included in the domain of the function as constants or coefficients?

   A) $g(x) = \frac{3}{5x^2}$
   B) $g(x) = \frac{3}{5x - 15}$
   C) $g(x) = \frac{3(x+2)}{5(x^2 - 4x + 3)}$
   D) $g(x) = \frac{3(x+2)}{5(x-1)(x-3)}$

110

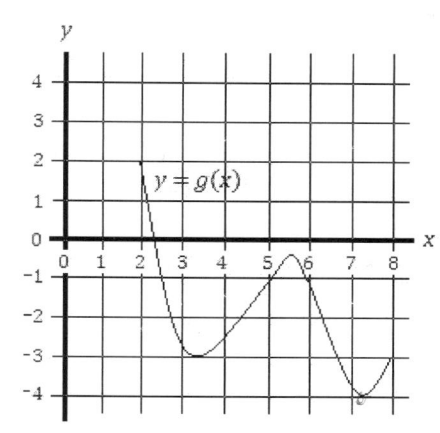

x	h(x)
−4	3
−3	1
−2	5
−1	2
0	0
1	7
2	6

9. The graph of the function g and a table of values for the function h are shown above. The minimum value of g is a. What is the value of $h(a)$?

11. For which of the following functions is it true that $f(-x) = -f(x)$ for all values of x ?

A) $f(x) = x^2 + 5$
B) $f(x) = x^2 + 5x$
C) $f(x) = x^3 + 5x$
D) $f(x) = x^3 + 5$

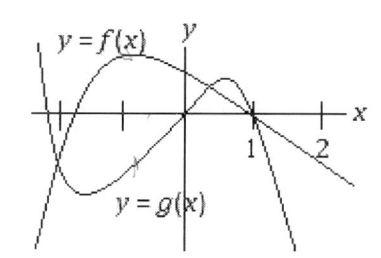

LEVEL 5

$$y = ax^2 - b$$

10. In the equation above, a and b are positive constants. Which of the following is an equivalent form of the equation?

A) $y = (ax - b)(ax + b)$
B) $y = (ax - \sqrt{b})(ax + \sqrt{b})$
C) $y = (\sqrt{a}x - \sqrt{b})(\sqrt{a}x + \sqrt{b})$
D) $y = (ax + b)^2$

12. Graphs of the functions f and g are shown in the xy-plane above. For which of the following values of x does $g(x) = -f(x)$?

A) $\frac{1}{2}$
B) 0
C) −1
D) −2

Answers

1. A   2. 10   3. A   4. D   5. C   6. C   7. 19   8. D   9. 3   10. C   11. C   12. C

LESSON 15 – PROBLEM SOLVING
ADDITIONAL PRACTICE 1

Full solutions to these problems are available for free download here:
www.SATPrepGet800.com/48SATy5

LEVEL 1

1. Johanna began filling a pitcher with water and then stopped for a short while. She then began filling the pitcher with water again, but at a slower rate than she had initially. Which of the following graphs could model the total amount of water in the pitcher versus time?

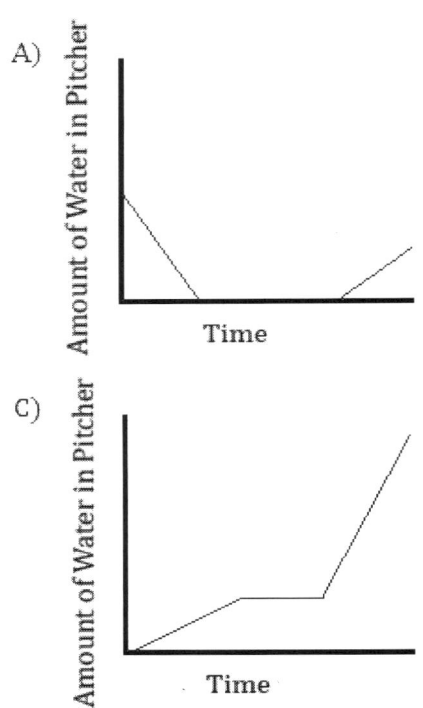

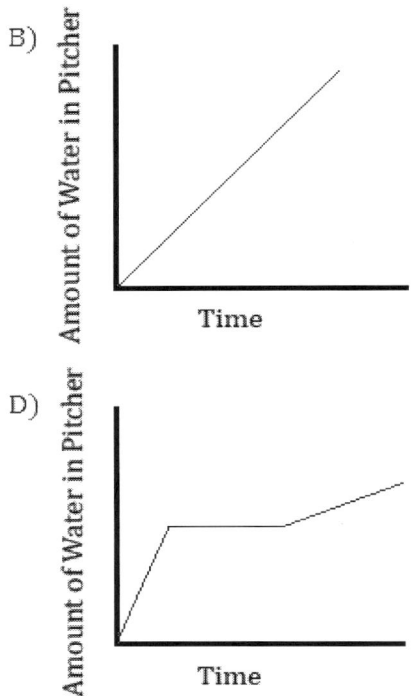

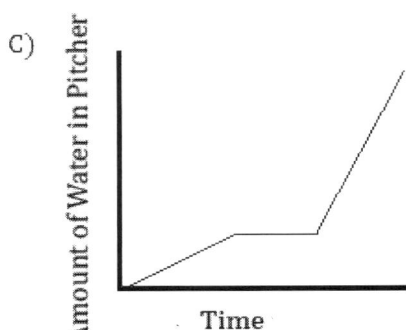

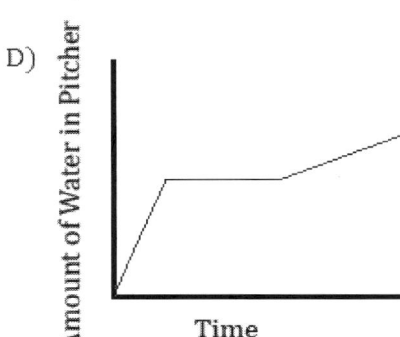

   A) [graph]
   B) [graph]
   C) [graph]
   D) [graph]

2. There are 4 atoms of carbon and 10 atoms of hydrogen in one molecule of butane. How many atoms of carbon are there in 17 molecules of butane?

LEVEL 2

3. * A *ream* of paper consists of 500 sheets stacked one on top of the other. Given that a ream of paper is 2 inches tall, which of the following is closest to the number of sheets of paper that need to be stacked to attain a height of $5\frac{3}{8}$ inches?

   A) 11
   B) 185
   C) 1340
   D) 5375

4. A store owner buys and sells watches, always keeping track of how many watches he has available for sale in his store. This data is shown on the graph below.

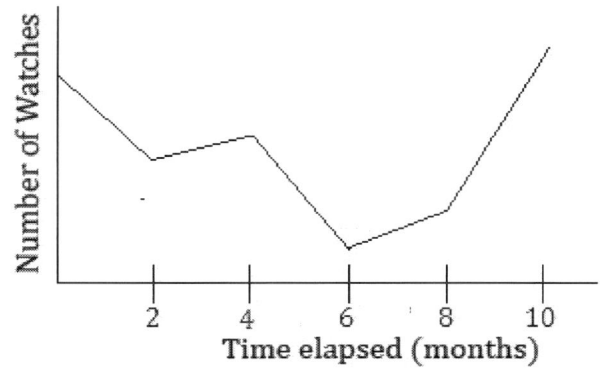

   On what interval did the number of watches increase the fastest?

   A) Between 2 and 4 months
   B) Between 4 and 6 months
   C) Between 6 and 8 months
   D) Between 8 and 10 months

LEVEL 3

5. * After adding 5% sales tax, a hat costs $12.60. What is the price of the hat before adding the sales tax?

   A) $11.80
   B) $12.00
   C) $12.10
   D) $12.20

Questions 6 - 7 refer to the following information.

	Annual Donations for a Corporation, 2000-2003			
	2000	**2001**	**2002**	**2003**
Animals	30	32	35	37.5
Children	380	410	425	438
Environment	36	37.5	38.25	40.1
Doctors	52	57	68	64
Scholarships	80	72	90.5	120.5

The table above lists the money donated annually by a corporation, in hundreds of dollars, to each of five causes from 2000 to 2003.

6. * Of the following, which ratio of the money donated to a cause in 2003 to the money donated to the same cause in 2000 is closest to the ratio of the money donated to animals in 2003 to the money donated to animals in 2000 ?

   A) Children
   B) Environment
   C) Doctors
   D) Scholarships

7. Find the average rate of change per year in the money donated to the environment from 2000 to 2003, to the nearest whole number of dollars.

LEVEL 4

Questions 8 - 11 refer to the following information.

A wheel with a diameter of 6 feet is rolling on the ground at a constant rate of 4 feet per second in a straight line from point *a* to point *b*.

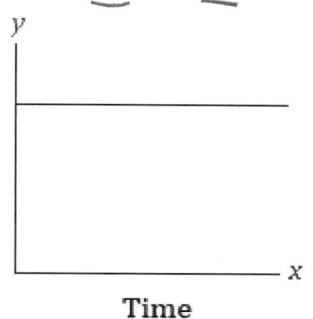

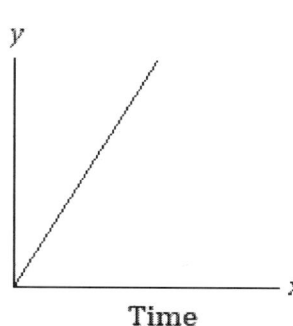

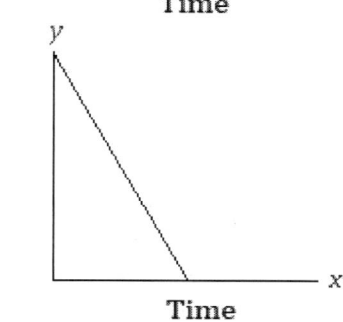

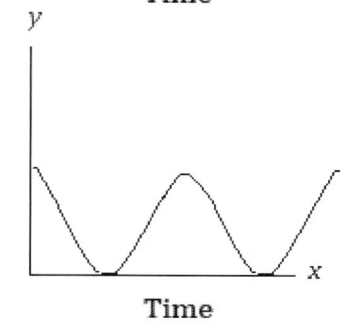

I. [Graph: horizontal line, y vs Time]

II. [Graph: line increasing from origin, y vs Time]

III. [Graph: line decreasing from y-axis to x-axis, y vs Time]

IV. [Graph: wave oscillating between 0 and a maximum, y vs Time]

8. Which of the graphs above could represent the distance of the center of the wheel from point *a* ?

   A) I
   B) II
   C) III
   D) IV

9. Which of the graphs above could represent the speed at which the wheel is rolling?

   A) I
   B) II
   C) III
   D) IV

10. Which of the graphs above could represent the distance from the center of the wheel to a fixed point on the rim?

    A) I
    B) II
    C) III
    D) IV

11. Which of the graphs above could represent the distance from the ground to a fixed point on the rim?

    A) I
    B) II
    C) III
    D) IV

LEVEL 5

12. Tom drives an average of 150 miles each day. His car can travel an average of 22 miles per gallon of gasoline. Tom would like to reduce his daily expenditure on gasoline by $6. Assuming gasoline costs $3 per gallon, which equation can Tom use to determine how many fewer average miles, d, he should drive each day?

   A) $\frac{22}{3}d = 146$

   B) $\frac{22}{3}d = 6$

   C) $\frac{3}{22}d = 146$

   D) $\frac{3}{22}d = 6$

Answers

1. D   2. 68   3. C   4. D   5. B   6. C   7. 137   8. B   9. A   10. A   11. D   12. D

LESSON 16 – GEOMETRY
ADDITIONAL PRACTICE 1

Full solutions to these problems are available for free download here:
www.SATPrepGet800.com/48SATy5

LEVEL 1

1. In isosceles triangle $\triangle PQR$, $\angle P$ and $\angle Q$ are congruent and the measure of $\angle R$ is 72°. What is the measure of $\angle P$? (Disregard the degree symbol when gridding your answer.)

   A) 18°
   B) 36°
   C) 54°
   D) 108°

2. What is the radius of a circle whose circumference is 15π?

LEVEL 2

3. C is the midpoint of line segment $\overline{AB}$, and D and E are the midpoints of $\overline{AC}$ and $\overline{CB}$, respectively. If the length of $\overline{CB}$ is 3, what is the length of $\overline{DB}$?

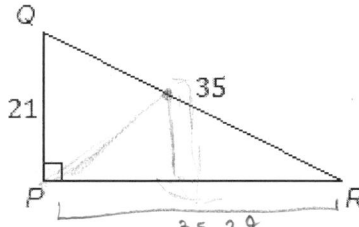

4. The lengths of two sides of right triangle $\triangle QPR$ shown above are given in centimeters. The midpoint of $\overline{PR}$ is how many centimeters from R?

117

5. An angle with a measure of $\frac{5\pi}{3}$ radians has a measure of x degrees, where $0 \leq x < 360$. What is the value of x ?

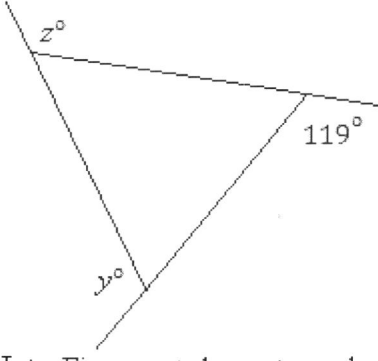

LEVEL 3

6. In $\triangle ABC$, the length of $\overline{AB}$ is 7 centimeters, and the length of $\overline{BC}$ is 9 centimeters. If it can be determined, what is the length, in centimeters, of $\overline{AC}$?

    A) 2
    B) $4\sqrt{2}$
    C) $\sqrt{130}$
    D) It cannot be determined from the given information.

Note: Figure not drawn to scale.

7. In the figure above, what is the value of $y + z$?

8. The number of radians in a 900-degree angle is equal to $k\pi$, where k is a positive constant. What is the value of k ?

LEVEL 4

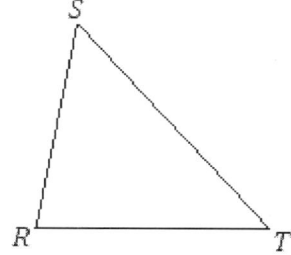

9. In the triangle above, $RS = RT = 10$ and $ST = 12$. What is the area of the triangle?

10. In a circle with center O, central angle POQ has a measure of $\frac{5\pi}{6}$ radians. The area of the sector formed by central angle POQ is what fraction of the area of the circle?

LEVEL 5

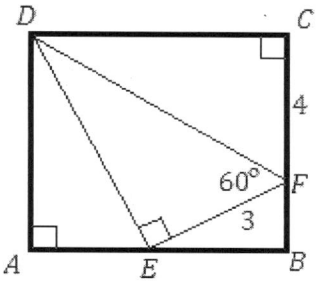

11. $ABCD$ shown above is a square, $m\angle DFE = 60°$, $EF = 3$, and $CF = 4$. What is the area of square $ABCD$?

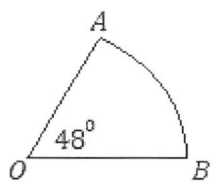

12. * In the figure above, AB is the arc of a circle with center O. If the length of arc AB is π, what is the area of region OAB, to the nearest tenth?

Answers

1. C 2. 15/2, 7.5 3. 4.5 4. 14 5. 300 6. D 7. 241 8. 5 9. 48 10. 5/12, .416, .417
11. 20 12. 5.9

119

LESSON 17 – HEART OF ALGEBRA
EQUATIONS OF LINES AND THEIR GRAPHS

Slippery Slopes

The **slope** of a line is

$$\text{Slope} = m = \frac{\text{rise}}{\text{run}} = \frac{y_2 - y_1}{x_2 - x_1}$$

Example: Let's find the slope of the line passing through the points $(3, -5)$ and $(7, 2)$.

Method 1: $\frac{2-(-5)}{7-3} = \frac{2+5}{7-3} = \frac{7}{4}$.

Method 2: We plot the two points as shown to the right and observe that to get from $(3, -5)$ to $(7, 2)$ we move up 7 and right 4. Therefore, the slope is $\frac{7}{4}$.

Note: If you cannot see where the 7 and 4 come from visually, then you can formally find the differences: $2 - (-5) = 7$ and $7 - 3 = 4$.

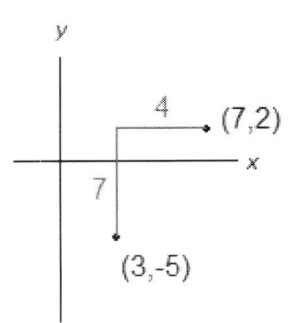

Moving on Up (or Down or Straight)

Lines with positive slope have graphs that go upwards from left to right. Lines with negative slope have graphs that go downwards from left to right. If the slope of a line is zero, it is horizontal. Vertical lines have **no** slope (also known as **infinite** slope or **undefined** slope).

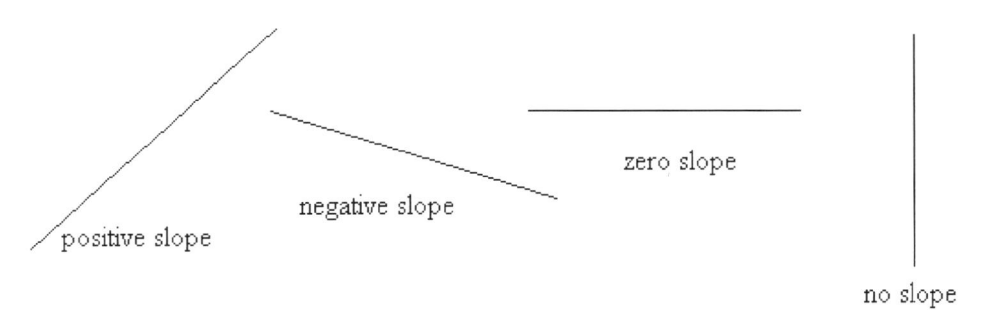

A Unique Equation for Every Line

The **slope-intercept form of an equation of a line** is $y = mx + b$, where m is the slope of the line and b is the y-intercept, ie., the point $(0, b)$ is on the line. Note that this point lies on the y-axis.

Examples: (1) $y = 2x + 7$ is an equation of a line with slope 2 and y-intercept 7.

(2) $y = -x - 5$ is an equation of a line with slope -1 and y-intercept -5 (Note: $-x = (-1)x$)

(3) $y = -6$ is an equation of a line with slope 0 and y-intercept -6 ($y = 0x - 6$)

(4) $x = 3$ is an equation of a line with **no** slope and **no** y-intercept.

Lines Deserve Multiple Equations

The **point-slope form of an equation of a line** is $y - y_0 = m(x - x_0)$, where m is the slope of the line and (x_0, y_0) is any point on the line.

Time to Practice

LEVEL 1: HEART OF ALGEBRA – EQUATIONS OF LINES AND THEIR GRAPHS

1. In the xy-plane, what is the y-intercept of the line with equation $y = -2x - 3$?

    A) $-\frac{1}{2}$
    B) -2
    C) $-\frac{3}{2}$
    D) -3

2. In the standard (x, y) coordinate plane, what is the slope of the line segment joining the points $(-3, -4)$ and $(5, -2)$?

LEVEL 2: HEART OF ALGEBRA – EQUATIONS OF LINES AND THEIR GRAPHS

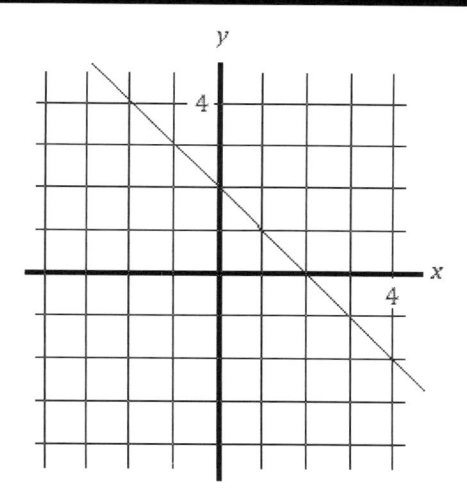

3. Which of the following is an equation of the line shown in the xy-plane above?

    A) $y = 2$
    B) $x = 2$
    C) $y = -x$
    D) $y = -x + 2$

4. What is the slope of the line with equation $y = \frac{x-5}{3}$?

121

LEVEL 3: HEART OF ALGEBRA – EQUATIONS OF LINES AND THEIR GRAPHS

5. The graph of the linear function h has intercepts at $(a, 0)$ and $(0, b)$ in the xy-plane. If a and b are opposite in sign, which of the following is true about te slope of the graph of h ?

   A) It is zero.
   B) It is positive.
   C) It is negative.
   D) It is undefined.

x	$g(x)$
0	-2
3	9
5	20

6. Some values of the linear function g are shown in the table above. Which of the foll⁄ defines g ?

   A) $g(x) = \frac{10}{3}x - 2$
   B) $g(x) = \frac{11}{3}x - 2$
   C) $g(x) = 4x + 2$
   D) $g(x) = -2x$

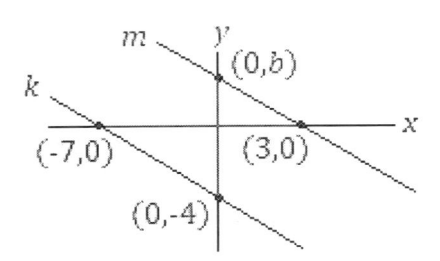

7. In the xy-plane above, line k is parallel to line m. What is the value of b ?

LEVEL 4: HEART OF ALGEBRA – EQUATIONS OF LINES AND THEIR GRAPHS

$$-5x + 2y = 3$$

8. In the xy-plane, the graph of which of the following equations is perpendicular to the graph of the equation above?

   A) $5x + 2y = 1$
   B) $5x - 2y = 1$
   C) $2x + 5y = 1$
   D) $2x - 5y = 1$

9. The graph of a line in the (x, y)-plane passes through the points $(-1, 2)$ and $(3, -4)$. The graph of a second line has slope 1 and contains the point $(-2, 5)$. If the two lines intersect at the point (x, y), what is the value of $x + 3$?

LEVEL 5: HEART OF ALGEBRA – EQUATIONS OF LINES AND THEIR GRAPHS

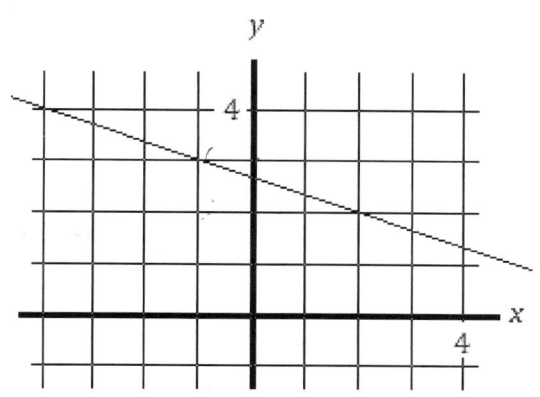

10. The graph of the linear function g is shown in the xy-plane above. The slope of the graph of the linear equation f is 5 times the slope of the graph of g. If the graph of f passes through the point $(0, 2)$, what is the value of $f(6)$?

A) -8
B) -4
C) 0
D) 12

Answers

1. D 2. 1/4, .25 3. D 4. 1/3, .333 5. B 6. B 7. 12/7, 1.71 8. C 9. 2/5, .4 10. A

Full Solutions

1.
* Solution using the slope-intercept form of a line: In the given equation, $b = -3$, choice **D**.

2.
Solution by drawing a picture: We plot the two points as shown to the right and observe that to get from $(-3, -4)$ to $(5, -2)$ we move up 2 and right 8. So, the answer is $\frac{2}{8} =$ **1/4** or **.25**.

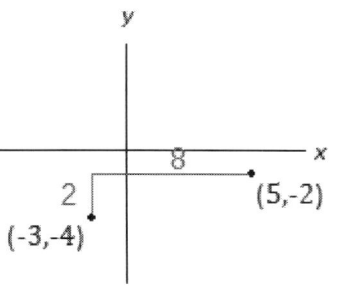

* Solution using the slope formula: $\frac{-2-(-4)}{5-(-3)} = \frac{-2+4}{5+3} = \frac{2}{8} =$ **1/4** or **.25**.

3.
* The y-intercept is $b = 2$ and the slope is $m = \frac{-1}{1} = -1$. So, an equation in slope-intercept form is $y = -x + 2$, choice **D**.

Notes: (1) In the picture on the left, we have circled the y-intercept, and showed how to compute the slope by starting at any point on the line and moving down 1 unit and then right 1 unit to get to another point (we used the points $(1, 1)$ and $(2, 0)$.

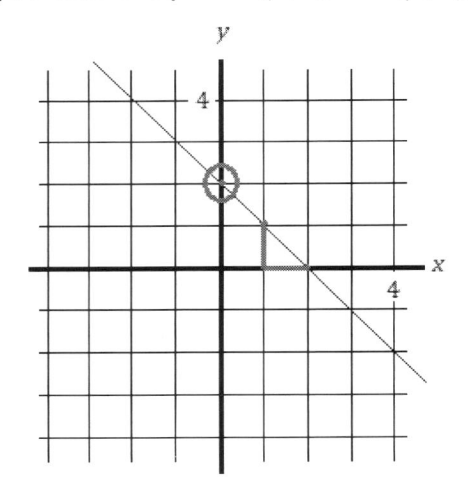

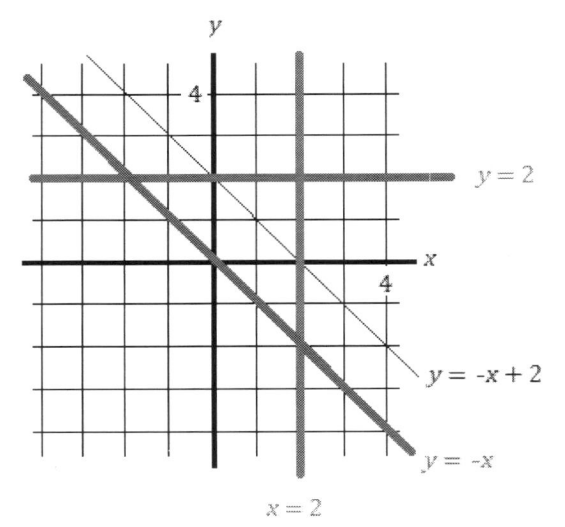

(2) In the picture on the right, we have sketched the graphs of all four answer choices on the same set of axes.

4.

* Solution using the slope-intercept form of a line: $\frac{x-5}{3} = \frac{x}{3} - \frac{5}{3} = \frac{1}{3}x - \frac{5}{3}$.

The slope of the line is $m = \mathbf{1/3}$ or $\mathbf{.333}$.

5.

Solution by picking numbers: Let's choose values for a and b, say $a = 2$ and $b = -3$. Then the line passes through the points $(2, 0)$ and $(0, -3)$. So, the slope of the line is $m = \frac{-3-0}{0-2} = \frac{-3}{-2} = \frac{3}{2}$. We see that the slope is positive, choice **B**.

Note: Instead of using the slope formula we can plot the two points, draw the line passing through them, and observe that the line is moving upward from left to right.

* Direct solution: The slope of the line passing through the points $(a, 0)$ and $(0, b)$ is $\frac{b-0}{0-a} = \frac{b}{-a} = -\frac{b}{a}$. Since a and b have opposite signs, $\frac{b}{a}$ is negative. It follows that $-\frac{b}{a}$ is positive, choice **B**.

6.

* Direct solution: The first row of the table gives that the y-intercept of the line is $b = -2$.

We can find the slope using any two rows of the table. Let's use the first two rows. These two rows give us the points $(0, -2)$ and $(3, 9)$, respectively. The slope is $m = \frac{9-(-2)}{3-0} = \frac{9+2}{3} = \frac{11}{3}$.

So, an equation of the line in slope-intercept form is $y = \frac{11}{3}x - 2$, and the answer is choice **B**.

Notes: (1) The table tells us that $g(0) = -2$, $g(3) = 9$, and $g(5) = 20$.

(2) Recall from Lesson 10 that $g(a) = b$ is equivalent to "the point (a, b) lies on the graph of g." So, from note (1), we see that the points $(0, -2)$, $(3, 9)$, and $(5, 20)$ lie on the graph of g.

(3) The point $(0, -2)$ is on the y-axis. So, $b = -2$.

(4) We can use any two of these three points to find the slope of the line. In the above solution, we used the first two points.

"Plug It In" Strikes Yet Again – This Time with Points!

If the graph of a function or other equation passes through certain points, plug those points into the equation to eliminate answer choices.

Solution by plugging in points: The first row of the table tells us that the point $(0, -2)$ is on the line, or equivalently, $g(0) = -2$. We evaluate $g(0)$ in all four answer choices.

A) $g(0) = -2$
B) $g(0) = -2$
C) $g(0) = 2$
D) $g(0) = 0$

Since choices C and D did not come out to -2, we can eliminate them. Let's use the second row of the table next. The second row tells us that $g(3) = 9$. We need only check choices A and B now.

A) $g(3) = \frac{10}{3} \cdot 3 - 2 = 10 - 2 = 8$
B) $g(3) = \frac{11}{3} \cdot 3 - 2 = 11 - 2 = 9$

Since choice A did not come out to 9, we can eliminate it, and the answer is choice **B**.

7.
LINES FACT 1: Parallel lines have the same slope.

Solution using LINES FACT 1: The slope of line k is $\frac{-4-0}{0-(-7)} = \frac{-4}{7}$ and the slope of line m is $\frac{b-0}{0-3} = \frac{b}{-3}$. Since parallel lines have the same slope, we have $\frac{-4}{7} = \frac{b}{-3}$. We cross multiply to get $7b = 12$. Finally, we divide each side by 7 to get $b = \mathbf{12/7}$ or $\mathbf{1.71}$.

8.
LINES FACT 2: Perpendicular lines have slopes that are negative reciprocals of each other.

Solution using LINES FACT 2: We first rewrite the given equation in slope-intercept form. We start by adding $5x$ to each side of the equation to get $2y = 5x + 3$. We then divide each side of the equation by 2 to get $y = \frac{5}{2}x + \frac{3}{2}$. So, the slope of the given line is $\frac{5}{2}$.

Since we want an equation of a line perpendicular to the given line, it's slope should be $-\frac{2}{5}$. So, the equation of the line in slope-intercept form is $y = -\frac{2}{5}x + b$ for some constant b. We multiply each side of this equation by 5 to get $5y = -2x + 5b$. We then add $2x$ to each side of this last equation to get $2x + 5y = 5b$. This matches choice **C**.

* **Quick solution:** If a line is written in the **general form** $ax + by = c$, then the slope of the line is $m = -\frac{a}{b}$. In this problem, the given line is in general form with $a = -5$ and $b = 2$. Therefore, the slope of the given line is $\frac{5}{2}$.

We can use the same method to get the slopes of the lines whose equations are in the answer choices.

  A) $-\frac{5}{2}$

  B) $\frac{5}{2}$

  C) $-\frac{2}{5}$

  D) $\frac{2}{5}$

Since choice C gave the negative reciprocal of $\frac{5}{2}$, the answer is choice **C**.

9.
* The slope of the first line is $m = \frac{-4-2}{3-(-1)} = \frac{-6}{4} = -\frac{3}{2}$. Using the point $(-1, 2)$, we can write an equation of the line in point-slope form as

$$y - 2 = -\frac{3}{2}(x - (-1)), \text{ or equivalently, } y = -\frac{3}{2}x + \frac{1}{2} \text{ (check this!)}$$

We can write an equation of the second line in point-slope form as

$$y - 5 = 1(x - (-2)), \text{ or equivalently, } y = x + 7 \text{ (check this!)}$$

Since both equations have y by itself, let's solve the system of equations using the *substitution method*.

We have $-\frac{3}{2}x + \frac{1}{2} = x + 7$. We multiply each side of this equation by 2 to get $-3x + 1 = 2x + 14$. Adding $3x$ to each side of the equation and subtracting 14 from each side of the equation gives us $-13 = 5x$. So, $x = -\frac{13}{5}$. It follows that $x + 3 = -\frac{13}{5} + \frac{15}{5} = \mathbf{2/5}$ or $\mathbf{.4}$.

Notes: (1) We can change a line from point-slope form to slope-intercept form simply by solving the equation for y.

For example, the equation $y - 5 = 1(x + 2)$ is in point-slope form. We simply add 5 to each side of the equation to get $y = x + 7$. This last equation is now in slope-intercept form.

(2) We needed to solve the following system of equations:

$$y = -\frac{3}{2}x + \frac{1}{2}$$
$$y = x + 7$$

In the above solution, we chose to use the *substitution method*. Since y is equal to both $-\frac{3}{2}x + \frac{1}{2}$ and $x + 7$, we must have these two quantities equal to each other.

10.

* By looking at the graph of g, we can see that the line passes through the points $(-1, 3)$ and $(2, 2)$. So, the slope of the graph of g is $\frac{2-3}{2-(-1)} = -\frac{1}{3}$. Since the slope of the graph of f is 5 times the slope of the graph of g, the slope of the graph of f is $-\frac{5}{3}$. We are also given that the y-intercept of the graph of f is $b = 2$. So, an equation for f is $f(x) = -\frac{5}{3}x + 2$. Finally, $f(6) = -\frac{5}{3} \cdot 6 + 2 = -10 + 2 = -8$, choice **A**.

LESSON 18 – PASSPORT TO ADVANCED MATH
OPERATIONS ON POLYNOMIALS

Polynomials, More or Less…

We **add polynomials** by simply combining like terms. We can change any **subtraction problem** to an addition problem by first distributing the minus sign. For example,

$$(-5x^2 + 3x) - (-5x^2 - 3x) = -5x^2 + 3x + 5x^2 + 3x = 6x.$$

FOILed Again, But Still We Multiply!

Most students are familiar with the mnemonic FOIL to help them **multiply** two binomials (polynomials with 2 terms) together. As a simple example, we have

$$(x+1)(x-2) = x^2 - 2x + x - 2 = x^2 - x - 2$$

Unfortunately, this method works ONLY for binomials. It does not extend to polynomials with more than 2 terms. Let's demonstrate another way to multiply polynomials with the same example.

We begin by lining up the polynomials vertically:

$$\begin{array}{r} x+1 \\ \underline{x-2} \end{array}$$

We multiply the -2 on the bottom by each term on top, moving from right to left. First note that -2 times 1 is -2:

$$\begin{array}{r} x+1 \\ \underline{x-2} \\ -2 \end{array}$$

Next note that -2 times x is $-2x$:

$$\begin{array}{r} x+1 \\ \underline{x-2} \\ -2x-2 \end{array}$$

Now we multiply the x on the bottom by each term on top, moving from right to left. This time as we write the answers we leave one blank space on the right:

$$\begin{array}{r} x+1 \\ \underline{x-2} \\ -2x-2 \\ \underline{x^2+x} \end{array}$$

Finally, we add:

$$\begin{array}{r} x+1 \\ \underline{x-2} \\ -2x-2 \\ \underline{x^2+x} \\ x^2-x-2 \end{array}$$

Products of Binomials

The following **special factoring formulas** are not necessary, but useful for saving a bit of time.

$$(x + y)^2 = x^2 + y^2 + 2xy$$
$$(x - y)^2 = x^2 + y^2 - 2xy$$
$$(x + y)(x - y) = x^2 - y^2$$

The last formula should be familiar. It's the difference of two squares. The other two are similar to each other and they are just the simplified result of multiplying the expression in parentheses by itself.

Example: $(2x - 5)^2 = (2x)^2 + (-5)^2 - 2(2x)(5) = 4x^2 + 25 - 20x = 4x^2 - 20x + 25$

Leftovers

The **remainder theorem** says that $p(r) = a$ if and only if the remainder when $p(x)$ is divided by $x - r$ is a.

Example: Let $p(x) = 3x^2 - 2x + 5$. Since $p(2) = 3 \cdot 2^2 - 2 \cdot 2 + 5 = 3 \cdot 4 - 4 + 5 = 12 + 1 = 13$, the remainder when $3x^2 - 2x + 5$ is divided by $x - 2$ is 13.

Factør Theørem

The **factor theorem** says that $p(r) = 0$ if and only if $x - r$ is a factor of the polynomial p. (Note that this is just the special case of the remainder theorem where $a = 0$.)

Example: Let $p(x) = 2x^3 - 3x + 1$. Since $p(1) = 2 - 3 + 1 = 0$, we know that $x - 1$ is a factor of p.

LEVEL 1: PASSPORT TO ADVANCED MATH – OPERATIONS ON POLYNOMIALS

1. Which of the following is equivalent to the sum of $2x^2 - 3$ and $5x + 3$?

   A) $10x^3 + 3x$
   B) $10x^3$
   C) $7x^3$
   D) $2x^2 + 5x$

LEVEL 2: PASSPORT TO ADVANCED MATH – OPERATIONS ON POLYNOMIALS

$$3x^2 + 5x - 2$$
$$4x^2 - 8x + 3$$

2. Which of the following is the sum of the two polynomials shown above?

   A) $7x^2 - 3x + 1$
   B) $7x^2 + 3x + 1$
   C) $7x^4 - 3x^2 + 1$
   D) $7x^4 + 3x^2 + 1$

$$(-3x^3 + 2x) - (-3x^3 - 2x)$$

3. Which of the following is equivalent to the expression above?

   A) 0
   B) $-6x^3$
   C) $4x$
   D) $-6x^3 + 4x$

4. When we subtract $-3x^2 + 2x - 5$ from $5x^2 + x - 3$, the result can be written $ax^2 + bx + c$, where a, b, and c are real numbers. What is the value of ac ?

LEVEL 3: PASSPORT TO ADVANCED MATH – OPERATIONS ON POLYNOMIALS

$$(3217 + x + 1000x^2) + 200(30x^2 - x + 10)$$

5. The expression above can be written in the form $ax^2 + bx + c$, where a, b, and c are constants. What is the value of $a + b - c$?

LEVEL 4: PASSPORT TO ADVANCED MATH – OPERATIONS ON POLYNOMIALS

6. * Which of the following is an equivalent form of $(3.5x^2 - 1.6) - (1.2x - 3.2)^2$?

   A) $2.06x^2 + 7.68x - 11.84$
   B) $2.06x^2 + 7.68x - 8.64$
   C) $4.94x^2 + 11.84$
   D) $4.94x^2 - 8.64$

LEVEL 5: PASSPORT TO ADVANCED MATH – OPERATIONS ON POLYNOMIALS

7. Which of the following expressions is equivalent to $\left(\frac{x}{3} + \frac{y}{4}\right)^2$?

   A) $\frac{x^2}{3} + \frac{y^2}{4}$
   B) $\frac{x^2}{9} + \frac{y^2}{16}$
   C) $\frac{x^2}{9} + \frac{xy}{12} + \frac{y^2}{16}$
   D) $\frac{x^2}{9} + \frac{xy}{6} + \frac{y^2}{16}$

$$\frac{x^2 - 4x + 3}{x - 5}$$

8. Which of the following is equivalent to the expression above?

   A) $x + 3 - \frac{24}{x-5}$
   B) $x + 3 - \frac{12}{x-5}$
   C) $x + 1 + \frac{8}{x-5}$
   D) $x + 1 + \frac{3}{x-5}$

9. For a polynomial $p(x)$, the value of $p(2)$ is -5. Which of the following must be true about $p(x)$?

   A) $x - 7$ is a factor of $p(x)$.
   B) $x - 5$ is a factor of $p(x)$.
   C) $x + 5$ is a factor of $p(x)$.
   D) The remainder when $p(x)$ is divided by $x - 2$ is -5.

$$g(x) = x^2 + 4x - 1$$
$$h(x) = 2x^3 + 3x^2 + x$$

10. The polynomials g and h are defined above. Which of the following polynomials is divisible by $2x - 1$?

    A) $k(x) = g(x) - h(x)$
    B) $k(x) = 12g(x) - h(x)$
    C) $k(x) = g(x) - 10h(x)$
    D) $k(x) = 12g(x) - 10h(x)$

Answers

1. D   2. A   3. C   4. 16   5. 1584   6. A   7. D   8. C   9. D   10. D

Full Solutions

1.
* **Algebraic solution:** $(2x^2 - 3) + (5x + 3) = 2x^2 + 5x - 3 + 3 = 2x^2 + 5x$, choice **D**.

2.
* **Algebraic solution:**

$$3x^2 + 5x - 2$$
$$4x^2 - 8x + 3$$
$$7x^2 - 3x + 1$$

This is choice **A**.

131

3.

Algebraic solution:
$$(-3x^3 + 2x) - (-3x^3 - 2x) = -3x^3 + 2x + 3x^3 + 2x$$
$$= (-3x^3 + 3x^3) + (2x + 2x) = 0 + 4x = 4x$$

This is choice **C**.

4.

Algebraic solution:
$$(5x^2 + x - 3) - (-3x^2 + 2x - 5) = 5x^2 + x - 3 + 3x^2 - 2x + 5$$
$$= (5x^2 + 3x^2) + (x - 2x) + (-3 + 5) = 8x^2 - x + 2$$

So, $a = 8$, $c = 2$, and therefore, $ac = 8 \cdot 2 = \mathbf{16}$.

5.

Algebraic solution: $(3217 + x + 1000x^2) + 200(30x^2 - x + 10)$
$$= (3217 + x + 1000x^2) + (6000x^2 - 200x + 2000) = 7000x^2 - 199x + 5217$$

So, $a = 7000$, $b = -199$, $c = 5217$, and therefore, $a + b - c = 7000 - 199 - 5217 = \mathbf{1584}$.

6.

Algebraic solution: $(1.2x - 3.2)^2 = (1.2x - 3.2)(1.2x - 3.2) = 1.44x^2 - 3.84x - 3.84x + 10.24$
$$= 1.44x^2 - 7.68x + 10.24$$

So, $(3.5x^2 - 1.6) - (1.2x - 3.2)^2 = (3.5x^2 - 1.6) - (1.44x^2 - 7.68x + 10.24)$
$$= 3.5x^2 - 1.6 - 1.44x^2 + 7.68x - 10.24 = 2.06x^2 + 7.68x - 11.84$$

This is choice **A**.

Note: We can do this a little faster by using the second special factoring formula:
$$(1.2x - 3.2)^2 = 1.44x^2 + 10.24 - 7.68x.$$

7.

* Solution using the first special factoring formula:
$$\left(\frac{x}{3} + \frac{y}{4}\right)^2 = \frac{x^2}{9} + \frac{y^2}{16} + \frac{2xy}{12} = \frac{x^2}{9} + \frac{y^2}{16} + \frac{xy}{6} = \frac{x^2}{9} + \frac{xy}{6} + \frac{y^2}{16}$$

This is choice **D**.

Note: If you do not remember the special factoring formula, you can multiply by FOIL or by using the algorithm from this section: $\left(\frac{x}{3} + \frac{y}{4}\right)^2 = \left(\frac{x}{3} + \frac{y}{4}\right)\left(\frac{x}{3} + \frac{y}{4}\right) = \frac{x^2}{9} + \frac{2xy}{12} + \frac{y^2}{16} = \frac{x^2}{9} + \frac{xy}{6} + \frac{y^2}{16}$

8.

* Solution using synthetic division: We can divide any polynomial by a linear polynomial of the form $x - r$ by using a simple procedure called **synthetic division**. We start by writing r in the upper left-hand corner. In this case, $r = 5$.

Next, we make sure that the polynomial we are dividing is written in descending order of exponents (which it is) and that every exponent is accounted for (which they are). We then write down the coefficients of this polynomial. So, we have the following:

$$5 \rfloor \quad 1 \quad -4 \quad 3$$

We begin by bringing down the first 1.

$$5 \rfloor \quad 1 \quad -4 \quad 3$$
$$\overline{}$$
$$1$$

We now multiply this number by the number in the upper left. So, we have $1 \cdot 5 = 5$. We place this number under the -4.

$$5 \rfloor \quad 1 \quad -4 \quad 3$$
$$5$$
$$\overline{}$$
$$1$$

Next, we add -4 and 5.

$$5 \rfloor \quad 1 \quad -4 \quad 3$$
$$5$$
$$\overline{}$$
$$1 \quad 1$$

We repeat this procedure to get $1 \cdot 5 = 5$, then add 3 and 5 to get 8.

$$5 \rfloor \quad 1 \quad -4 \quad 3$$
$$5 \quad 5$$
$$\overline{}$$
$$1 \quad 1 \quad 8$$

The bottom row gives the coefficients of the quotient (which is a polynomial of 1 degree less than the dividend) and the remainder.

So, the quotient polynomial is $1x^1 + 1$ and the remainder is 8. Note that the degree of this polynomial is 1, which is 1 less than the degree of the polynomial $x^2 - 4x + 3$.

We put the remainder over the linear divisor and add it to the quotient.

So, we have $\frac{x^2 - 4x + 3}{x - 5} = x + 1 + \frac{8}{x - 5}$, choice **C**.

Note: This problem can also be solved using long division. This procedure is more time consuming than synthetic division, so I will omit it here and leave it as an optional exercise for the interested reader.

9.

* **Solution using the remainder theorem:** Since $p(2) = -5$, by the remainder theorem, the remainder when $p(x)$ is divided by $x - 2$ is -5, choice **D**.

Note: In this problem, we are using the remainder theorem with $r = 2$ and $a = -5$.

Solution by picking a polynomial: If we let $p(x) = x^2 - 9$, then we have $p(2) = 2^2 - 9 = -5$. Since $x - 7$, $x - 5$, and $x + 5$ are not factors of this polynomial, we can eliminate choices A, B, and C. Therefore, the answer is choice **D**.

Notes: (1) $p(x) = x^2 - 9$ is a second-degree polynomial (or quadratic polynomial). It has *at most* two linear factors. It should be clear that $x - 7$, $x - 5$, and $x + 5$ cannot be factors of this polynomial. In fact, the two linear factors of this polynomial are $x - 3$ and $x + 3$.

(2) It might seem more reasonable to pick a linear polynomial instead of a quadratic one. In this case, the simplest linear polynomial satisfying the given condition is $p(x) = x - 7$ ($p(2) = 2 - 7 = -5$). Although we can eliminate choices B and C using this polynomial, we cannot eliminate choice A. If you actually divide $x - 7$ by $x - 2$ (using either long division or synthetic division) you will see that the result is -5. So, we cannot eliminate choice D either.

This is why I chose to use a quadratic polynomial instead of a linear one.

(3) We can actually use the constant function $p(x) = -5$. This is a polynomial of degree zero, and the given condition is trivially satisfied. Clearly this polynomial has no linear factors, and so we can eliminate choices A, B, and C.

10.
* **Solution using the factor theorem:** We note that $2x - 1 = 2\left(x - \frac{1}{2}\right)$, and use $r = \frac{1}{2}$. We have

$$g\left(\frac{1}{2}\right) = \left(\frac{1}{2}\right)^2 + 4\left(\frac{1}{2}\right) - 1 = \frac{1}{4} + 2 - 1 = \frac{1}{4} + 1 = \frac{5}{4}$$

$$h\left(\frac{1}{2}\right) = 2\left(\frac{1}{2}\right)^3 + 3\left(\frac{1}{2}\right)^2 + \frac{1}{2} = 2\left(\frac{1}{8}\right) + 3\left(\frac{1}{4}\right) + \frac{1}{2} = \frac{1}{4} + \frac{3}{4} + \frac{1}{2} = \frac{3}{2}$$

Since $12\left(\frac{5}{4}\right) - 10\left(\frac{3}{2}\right) = 15 - 15 = 0$, we see that if $k(x) = 12g(x) - 10h(x)$, then $k\left(\frac{1}{2}\right) = 0$, and it follows that $2x - 1$ is a factor of k. So, the answer is choice **D**.

Note: To use the factor theorem, we need to divide by a linear polynomial of the form $x - r$. So, we rewrite $2x - 1$ as $2\left(x - \frac{1}{2}\right)$. We see that $2x - 1$ is a factor of the polynomial if and only if $x - \frac{1}{2}$ is a factor of the polynomial. So, we use $r = \frac{1}{2}$.

LESSON 19 – PROBLEM SOLVING
STATISTICS

Don't Be Average

The **average (arithmetic mean)** of a list of numbers is the sum of the numbers in the list divided by the quantity of the numbers in the list.

$$\text{Average} = \frac{\text{Sum}}{\text{Number}}$$

The **median** of a list of numbers is the middle number when the numbers are arranged in increasing order. If the total number of values in the list is even, then the median is the average of the two middle values.

The **mode** of a list of numbers is the number that occurs most frequently. There can be more than one mode if more than one number occurs with the greatest frequency.

The **range** of a list of numbers is the positive difference between the greatest number and smallest number in the list.

Example 1: Let's compute the average (arithmetic mean), median, mode, and range of 1, 1, 6, 10, 12.

$$\text{Average} = \frac{1+1+6+10+12}{5} = \frac{30}{5} = 6 \quad \text{Median} = \mathbf{6} \quad \text{Mode} = \mathbf{1} \quad \text{Range} = 12 - 1 = \mathbf{11}$$

Example 2: Let's do the same for this set of data: 7, 2, 5, 18, 10, 3.

$$\text{Average} = \frac{7+2+5+18+10+3}{6} = \frac{45}{6} = \frac{15}{2} \text{ or } \mathbf{7.5}$$

To find the median it is helpful to rewrite the numbers in increasing order: 2, 3, 5, 7, 10, 18. Then the median is $\frac{5+7}{2} = \frac{12}{2} = \mathbf{6}$.

There is **no mode**, and the range is $18 - 2 = \mathbf{16}$.

From AVERAGE to SUM-thing Better

A problem involving averages often becomes much easier when we first convert the averages to sums. We can easily change an average to a sum using the following simple formula.

$$\textbf{Sum} = \textbf{Average} \cdot \textbf{Number}$$

Many problems with averages involve one or more conversions to sums, followed by a subtraction.

Note: The above formula comes from eliminating the denominator in the definition of average:

$$\text{Average} = \frac{\text{Sum}}{\text{Number}}$$

Let's try an example.

LEVEL 1: PROBLEM SOLVING – STATISTICS

1. * The average (arithmetic mean) of four numbers is 73.6. If three of the numbers are 76.4, 92.3, and 85.2, what is the fourth number?

* Solution by changing averages to sums: In this case we are averaging 4 numbers. Thus, the **Number** is 4. The **Average** is given to be 73.6. So, the **Sum** of the 4 numbers is $73.6 \cdot 4 = 294.4$. Since we know that three of the numbers are 76.4, 92.3, and 85.2, the fourth number must be

$$294.4 - 76.4 - 92.3 - 85.2 = \mathbf{40.5}.$$

Time to Practice

LEVEL 1: PROBLEM SOLVING – STATISTICS

2. What is the median of the following 9 test grades?

   89, 66, 75, 91, 56, 92, 76, 71, 76

| Exam Grade for Classes in a Middle School ||
Class	Median grade (out of 100)
Algebra	65.5
Geometry	62
Chemistry	58.5
Physics	67
Spanish	75
History	82.5

3. What is the range of the median grades from the classes in the table above?

LEVEL 2: PROBLEM SOLVING – STATISTICS

Height of Student (in inches)

48	60	60	60	61	61	62
63	63	65	65	65	65	65
65	65	66	67	67	68	70
70	71	72	73	73	73	74

4. The table above lists the heights, to the nearest inch, of a random sample of 28 students. The outlier height of 48 inches is an error. Of the mean, median, mode, and range of the values listed, which will change the most if the 48-inch outlier is removed from the data?

   A) Mean
   B) Median
   C) Mode
   D) Range

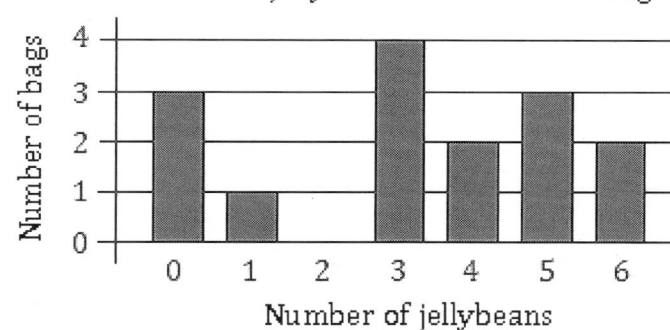

5. * Based on the histogram above, what is the average (arithmetic mean) number of jellybeans per bag?

LEVEL 3: PROBLEM SOLVING – STATISTICS

6. Vlada is preparing for the SAT. Her goal is to study an average of at least 6 hours per week for 5 weeks. She studied 4 hours the first week, 7 hours the second week, 8 hours the third week, and 3 hours the fourth week. Which inequality can be used to represent the number of hours, h, Vlada could study on the fifth week to reach her goal?

   A) $\frac{4+7+8+3}{4} + h \geq 6$
   B) $4 + 7 + 8 + 3 \geq h \cdot 6$
   C) $\frac{4}{5} + \frac{7}{5} + \frac{8}{5} + \frac{3}{5} + h \geq 6$
   D) $4 + 7 + 8 + 3 + h \geq 5 \cdot 6$

Time on Treadmill (minutes)	Frequency
15	1
20	3
25	2
30	1
35	2
40	3
45	3
50	1
55	1
60	1

7. A personal trainer with 18 clients recorded how much time each client spent on the treadmill at their last session. The results are shown in the table above. Based on the table, what was the median number of minutes that the trainer's clients spent on the treadmill?

LEVEL 4: PROBLEM SOLVING – STATISTICS

	Heights (inches)							
Jessie	5.3	4.1	4.7	6.2	3.8	4.5	4.8	5.9
Carl	3.8	2.7	4.9	6.1	x	5.1	2.9	3.9

8. * Jessie and Carl each collected eight plants, and the heights of the plants are given in the table above. The mean of the heights of the plants collected by Jessie is 0.3 inches more than the mean of the heights of the plants collected by Carl. What is the value of x?

LEVEL 5: PROBLEM SOLVING – STATISTICS

9. If x is the average (arithmetic mean) of a and b, y is the average of $2a$ and $3b$, and z is the average of $4a$ and $5b$, what is the average of x, y, and z in terms of a and b?

   A) $a + b$
   B) $\frac{a+b}{2}$
   C) $\frac{7a}{3} + 3b$
   D) $\frac{7a+9b}{6}$

10. In Dr. Steve's AP Calculus BC class, students are given a grade between 0 and 100, inclusive on each exam. Jason's average (arithmetic mean) for the first 3 exams was 90. What is the lowest grade Jason can receive on his 4th exam and still be able to have an average of 90 for all 7 exams that will be given?

Answers

1. 40.5   2. 76   3. 24   4. D   5. 16/5, 3.2   6. D   7. 75/2, 37.5   8. 15/2, 7.5   9. D   10. 60

Full Solutions

2.

* Let's rewrite the list of numbers in increasing order.

$$56, 66, 71, 75, 76, 76, 89, 91, 92$$

There are 9 numbers in the list. Since 9 is odd, we take the middle number, which is **76**.

3.

* The range is $82.5 - 58.5 =$ **24**.

Note: It may seem confusing that the word "median" appears in this problem, but we are never taking a median to solve the problem. This is because the medians were already taken when the data was compiled. Each number in the table represents the median for a collection of grades. We simply need to take the range of all the numbers in the list.

4.

* The median and mode do not change at all if we remove the 48, and the mean will change just a bit. The range however changes from 26 to 14 (a change of 12). So, the answer is **D**.

Notes: (1) We can find the median (of the original set of data) quite easily by crossing out the top and bottom row, and then crossing out the first 6 entries of the second row and the last 6 entries of the third row.

48	60	60	60	61	61	62
63	63	65	65	65	65	65
65	65	66	67	67	68	70
70	71	72	73	73	73	74

Now note that if we remove the 48 from the data, then the median will still be 65 (it will be the entry in the first column and third row).

(2) The mode of the data is 65 because 65 appears 7 times, and no other number appears that many times. Deleting the 48 does not affect this, and so the mode remains 65.

(3) The range of the original data is $74 - 48 = 26$. When we remove the 48, the range becomes $74 - 60 = 14$.

(4) Computing the exact mean here would be quite tedious. But there is no need to do so. We need only be convinced that the mean will not change by 12 or more ($26 - 14 = 12$) when we remove the 48.

This should be somewhat obvious, but in case it is not, let's analyze this a bit. To compute the mean, we add up all the data, and then divide by the number of data points.

So, to get the mean of all the data, we add everything up and divide by 28. For example, if all those numbers added up to 1200, we would get a mean of $\frac{1200}{28} \approx 42.86$.

To get the mean of the data with the 48 removed, we add everything except the 48, and divide by 27. So, using our rough estimate for a sum of 1200 for all the data, when we remove the 48 we get a sum of 1152, and so we get a new mean of $\frac{1152}{27} \approx 42.67$.

The change in the mean was approximately 0.19, a change that is much smaller than the change in range.

(5) It should be clear that even if our estimate was way off, the mean could not possibly have changed more than the range.

5.
* $\frac{3 \cdot 0 + 1 \cdot 1 + 0 \cdot 2 + 4 \cdot 3 + 2 \cdot 4 + 3 \cdot 5 + 2 \cdot 6}{3+1+4+2+3+2} = \frac{1+12+8+15+12}{15} = \frac{48}{15} = \mathbf{3.2}$.

Notes: (1) According to the graph, 0 occurs 3 times, 1 occurs 1 time, 2 occurs 0 times, 3 occurs 4 times, 4 occurs 2 times, 5 occurs 3 times, and 6 occurs 2 times.

(2) A complete list of the data is

$$0, 0, 0, 1, 3, 3, 3, 3, 4, 4, 5, 5, 5, 6, 6$$

(3) Average $= \frac{\text{Sum}}{\text{Number}}$. In other words, to compute an average, we add up all the data, and then divide by the number of data points.

6.
* **Solution by changing averages to sums:** We want the average for 5 weeks to be at least 6. So, we want the sum to be at least $5 \cdot 6$. The sum for the 5 weeks is $4 + 7 + 8 + 3 + h$. So, we need to have $4 + 7 + 8 + 3 + h \geq 5 \cdot 6$. This is choice **D**.

7.
* Let's list all the data in increasing order.

$$15, 20, 20, 20, 25, 25, 30, 35, \mathbf{35, 40}, 40, 40, 45, 45, 45, 50, 55, 60$$

Since there is an even number of minutes, we have to take the mean of the middle two numbers. So, the median is $\frac{35+40}{2} = \mathbf{75/2}$ or $\mathbf{37.5}$.

Notes: (1) Since there are 18 data points, we can find the middle by dividing 18 by 2 to get $\frac{18}{2} = 9$. So, the median is the mean of the 9th and 10th numbers in the list.

(2) If you aren't confident about finding the middle, you can strike off two numbers at a time simultaneously, one from each end until just two numbers are left.

$$\cancel{15}, \cancel{20}, \cancel{20}, \cancel{20}, \cancel{25}, \cancel{25}, \cancel{30}, \cancel{35}, \mathbf{35, 40}, \cancel{40}, \cancel{40}, \cancel{45}, \cancel{45}, \cancel{45}, \cancel{50}, \cancel{55}, \cancel{60}$$

(3) To save time, we can just cross numbers off the table from both ends. For example, we can cross off the first four rows. This eliminates the first $1 + 3 + 2 + 1 = 7$ data points. So, we get rid of the last 7 data points as well. This is the last 4 rows and 1 data point from the row above them. Here's how the mark-up might look.

Time on Treadmill (minutes)	Frequency
~~15~~	~~1~~
~~20~~	~~3~~
~~25~~	~~2~~
~~30~~	~~1~~
35	2
40	2
~~45~~	~~2~~
~~50~~	~~1~~
~~55~~	~~1~~
~~60~~	~~1~~

Now it's easy to see that the median is the mean of 35 and 40.

8.
* The mean of the heights of the plants collected by Jessie is

$$\frac{5.3 + 4.1 + 4.7 + 6.2 + 3.8 + 4.5 + 4.8 + 5.9}{8} = \frac{39.3}{8} = 4.9125$$

It follows that the mean of the heights of the plants collected by Carl is $4.9125 - 0.3 = 4.6125$.

We can now compute the sum of the heights of the plants collected by Carl in two ways.

First, we can change the mean to a sum: Sum $= 4.6125 \cdot 8 = 36.9$.

Second, we can add up the entries in the second row of the table:

$$3.8 + 2.7 + 4.9 + 6.1 + x + 5.1 + 2.9 + 3.9 = 29.4 + x$$

So, we have $29.4 + x = 36.9$, and therefore, $x = 36.9 - 29.4 = \mathbf{7.5}$.

Notes: We saved a little time here by using the strategy of changing averages to sums. We can also work directly with the mean of the heights of the plants collected by Carl.

$$\frac{29.4 + x}{8} = 4.6125$$

We would then multiply each side of this equation by 8 to get $29.4 + x = 4.6125 \cdot 8 = 36.9$, and then subtract 29.4 to get $x = 7.5$.

9.

*** Solution by changing averages to sums:** The sum of a and b is $a + b = 2x$, the sum of $2a$ and $3b$ is $2a + 3b = 2y$, and the sum of $4a$ and $5b$ is $4a + 5b = 2z$. We now add these three equations.

$$a + b = 2x$$
$$2a + 3b = 2y$$
$$\underline{4a + 5b = 2z}$$
$$7a + 9b = 2x + 2y + 2z$$

We factor 2 on the right to get $7a + 9b = 2(x + y + z)$. Finally, we divide each side of this last equation by 6 to get $\frac{7a+9b}{6} = \frac{x+y+z}{3}$, and we see that the average of x, y, and z is $\frac{7a+9b}{6}$, choice **D**.

10.

*** Solution by changing averages to sums:** The sum of the first 3 exam grades was $90 \cdot 3 = 270$. We want the sum of Jason's 7 exam grades to be $90 \cdot 7 = 630$. So, we need the sum of the grades on the last four exams to be $630 - 270 = 360$. The maximum grade is 100, and so the most Jason can score on the last 3 exams is $100 \cdot 3 = 300$. Therefore, on the 4th exam he must score at least $360 - 300 = \mathbf{60}$.

LESSON 20 – GEOMETRY
SOLID GEOMETRY

What Do Boxes, Soda Cans, and the Great Pyramids Have in Common?

Solid geometry problems on the SAT usually involve the volume or surface area of three-dimensional figures. The following volume formulas appear at the beginning of every math section on the SAT.

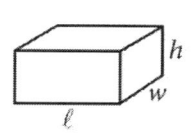

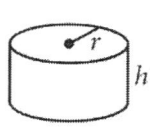

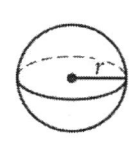

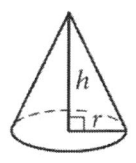

$V = \ell wh$ $V = \pi r^2 h$ $V = \frac{4}{3}\pi r^3$ $V = \frac{1}{3}\pi r^2 h$ $V = \frac{1}{3}\ell wh$

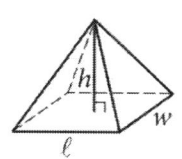

Let's jump right into some problems.

LEVEL 1: GEOMETRY – SOLID GEOMETRY

1. After being inflated, a spherical balloon has a radius of 9 inches. Which of the following is equal to the volume of the balloon, in cubic inches?

   A) 18π
   B) 81π
   C) 729π
   D) 972π

LEVEL 2: GEOMETRY – SOLID GEOMETRY

5 inches

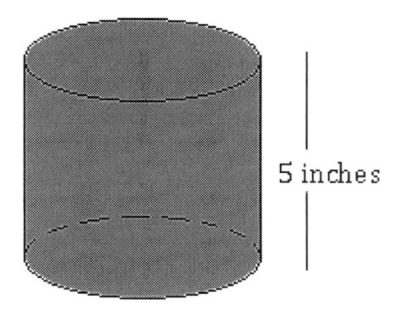

2. * A can in the shape of a right circular cylinder is completely filled with soda as shown above. If the volume of the can is 8.45π cubic inches, what is the <u>diameter</u> of the base of the cylinder, in inches?

3. A box in the shape of a right rectangular prism has a volume of 252 cubic centimeters. If the dimensions of the box are 7 centimeters by 3 centimeters by w centimeters, what is the value of w?

143

LEVEL 3: GEOMETRY – SOLID GEOMETRY

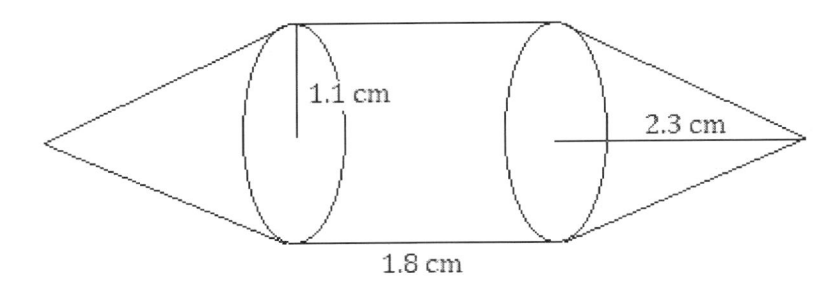

4. * An NAID is a type of medication used to reduce inflammation. Suppose an NAID is created in pill form using two congruent right circular cones and a right circular cylinder with measurements shown in the figure above. Of the following, which is closest to the volume of the pill, in cubic centimeters?

   A) 2.91
   B) 5.83
   C) 6.84
   D) 12.67

5. A toy manufacturer makes spherical balls, each with a radius between 5.8 inches and 6.1 inches. What is one possible volume, rounded to the nearest cubic inch, of a toy ball produced by this manufacturer?

6. * Sydney has identical containers each in the shape of a cone with internal diameter 7 inches. She pours liquid from a two-gallon bottle into each container until it is full. If the height of liquid in each container is 10 inches, what is the largest number of full containers into which she can pour two gallons of liquid? (Note: There are 231 cubic inches in 1 gallon.)

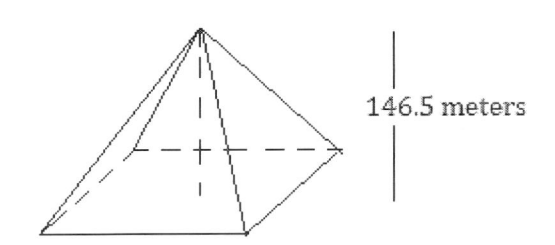

7. * Before erosion and other factors had taken its toll, the *Great Pyramid of Giza* shown above had a square base and a volume of 2,592,276.48 cubic meters. What was the length of a side of the base, to the nearest meter?

LEVEL 4: GEOMETRY – SOLID GEOMETRY

8. The volume of right circular cylinder C is V cubic inches. Right circular cylinder D has twice the height and half the radius of right circular cylinder C. Which of the following expresses the volume of right circular cylinder D in terms of V ?

   A) $4V$
   B) $2V$
   C) V
   D) $\frac{V}{2}$

9. A storage facility stores containers shaped liked rectangular prisms that satisfy certain dimensional conditions. Specifically, the conditions state that the sum of the area of the base of the container (determined using the length and width of the container) and the height of the container cannot exceed 37 feet. If a certain container has a height of $24\frac{1}{2}$ feet, and a width that is half of its length, which of the following inequalities gives the possibilities for the length, L, in feet, of the container?

   A) $0 \leq L \leq 2\frac{1}{2}$
   B) $0 \leq L \leq 5$
   C) $0 \leq L \leq 7\frac{1}{2}$
   D) $0 \leq L \leq 10$

LEVEL 5: GEOMETRY – SOLID GEOMETRY

10. The surface area of a cube is $6\left(\frac{c}{4d}\right)^2$, where c and d are positive constants. Which of the following gives the area of one face of the cube?

    A) $\frac{4c}{d}$
    B) $\frac{c}{d}$
    C) $\frac{c^2}{4d^2}$
    D) $\frac{c^2}{16d^2}$

Answers

1. D   2. 2.6   3. 12   4. D   5. 905   6. 3   7. 230   8. D   9. B   10. D

Full Solutions

1.

* Since the balloon is shaped like a sphere, it's volume is $V = \frac{4}{3}\pi r^3 = \frac{4}{3}\pi \cdot 9^3 = 972\pi$, choice **D**.

Note: The volume of a sphere with radius r is $V = \frac{4}{3}\pi r^3$.

2.

* **Algebraic solution:** $V = \pi r^2 h \Rightarrow 8.45\pi = \pi r^2(5) \Rightarrow 1.69 = r^2 \Rightarrow 1.3 = r$. So, $d = 2 \cdot 1.3 = \mathbf{2.6}$.

Notes: (1) The volume of a cylinder is $V = \pi r^2 h$, where r is the radius of a base of the cylinder and h is the height of the cylinder.

(2) To get from the second to the third equation, we divided each side of the equation by 5π.

(3) The equation $1.69 = r^2$ would normally have the two solutions $\pm 1.3 = r$. But the radius of a circle must be positive, and so we reject the negative solution.

(4) The diameter of a circle is twice the radius. Symbolically, $d = 2r$.

3.

* Using $V = lwh$, we have $252 = 7 \cdot 3 \cdot w = 21w$. So, $w = \frac{252}{21} = \mathbf{12}$.

4.

* The volume is $V = \pi(1.1)^2 \cdot 1.8 + 2\left(\frac{1}{3}\right)\pi(1.1)^2 \cdot 2.3 \approx 12.67$. This is choice **D**.

Notes: (1) The pill consists of a cylinder and two cones. We get the volume of the pill by adding up the volumes of the three individual solids.

(2) The formulas for the volume of a cylinder and the volume of a cone are given in the beginning of each math section on the SAT.

(3) The volume of a cylinder is $V = \pi r^2 h$, where r is the radius of each circular base of the cylinder and h is the height of the cylinder.

In this problem, the radius of a base is $r = 1.1$ and the height is $h = 1.8$. Therefore, the volume of the cylinder is $V = \pi(1.1)^2 \cdot 1.8 \approx 6.84$.

(4) The volume of a cone is $V = \frac{1}{3}\pi r^2 h$, where r is the radius of the circular base of the cone and h is the height of the cone.

In this problem, the radius of the base is $r = 1.1$ and the height is $h = 2.3$. Therefore, the volume of the cone is $V = \frac{1}{3}\pi(1.1)^2 \cdot 2.3 \approx 2.91$.

(5) To get the total volume of the pill, we add the volume of the cylinder and the volume of the two cones to get approximately $6.84 + 2 \cdot 2.91 \approx 12.66$. This is closest to choice **D**.

5.

* Let's choose the radius to be 6 inches. Then $V = \frac{4}{3}\pi r^3 = \frac{4}{3}\pi \cdot 6^3 \approx 904.7787$. To the nearest inch, this is **905**.

Note: $\frac{4}{3}\pi(5.8)^3 \approx 817.28$ and $\frac{4}{3}\pi(6.1)^3 \approx 950.78$. So, we can grid in any whole number between 817 and 951, inclusive. To be safe, you can avoid the extreme values of 817 and 951. However, both of those numbers are acceptable answers. Do you understand why they are okay?

6.

* The volume of 1 container is $V = \frac{1}{3}\pi r^2 h = \frac{1}{3}\pi \left(\frac{7}{2}\right)^2 \cdot 10 \approx 128.2817$ cubic inches.

The volume of two gallons of liquid, in cubic inches, is $2 \cdot 231 = 462$.

We divide the two volumes to get the number of containers: $\frac{462}{128.2817} \approx 3.60145$

So, the largest number of *full* containers is **3**.

7.

* Using $V = \frac{1}{3}lwh$, we have $2{,}592{,}276.48 = \frac{1}{3}146.5x^2$, where we use x to represent both the length and width of the base (since they are equal). We multiply by 3 and divide by 146.5 to get $x^2 = 53{,}084.16$. We then take the square root of each side to get $x = 230.4$. To the nearest meter, this is **230**.

8.

Algebraic solution: The volume of cylinder C is $V = \pi r^2 h$, where r is the radius of C and h is the height of C. It follows that the radius of cylinder D is $\frac{r}{2}$ and the height of cylinder D is $2h$. So, the volume of cylinder D is $W = \pi \left(\frac{r}{2}\right)^2 (2h) = \pi \frac{r^2}{4} \cdot 2h = \frac{\pi r^2 h}{2} = \frac{V}{2}$, choice **D**.

* **Quick solution:** In the formula for the volume of a cylinder, r is squared. It follows that multiplying the radius by $\frac{1}{2}$ multiplies the volume by $\left(\frac{1}{2}\right)^2 = \frac{1}{4}$. Since h does not have any power, multiplying the height by 2, multiplies the volume by 2. So, when we take half of the radius and double the height, the volume is multiplied by $\frac{1}{4} \cdot 2 = \frac{1}{2}$. Therefore, the answer is choice **D**.

Note: This problem can also be solved by picking numbers. I leave the details of this solution to the reader.

9.

* Since the width of the container is half of its length, we have that the width of the container is $W = \frac{1}{2}L$, and therefore the area of the base of the container is $A = LW = L\left(\frac{1}{2}L\right) = \frac{1}{2}L^2 = \frac{L^2}{2}$. The given condition tells us that we must have $A + h \leq 37$, or equivalently, $\frac{L^2}{2} + \frac{49}{2} \leq 37$. Multiplying each side of this inequality by 2 gives $L^2 + 49 \leq 74$. We subtract 49 from each side to get $L^2 \leq 25$. So, we must have $|L| \leq 5$, or equivalently, $-5 \leq L \leq 5$. Since the length of a container cannot be negative, this is equivalent to $0 \leq L \leq 5$, choice **B**.

Notes: (1) $24\frac{1}{2} = 24 + \frac{1}{2} = \frac{48}{2} + \frac{1}{2} = \frac{49}{2}$.

(2) Alternatively, we can quickly change the mixed numeral $a\frac{b}{c}$ to an improper fraction by multiplying a and c, adding the result to b, and then placing this final result over c. Symbolically, $a\frac{b}{c} = \frac{ac+b}{c}$.

In this problem, we have $24\frac{1}{2} = \frac{24 \cdot 2 + 1}{2} = \frac{48+1}{2} = \frac{49}{2}$.

(3) The inequality $x^2 \leq a^2$ is equivalent to the absolute value inequality $|x| \leq a$. This absolute value inequality is equivalent to $-a \leq x \leq a$.

For example, the following inequalities are all equivalent: $L^2 \leq 25$, $|L| \leq 5$, and $-5 \leq L \leq 5$.

10.

* To find the surface area of a cube, we add up the areas of the 6 faces. Since all 6 faces are the same, the surface area of a cube is $S = 6A$, where A is the area of a face of the cube. So, we have $6A = 6\left(\frac{c}{4d}\right)^2$, and therefore, $A = \left(\frac{c}{4d}\right)^2 = \frac{c^2}{16d^2}$, choice **D**.

LESSON 21 – HEART OF ALGEBRA
INTERPRETING LINEAR EXPRESSIONS

More Than Words Is All You Need

Let's jump right into some problems.

LEVEL 1: HEART OF ALGEBRA – INTERPRETING LINEAR EXPRESSIONS

$$s + b = 7$$

1. The equation above relates the number of strawberries, s, and the number of bananas, b, that are in Jonathon's fruit salad. What does the number 7 represent?

   A) The number of strawberries in the fruit salad
   B) The number of bananas in the fruit salad
   C) The total number of strawberries and bananas in the fruit salad
   D) The number of strawberries in the fruit salad for each banana in the fruit salad

2. Express Painting is hired to paint the walls in n rooms of equal size. Express Painting's fee, in dollars can be calculated by the expression $2nCh(\ell+w)$, where n is the number of rooms, C is the cost per square foot of the paint in dollars, ℓ is the length of each room in feet, w is the width of each room in feet, and h is the height of each room, in feet. If the customer chooses to use more expensive paint, which of the factors in the expression would change?

   A) n
   B) h
   C) $\ell+w$
   D) C

LEVEL 2: HEART OF ALGEBRA – INTERPRETING LINEAR EXPRESSIONS

3. A cable company charges two types of fees: a one-time setup fee and a monthly service fee. The equation $C = 90x + 45$ represents the total cost, C, in dollars, for x months of cable service. What does 45 represent in the equation?

   A) The price of one typical month of service
   B) The total amount, in dollars, for cable access for one month
   C) The total amount, in dollars, for cable access for x months
   D) The cost of the setup fee, in dollars

LEVEL 3: HEART OF ALGEBRA – INTERPRETING LINEAR EXPRESSIONS

4. The number of decks of cards, d, that a convenience store can sell per week at a price of p dollars is given by $d = 90 - 15p$. What is the meaning of the value 90 in this equation?

    A) 90 cents is the maximum that someone would pay for a deck of cards.
    B) 90 people per week would take a deck of cards for free.
    C) If the price of a deck of cards is decreased by 1 dollar, then 90 more people will make a purchase.
    D) If the price of a deck of cards is decreased by 90 cents, then 90 more people will make a purchase.

5. Premium Printing estimates the price of a printing job, in dollars, using the expression $2pt + 3$, where p is the number of printers and t is the total time, in minutes, needed to complete the job using p printers. Which of the following is the best interpretation of the number 2 in the expression?

    A) Each printer prints for 2 minutes.
    B) The price of the job increases by $2 every minute.
    C) At least 2 printers are needed to complete the job.
    D) Premium Printing charges $2 per minute for each printer.

$$L = 0.01x + 1.3$$

6. An entomologist uses the model above to estimate the length L of a certain species of insect, in centimeters, in terms of the insect's age x, in days. Based on the model, what is the estimated increase, in <u>millimeters</u>, of the insect's length each day? (1 centimeter = 10 millimeters)

    A) 0.001
    B) 0.01
    C) 0.1
    D) 1

7. The *femur*, or thigh bone, is the longest bone in the human body. The height of an adult male h, in inches, can be estimated by the linear function $h(x) = 1.88x + 32.01$, where x is the length of the adult male's femur, in inches. Which of the following statements is the best interpretation of the number 1.88 in this context?

    A) The height of an adult male, in inches, whose femur is 32.01 inches long
    B) The increase in the height of an adult male, in inches, that corresponds to a 1 inch increase in the length of the femur
    C) The increase in the length of an adult male's femur, in inches, that corresponds to a 1 inch increase in the height of the adult male
    D) The increase in the height of an adult male, in inches, that corresponds to a 32.01 inch increase in the length of the femur

LEVEL 4: HEART OF ALGEBRA – INTERPRETING LINEAR EXPRESSIONS

8. While training for a competition, a swimmer decided to increase the number of laps he swam each day by a constant amount for 12 days. If he swam 14 laps on day 5 and 32 laps on day 11, which of the following best describes how the number of laps changed during his first 12 days of training?

    A) The swimmer increased the number of laps he swam by 1 per day.
    B) The swimmer increased the number of laps he swam by 3 per day.
    C) The swimmer increased the number of laps he swam by 1 every 3 days.
    D) The swimmer increased the number of laps he swam by 3 every 2 days.

9. At a factory, w workers are needed to build a appliances. If $w = 2a + 3$, how many additional workers are needed to make each additional appliance?

    A) None
    B) One
    C) Two
    D) Three

$$A = 20t + 100$$

10. The equation above gives the amount of money A deposited into a checking account, in dollars, after t months. Based on the equation, which of the following must be true?

    I. Each month, $20 is deposited into the account.
    II. $1 is deposited into the account every 20 months.
    III. The initial deposit into the account was $20.

    A) I only
    B) II only
    C) III only
    D) I and III only

Answers

1. C   2. D   3. D   4. B   5. D   6. C   7. B   8. B   9. C   10. A

Full Solutions

1.

* s is the number of strawberries in the fruit salad and b is the number of bananas in the fruit salad. So, $s + b$ is the total number of strawberries and bananas in the fruit salad. Since $s + b = 7$, the number 7 also represents the total number of strawberries and bananas in the fruit salad, choice **C**.

Note: Let's choose specific values for s and b just to make sure we can clearly see what is going on here. If we put 3 strawberries and 4 bananas in Jonathon's fruit salad, then we have $s = 3$, $b = 4$, and $s + b = 7$. We see that the number 7 does NOT represent the number of strawberries or bananas individually. This eliminates choices A and B. Also, choice D doesn't make sense here because there are more bananas than strawberries in the fruit salad. The number 7 does represent the total number of strawberries and bananas in the fruit salad.

2.

* C is the cost per square foot of the paint in dollars. If a customer chooses to use more expensive paint, then C will increase. So, the answer is choice **D**.

Notes: (1) n would increase if the customer decided to have more rooms painted (the rooms would need to be of equal size), and n would decrease if the customer decided to have less rooms painted.

(2) h would increase if the customer decided to paint rooms that were higher, and h would decrease if the customer decided to paint rooms that were less high.

(3) $\ell+w$ would increase if the customer decided to paint rooms whose length and width had a greater sum, and $\ell+w$ would decrease if the customer decided to paint rooms whose length and width had a smaller sum.

3.

* When $x = 0$, $C = 45$. This means that it costs \$45 for 0 months of service. In other words, 45 is the setup fee, in dollars, choice **D**.

Notes: (1) The number 90 in the equation is the monthly fee. In other words, it is the price of one typical month of service.

(2) If we substitute 1 for x, we get $C = 90 \cdot 1 + 45 = 135$. This is the cost for 1 month plus the setup fee. In other words, this is the total amount, in dollars, for cable access for one month.

(3) In general, $90x + 45$ is the total amount, in dollars, for cable access for x months.

4.

* $d = 90$ when $p = 0$. This means that the convenience store can sell 90 decks of cards per week at a price of 0 dollars. In other words, 90 people per week would take a deck of cards for free, choice **B**.

Notes: (1) In the equation $d = 90 - 15p$, we are thinking of p as the **independent variable**, and d as the **dependent variable**. In other words, we input a value for p, and we get a d value as an output.

For example, if the input is a price of $p = 0$ dollars, then the output is a quantity of $d = 90 - 15(0) = 90$ decks of cards.

(2) What if the question instead asked for the meaning of the number 15 in the equation?

First recall that the slope of a line is

$$\text{Slope} = m = \frac{\text{change in the dependent variable}}{\text{change in the independent variable}} = \frac{\text{change in } d}{\text{change in } p}$$

Also recall that the **slope-intercept form of an equation of a line** is $y = mx + b$ where m is the slope of the line. The given equation can be written $d = -15p + 90$, and we see that the slope is $m = -15 = -\frac{15}{1}$. So, we see that a change in p by 1 unit corresponds to a change in d by 15 units.

Since the sign of -15 is negative, there is a **negative association** between p and d. It follows that an increase in p corresponds to a decrease in d. So, if the price p of a deck of cards is increased by 1 dollar, then 15 less people will make a purchase per week.

5.
* **Algebraic solution:** 3 is the fixed price and $2pt$ is the variable price. For the variable price, we are multiplying three quantities together: 2, p and t. So, this quantity depends on both the number of printers, p, and the time t, in minutes, needed to complete the job using those p printers. Now pt is the total number of minutes of work done using p printers, each working for t minutes. The cost of the job increases by \$2 for each minute a printer works. Therefore, of the choices given, the best interpretation of the number 2 is that Premium Printing charges \$2 per minute for each printer, choice **D**.

Notes: (1) Each printer prints for t minutes. Since there is no reason that t needs to be 2, we can eliminate choice A.

(2) If there is only one printer ($p = 1$), then then the variable price is $2t$, and the price of the job increases by \$2 every minute. If, however, there are two printers ($p = 2$), then the variable price is $2t \cdot 2 = 4t$, and the price of the job increases by \$4 every minute. This shows that we can eliminate choice B.

In this last example, we see that the price of the job is \$4 per minute for 2 printers, or equivalently, the price of the job is \$2 per minute for each printer. This gives evidence to support that choice D is correct.

(3) The number of printers is p. Since there is no reason that p cannot be 1, we can eliminate C.

6.
Solution by picking numbers: If $x = 1$, then $L = 0.01 + 1.3 = 1.31$.

If $x = 2$, then $L = 0.01 \cdot 2 + 1.3 = 0.02 + 1.3 = 1.32$.

So, when the insect's age increases by 1 day, the estimated length of the insect increases by $1.32 - 1.31 = 0.01$ centimeters. This is equivalent to $10 \cdot 0.01 = 0.1$ millimeters, choice **C**.

* **Algebraic solution:** The equation is linear with a slope of $0.01 = \frac{0.01}{1}$. This means that an increase in x by 1 day corresponds to an increase in L by 0.01 centimeters. This is equivalent to 0.1 millimeters, choice **C**.

Notes: (1) In the equation $L = 0.01x + 1.3$, we are thinking of x as the **independent variable**, and L as the **dependent variable**. In other words, we input a value for x and we get an L value as an output. For example, if the input is $x = 2$ days, then the output is a length of $L = 0.01 \cdot 2 + 1.3 = 1.32$ centimeters.

(2) The equation $L = 0.01x + 1.3$ is in slope-intercept form, with slope 0.01 and L-intercept 1.3. Here, we have Slope $= m = \frac{\text{change in the dependent variable}}{\text{change in the independent variable}} = \frac{\text{change in } L}{\text{change in } x}$. So, a change in x by 1 day corresponds to a change in L by 0.01 centimeters.

(3) Since the sign of 0.01 is positive ($0.01 = +0.01$), there is a **positive association** between x and L. It follows that an increase in x corresponds to an increase in L. See problem 4 for an example of a **negative association** between two variables.

7.
Solution by picking numbers: $h(1) = 1.88 + 32.01 = 33.89$. So, according to the function, if an adult male has a 1 inch femur, his height will be 33.89 inches. $h(2) = 1.88 \cdot 2 + 32.01 = 35.77$. So, again according to the function, if an adult male has a 2 inch femur, his height will be 35.77 inches. So, when we increase an adult male's femur by 1 inch, his height increases by $35.77 - 33.89 = 1.88$ inches. This is choice **B**.

* **Algebraic solution:** The equation is linear with a slope of 1.88. This means that an increase in x by 1 inch corresponds to an increase in $h(x)$ by 1.88 inches. This is choice **B**.

See problems 4 and 6 for more information on how this solution works.

8.
* **Algebraic solution:** The equation is linear with a slope of

$$\frac{\text{change in number of laps}}{\text{change in number of days}} = \frac{32 - 14}{11 - 5} = \frac{18}{6} = 3 = \frac{3}{1}$$

This means that an increase by 1 day corresponds to an increase in 3 laps. This is choice **B**.

Notes: (1) We have a linear relationship between the independent variable t, the number of days, and the dependent variable L, the number of laps the swimmer swam. **The expression "constant amount" in the problem gives away that the relationship is linear.**

(2) If the input is $t = 5$ days, then the output is $L = 14$ laps. Similarly, if the input is $t = 11$ days, then the output is $L = 32$ laps. It follows that the graph of this linear function passes through the points $(5, 14)$ and $(11, 32)$.

(3) We can now find the slope of the line passing through these points in the usual way (as was done in the solution).

(4) Since the slope is $\frac{3}{1}$, we know that for each change in the independent variable by 1 unit, the dependent variable changes by 3 units.

In this case, the independent variable is the number of days, and the dependent variable is the number of laps. So, a change by 1 day corresponds with a change of 3 laps. In other words, the number of laps increases by 3 each day.

(5) Since the slope is positive ($3 = +3$), there is a **positive association** between t and L. It follows that an increase in t corresponds to an increase in L.

9.

Solution by picking numbers: To build $a = 1$ appliance requires $w = 2 \cdot 1 + 3 = 5$ workers. To build $a = 2$ appliances requires $w = 2 \cdot 2 + 3 = 4 + 3 = 7$ workers. So, to make 1 additional appliance requires $7 - 5 = 2$ additional workers, choice **C**.

* Algebraic Solution: We are given a linear relationship between the independent variable a and the dependent variable w. The slope is $\frac{\text{change in number of workers}}{\text{change in number of appliances}} = 2 = \frac{2}{1}$. It follows that each additional appliance requires 2 more workers, choice **C**.

10.

* Algebraic Solution: We are given a linear relationship between the independent variable t and the dependent variable A. The slope is

$$\frac{\text{change in } A}{\text{change in } t} = \frac{\text{change in amount of money deposited into account}}{\text{change in number of months}} = 20 = \frac{20}{1}$$

It follows that each month, $20 is deposited into the account. So, I is true (and II is false). So, the answer is A or D.

We get the initial deposit by substituting 0 for t to get $20 \cdot 0 + 100 = 100$. So, the initial deposit into the account was $100 and III is false. So, the answer is choice **A**.

LESSON 22 – PASSPORT TO ADVANCED MATH
EXPONENTS AND ROOTS

Don't Break Any Laws (of Exponents)

Here is a brief review of the laws of exponents you should know for the SAT.

Law	Example
$x^0 = 1$	$3^0 = 1$
$x^1 = x$	$9^1 = 9$
$x^a x^b = x^{a+b}$	$x^3 x^5 = x^8$
$x^a / x^b = x^{a-b}$	$x^{11}/x^4 = x^7$
$(x^a)^b = x^{ab}$	$(x^5)^3 = x^{15}$
$(xy)^a = x^a y^a$	$(xy)^4 = x^4 y^4$
$(x/y)^a = x^a/y^a$	$(x/y)^6 = x^6/y^6$
$x^{-1} = 1/x$	$3^{-1} = 1/3$
$x^{-a} = 1/x^a$	$9^{-2} = 1/81$
$x^{1/n} = \sqrt[n]{x}$	$x^{1/3} = \sqrt[3]{x}$
$x^{m/n} = \sqrt[n]{x^m} = \left(\sqrt[n]{x}\right)^m$	$x^{9/2} = \sqrt{x^9} = \left(\sqrt{x}\right)^9$

Let's jump right into some problems.

LEVEL 1: PASSPORT TO ADVANCED MATH – EXPONENTS AND ROOTS

1. Which of the following is equivalent to $\dfrac{x^5 \cdot x^3}{x^8}$ for $x \neq 0$?

   A) 1
   B) x
   C) $x^{\frac{15}{8}}$
   D) $x^{\frac{5}{8}} \cdot x^{\frac{3}{8}}$

LEVEL 2: PASSPORT TO ADVANCED MATH – EXPONENTS AND ROOTS

2. Which of the following is equal to $\dfrac{(xy)^7 (yz)^2}{y^9}$ for $y \neq 0$?

   A) 1
   B) xyz
   C) $x^7 z^2$
   D) $x^7 y^5 z^2$

LEVEL 3: PASSPORT TO ADVANCED MATH – EXPONENTS AND ROOTS

3. Which of the following is equivalent to $(\frac{2}{3})^3(\frac{9}{4})^2$?

   A) 0
   B) $\frac{2}{3}$
   C) 1
   D) $\frac{3}{2}$

4. If $(5^7)^x = (5^3)^5$, what is the value of x ?

   A) $\frac{1}{8}$
   B) $\frac{6}{7}$
   C) $\frac{15}{7}$
   D) 8

LEVEL 4: PASSPORT TO ADVANCED MATH

5. Which of the following is equivalent to $4^{\frac{5}{4}}$?

   A) $\sqrt[5]{4}$
   B) $\sqrt[4]{4}$
   C) $\sqrt{2}$
   D) $4\sqrt{2}$

6. Which of the following is equivalent to $7^{-\frac{11}{3}}$?

   A) $\sqrt[3]{7^{11}}$
   B) $\frac{1}{\sqrt[3]{7^{11}}}$
   C) $-\sqrt[3]{7^{11}}$
   D) $-\frac{1}{\sqrt[3]{7^{11}}}$

7. If $\sqrt[5]{k^3} \cdot \sqrt[3]{k^2} = k^m$ for all values of k, what is the value of m ?

8. If $x = 4\sqrt{3}$ and $3x = \sqrt{6y}$, what is the value of y ?

157

LEVEL 5: PASSPORT TO ADVANCED MATH – EXPONENTS AND ROOTS

9. Which of the following is equivalent to $\dfrac{x^{-\frac{5}{2}} \cdot x^{-1}}{x^{-\frac{4}{3}}}$?

   A) $\sqrt[6]{x^{13}}$

   B) $\sqrt[13]{x^{6}}$

   C) $\dfrac{1}{\sqrt[6]{x^{13}}}$

   D) $\dfrac{1}{\sqrt[13]{x^{6}}}$

10. If $5a - 30b = 3$, what is the value of $\dfrac{4^a}{16^{3b}}$?

    A) 4^3

    B) $\sqrt{4^3}$

    C) $4^{\frac{3}{5}}$

    D) The value cannot be determined from the information given.

Answers

1. A 2. C 3. D 4. C 5. D 6. B 7. 1.26, 1.27 8. 72 9. C 10. C

Full Solutions

1.
Solution using a law of exponents:
$$\frac{x^5 \cdot x^3}{x^8} = \frac{x^8}{x^8} = 1$$

The answer is choice **A**.

Notes: (1) We used the law of exponents in the third row of the table to write $x^5 \cdot x^3 = x^{5+3} = x^8$.

(2) A positive integer exponent of n indicates that the **base** is being multiplied by itself n times. For example, $x^5 = x \cdot x \cdot x \cdot x \cdot x$ and $x^3 = x \cdot x \cdot x$. So, $x^5 \cdot x^3 = (x \cdot x \cdot x \cdot x \cdot x)(x \cdot x \cdot x) = x^8$. This kind of reasoning can be used if you ever forget an exponential law.

(3) The last step in the computation above can be thought of in two different ways: (i) $\dfrac{x^8}{x^8} = 1$ because the numerator and denominator are the same; (ii) $\dfrac{x^8}{x^8} = x^{8-8} = x^0 = 1$ by the laws of exponents in the fourth and first rows.

(4) This problem can also be solved by picking numbers. I leave the details to the reader.

2.

Solution using laws of exponents:

$$\frac{(xy)^7(yz)^2}{y^9} = \frac{x^7 y^7 y^2 z^2}{y^9} = \frac{x^7 y^9 z^2}{y^9} = x^7 z^2$$

This is choice **C**.

Notes: (1) For the first step, we used the law of exponents in the sixth row of the table two times.

(2) For the second step, we used the law of exponents in the third row of the table.

(3) For the third step, see note (3) from problem 1.

(4) This problem can also be solved by picking numbers. I leave the details to the reader.

3.

Solution using laws of exponents:

$$\left(\frac{2}{3}\right)^3 \left(\frac{9}{4}\right)^2 = \frac{2^3}{3^3} \cdot \frac{9^2}{4^2} = \frac{2^3}{3^3} \cdot \frac{(3^2)^2}{(2^2)^2} = \frac{2^3}{3^3} \cdot \frac{3^4}{2^4} = \frac{2^3}{2^4} \cdot \frac{3^4}{3^3} = \frac{3^1}{2^1} = \frac{3}{2}$$

This is choice **D**.

Notes: (1) For the first step, we used the law of exponents in the seventh row of the table two times.

(2) For the second step, we wrote $9 = 3^2$ and $4 = 2^2$.

(3) For the third step, we used the law of exponents in the fifth row of the table two times.

(4) For the fourth step, we just rearranged the factors in the denominator.

(5) For the fifth step, we used the law of exponents in the fourth row of the table two times.

4.

Solution using laws of exponents: We use the law of exponents in the fifth row of the table to write $(5^7)^x = 5^{7x}$ and $(5^3)^5 = 5^{15}$. So, we have $5^{7x} = 5^{15}$. Therefore, $7x = 15$, and so $x = \frac{15}{7}$, choice **C**.

Note: In the expression 5^{7x}, the number 5 is called the **base** of the exponential expression. In the equation $5^{7x} = 5^{15}$, observe that each side of the equation consists of an exponential expression with the same base. Whenever these bases are equal, the exponents must be equal as well. It follows that $7x = 15$.

5.

Solution using laws of exponents:

$$4^{\frac{5}{4}} = 4^{\frac{1}{2} \cdot \frac{5}{2}} = \left(4^{\frac{1}{2}}\right)^{\frac{5}{2}} = \left(\sqrt{4}\right)^{\frac{5}{2}} = 2^{\frac{5}{2}} = (2^5)^{\frac{1}{2}} = (2^4 \cdot 2^1)^{\frac{1}{2}} = (2^4)^{\frac{1}{2}}(2^1)^{\frac{1}{2}} = 2^2 \cdot 2^{\frac{1}{2}} = 4\sqrt{2}$$

This is choice **D**.

Notes: (1) Make sure you recognize which law of exponents was used at each step of this computation.

(2) We can change fractional exponents to roots at any time using the law in the tenth or eleventh row of the table. For example, we can write $2^{\frac{5}{2}}$ as $\sqrt{2^5}$ and then proceed to finish the computation as follows: $\sqrt{2^5} = \sqrt{2^4 \cdot 2^1} = \sqrt{2^4}\sqrt{2} = 2^2\sqrt{2} = 4\sqrt{2}$.

(3) All the laws given in the table work for roots as well (since they are just fractional exponents). For example, since $(xy)^{\frac{1}{2}} = x^{\frac{1}{2}}y^{\frac{1}{2}}$, we have $\sqrt{xy} = \sqrt{x}\sqrt{y}$. We used this in the second step in the computation in note (2).

6.
* **Solution using laws of exponents:**
$$7^{-\frac{11}{3}} = \frac{1}{7^{\frac{11}{3}}} = \frac{1}{\sqrt[3]{7^{11}}}$$

This is choice **B**.

Notes: (1) For the first step, we used the law of exponents in the ninth row of the table.

(2) For the second step, we used the law of exponents in the eleventh row of the table.

7.
* **Solution using laws of exponents:**
$$\sqrt[5]{k^3} \cdot \sqrt[3]{k^2} = k^{\frac{3}{5}} \cdot k^{\frac{2}{3}} = k^{\frac{3}{5}+\frac{2}{3}} = k^{\frac{3\cdot3+5\cdot2}{5\cdot3}} = k^{\frac{9+10}{15}} = k^{\frac{19}{15}}$$

So, $m = \frac{19}{15}$. We can grid in **1.26** or **1.27**.

Notes: (1) We used the law of exponents $x^a x^b = x^{a+b}$ (third row of the table) to get $k^{\frac{3}{5}} \cdot k^{\frac{2}{3}} = k^{\frac{3}{5}+\frac{2}{3}}$.

(2) We can rewrite the expression $\sqrt[c]{a^b}$ using only an exponent as $a^{\frac{b}{c}}$ (eleventh row of the table). In the expression $a^{\frac{b}{c}}$, a is the base, b is the power, and c is the root.

For example, $\sqrt[5]{k^3} = k^{\frac{3}{5}}$ and $\sqrt[3]{k^2} = k^{\frac{2}{3}}$.

(3) If we are allowed to use a calculator for this problem, then we can add $\frac{3}{5}$ and $\frac{2}{3}$ by typing the following into our TI-84 calculator: $3/5 + 2/3$
The output will be approximately 1.26666666.

(4) If a calculator is not allowed, we can use the following: $\frac{a}{b} + \frac{c}{d} = \frac{ad+bc}{bd}$

For example, $\frac{3}{5} + \frac{2}{3} = \frac{3\cdot3+5\cdot2}{5\cdot3} = \frac{9+10}{15} = \frac{19}{15}$.

8.
* Squaring each side of the equation $3x = \sqrt{6y}$ gives $9x^2 = 6y$. So, we have $y = \frac{9x^2}{6} = \frac{3}{2}x^2 = \frac{3}{2}(4\sqrt{3})^2 = \frac{3}{2} \cdot 16 \cdot 3 = \mathbf{72}$.

Note: $(4\sqrt{3})^2 = (4\sqrt{3})(4\sqrt{3}) = 4 \cdot 4 \cdot \sqrt{3} \cdot \sqrt{3} = 16 \cdot 3 = 48.$

9.

* Solution using laws of exponents:

$$\frac{x^{-\frac{5}{2}} \cdot x^{-1}}{x^{-\frac{4}{3}}} = \frac{x^{-\frac{5}{2}-1}}{x^{-\frac{4}{3}}} = \frac{x^{-\frac{5}{2}-\frac{2}{2}}}{x^{-\frac{4}{3}}} = \frac{x^{-\frac{7}{2}}}{x^{-\frac{4}{3}}} = x^{-\frac{7}{2}-(-\frac{4}{3})} = x^{-\frac{7}{2}+\frac{4}{3}} = x^{\frac{-21+8}{6}} = x^{-\frac{13}{6}} = \frac{1}{x^{\frac{13}{6}}} = \frac{1}{\sqrt[6]{x^{13}}}$$

This is choice **C**.

Notes: (1) Make sure you recognize which law of exponents was used at each step of this computation.

(2) If a calculator is allowed for the problem, then you can use it for all the computations in the above solution, or you can solve the problem by picking numbers.

(3) See note (4) from problem 7 for an explanation how to add fractions without a calculator.

10.

Algebraic solution 1:

$$\frac{4^a}{16^{3b}} = \frac{4^a}{(4^2)^{3b}} = \frac{4^a}{4^{6b}} = 4^{a-6b} = 4^{\frac{5a-30b}{5}} = (4^{5a-30b})^{\frac{1}{5}} = (4^3)^{\frac{1}{5}} = 4^{\frac{3}{5}}$$

This is choice **C**.

Notes: (1) For the first step, we simply wrote $16 = 4^2$.

(2) For the second step, we used the rule of exponents in the fifth row of the table to write $(4^2)^{3b} = 4^{2 \cdot 3b} = 4^{6b}$.

(3) For the third step, we used the law of exponents in the fourth row of the table to get $\frac{4^a}{4^{6b}} = 4^{a-6b}$.

(4) For the fourth step, we did the following: $\frac{5a-30b}{5} = \frac{5(a-6b)}{5} = a - 6b$.

(5) For the fifth step, we used the law of exponents in the fifth row of the table again.

(6) For the sixth step, we used the given information that $5a - 30b = 3$.

(7) For the last step, we used the law of exponents in the fifth row of the table again.

* Algebraic solution 2: We start by writing $5a - 30b = 5(a - 6b)$, so that the given equation becomes $5(a - 6b) = 3$. Dividing each side of this equation by 5 yields $a - 6b = \frac{3}{5}$. We can now solve the problem as follows:

$$\frac{4^a}{16^{3b}} = \frac{4^a}{(4^2)^{3b}} = \frac{4^a}{4^{6b}} = 4^{a-6b} = 4^{\frac{3}{5}}$$

This is choice **C**.

LESSON 23 – PROBLEM SOLVING
DATA ANALYSIS

Don't Be a Deviant

The **standard deviation** of a set of numbers measures how far the numbers are from the arithmetic mean. If the data values are close to the mean, the standard deviation is small. If the data is far from the mean, the standard deviation is large.

For example, if all the data values were the same, then the mean would be that common value and the standard deviation would be 0.

You are not expected to ever actually compute standard deviation on the SAT. All you need to know is that the standard deviation is bigger when the data is "spread further apart."

Let's try an example.

LEVEL 3: PROBLEM SOLVING – DATA ANALYSIS

1. The tables below give the distribution of the grades received by a class of 35 students on a math exam and a chemistry exam.

Math Exam	
Grade	Frequency
100	7
95	5
90	5
85	4
80	6
75	8

Chemistry Exam	
Grade	Frequency
100	1
95	4
90	26
85	2
80	1
75	1

Which of the following is true about the data shown for these 35 students?

A) The standard deviation of grades on the math exam is larger.
B) The standard deviation of grades on the chemistry exam is larger.
C) The standard deviation of grades on the math exam is the same as that of the chemistry exam.
D) The standard deviation of grades on these two exams cannot be calculated with the data provided.

* The scores on the math exam are more "spread out" than the scores on the chemistry exam. It follows that the standard deviation of grades on the math exam is larger, choice **A**.

Notes: (1) The mean of the chemistry grades is approximately 90. Notice that most of the data are near this value (between 85 and 95). So, the standard deviation is small.

(2) The mean of the math grades is 87, but the grades are spread out with many values at the extremes 75 and 100. So, the standard deviation is large.

Sample High, Error Low

A **margin of error** occurs when a sample is taken from a larger population. On the SAT, you do not need to be able to compute a margin of error. The most important thing to understand is that *increasing* the sample size within the <u>same population</u> will *decrease* the margin of error.

Let's try an example.

LEVEL 3: PROBLEM SOLVING – DATA ANALYSIS

2. A data analyst was interested in the mean height of women in a small town. He randomly measured the heights of 200 women in that town, and found that the mean height of these women was 61 inches, and the margin of error for this estimate was 3 inches. The data analyst would like to repeat the procedure and attempt to reduce the margin of error. Which of the following samples would most likely result in a smaller margin of error for the estimated mean height of women in that same town?

   A) 100 randomly selected people from the same town.
   B) 100 randomly selected women from the same town.
   C) 400 randomly selected people from the same town.
   D) 400 randomly selected women from the same town.

* Increasing the sample size while keeping the population the same will most likely decrease the margin of error. So, the answer is choice **D**.

Notes: (1) Decreasing the sample size will increase the margin of error. This allows us to eliminate choices A and B.

(2) The original sample consisted of only women. If we were to allow the second sample to include all people (including men), then we have changed the population. We cannot predict what impact this would have on the mean and margin of error. This allows us to eliminate choice C. (See SAMPLING RULE 1 below.)

(3) The margin of error of 3 inches tells us that the *actual* mean for the *entire* population is most likely between $61 - 3 = 58$ inches and $61 + 3 = 64$ inches.

Sampling Errors

A sample from a population is surveyed to try to get results about the entire population. For example, if we want to get a result about 1 million adults in a city, we might survey 2000 adults from the city at random. The following rules will help to get these types of questions correct on the SAT.

SAMPLING RULE 1: Don't change the population. The results from one population DO NOT carry over to another population.

SAMPLING RULE 2: Make sure that the sample is random. If you want your results to generalize to an entire population, do not restrict your sample to people with specific characteristics. Otherwise the sample is **biased** and the results may not extend to the entire population.

SAMPLING RULE 3: Sampling does not give exact results for the entire population. A sample is used to estimate results about an entire population, and not to give exact results.

SAMPLING RULE 4: Two different samples may give two different results. Both samples may estimate results about the entire population, but they need not be identical to each other.

SAMPLING RULE 5: The location a survey is given could create bias. Certain types of people may be more likely to be found at certain places. Sampling at specific places could introduce bias, violating SAMPLING RULE 2.

SAMPLING RULE 6: A cause-effect relationship requires two different groups that are treated differently. If all participants are surveyed the same way, then a cause-effect cannot be determined.

Time to Practice

LEVEL 3: PROBLEM SOLVING – DATA ANALYSIS

3. A well-known animal organization wanted to analyze the opinions of residents in a certain city regarding the funding of an animal sanctuary within that city's limits. The organization surveyed a sample of 200 animal activists that live in the city. The survey showed that almost all those sampled fully supported the funding of the sanctuary. Which of the following is true about the organization's survey?

    A) The survey should have consisted only of residents that are not animal activists.
    B) The survey sample is biased because it is not representative of the residents living in the city.
    C) The survey sample should have included more than 200 animal activists.
    D) The survey shows that most of the residents in the city are in favor of funding the animal sanctuary.

4. A biologist was interested in the number of times a field cricket chirps each minute on a sunny day. He randomly selected 100 field crickets from a garden, and found that the mean number of chirps per minute was 112, and the margin of error for this estimate was 6 chirps. The biologist would like to repeat the procedure and attempt to reduce the margin of error. Which of the following samples would most likely result in a smaller margin of error for the estimated mean number of times a field cricket chirps each minute on a sunny day?

    A) 50 randomly selected crickets from the same garden.
    B) 50 randomly selected field crickets from the same garden.
    C) 200 randomly selected crickets from the same garden.
    D) 200 randomly selected field crickets from the same garden.

5. 1500 adults were selected at random from New York City and asked if they were satisfied with the condition of the roads in the city. Of those surveyed, 85 percent responded that they were not satisfied with the condition of the roads in the city. Based on the results of the survey, which of the following statements must be true?

   I.   If 1500 adults were surveyed from another city, 85 percent of them would report that they are not satisfied with the road conditions in the city.
   II. Of all adults in New York City, 85 percent are not satisfied with the city's road conditions.
   III. If another 1500 adults from New York City were surveyed, 85 percent of them would report that they are not satisfied with the road conditions in the city.

   A) None
   B) III only
   C) II and III only
   D) I, II, and III

6. A survey was conducted to determine how many single men in a large city wanted to get married. 250 single men who visited a local coffee shop on a Saturday were given the survey, and 20 men refused to respond. Which of the following factors makes it least likely that a reliable conclusion can be drawn about the percentage of single men in the city that want to get married.

   A) Population size
   B) Sample size
   C) Where the survey was given
   D) The number of people who refused to respond

7. A psychologist wanted to determine if there is an association between diet and stress levels for the population of middle aged women in New York. He surveyed a random sample of 1500 middle aged female New Yorkers and found substantial evidence of a positive association between diet and stress levels. Which of the following conclusions is well supported by the data?

   A) A dietary change causes an increase in stress levels for middle aged women from New York.
   B) An increase in stress levels causes middle aged women from New York to change their diets.
   C) There is a positive association between diet and stress levels for middle aged women in New York.
   D) There is a positive association between diet and stress levels for middle aged women in the world.

LEVEL 4: PROBLEM SOLVING – DATA ANALYSIS

8. 15 women went on a 6 month long weight loss program. They recorded their weights, in pounds, before and after completing the program. The results can be seen in the dot plots below (all weights have been rounded to the nearest 10 pounds).

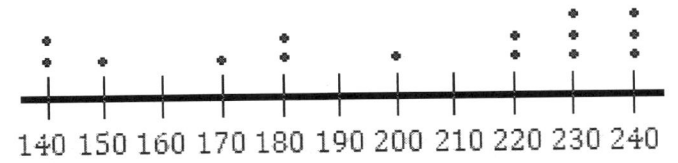

[Dot plot: Weight before starting weight loss program, axis 140–240]

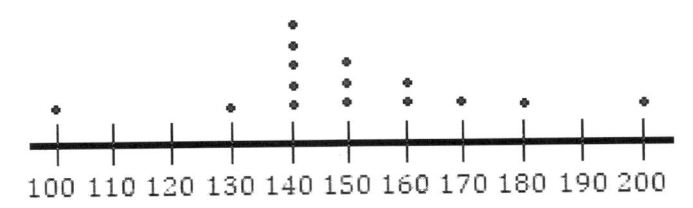

[Dot plot: Weight after completing weight loss program, axis 100–200]

Let R_1 and σ_1 be the range and standard deviation, respectively, of the weights before beginning the weight loss program, and let R_2 and σ_2 be the range and standard deviation, respectively, of the weights after completing the weight loss program. Which of the following is true?

A) $R_1 = R_2$ and $\sigma_1 \neq \sigma_2$
B) $R_1 = R_2$ and $\sigma_1 = \sigma_2$
C) $R_1 < R_2$ and $\sigma_1 < \sigma_2$
D) $R_1 > R_2$ and $\sigma_1 > \sigma_2$

9. A survey was conducted at a local dog park to determine the mean number of pets per family in a neighborhood. The mean number of pets from the 35 respondents was found to be 2.8. Which of the following statements must be true?

A) The mean number of pets per family in the neighborhood is 2.8.
B) The sampling method is flawed and may produce a biased estimate of the mean number of pets per family in the neighborhood.
C) The sampling method is not flawed and is likely to produce an unbiased estimate of the mean number of pets per family in the neighborhood.
D) A determination about the mean number of pets per family in the neighborhood should not be made because the sample size is too small.

LEVEL 5: PROBLEM SOLVING – DATA ANALYSIS

10. In a small city, a survey was taken to try to determine how much money families donate to charity each year. It was found that the median amount was $300 and the mean amount was $1700. Which of the following situations could explain the difference between the median and the mean gross income of families in the town?

A) There are a few families that donate much less money than the rest.
B) There are a few families that donate much more money than the rest.
C) All the families in the town donate approximately the same amount of money each year.
D) Many of the families donate between $300 and $1700 each year.

Answers

1. A 2. D 3. B 4. D 5. A 6. C 7. C 8. A 9. B 10. B

Full Solutions

3.

* This sample is not truly random, is it? It's clearly **biased**! Since animal activists were the only ones surveyed, we couldn't possibly get an idea about the opinions of *all* residents in the city. The answer is choice **B**.

Notes: (1) The idea here was to get an idea of how much of the population of the city would support the funding of an animal sanctuary within the city's limits. To serve this purpose, the sample of residents surveyed needed to be random. By choosing only animal activists to survey, the sample was not random. This eliminates choices C and D.

(2) Similarly, if animal activists were excluded from taking the survey, the sample would also not be random. This eliminates choice A.

(3) In this problem, we violated SAMPLING RULE 2.

4.

* Increasing the sample size while keeping the population the same will most likely decrease the margin of error. So, the answer is choice **D**.

Notes: (1) Decreasing the sample size will increase the margin of error. This allows us to eliminate choices A and B.

(2) The original sample consisted of only field crickets. If we were to allow the second sample to include all crickets, then we have changed the population (violating SAMPLING RULE 1). We cannot predict what impact this would have on the mean and margin of error. This allows us to eliminate choice C.

Technical note: In reality, there is a correlation between the frequency of cricket chirps and temperature. You can estimate the current temperature, in degrees Fahrenheit, by counting the number of times a cricket chirps in 15 seconds and adding 37 to the result.

5.

* Changing the population could change the results. There is no reason to expect that the same percentage of people from a different city responded the same way as New York City (see SAMPLING RULE 1). So, I does not need to be true.

It is unlikely that the percentage we got from a sample size of 1500 adults from New York City would be exactly the same as the percentage for all adults from New York City (see SAMPLING RULE 3). So, II does not need to be true.

It is also unlikely that taking a different sample would yield the exact same results, even if it is from the same population (see SAMPLING RULE 4). So, III does not need to be true either, and the answer is choice **A**.

6.
* In order to generalize the results of a survey to an entire population, the survey participants need to be randomly selected throughout that population. Since the survey was taken at a single coffee shop, it is unlikely that the sample represents a random sample from the entire city (see SAMPLING RULE 5). So, the answer is choice **C**.

7.
* A relationship in the given data should be generalized only to the population that the sample was drawn from (see SAMPLING RULE 1). In this case, that is middle aged women in New York. So, we can eliminate choice D.

Furthermore, choices A and B involve a **cause-effect relationship**. This type of relationship can be established only when the participants surveyed are randomly assigned to groups that are treated differently (see SAMPLING RULE 6). In this case, all the participants are surveyed the same way. So, we can eliminate choices A and B, and the answer is therefore choice **C**.

8.
* $R_1 = 240 - 140 = 100$ and $R_2 = 200 - 100 = 100$. So, $R_1 = R_2$ and we can eliminate choices C and D.

σ_1 is fairly large because the data is very "spread out," while σ_2 is smaller because overall the data is grouped more closely together. In particular, $\sigma_1 \neq \sigma_2$, and the answer is choice **A**.

9.
* In order to generalize the results of a survey to an entire population, the survey participants need to be randomly selected throughout that population. Since the survey was taken at a dog park, it is unlikely that the sample represents a random sample from the entire neighborhood (see SAMPLING RULE 5). So, the answer is choice **B**.

10.
* **Direct solution:** Since the median and mean are not equal, the data is not symmetrical. In particular, the mean is greater than the median. This means that there are large outliers in the data. In other words, there are a few families that donate much more money than the rest, choice **B**.

Notes: (1) A distribution is **symmetrical** when the mean and median of the data are equal. A normal distribution is an example of a symmetrical distribution.

(2) In this problem, the mean and median are not equal, and so it follows that the distribution is NOT symmetrical.

(3) A distribution that is not symmetrical contains **outliers**. These are a small group of data that are significantly larger or smaller than the rest of the data.

(4) If the outliers are larger than the rest of the data, then the mean will be greater than the median, and conversely. If the outliers are smaller than the rest of the data, then the mean will be less than the median, and conversely.

In this problem, the mean is greater than the median, and so the outliers are larger than the rest of the data.

Solution by picking numbers and changing averages to sums: To simplify things, let's use the numbers 3 and 17 for the median and mean, respectively, and let's use three data points. We will make two of the data points 1 and 3, and choose the third so that the mean is 17. Letting our data points be 1, 3, and x, we use the formula "Sum = Average · Number" to get that the sum of the three data points is $17 \cdot 3 = 51$. So, we have $1 + 3 + x = 51$, and therefore, $x = 51 - 1 - 3 = 47$. So, the three data points are 1, 3, and 47. Note that in this example there is one data point that is significantly greater than the rest, so that choice B is true. More importantly, observe that for these data, choices A, C, and D are false. Therefore, the answer is choice **B**.

LESSON 24 – GEOMETRY
PARALLEL LINES AND SIMILARITY

Parallel Lines

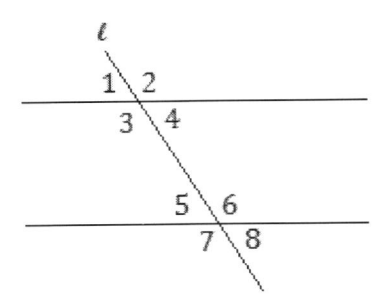

The figure above shows two **parallel lines** cut by the **transversal** ℓ.

Angles 1, 4, 5, and 8 all have the same measure. Also, angles 2, 3, 6, and 7 all have the same measure. Any two angles that do not have the same measure are supplementary, that is their measures add to 180°.

Technical notes: (1) Various pairs of these angles are given special names. Angles 3 and 6 are called **alternate interior angles**, angles 1 and 8 are called **alternate exterior angles**, and angles 1 and 5 are called **corresponding angles**. Each of these angle pairs are congruent precisely when the two lines cut by the transversal are parallel.

(2) Angles 1 and 4 are **vertical angles**. Recall that vertical angles are always congruent.

Angles 1 and 3 form a **linear pair**. Angles that form a linear pair are always **supplementary** (their angle measures sum to 180°).

Exercise: In the figure above, find one more pair of alternate interior angles, one more pair of alternate exterior angles, three more pairs of corresponding angles, three more pairs of vertical angles, and seven more linear pairs.

LEVEL 2: GEOMETRY – PARALLEL LINES AND SIMILARITY

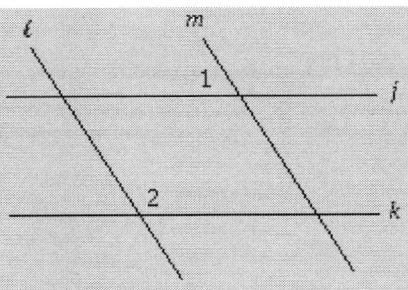

1. In the figure above, lines j and k are parallel and lines ℓ and m are parallel. If the measure of $\angle 1$ is 43°, what is the measure of $\angle 2$? (Disregard the degree sign when gridding in your answer.)

* $m\angle 2 = 180° - m\angle 1 = 180° - 43° = 137°$. So, we grid in **137**.

Note: ∠1 and ∠2 are clearly not congruent (∠1 is acute and ∠2 is obtuse). So, they must be supplementary. This means that $m\angle 1 + m\angle 2 = 180°$.

Same Shape, Different Size

Two triangles are **similar** if their angles are congruent. Note that similar triangles **do not** have to be the same size. Also, note that to show that two triangles are similar we need only show that two pairs of angles are congruent. We get the third pair for free because all triangles have angle measures summing to 180 degrees.

Example: In the figure to the right, assume that $\overline{BC}$ is parallel to $\overline{DE}$. It then follows that angles ADE and ABC are congruent (corresponding angles). Since triangles ADE and ABC share angle A, the two triangles are similar.

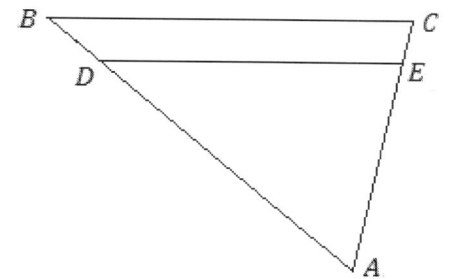

Important Fact: Corresponding sides of similar triangles are in proportion.

So, for example, in the figure to the right, $\frac{AD}{AB} = \frac{DE}{BC}$.

LEVEL 2: GEOMETRY – PARALLEL LINES AND SIMILARITY

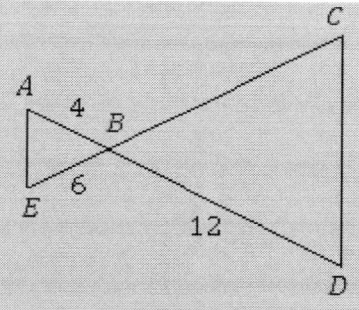

2. In the figure above, $AE \parallel CD$ and segment AD intersects segment CE at B. What is the length of segment CE ?

* $\frac{BC}{BD} = \frac{BE}{BA}$. So $\frac{BC}{12} = \frac{6}{4}$. Thus, $4BC = 72$, and so $BC = \frac{72}{4} = 18$.

It follows that $CE = BC + BE = 18 + 6 = \textbf{24}$.

Notes: (1) In this problem, we can use alternate interior angles and/or vertical angles to show the congruence of the various pairs of angles. For example, angles ABE and CBD are vertical angles, and angles BAE and BDC are alternate interior angles. It follows that the two triangles are similar.

(2) In problems involving similar triangles, it can be very helpful to redraw the triangles next to each other so that corresponding sides are in matching positions. This will eliminate the risk of setting up the proportion incorrectly.

Here is what this would look like for the two triangles in this problem.

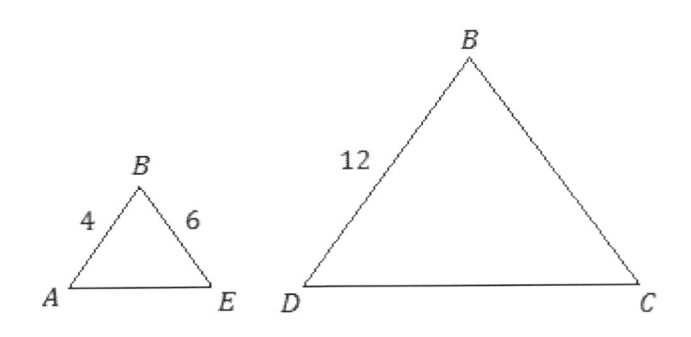

Time to Practice

LEVEL 2: GEOMETRY – PARALLEL LINES AND SIMILARITY

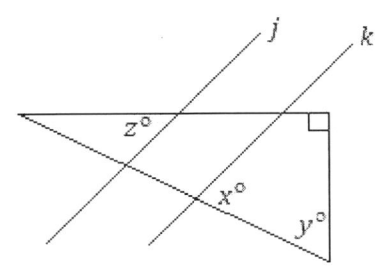

Note: Figure not drawn to scale.

3. In the figure above, lines j and k are parallel, $x = 100$, and $y = 35$. What is the value of z ?

   A) 35
   B) 45
   C) 55
   D) 80

LEVEL 3: GEOMETRY – PARALLEL LINES AND SIMILARITY

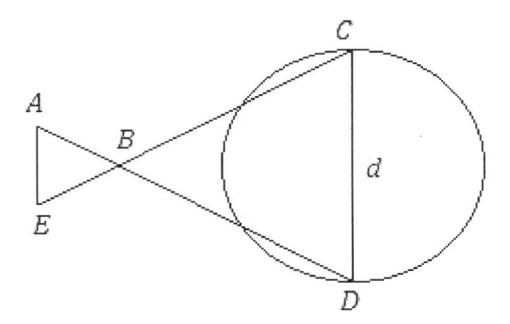

4. A surveyor wants to find the diameter, d, in meters, of a circular plot of land as represented in the sketch above. The lengths represented by AE, EB, BC, and BD on the sketch were determined to be 1200 meters, 1500 meters, 2500 meters, and 3100 meters, respectively. Segments AD and CE intersect at B, and $\angle EAB$ and $\angle CDB$ have the same measure. What is the value of d ?

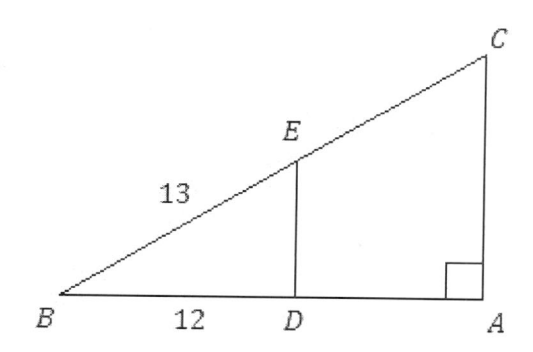

5. In the figure above, $\overline{DE}$ is parallel to $\overline{AC}$, D is the midpoint of $\overline{AB}$, $BD = 12$, and $BE = 13$. What is the length of $\overline{AC}$?

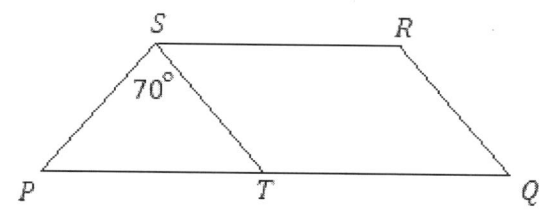

Note: Figure not drawn to scale.

6. In the figure above, $\overline{SR} \parallel \overline{PQ}$, $\overline{ST} \parallel \overline{RQ}$, $SP = ST$, and $m\angle PST = 70°$. What is $m\angle RST$? (disregard the degree symbol when gridding your answer.)

LEVEL 4: GEOMETRY – PARALLEL LINES AND SIMILARITY

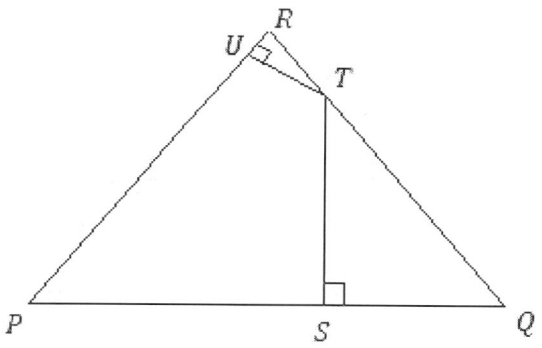

Note: Figure not drawn to scale.

7. Triangle PQR above is equilateral with $PQ = 44$. The ratio of ST to TU is $8:3$. What is the length of $\overline{SQ}$?

A) 6
B) 16
C) $16\sqrt{3}$
D) 32

173

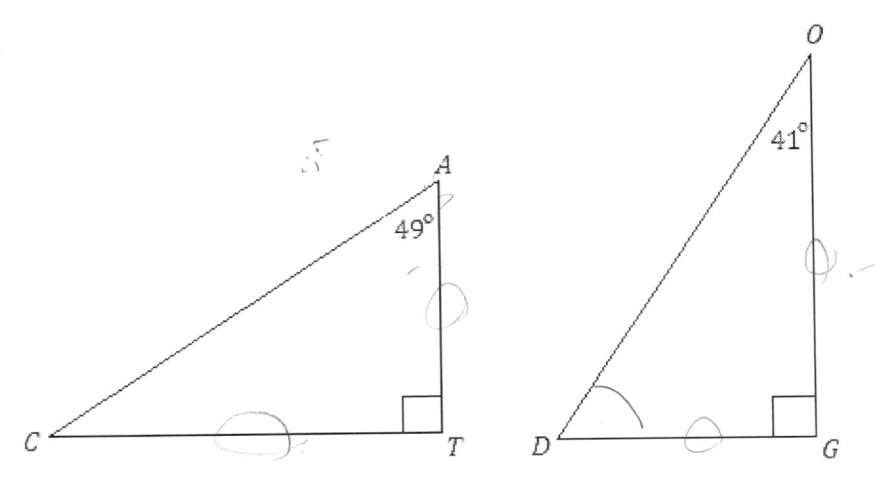

8. Triangles *CAT* and *DOG* are shown above. Which of the following is equal to the ratio $\frac{CT}{AT}$?

A) $\frac{DG}{DO}$

B) $\frac{DG}{OG}$

C) $\frac{OG}{DG}$

D) $\frac{DO}{OG}$

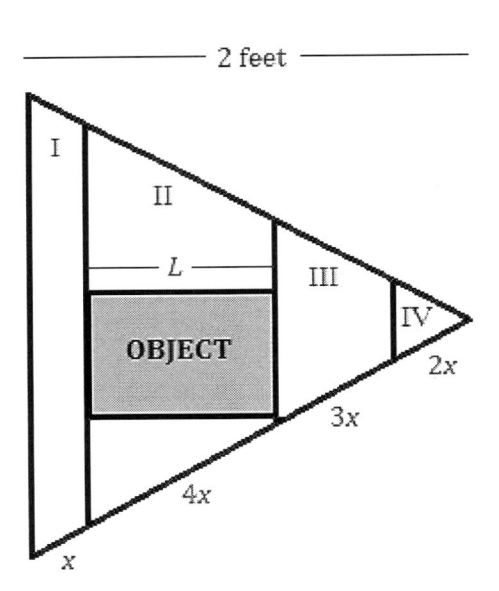

9. Tracy and Philip made a triangular shaped time capsule with 4 compartments as shown in the figure above. The total length is 2 feet. What is the maximum length *L*, in feet, of an object that can fit into compartment II?

LEVEL 5: GEOMETRY – PARALLEL LINES AND SIMILARITY

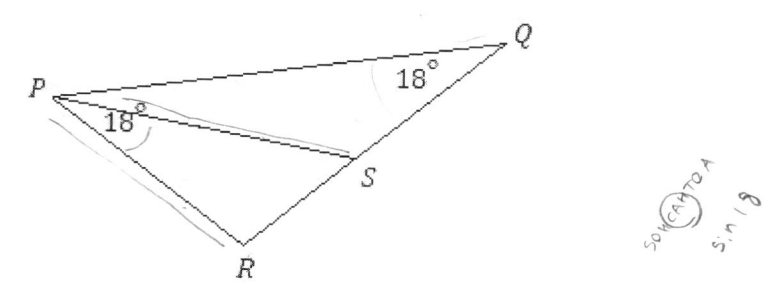

10. In the figure above, which of the following ratios has the same value as $\frac{PR}{PS}$?

   A) $\frac{PQ}{QR}$
   B) $\frac{PQ}{PR}$
   C) $\frac{QR}{PQ}$
   D) $\frac{QR}{PR}$

Answers

1. 137   2. 24   3. B   4. 2000   5. 10   6. 55   7. B   8. C   9. 4/5, .8   10. C

Full Solutions

3.
* Let's replace x by 100 and y by 35 in the figure. We also use corresponding angles to label the upper angle to the left of k with z. We show all this in the picture on the left.

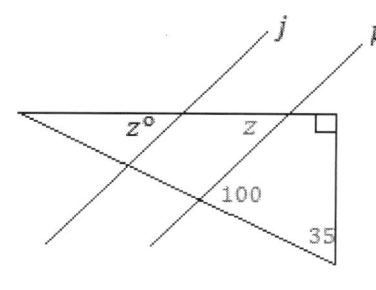

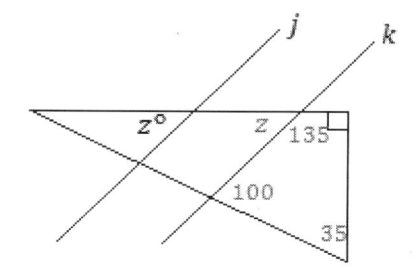

The rightmost part of the figure is a quadrilateral. Since the sum of the angle measures in a quadrilateral is $360°$, the unlabeled angle has measure $360 - 100 - 35 - 90 = 135°$. We show this in the figure on the right. Finally, $z = 180 - 135 = 45$, choice **B**.

Alternate solution: Again, let's replace x by 100 and y by 35 in the figure. Since the sum of the angle measures in a triangle is $180°$, the leftmost angle in the big triangle measures $180 - 35 - 90 = 55°$. We also use corresponding angles to label the lower angle to the right of j with $100°$. We show all this in the picture on the left.

175

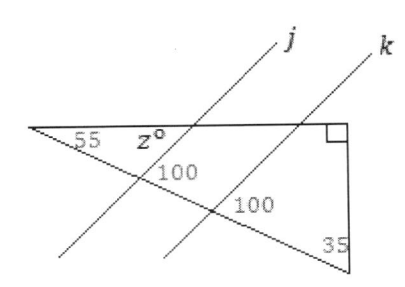

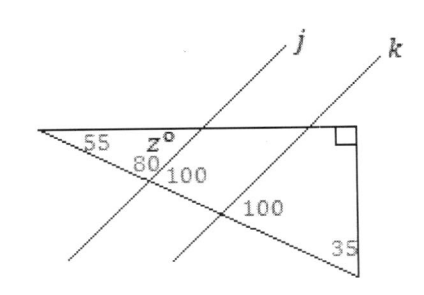

We now use supplementary angles to label the lower angle to the left of j as $180 - 100 = 80°$, as shown in the figure on the right. Finally, using the fact that the angle measures in a triangle sum to $180°$, we have $z = 180 - 55 - 80 = 45$, choice **B**.

4.

* $\frac{CD}{AE} = \frac{BC}{EB}$. Thus, $\frac{d}{1200} = \frac{2500}{1500} = \frac{5}{3}$. So, $d = \frac{5}{3} \cdot 1200 = \mathbf{2000}$.

Notes: (1) BD was not needed to answer the question.

(2) Don't forget to redraw the two triangles next to each other so that corresponding sides are in matching positions, as was done in problem 2. Also, make sure to label all the sides. This will ensure that you set up the proportion correctly.

5.

* Using the Pythagorean triple 5, 12, 13, we have that $DE = 5$. Since D is the midpoint of $\overline{AB}$, we have $AB = 2 \cdot 12 = 24$.

Finally, using the similarity of triangles BED and BCA, we have $\frac{AC}{DE} = \frac{BA}{BD}$. So, $\frac{AC}{5} = \frac{24}{12} = 2$. Therefore, $AC = 2 \cdot 5 = \mathbf{10}$.

Notes: (1) In this problem, we can use corresponding angles and/or the fact that $\angle B$ is shared by both triangles to show the congruence of the various pairs of angles. For example, angles BED and BCA are corresponding angles, and angle B is shared by both triangles. It follows that the two triangles are similar.

(2) If you're having trouble seeing how to set up the proportion, redraw triangles BED and BCA next to each other, and label all the sides and angles, as was done in problem 2.

6.

* Since the angle measures in a triangle sum to $180°$, $m\angle SPT + m\angle PTS = 180 - 70 = 110°$. Since $SP = ST$, $m\angle SPT = m\angle PTS = \frac{110}{2} = 55°$. Using alternate interior angles, $m\angle RST = 55°$. So, we grid in **55**.

Notes: (1) The symbol "∥" stands for parallel, and $\overline{SR} \parallel \overline{PQ}$ is read "line segment SR is parallel to line segment PQ."

(2) To get that $m\angle RST = 55°$, we used parallel lines $\overline{SR}$ and $\overline{PQ}$ cut by transversal ST. If you have trouble seeing it, it may help to extend the three line segments in the picture as shown below. In the leftmost figure, we lightened the part of the figure that is not needed for this part of the solution. In the rightmost figure, we added that information back in, together with the two congruent alternate interior angles.

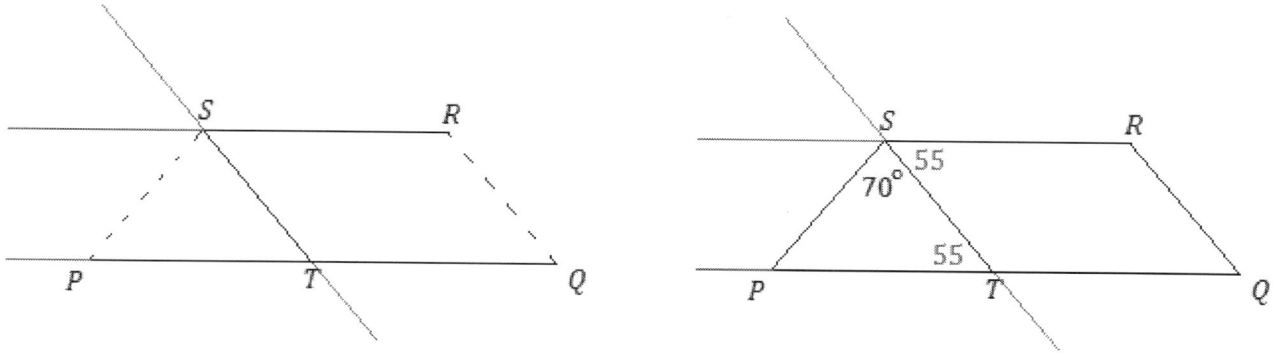

7.

* Since ΔPQR is equilateral, $\angle R \cong \angle Q$, and since all right angles are congruent, $\angle TSQ \cong \angle TUR$. It follows that $\Delta TSQ \sim \Delta TUR$. Therefore, $\frac{TQ}{TR} = \frac{ST}{TU} = \frac{8}{3}$.

So, we can write $TQ = 8x$ and $TR = 3x$ for some x, and therefore, we have

$$11x = 8x + 3x = TQ + TR = QR = PQ = 44.$$

So, $x = \frac{44}{11} = 4$.

It follows that $TQ = 8 \cdot 4 = 32$.

Since ΔPQR is equilateral, $m\angle TQS = 60°$, and so, $m\angle QTS = 30°$.

Since the hypotenuse of ΔTSQ has length 32, it follows that $SQ = 16$, choice **B**.

Notes: (1) The symbol $\cong$ stands for "congruent," so that $\angle R \cong \angle Q$ is read "angle R is congruent to angle Q."

Two angles are **congruent** if they have the same measure.

(2) An equilateral triangle is also equiangular. That is all three angles are congruent.

Since the angle measures of a triangle sum to $180°$, each angle of an equilateral triangle measures $60°$.

(3) The symbol $\sim$ stands for "similar," so that $\Delta TSQ \sim \Delta TUR$ is read "triangle TSQ is similar to triangle TUR."

(4) Since $m\angle Q = 60°$ and $m\angle TSQ = 90°$, we have $m\angle STQ = 180 - 60 - 90 = 30°$.

So, ΔTSQ is a 30, 60, 90 triangle. The side opposite the 30° angle always has half the length of the hypotenuse. See Lesson 8 for more on 30, 60, 90 triangles.

8.
* Since $90 - 49 = 41$, both triangles have the same angle measures, and therefore, they are similar. However, the way they are drawn, the corresponding sides are not matching up. Let's redraw the rightmost triangle so that the angles of the two triangles match up.

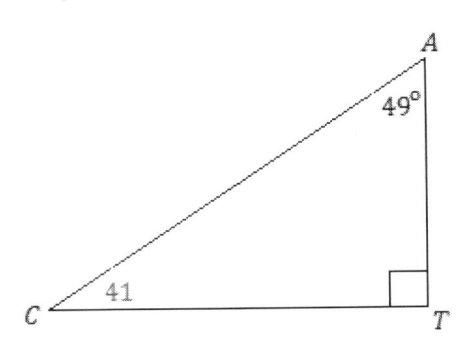

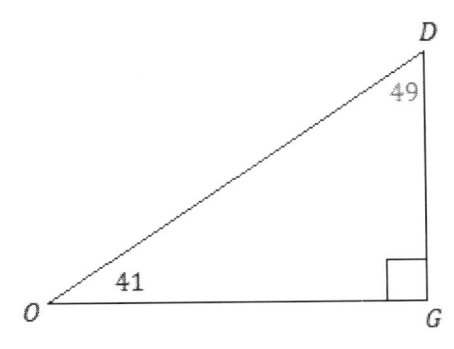

It is now easy to see that $\frac{CT}{AT} = \frac{OG}{DG}$, choice **C**.

9.
* There are 4 triangles in the picture that are all similar. It follows that the ratios of the heights of the triangles are the same as the ratios of the bottom sides of the triangles. So, if we let y be the horizontal distance between the two leftmost vertical segments, we have $y + 4y + 3y + 2y = 10y$. It follows that $10y = 2$, so that $y = \frac{2}{10} = \frac{1}{5}$ foot. Finally, $L = 4y = 4 \cdot \frac{1}{5} = \textbf{4/5}$ or $\textbf{.8}$.

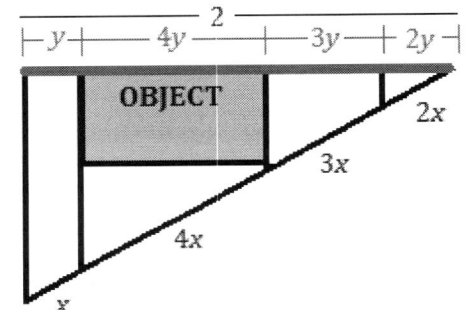

Note: The picture to the right shows the heights of the various parts of the big triangle in terms of y.

10.
* Observe that triangles PRS and QRP both have an $18°$ angle, and they share angle R. It follows that they are similar. However, the way they are drawn, the corresponding sides are not matching up. Let's redraw both triangles so that the angles of the two triangles match up.

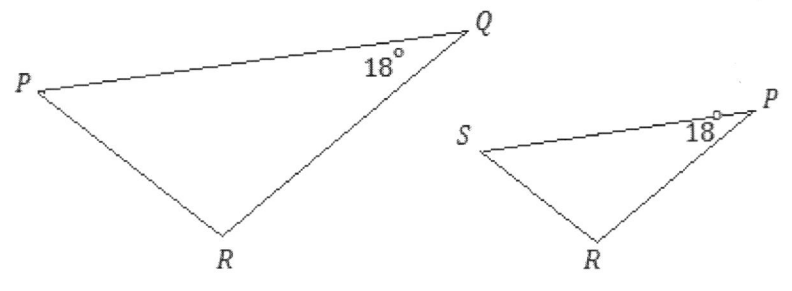

Notice that now both triangles have angle R at the same position and the $18°$ angles are at the same position.

It's now easy to see that $\frac{PR}{PS} = \frac{QR}{QP} = \frac{QR}{PQ}$, choice **C**.

LESSON 25 – HEART OF ALGEBRA
MANIPULATING LINEAR EXPRESSIONS

Being a Manipulator Isn't Always Bad

On the SAT, you will sometimes be asked to solve for one variable in terms of others. As a simple example, if $A = B + 1$, then we can isolate B by subtracting 1 from each side of the equation to get $A - 1 = B$. We would normally write this as $B = A - 1$.

Don't Break the Block!

We define a **block** to be an algebraic expression that appears more than once in a given problem. Very often in SAT problems a block can be treated just like a variable. In particular, blocks should usually NOT be manipulated—treat them as a single unit.

Let's try an example.

LEVEL 1: HEART OF ALGEBRA – MANIPULATING LINEAR EXPRESSIONS

1. If $2(x + y) = 7$, what is the value of $x + y$?

   A) $\frac{2}{7}$
   B) 2
   C) $\frac{7}{2}$
   D) 7

Formal substitution: There is a block of $(x + y)$ in this problem. Let's formally make the substitution $u = x + y$. The problem then becomes the following:

   If $2u = 7$, what is the value of u?

We divide each side of this equation by 2 to get $u = \frac{7}{2}$, choice **C**.

* **Quick solution:** We divide each side of the given equation by 2 to get $x + y = \frac{7}{2}$, choice **C**.

Note: Notice how we did NOT break the block. In this problem, we DO NOT want to distribute on the left. If we do, we get the equation $2x + 2y = 7$. It is now harder to figure out what $x + y$ is.

Time to Practice

LEVEL 1: HEART OF ALGEBRA – MANIPULATING LINEAR EXPRESSIONS

2. The formula below is used to compute C, the cost of goods sold, where B is the beginning inventory, P is the amount of inventory purchased, and E is the end inventory.

$$C = B + P - E$$

   Which of the following correctly gives B in terms of C, P, and E ?

   A) $B = E - P - C$
   B) $B = C + P - E$
   C) $B = C + P + E$
   D) $B = C - P + E$

3. Which of the following inequalities is equivalent to $10x - 15y \leq 20$?

   A) $x - y \leq 2$
   B) $3x - 2y \leq 4$
   C) $2x - 3y \leq 4$
   D) $3y - 2x \leq 4$

4. If $9x - 27 = 72$, what is the value of $x - 3$?

LEVEL 2: HEART OF ALGEBRA – MANIPULATING LINEAR EXPRESSIONS

$$0.7c = k$$

5. A 30% discount is given on a computer originally priced at c dollars. The new price is k and the relationship between c and k is given in the equation above. What is c in terms of k ?

   A) $c = 0.7k$
   B) $c = \dfrac{0.7}{k}$
   C) $c = \dfrac{k}{0.7}$
   D) $c = k - 0.7$

Questions 6 and 7 refer to the following information.

$$s = 127 + 2.37p$$

In the equation above, s represents the supply (the quantity a supplier is willing to make available), in units, of a certain item with a price of p dollars.

6. Which of the following expresses the price of the item in terms of the supply?

   A) $p = \frac{s+127}{2.37}$

   B) $p = \frac{s-127}{2.37}$

   C) $p = \frac{127-s}{2.37}$

   D) $p = \frac{2.37}{s+127}$

7. * For which of the following prices will the supply be closest to 283 units?

   A) $63
   B) $65
   C) $66
   D) $67

LEVEL 3: HEART OF ALGEBRA – MANIPULATING LINEAR EXPRESSIONS

Questions 8 - 10 refer to the following information.

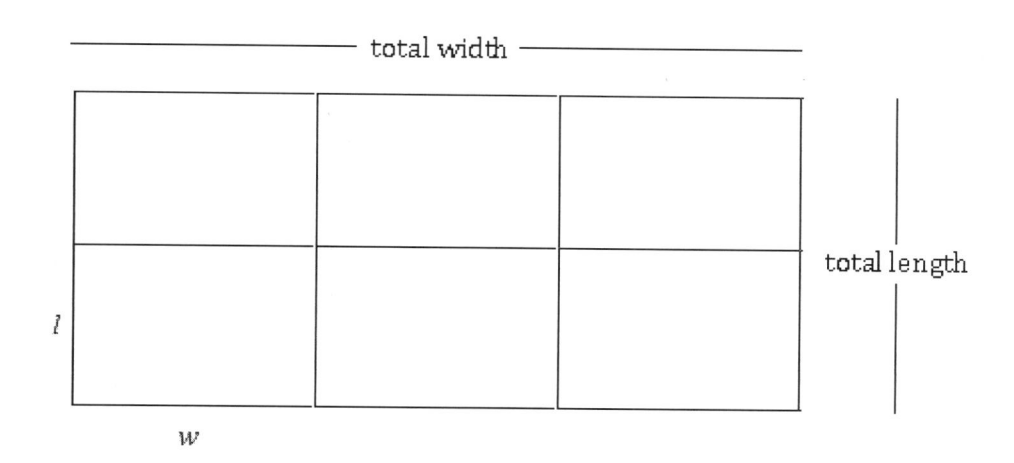

Kelly is planning to add a garden to her backyard. The garden will be partitioned into rectangular blocks so that $3l + w = 16$, where l is the length and w is the width of each block, in feet. The lengths of all the blocks will be the same, and similarly for the widths.

8. Which of the following expresses the length of a block in terms of its width?

   A) $l = -\frac{1}{3}(16 + w)$

   B) $l = -\frac{1}{3}(16 - w)$

   C) $l = \frac{1}{3}(16 + w)$

   D) $l = \frac{1}{3}(16 - w)$

LEVEL 4: HEART OF ALGEBRA – MANIPULATING LINEAR EXPRESSIONS

9. Kelly has decided that she would like the width of each block to be at least 7 feet and the length of each block to be at least 2 feet. Which of the following inequalities represents the set of all possible values for the length of the block that meets these requirements?

    A) $0 \leq l \leq 3$
    B) $2 \leq l \leq 3$
    C) $3 \leq l \leq 7$
    D) $l \geq 3$

LEVEL 5: HEART OF ALGEBRA – MANIPULATING LINEAR EXPRESSIONS

10. Kelly decides that she would like the total length of the garden to be 34 feet, with the length of each block between 3 and 4 feet. She also wants there to be 2 rows of blocks with an even number of blocks in each row. Which of the following must be the width of each block, in feet?

    A) 3.4
    B) 4.6
    C) 5.8
    D) 8.5

Answers

1. C   2. D   3. C   4. 8   5. C   6. B   7. C   8. D   9. B   10. C

Full Solutions

2.
* We subtract P from and add E to each side of the equation to get $B = C - P + E$, choice **D**.

3.
* We can factor out 5 from the left-hand side to get $5(2x - 3y) \leq 20$. We now divide each side of this last inequality by 5 to get $2x - 3y \leq \frac{20}{5} = 4$, choice **C**.

4.
* We can factor out 9 from the left-hand side to get $9(x - 3) = 72$. We now divide each side of this last equation by 9 to get $x - 3 = \frac{72}{9} = \mathbf{8}$.

5.
* We divide each side of the given equation by 0.7 to get $c = \frac{k}{0.7}$, choice **C**.

6.
* **Algebraic solution:** To get p by itself we begin by subtracting 127 from each side of the equation to get $s - 127 = 2.37p$. We then divide each side of this last equation by 2.37 to get $p = \frac{s-127}{2.37}$. This is choice **B**.

Note: If a calculator is allowed, then this problem can also be solved by picking numbers. In this case, it is easiest to choose a value for p, and then determine the corresponding value for s in the original equation. We would then substitute the s value into each answer choice and eliminate any choices for which p comes out incorrect. I leave the details of this solution to the reader.

7.

Solution by starting with choice C: We start with choice C and guess that $p = 66$. It follows that $s = 127 + 2.37 \cdot 66 = 283.42$. Since this is 283 to the nearest whole number, it seems likely that this is the answer.

To be safe, we should make sure that choice B doesn't give an answer closer to 283. So, let's let $p = 65$. Then $s = 127 + 2.37 \cdot 65 = 281.05$. Since this is NOT closer, the answer is choice **C**.

* **Solution by using the answer to the last problem:** From the last problem, we know that $p = \frac{s-127}{2.37}$. We substitute 283 in for s to get

$$p = \frac{283 - 127}{2.37} = \frac{156}{2.37} \approx 65.82$$

So, the answer is choice **C**.

8.

***Algebraic solution:** $3l + w = 16 \Leftrightarrow 3l = 16 - w \Leftrightarrow l = \frac{1}{3}(16 - w)$. This is choice **D**.

Note: We first subtracted w from each side of the equation to get $3l = 16 - w$. We then multiplied each side of the resulting equation by $\frac{1}{3}$ to get $l = \frac{1}{3}(16 - w)$.

9.

***Algebraic solution:** We are given that Kelly would like $w \geq 7$ and $l \geq 2$. Since $w = 16 - 3l$, from the first inequality, we want $16 - 3l \geq 7$. Subtracting 16 from each side of this inequality gives us $-3l \geq 7 - 16 = -9$. We now divide each side of this last inequality by -3 to get $l \leq \frac{-9}{-3} = 3$. Combining the inequalities $l \geq 2$ and $l \leq 3$ yields $2 \leq l \leq 3$, choice **B**.

Note: When we multiply or divide each side of an inequality by a negative number, the inequality reverses.

In this problem, we divided by -3, and so the inequality changed from "greater than or equal to" to "less than or equal to."

10.

***Algebraic solution:** The number of blocks in a row must be between $\frac{34}{4} = 8.5$ and $\frac{34}{3} \approx 11.3$. Since Kelly wants an even number of blocks in each row, there must be **10** blocks in each row.

So, the length of each block is $\frac{34}{10} = 3.4$ feet. Since $3l + w = 16$, we have $w = 16 - 3l$.

It follows that the width of each block must be $16 - 3 \cdot 3.4 = 16 - 10.2 = 5.8$ feet, choice **C**.

LESSON 26 – PASSPORT TO ADVANCED MATH
MANIPULATING NONLINEAR EXPRESSIONS

More Ways to Manipulate

Let's jump right into some problems.

LEVEL 2: PASSPORT TO ADVANCED MATH – MANIPULATING NONLINEAR EXPRESSIONS

1. A rectangle has area A, length x and width y. Which of the following represents y in terms of A and x?

   A) $y = \frac{A}{2x}$
   B) $y = \frac{A}{x}$
   C) $y = \frac{2A}{x}$
   D) $y = \frac{\sqrt{A}}{x}$

LEVEL 3: PASSPORT TO ADVANCED MATH – MANIPULATING NONLINEAR EXPRESSIONS

$$a = \frac{rP}{1-(1+r)^{-n}}$$

2. An *annuity* is a series of periodic payments that are received at a future date. In the formula above, a is the periodic payment on an annuity, P is the present value of the annuity, r is the interest rate per period, and n is the number of payment periods. Which of the following gives P in terms of a, r, and n.

   A) $P = ra$
   B) $P = (1+r)^n a$
   C) $P = \frac{ra}{1-(1+r)^{-n}}$
   D) $P = a\frac{1-(1+r)^{-n}}{r}$

$$F(x) = |x^2 - 2| + 2$$

3. For what value of x is $F(x)$ equal to 0 ?

   A) 0
   B) 2
   C) $\sqrt{2}$
   D) There is no such value of x.

4. If $x \neq -\frac{3}{2}$, what is the value of $(10x + 15)\left(\frac{1}{2x+3}\right)$?

184

LEVEL 4: PASSPORT TO ADVANCED MATH – MANIPULATING NONLINEAR EXPRESSIONS

$$P = \frac{A}{A + N}$$

5. The formula above is used to compute the percentage P of people in a population that have anemia, where A is the number of people from the population that have anemia, and N is the number of people from the population that do not have anemia. Which of the following expresses the number of people that have anemia in terms of the other variables?

   A) $A = \frac{N}{P-1}$
   B) $A = \frac{N}{1-P}$
   C) $A = \frac{PN}{1-P}$
   D) $A = \frac{PN}{P-1}$

6. If $\frac{3}{x} = \frac{6}{x+9}$, what is the value of $\frac{x}{3}$?

   A) 3
   B) 6
   C) 9
   D) 12

7. A soda can manufacturer uses the formula $M = 2\pi r^2 n + \pi r h n$ to calculate the amount of material, M, needed to manufacture n cylindrical soda cans of height h and base radius r. Which of the following correctly expresses h in terms of M, n, and r?

   A) $h = \frac{\pi r n}{M - 2\pi r^2}$
   B) $h = \frac{M - 2\pi r^2}{\pi r n}$
   C) $h = M - \frac{2r}{n}$
   D) $h = \frac{M}{\pi r n} - 2r$

LEVEL 5: PASSPORT TO ADVANCED MATH – MANIPULATING NONLINEAR EXPRESSIONS

8. If $k > -1$, which of the following is equivalent to $\frac{1}{\frac{1}{k+1} + \frac{1}{k+2}}$.

   A) $2k + 3$
   B) $k^2 + 3k + 2$
   C) $\frac{k^2 + 3k + 2}{2k + 3}$
   D) $\frac{2k + 3}{k^2 + 3k + 2}$

9. An encyclopedia salesman has a boxes, each containing 7 encyclopedias. After visiting b families and selling c encyclopedias to each of them, he has d encyclopedias remaining. Which of the following expresses b in terms of a, c, and d ?

A) $\frac{7a-d}{c}$
B) $\frac{7a+d}{c}$
C) $\frac{7a}{c} - d$
D) $\frac{7c-d}{a}$

10. The equation $\frac{36x^2+81x-15}{kx-7} = -3x - 5 - \frac{50}{kx-7}$ is true for all values of $x \neq \frac{7}{k}$, where k is a constant. What is the value of $|k|$?

Answers

1. B   2. D   3. D   4. 5   5. C   6. A   7. D   8. C   9. A   10. 12

Full Solutions

1.
* **Algebraic solution:** The area of the rectangle is $A = xy$. Dividing each side of this equation by x gives $y = \frac{A}{x}$, choice **B**.

Solution by picking numbers: Let's let $x = 2$ and $y = 3$, so that $A = 6$. Put a nice big dark circle around 3 so you can find it easier later. We now substitute $A = 6$ and $x = 2$ into each answer choice:

A) $y = \frac{6}{2 \cdot 2} = \frac{3}{2} = 1.5$
B) $y = \frac{6}{2} = 3$
C) $y = \frac{2 \cdot 6}{2} = 6$
D) $y = \frac{\sqrt{6}}{2}$

Since A, C, and D each came out incorrect, the answer is choice **B**.

Notes: (1) B is **not** the correct answer simply because it is equal to 3. It is correct because all three of the other choices are **not** 3. **You must check all four choices!**

(2) All the above computations can be done in a single step with your calculator (if a calculator is allowed for this problem).

2.
* **Algebraic solution:** To get P by itself we multiply each side of the equation by the reciprocal of $\frac{r}{1-(1+r)^{-n}}$ which is $\frac{1-(1+r)^{-n}}{r}$.

$$a\frac{1-(1+r)^{-n}}{r} = \frac{rP}{1-(1+r)^{-n}} \cdot \frac{1-(1+r)^{-n}}{r}$$

$$a\frac{1-(1+r)^{-n}}{r} = P$$

This is choice **D**.

3.

Solution by starting with choice C: We start with choice C and compute

$$F(\sqrt{2}) = |(\sqrt{2})^2 - 2| + 2 = |2 - 2| + 2 = 0 + 2 = 2$$

So, we can eliminate choice C.

Let's try B: $F(2) = |2^2 - 2| + 2 = |4 - 2| + 2 = |2| + 2 = 2 + 2 = 4$.

So, we can eliminate choice B.

Let's try A: $F(0) = |-2| + 2 = 2 + 2 = 4$.

So, we can eliminate choice A and the answer is choice **D**.

* **Direct solution:** $|x^2 - 2| \geq 0$ no matter what x is. It follows that $|x^2 - 2| + 2 \geq 2$.

In particular, $|x^2 - 2| + 2$ could never be 0, and so the answer is **D**.

Recall: $|x|$ is the **absolute value** of x. If x is nonnegative, then $|x| = x$. If x is negative, then $|x| = -x$ (in other words, if x is negative, then taking the absolute value just eliminates the minus sign). For example, $|12| = 12$ and $|-12| = 12$.

4.

* **Algebraic solution:** We have $10x + 15 = 5(2x + 3)$. It follows that we have the following.

$$(10x + 15)\left(\frac{1}{2x+3}\right) = 5(2x+3)\left(\frac{1}{2x+3}\right) = 5$$

5.

* **Algebraic solution:** We start by multiplying each side of the given equation by $A + N$ to get $P(A + N) = A$.

Distributing on the left gives us $PA + PN = A$.

We now subtract PA from each side of the equation to get

$$PN = A - PA.$$

We factor out A on the right to get $PN = A(1 - P)$.

Finally, we divide each side of the equation by $1 - P$ to get $\frac{PN}{1-P} = A$.

This is equivalent to choice **C**.

Notes: (1) When solving an equation that has denominators, it is always a good idea to eliminate the denominators first.

In this problem, the only denominator is $A + N$. The easiest way to eliminate this denominator is to multiply each side of the equation by it.

(2) The reason we subtract PA from each side of the equation in the third step is because we want to get all terms with A to one side of the equation (because we are solving for A).

This allows us to factor out the A in the next step, and then perform a division to isolate A.

6.
* **Algebraic solution:** We cross multiply the given equation to get $3(x + 9) = 6x$, or equivalently, $3x + 27 = 6x$. Subtracting $3x$ from each side of this equation yields $27 = 3x$. Dividing by 3 gives us $x = \frac{27}{3} = 9$. It follows that $\frac{x}{3} = \frac{9}{3} = 3$, choice **A**.

Note: We can save one step by dividing each side of the equation $27 = 3x$ by 9 to get $\frac{27}{9} = \frac{3x}{9}$, or equivalently, $3 = \frac{x}{3}$.

Solution by starting with choice C: We start with choice C and guess that $\frac{x}{3} = 9$. It follows that $x = 9 \cdot 3 = 27$. Now, $\frac{3}{x} = \frac{3}{27} = \frac{1}{9}$ and $\frac{6}{x+9} = \frac{6}{36} = \frac{1}{6}$. These do not match up, and so C is NOT the answer.

Let's try choice A next and guess that $\frac{x}{3} = 3$. Then $x = 3 \cdot 3 = 9$. Now, $\frac{3}{x} = \frac{3}{9} = \frac{1}{3}$ and $\frac{6}{x+9} = \frac{6}{18} = \frac{1}{3}$. These do match up, and so the answer is choice **A**.

7.
* **Algebraic solution:** We subtract $2\pi r^2 n$ from each side of the equation to get $M - 2\pi r^2 n = \pi r h n$. We now divide by $\pi r n$ to get $h = \frac{M - 2\pi r^2 n}{\pi r n} = \frac{M}{\pi r n} - \frac{2\pi r^2 n}{\pi r n} = \frac{M}{\pi r n} - 2r$, choice **D**.

Note: $h = \frac{M - 2\pi r^2 n}{\pi r n}$ would also be a correct answer. This is not one of the choices though. It would be easy to accidentally choose choice B because it looks a lot like this expression. However, in choice B the second term in the numerator is missing an n.

8.
Solution by picking a number: Let's choose a value for k, say $k = 2$. Then

$$\frac{1}{\frac{1}{k+1} + \frac{1}{k+2}} = \frac{1}{\frac{1}{2+1} + \frac{1}{2+2}} = \frac{1}{\frac{1}{3} + \frac{1}{4}} = \frac{1}{\frac{4}{12} + \frac{3}{12}} = \frac{1}{\frac{7}{12}} = \boxed{\frac{12}{7}}$$

Put a nice big, dark circle around this number so that you can find it easily later. We now substitute 2 in for k into **all** four answer choices (we use our calculator if we're allowed to).

A) $2 \cdot 2 + 3 = 7$
B) $2^2 + 3 \cdot 2 + 2 = 12$
C) $(2^2 + 3 \cdot 2 + 2)/(2 \cdot 2 + 3) = 12/7$
D) $(2 \cdot 2 + 3)/(2^2 + 3 \cdot 2 + 2) = 7/12$

Since C is the only choice that has become $\frac{12}{7}$, we conclude that **C** is the answer.

Note: C is **not** the correct answer simply because it is equal to $\frac{12}{7}$. It is correct because all the other choices are **not** $\frac{12}{7}$.

Algebraic solution: We multiply the numerator and denominator of the complex fraction by $(k+1)(k+2)$ to get

$$\frac{1}{\frac{1}{k+1} + \frac{1}{k+2}} \cdot \frac{(k+1)(k+2)}{(k+1)(k+2)} = \frac{(k+1)(k+2)}{(k+2)+(k+1)} = \frac{k^2 + 3k + 2}{2k+3}$$

This is choice **C**.

Notes: (1) The three simple fractions within the given complex fraction are $1 = \frac{1}{1}$, $\frac{1}{k+1}$, and $\frac{1}{k+2}$.

The least common denominator (LCD) of these three fractions is

$$(k+1)(k+2)$$

Note that the least common denominator is just the least common multiple (LCM) of the three denominators. In this problem, the LCD is the same as the product of the denominators.

(2) To simplify a complex fraction, we multiply each of the numerator and denominator of the fraction by the LCD of all the simple fractions that appear.

(3) Make sure to use the distributive property correctly here.

$$\left(\frac{1}{k+1} + \frac{1}{k+2}\right) \cdot (k+1)(k+2)$$
$$= \left(\frac{1}{k+1}\right) \cdot (k+1)(k+2) + \left(\frac{1}{k+2}\right) \cdot (k+1)(k+2)$$
$$= (k+2) + (k+1)$$

This is how we got the denominator in the second expression in the solution.

9.
Solution by picking numbers: Let's let $a = 2$, $b = ③$, and $c = 4$. So, the salesman has $2 \cdot 7 = 14$ encyclopedias. He sells 4 encyclopedias to each of 3 families for a total of $4 \cdot 3 = 12$ encyclopedias. It follows that he has $14 - 12 = 2$ left. So, $d = 2$.

Since we are trying to find b we put a nice big, dark circle around $b = 3$. We now check each answer choice.

A) $\frac{7a-d}{c} = \frac{14-2}{4} = \frac{12}{4} = 3$

B) $\frac{7a+d}{c} = \frac{14+2}{4} = \frac{16}{4} = 4$

C) $\frac{7a}{c} - d = \frac{14}{4} - 2 = 3.5 - 2 = 1.5$

D) $\frac{7c-d}{a} = \frac{28-2}{2} = \frac{26}{2} = 13$

Since choices B, C, and D came out incorrect we can eliminate them. So, the answer is choice **A**.

* **Algebraic solution:** The salesman has a total of $a \cdot 7 = 7a$ encyclopedias (a boxes with 7 encyclopedias per box). He sells a total of bc encyclopedias (b families and c encyclopedias per family). So, the number of encyclopedias he has remaining is $d = 7a - bc$.

We need to solve this last equation for b. We subtract $7a$ from each side of the equation to get $d - 7a = -bc$. We now divide each side of this last equation by $-c$: $b = \frac{d-7a}{-c} = \frac{-(d-7a)}{c} = \frac{7a-d}{c}$, choice **A**.

Note: To avoid all the minus signs, we can also solve the equation $d = 7a - bc$ by adding bc to each side of the equation while simultaneously subtracting d from each side of the equation to get $bc = 7a - d$. We then just divide by c to get $b = \frac{7a-d}{c}$.

10. The equation $\frac{36x^2+81x-15}{kx-7} = -3x - 5 - \frac{50}{kx-7}$ is true for all values of $x \neq \frac{7}{k}$, where k is a constant. What is the value of $|k|$?

Solution by picking a number: Let's let $x = 1$. We substitute 1 in for x in the equation to get $\frac{36+81-15}{k-7} = -3 - 5 - \frac{50}{k-7}$, or equivalently, $\frac{102}{k-7} = -8 - \frac{50}{k-7}$. We multiply each side of this equation by $k - 7$ to get $102 = -8(k-7) - 50$, or equivalently, $102 = -8k + 56 - 50$. So, $96 = -8k$, and therefore, $k = \frac{96}{-8} = -12$. Therefore, $|k| = \mathbf{12}$.

* **Quick algebraic solution:** We multiply each side of the equation by $kx - 7$ to get

$$36x^2 + 81x - 15 = (-3x - 5 - \frac{50}{kx-7})(kx-7)$$
$$36x^2 + 81x - 15 = (-3x - 5)(kx - 7) - 50$$
$$36x^2 + 81x - 15 = -3kx^2 + 21x - 5kx + 35 - 50$$
$$36x^2 + 81x - 15 = -3kx^2 + (21 - 5k)x - 15.$$

So, we must have $-3k = 36$, and so $k = -12$. Therefore, $|k| = \mathbf{12}$.

Note: We could also solve $21 - 5k = 81$ to get $k = -12$.

LESSON 27 – PROBLEM SOLVING
SCATTERPLOTS

A Scattered Mess

A scatterplot is a graph of plotted points that shows the relationship between two sets of data. On the SAT, the "line of best fit" is sometimes drawn over a given scatterplot.

Example: Take a look at the following scatterplot.

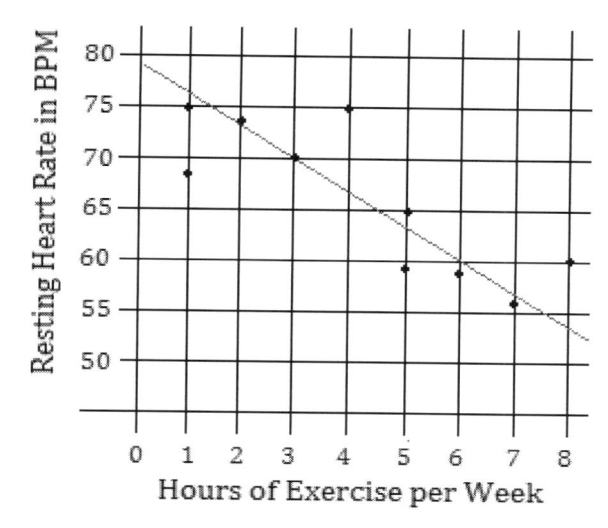

There are 10 data points in this scatterplot. Each point represents a person. The x-coordinate of the point tells us how many hours that person exercises per week, and the y-coordinate of the point tells us the resting heart rate of that person. For example, there is a person that exercises 1 hour per week with a resting heart rate of 75 BPM (beats per minute), and there is also another person that exercises 1 hour per week with a resting heart rate of approximately 68 BPM.

The line that is drawn in the figure is the line of best fit. It is the line that gives the best overall approximation of all the data points.

Ordering the Scatter

The following scatterplots show **positive associations**.

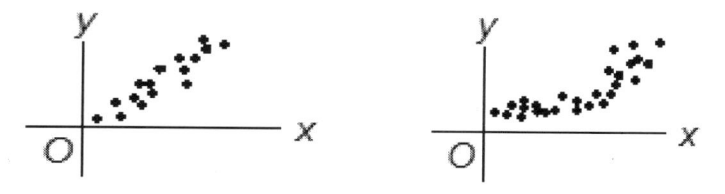

The scatterplot on the left shows a linear positive association, whereas the scatterplot on the right shows a nonlinear positive association. The rightmost scatterplot looks like it might show an exponential positive association.

Here are a few more scatterplots.

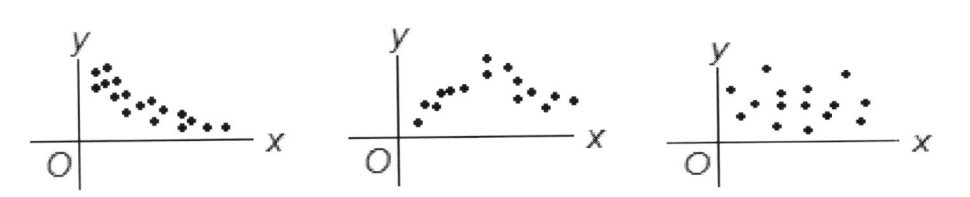

The leftmost scatterplot shows a nonlinear (possibly exponential) **negative association**, whereas the other two show **no association**.

Time to Practice

LEVEL 1: PROBLEM SOLVING – SCATTERPLOTS

Questions 1 - 4 refer to the following information.

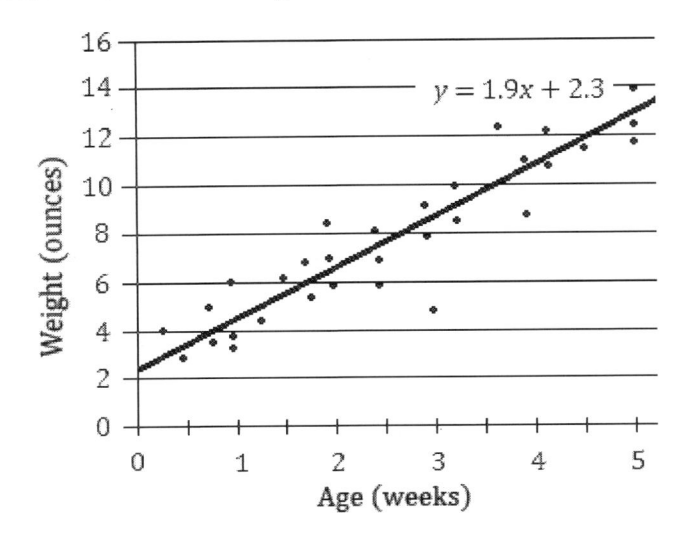

* The scatterplot above shows data collected on the age and weights of several kittens, and the line of best fit for the data is shown.

1. Which of the following is the best approximation to the weight, in ounces, of the youngest kitten for which there is a data point appearing in the scatterplot?

    A) 0.25
    B) 0.5
    C) 3
    D) 4

2. What is the age, in weeks, of the kitten represented by the data point that is farthest from the line of best fit?

    A) 3
    B) 4
    C) 5
    D) 6

LEVEL 2: PROBLEM SOLVING – SCATTERPLOTS

3. * Based on the line of best fit, if a kitten is 6 weeks old, what is the predicted weight, in ounces, of the kitten?

    A) 11.8
    B) 13.7
    C) 14.65
    D) 15.6

LEVEL 3: PROBLEM SOLVING – SCATTERPLOTS

4. Which of the following is the best interpretation of the slope of the line of best fit in the context of this problem?

    A) The predicted weight of a kitten that is 5 weeks old
    B) The predicted age of a kitten that was just born
    C) The predicted increase in weight, in ounces, for each week that a kitten ages
    D) The predicted increase in the age of a kitten needed to increase the kitten's weight by 1 ounce

5. Which of the following graphs best shows a strong positive association between x and y?

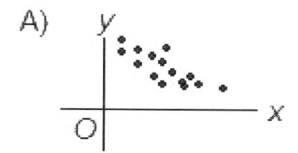

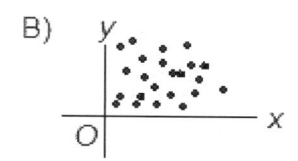

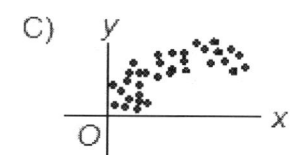

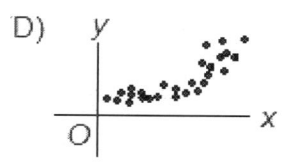

    A)
    B)
    C)
    D)

193

Questions 6 - 8 refer to the following information.

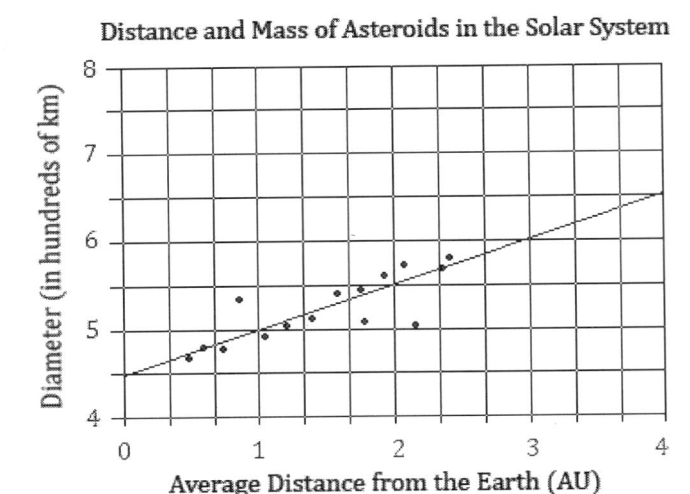

Distance and Mass of Asteroids in the Solar System

The scatterplot above shows the diameters of 15 asteroids, in hundreds of kilometers, with respect to their average distance from the earth in astronomical units (AU). The line of best fit is drawn.

6. A scientist has discovered a new asteroid about 2 AU from the Earth. According to the line of best fit, which of the following best approximates the diameter of the asteroid, in kilometers?

    A) 5.5
    B) 55
    C) 550
    D) 5500

7. 1 astronomical unit is equal to approximately 150 million kilometers. Which of the following gives the best estimate for the minimum possible distance, in millions of kilometers, between the largest and smallest asteroid whose data points appear in the scatterplot?

    A) 160
    B) 285
    C) 368
    D) 435

LEVEL 4: PROBLEM SOLVING – SCATTERPLOTS

8. According to the scatterplot, which of the following statements is true about the relationship between an asteroid's average distance from the Earth and its size?

    A) The distance from an asteroid to the Earth is unrelated to its size.
    B) An asteroid that is further from the Earth is smaller than an asteroid that is closer to the Earth.
    C) An asteroid that is closer to the Earth is smaller than an asteroid that is further from the Earth.
    D) An asteroid that is further from the Earth is more likely to be larger than an asteroid that is closer to the Earth.

9. Which scatterplot shows a relationship that is appropriately modeled with the equation $y = ab^x$, where $a > 0$ and $0 < b < 1$?

A)
B)
C)
D)

LEVEL 5: PROBLEM SOLVING – SCATTERPLOTS

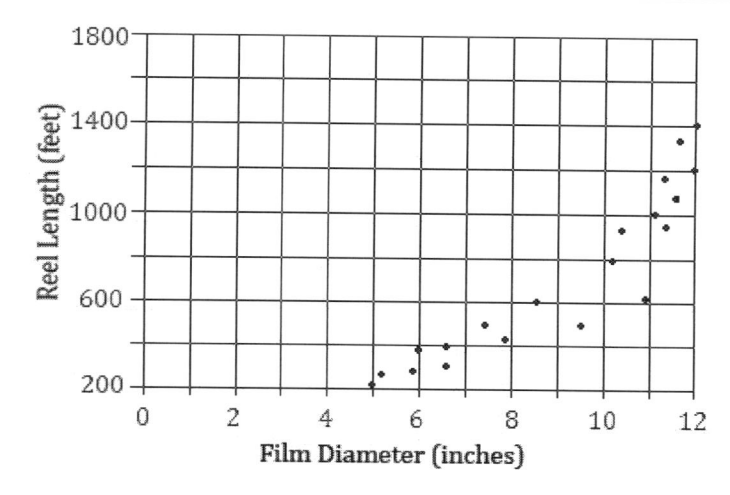

10. * The scatterplot above shows the lengths of several film reels, in feet, versus the diameters of the film on those reels, in inches. Of the following equations, which best models the data in the scatterplot?

A) $y = -14.5x^2 - 112.3x + 430.2$
B) $y = 14.5x^2 - 112.3x + 430.2$
C) $y = -14.5x^2 + 112.3x - 430.2$
D) $y = 14.5x^2 + 112.3x - 430.2$

Answers

1. D 2. A 3. B 4. C 5. D 6. C 7. B 8. D 9. B 10. B

Full Solutions

1.
* A point with approximate coordinates $(0.25, 4)$ appears to be in the scatterplot. 0.25 is the age of the kitten and 4 is the corresponding weight. So, the answer is 4, choice **D**.

195

Notes: (1) We are looking for the weight of the kitten and not the kitten's age. The weight is given by the y-coordinate of the point.

(2) The question implies that we want the *actual* weight of the kitten and not the weight of the kitten that is *predicted* by the line of best fit. The predicted weight of the kitten looks to be closer to 3 (corresponding to the point $(0.25, 3)$ on the line). But the actual weight is the y-coordinate of the point that is *not* on the line of best fit.

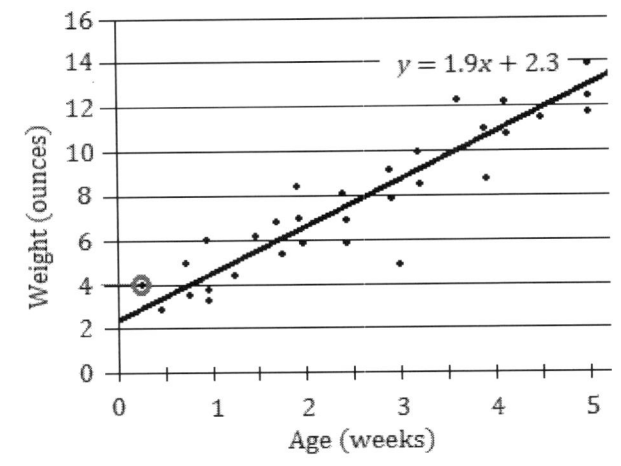

(3) To the right is a picture of the graph with a circle around the appropriate data point needed to answer this question.

    2.
* The data point that is furthest from the line of best fit is at $(3, 5)$. This point represents a kitten with an age of 3 weeks, choice **A**.

    3.
* The equation of the line of best fit is written right over the graph: $y = 1.9x + 2.3$, where x is the age of a kitten, and y is the predicted weight of the same kitten. When the age of a kitten is $x = 6$, we have that the predicted weight of the kitten is $y = 1.9 \cdot 6 + 2.3 = 13.7$, choice **B**.

    4.
* The slope of the line is $\frac{\text{change in weight}}{\text{change in age}}$. If we make the denominator a 1 week increase, then the fraction is the change in weight per 1 week increase. Since the line is moving upward from left to right, we can replace "change" in the numerator by "increase." So, the answer is choice **C**.

Note: Recall that the slope of a line is

$$\text{Slope} = m = \frac{\text{rise}}{\text{run}} = \frac{\text{change in vertical distance}}{\text{change in horizontal distance}}$$

In this problem, the change in vertical distance is the change in weight, in ounces, and the change in horizontal distance is the change in age, in weeks.

    5.
* Only the scatterplot in choice D is continually moving upward from left to right. So, the answer is choice **D**.

    6.
* It looks like the point $(2, 5.5)$ is on the line of best fit. But the answer is NOT 5.5. According to the label on the y-axis and the text in the paragraph, diameters are given in hundreds of kilometers. So, we need to multiply 5.5 by 100 to get $5.5 \cdot 100 = 550$, choice **C**.

7.

* The minimum possible distance will occur if both asteroids are on the same side of the Earth and the centers of the two asteroids and the Earth all lie on the same line (as shown in the figure on the right). In this case, the distance between the two asteroids is about $2.4 - 0.5 = 1.9$ AU. We change this to millions of kilometers by multiplying by 150. We get $1.9 \cdot 150 = 285$, choice **B**.

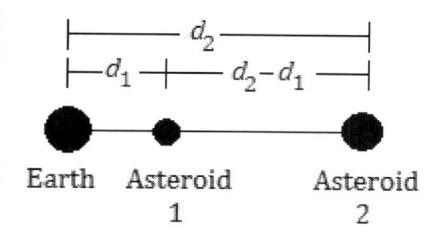

8.

* **Solution by process of elimination:** This is a bit tricky. From the scatterplot, it does seem like asteroids that are further from the Earth tend to be larger than asteroids that are closer to the Earth. This eliminates choices A and B.

Although the asteroids do tend to get larger overall as we move further away from the Earth, there are examples of closer asteroids being larger than asteroids that are further. For example, there is an asteroid that is about 2.2 AU from the Earth that has a smaller diameter than many asteroids whose data points appear to the left of its data point. So, we can eliminate choice C, and the answer is **D**.

9.

* Choices B and C have the basic shape of exponential graphs. Choice B has a base between 0 and 1. So, the answer is choice **B**.

Note: Exponential graphs have one of the basic shapes shown in the figures to the right. The top figure is an exponential graph with $b > 1$, and the bottom figure is an exponential graph with $0 < b < 1$. We can pick values for a and b, and use our graphing calculator to check that we have the right graph. For example, if we let $a = 2$, $b = \frac{1}{3}$, and put $Y1 = 2(\frac{1}{3})\wedge X$ in our graphing calculator, we get a graph like the one in the bottom figure. The scatterplot in choice B is closest to this.

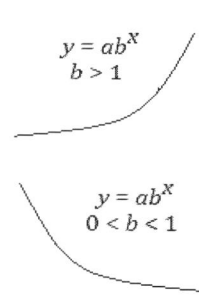

10.

* **Solution by picking a number:** Let's substitute in a value for x to try to eliminate answer choices. It's looks like when $x = 5$, we should get a y-value close to 200. Let's substitute $x = 5$ into each answer choice (using our calculator).

 A) -493.8
 B) 231.2
 C) -231.2
 D) 493.8

Choices A, C, and D did not come out close to 200, and so we can eliminate them. The answer is **B**.

Notes: (1) A function of the form $y = ax^2 + bx + c$ with $a \neq 0$ is called a quadratic function. The graph of a quadratic function is a **parabola**. If $a > 0$, the parabola opens upwards and if $a < 0$, the parabola opens downwards. We will review everything that you need to know about quadratic functions and their graphs in Lesson 42.

(2) The scatterplot given in this problem seems to have the basic shape of an upward facing parabola. So, we might model it with an equation of the form $y = ax^2 + bx + c$, where $a > 0$. Since choices A and C have $a < 0$, their graphs are downward facing parabolas, and so we can eliminate A and C.

LESSON 28 – COMPLEX NUMBERS
OPERATIONS

Are Complex Numbers Really That Complex?

A **complex number** has the form $a + bi$ where a and b are real numbers and $i = \sqrt{-1}$.

Example: The following are complex numbers:

$$3 + 7i \qquad \frac{5}{3} + (-4i) = \frac{5}{3} - 4i \qquad -\pi + 3.7i \qquad \sqrt{-25} = 5i$$

$0 + 8i = 8i$ This is called a **pure imaginary** number.

$12 + 0i = 12$ This is called a **real number.**

$0 + 0i = 0$ This is **zero**.

Addition and subtraction: We add two complex numbers simply by adding their real parts, and then adding their imaginary parts.

$$(a + bi) + (c + di) = (a + c) + (b + d)i$$

Example: $(5 + 2i) + (3 + 7i) = (5 + 3) + (2 + 7)i = \mathbf{8 + 9i}$

Multiplication: We can multiply two complex numbers by formally taking the product of two binomials and then replacing i^2 by -1.

$$(a + bi)(c + di) = (ac - bd) + (ad + bc)i$$

Example: $(5 + 2i)(3 + 7i) = (15 - 14) + (35 + 6)i = \mathbf{1 + 41i}$

The **conjugate** of the complex number $a + bi$ is the complex number $a - bi$.

Example: The conjugate of $5 + 2i$ is $\mathbf{5 - 2i}$.

Note that when we multiply conjugates together we always get a nonnegative real number. In fact, we have

$$(a + bi)(a - bi) = a^2 + b^2$$

Division: We can put the quotient of two complex numbers into standard form by multiplying both the numerator and denominator by the conjugate of the denominator. This is best understood with an example.

Example:

$$\frac{5 + 2i}{3 + 7i} = \frac{(5 + 2i)}{(3 + 7i)} \cdot \frac{(3 - 7i)}{(3 - 7i)} = \frac{(15 + 14) + (-35 + 6)i}{3^2 + 7^2} = \frac{29 - 29i}{9 + 49} = \frac{29 - 29i}{58} = \mathbf{\frac{29}{58} - \frac{29}{58}i}$$

POWERS of i

Since $i = \sqrt{-1}$, we have the following:

$i^2 = \sqrt{-1}\sqrt{-1} = -1$

$i^3 = i^2 i = -1i = -i$

$i^4 = i^2 i^2 = (-1)(-1) = 1$

$i^5 = i^4 i = 1i = i$

Notice that the pattern begins to repeat.

Starting with $i^0 = 1$, we have

$i^0 = 1$	$i^1 = i$	$i^2 = -1$	$i^3 = -i$
$i^4 = 1$	$i^5 = i$	$i^6 = -1$	$i^7 = -i$
$i^8 = 1$	$i^9 = i$	$i^{10} = -1$	$i^{11} = -i$

...

In other words, when we raise i to a nonnegative integer, there are only four possible answers:

$$1, i, -1, \text{ or } -i$$

To decide which of these values is correct, we find the remainder upon dividing the exponent by 4.

LEVEL 4: COMPLEX NUMBERS – OPERATIONS

1. Which of the following is equal to i^{73}?

   A) -1
   B) $-i$
   C) 1
   D) i

* $i^{73} = i^1 = i$ because when we divide 73 be 4 we get a remainder of 1. So, the answer is choice **D**.

Notes: (1) To get the remainder upon dividing 73 by 4, you **cannot** just divide 73 by 4 in your calculator. This computation produces the answer 18.25 which does not say anything about the remainder.

To find a remainder you must either do the division by hand, or use the Calculator Algorithm below.

(2) This computation can also be done quickly in your calculator, but be careful. Your calculator may sometimes "disguise" the number 0 with a tiny number in scientific notation. For example, when we type $i \wedge 73$ ENTER into our TI-84, we get an output of $-2.3\text{E} - 12 + i$. The expression $-2.3\text{E} - 12$ represents a tiny number in scientific notation which is essentially 0. So, it should be read as $0 + i = i$.

(3) Calculator Algorithm for computing a remainder: Although performing division in your calculator never produces a remainder, there is a simple algorithm you can perform which mimics long division. Let's find the remainder when 73 is divided by 4 using this algorithm.

Step 1: Perform the division in your calculator: $73/4 = 18.25$
Step 2: Multiply the integer part of this answer by the divisor: $18 \cdot 4 = 72$
Step 3: Subtract this result from the dividend to get the remainder: $73 - 72 = \mathbf{1}$

Time to Practice

LEVEL 1: COMPLEX NUMBERS – OPERATIONS

2. For $i = \sqrt{-1}$, the sum $(-3 + 2i) + (-5 - 7i)$ is equal to

   A) $-8 + 9i$
   B) $-8 - 5i$
   C) $2 + 9i$
   D) $2 - 5i$

3. If $(-3 + 5i) + (-2 - 7i) = a + bi$ and $i = \sqrt{-1}$, then what is the value of ab?

LEVEL 2: COMPLEX NUMBERS – OPERATIONS

4. When we subtract $7 - i$ from $-3 + 5i$ we get which of the following complex numbers?

   A) $-10 - 6i$
   B) $-10 + 6i$
   C) $4 + 4i$
   D) $4 - 4i$

5. Which of the following complex numbers is equal to $(5i^2 + 3i) - (2 - 7i)$?

   A) $-7 + 10i$
   B) $3 + 4i$
   C) $-3 - 4i$
   D) $7 - 10i$

6. Let a and b be real numbers and $i = \sqrt{-1}$. When we add $a + bi$ to $7 - 2i$, we get $-3 + 5i$. What is the value of b?

LEVEL 3: COMPLEX NUMBERS – OPERATIONS

7. If $i = \sqrt{-1}$, which of the following complex numbers is equivalent to $(5 - 2i)(-2 + 7i)$?

   A) $4 + 39i$
   B) $4 - 39i$
   C) $-10 + 14i$
   D) $-10 - 14i$

LEVEL 4: COMPLEX NUMBERS – OPERATIONS

8. Which of the following complex numbers is equivalent to $\frac{2-3i}{3+5i}$, where $i = \sqrt{-1}$?

   A) $\frac{2}{3} + \frac{3}{5}i$

   B) $\frac{2}{3} - \frac{3}{5}i$

   C) $\frac{9}{34} + \frac{19}{34}i$

   D) $-\frac{9}{34} - \frac{19}{34}i$

$$i^3 + i^4 + i^5 + i^8$$

9. The complex number expression above is equivalent to a real number a. What is the value of a? (Note: $i = \sqrt{-1}$)

LEVEL 5: COMPLEX NUMBERS – OPERATIONS

10. If $(x - 3i)(5 + yi) = 28 - 3i$ then what is one possible value of $x + y$? (Note: $i = \sqrt{-1}$)

Answers

1. D 2. B 3. 10 4. B 5. A 6. 7 7. A 8. D 9. 2 10. 8

Full Solutions

2.
* $(-3 + 2i) + (-5 - 7i) = (-3 - 5) + (2 - 7)i = -8 - 5i$, choice **B**.

3.
* $(-3 + 5i) + (-2 - 7i) = (-3 - 2) + (5 - 7)i = -5 - 2i$. So $a = -5$, $b = -2$, and therefore, $ab = (-5)(-2) = \mathbf{10}$.

4.
* $(-3 + 5i) - (7 - i) = -3 + 5i - 7 + i = -10 + 6i$, choice **B**.

5.
* First note that $i^2 = (\sqrt{-1})^2 = -1$, so that $5i^2 = 5(-1) = -5$. So, we have
$$(5i^2 + 3i) - (2 - 7i) = (-5 + 3i) - (2 - 7i) = -5 + 3i - 2 + 7i = -7 + 10i$$
This is choice **A**.

6.
* **Solution by adding:** We solve the following equation for a.
$$(a + bi) + (7 - 2i) = -3 + 5i$$

We need only the imaginary parts: $b - 2 = 5$. So, $b = 5 + 2 = \mathbf{7}$.

* Solution by subtracting: $(-3 + 5i) - (7 - 2i) = -3 + 5i - 7 + 2i = -10 + 7i$

So, $b = \mathbf{7}$.

7.

* $(5 - 2i)(-2 + 7i) = (-10 + 14) + (35 + 4)i = 4 + 39i$, choice **A**.

Notes: (1) Here we used the following formula for multiplying two complex numbers:
$$(a + bi)(c + di) = (ac - bd) + (ad + bc)i$$
One option is to have this formula memorized, although this is not necessary (see note (3) below).

(2) Since $i = \sqrt{-1}$, it follows that $i^2 = \left(\sqrt{-1}\right)^2 = -1$.

(3) We can multiply the two complex numbers by using the distributive property and letting $i^2 = -1$.
$$(5 - 2i)(-2 + 7i) = (5 - 2i)(-2) + (5 - 2i)(7i)$$
$$= -10 + 4i + 35i - 14i^2 = -10 + 39i - 14(-1) = -10 + 14 + 39i = 4 + 39i$$

(4) We can also use the shortcut of FOILing like many of us do for multiplication of binomials.
$$(5 - 2i)(-2 + 7i) = (5)(-2) + 5(7i) + (-2i)(-2) + (-2i)(7i)$$
$$= -10 + 35i + 4i - 14i^2 = -10 + 39i - 14(-1) = -10 + 14 + 39i = 4 + 39i$$

8.

*
$$\frac{(2 - 3i)}{(3 + 5i)} = \frac{(2 - 3i)}{(3 + 5i)} \cdot \frac{(3 - 5i)}{(3 - 5i)} = \frac{(6 - 15) + (-10 - 9)i}{9 + 25} = \frac{-9 - 19i}{34} = -\frac{9}{34} - \frac{19}{34}i$$

The answer is choice **D**.

9.

* $i^3 = -i$, $i^4 = 1$, $i^5 = i$, and $i^8 = 1$. So, $i^3 + i^4 + i^5 + i^8 = -i + 1 + i + 1 = \mathbf{2}$.

Note: See problem 1 above for details on how to raise i to the various powers that appear in this question.

10.

* $(x - 3i)(5 + yi) = (5x + 3y) + (xy - 15)i$. So, $5x + 3y = 28$ and $xy - 15 = -3$. Therefore, $xy = 12$. We need to solve the following system of equations:
$$5x + 3y = 28$$
$$xy = 12$$
There are several ways to solve this formally, but we can also just try guessing. We are looking for two numbers that multiply to 12. If we try $x = 2$ and $y = 6$, then we have
$$5x + 3y = 5(2) + 3(6) = 10 + 18 = 28$$
So, a possible solution to the system is $x = 2$, $y = 6$, and in this case, $x + y = \mathbf{8}$.

LESSON 29 – HEART OF ALGEBRA
ADDITIONAL PRACTICE 2

Full solutions to these problems are available for free download here:
www.SATPrepGet800.com/48SATy5

LEVEL 1

1. If $y = \frac{3}{5}x + 1$ and $x = 20$, what is the value of $x - y$?

   A) 7
   B) 13
   C) 17
   D) 22

2. The formula $d = rt$ is used to find the distance an object travels over a span of time, t, at a constant rate, r. What is the time, t, expressed in terms of d and r.

   A) $t = dr$
   B) $t = \frac{d}{r}$
   C) $t = \frac{r}{d}$
   D) $t = d - r$

LEVEL 2

3. Saline solution X contains 10% salt and saline solution Y contains 15% salt. Together, the 2 solutions contain a total of 5 ounces of salt. Which of the following equations models this relationship, where x is the number of ounces of saline solution X and y is the number of ounces of saline solution Y?

   A) $0.1x + 0.15y = 5$
   B) $0.15x + 0.1y = 5$
   C) $10x + 15y = 5$
   D) $15x + 10y = 5$

$$A = 17t + 20$$

4. After making an initial deposit into a savings account in January, Candice proceeded to deposit a fixed amount of money into the same savings account each month, beginning in February. The equation above models the amount A, in dollars, that Candice has deposited after t monthly deposits. According to the model, how many dollars was Candice's initial deposit? (Disregard the $ sign when gridding your answer.)

LEVEL 3

5. The line k in the xy-plane contains points from each of Quadrants I and IV, but no points from Quadrants II and III. Which of the following must be true?

   A) The slope of line k is positive.
   B) The slope of line k is negative.
   C) The slope of line k is zero.
   D) The slope of line k is undefined.

6. Which of the following mathematical expressions is equivalent to the verbal expression "A number, k, doubled is 24 less than the product of k and 3"?

   A) $2k = 3k - 24$
   B) $k^2 = 3k - 24$
   C) $2k = 24 - 3k$
   D) $2k = 24 + 3k$

$$3(7x - 15) - (11 - 3x) = 4$$

7. What value of x satisfies the equation above?

8. When 11 is decreased by $3x$, the result is more than 5. What is the greatest possible integer value for x?

LEVEL 4

9. In the xy-plane, the line determined by the points $(5a, 3)$ and $(15, a)$ passes through the origin. Which of the following could be the value of a ?

   A) -3
   B) 0
   C) 2
   D) 6

10. A person's weight on the Moon increases by approximately 1 pound for each 6 pound increase on Earth, and a person that weighs 102 pounds on Earth weighs approximately 17 pounds on the Moon. Which of the following equations best models the relationship between the weight of a person on Earth, e, and the weight of the person on the moon, m ?

    A) $e = 6m$
    B) $e = \frac{m}{6}$
    C) $e = 6m + 102$
    D) $e = \frac{m}{6} + 102$

11. * The monthly membership fee for a fitness center is $49.99. The cost includes the usage of all equipment and classes with the exception of Pilates classes for which there is an additional fee of $1.30 per class. For one month, Cindy's total membership fees were $68.19. How many Pilates classes did Cindy take that month?

LEVEL 5

12. * The ionosphere is the layer of the earth's atmosphere that contains a high concentration of ions and free electrons and is able to reflect radio waves. It lies between about 40 to 620 miles above the Earth's surface. At a distance of 40 miles above the Earth's surface, the temperature is $-100°$ Fahrenheit, and at a distance of 600 miles above the Earth's surface, the temperature is $440°$ Fahrenheit. Given that the relationship between the distance above the Earth's surface, d, and the temperature, t, is linear, which of the following equations relates t and d ?

    A) $d - t = 140$
    B) $27d - 8t = 1880$
    C) $d - 28t = 2840$
    D) $27d - 28t = 3880$

Answers

1. A   2. B   3. A   4. 20   5. D   6. A   7. 5/2, 2.5   8. 1   9. A   10. A   11. 14   12. D

LESSON 30 – PASSPORT TO ADVANCED MATH
ADDITIONAL PRACTICE 2

Full solutions to these problems are available for free download here:
www.SATPrepGet800.com/48SATy5

LEVEL 1

$$f(x) = 5x^2 - 7$$
$$g(x) = \frac{2}{3}x^3 + 5$$

1. The functions f and g are defined above. What is the value of $g(3) - f(1)$?

LEVEL 2

k	-2	2	3
$f(k)$	-7	1	3

2. The table above shows some values of the linear function f. Which of the following defines f ?

   A) $f(k) = k - 3$
   B) $f(k) = 2k - 3$
   C) $f(k) = 2k - 7$
   D) $f(k) = 4k - 1$

LEVEL 3

3. Which of the following is equivalent to $18a^4 - 32b^2$?

   A) $(9a^2 - 16b)(9a^2 + 16b)$
   B) $2(3a^2 - 4b)(3a^2 + 4b)$
   C) $2(6a^2 - 8b)(6a^2 + 8b)$
   D) $2(a^2 - 4b)(9a^2 + 4b)$

4. If $\sqrt{16} + \sqrt{k} = \sqrt{49}$, what is the value of k ?

   A) $\sqrt{3}$
   B) 3
   C) 9
   D) 3

$$\frac{x-y}{y} = z$$

5. In the equation above, if x and y are both negative, which of the following must be true?

   A) $z < -1$
   B) $z = -1$
   C) $z > -1$
   D) $z > 1$

LEVEL 4

6. If $xy = z$ and $x^2 + y^2 = w$, which of the following is equivalent to $w - 2z$?

   A) $(x+y)^2$
   B) $(x-y)^2$
   C) $(2x-2y)^2$
   D) $2(x-y)^2$

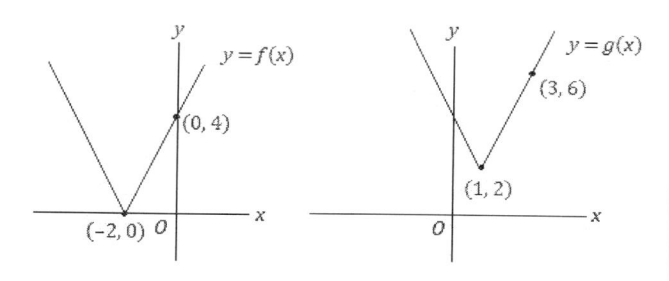

7. A cone has volume V, height h, and base diameter d. Which of the following represents d in terms of V and h?

   A) $d = 2\sqrt{V\pi h}$
   B) $d = \sqrt{\dfrac{V}{3\pi h}}$
   C) $d = \sqrt{\dfrac{3V}{\pi h}}$
   D) $d = 2\sqrt{\dfrac{3V}{\pi h}}$

$$x^3 + x^2 + x - 3 = (x-1)(x^2 + kx + 3)$$

8. In the equation above, k is a constant. If the equation is true for all values of x, what is the value of k?

LEVEL 5

9. The expression $\frac{7x-3}{x+4}$ is equivalent to which of the following?

    A) $\frac{7-3}{4}$

    B) $7 - \frac{3}{4}$

    C) $7 - \frac{3}{x+4}$

    D) $7 - \frac{31}{x+4}$

10. If $\frac{(x^a)^b x^c}{x^d} = x^4$ for all $x \neq 0$, which of the following must be true?

    A) $ab + c - d = 4$

    B) $\frac{ab+c}{d} = 4$

    C) $ab - cd = 4$

    D) $ab - c^d = 4$

11. The figures above show the graphs of the functions f and g. The function f is defined by $f(x) = 2|x+2|$ and the function g is defined by $g(x) = f(x+h) + k$, where h and k are constants. What is the value of $|h-k|$?

$$\frac{7}{x+1} - \frac{3x-5}{(x+1)^2}$$

12. The expression above is equivalent to $\frac{ax+b}{(x+1)^2}$, where $x \neq -1$ and a and b are positive constants. What is the value of ab?

Answers

1. 25   2. B   3. B   4. C   5. C   6. B   7. D   8. 2   9. D   10. A   11. 5   12. 48

LESSON 31 – PROBLEM SOLVING
ADDITIONAL PRACTICE 2

Full solutions to these problems are available for free download here:
www.SATPrepGet800.com/48SATy5

LEVEL 1

1. If a 6-pound quiche is cut into three equal pieces and each of those pieces is cut into four equal pieces, what is the weight, in ounces, of each piece of quiche?
   (1 pound = 16 ounces)

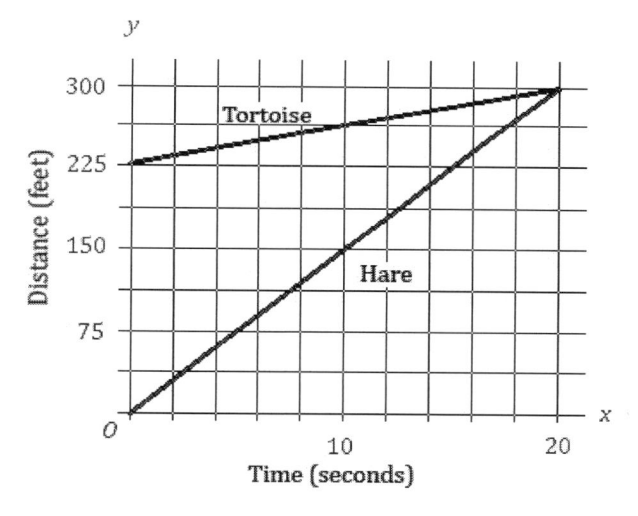

2. A tortoise and a hare had a race. The tortoise was given a head start and each ran at a constant rate. Both animals finished the race in 20 seconds, and so the result was a tie. The graph above shows the positions of the tortoise and the hare throughout the race. According to the graph, the tortoise was given a head start of how many feet?

LEVEL 2

3. * The distance traveled by Venus in one orbit around the Sun is about 420,000,000 miles. Venus makes one complete orbit around the sun in approximately seven Earth months. Of the following, which is the closest to the average speed of Venus, in miles per hour, as it orbits the Sun?

   A) 60,000
   B) 85,000
   C) 100,000
   D) 200,000

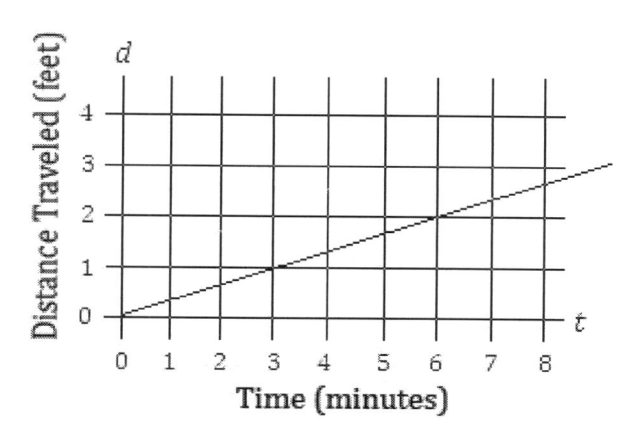

4. The graph above shows the distance travelled d, in feet, by a freight elevator t minutes after the freight elevator begins moving. Which of the following equations gives the correct relationship between d and t ?

   A) $d = \frac{1}{3}t$
   B) $d = 3t$
   C) $d = t + 3$
   D) $d = 3t + 3$

LEVEL 3

Age of 16 Tigers in a Sanctuary	
Age	Frequency
15	3
16	4
17	2
18	3
19	2
20	2

5. * The table above shows the distribution of the ages of 16 tigers, in years, living in an animal sanctuary. Which of the following gives the correct order of the mean, median, and mode of the tigers' ages?

   A) median < mode < mean
   B) mean < mode < median
   C) mode < mean < median
   D) mode < median < mean

6. Which of the following graphs best shows a strong negative association between x and y?

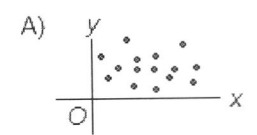

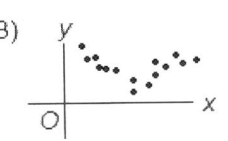

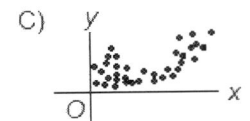

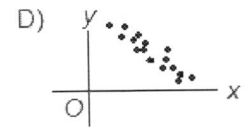

   A)
   B)
   C)
   D)

LEVEL 4

7. A study was done on the flight speed of different types of birds in a sanctuary. A random sample of birds was selected and these birds were implanted with a tracker. 200 albatrosses were part of the sample, and it was observed that 25% of them flew faster than 75 miles per hour. Which of the following conclusions is best supported by the sample data?

   A) The average flight speed of all birds in the sanctuary is approximately 75 miles per hour.
   B) Most birds in the sanctuary cannot fly faster than 75 miles per hour.
   C) Approximately 25% of all albatrosses in the sanctuary can fly faster than 75 miles per hour.
   D) Approximately 25% of all birds in the sanctuary can fly faster than 75 miles per hour.

Questions 8 - 12 refer to the following information.

Machine	Depreciation Rate
Machine A	2.3%
Machine B	3.1%
Machine C	1.7%
Machine D	4.2%

To estimate the current value, V, of a machine, we use the formula $V = P\left(1 - \frac{r}{100}\right)^t$, where P is the original price of the machine, r is the approximate depreciation rate of the machine, and t is the age of the machine, in years. The table above gives the approximate depreciation rates for four different machines.

8. * Machine C is 3 years old and its original price was $5000. According to the information in the table, which of the following is closest to the current value of Machine C?

   A) $4951.28
   B) $4749.31
   C) $4549.27
   D) $4396.09

9. * If Machine A had an original price of $50,000, and now has a value of $47,750, which of the following will be closest to the age of Machine A, in years?

   A) 1
   B) 2
   C) 3
   D) 4

10. * A machine had an original price of $7500 four years ago, and its current value is $6612.36. The machine is most likely to be which of the following?

    A) Machine A
    B) Machine B
    C) Machine C
    D) Machine D

LEVEL 5

11. * If Machines A and B both have original values of $2000, which of the following will be closest to the difference, in dollars, of their prices when they are each 7 years old?

    A) $85
    B) $90
    C) $95
    D) $100

211

Machine Age versus Value

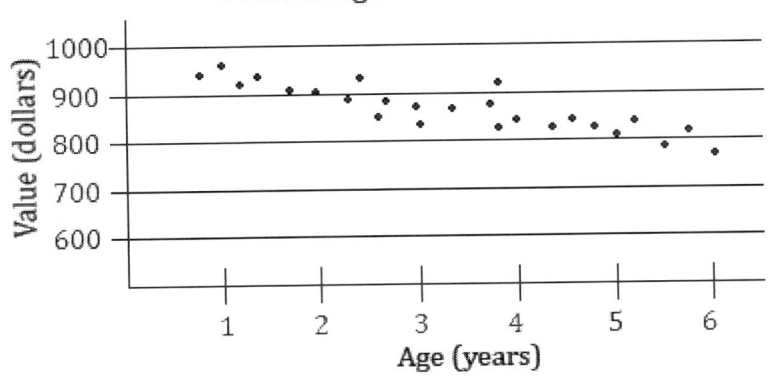

12. * The scatterplot above gives the age of 25 machines with original prices of $1000 plotted against their values. The depreciation rates of these machines are most likely closest to that of which of the following machines?

    A) Machine A
    B) Machine B
    C) Machine C
    D) Machine D

Answers

1. 8   2. 225   3. B   4. A   5. D   6. D   7. C   8. B   9. B   10. B   11. C   12. D

LESSON 32 – GEOMETRY AND COMPLEX NUMBERS
ADDITIONAL PRACTICE 2

Full solutions to these problems are available for free download here:
www.SATPrepGet800.com/48SATy5

LEVEL 1

1. In the standard (x, y) coordinate plane, point M with coordinates $(3, 7)$ is the midpoint of $\overline{PQ}$, and P has coordinates $(1, 9)$. What are the coordinates of Q?

   A) $(5, 5)$
   B) $(-5, -5)$
   C) $(-1, 11)$
   D) $(4, 16)$

2. The circular base of a cone has a radius of 5 inches and the height of the cone is 3 inches. Which of the following is equal to the volume of the cone?

   A) 25
   B) 75
   C) 25π
   D) 75π

3. If $(7 - i) + (-1 + 3i) = a + bi$ and $i = \sqrt{-1}$, then what is the value of $\frac{a}{b}$?

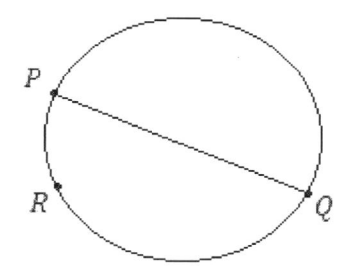

LEVEL 2

4. In the circle above, segment PQ is a diameter. If the length of arc $\overparen{PRQ}$ is 5π, what is the length of the diameter of the circle?

   A) 5
   B) 8
   C) 10
   D) 12

LEVEL 3

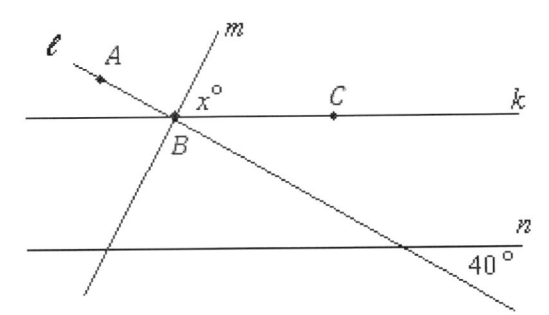

Note: Figure not drawn to scale.

5. In the figure above, line k is parallel to line n. If line m bisects angle ABC, what is the value of x ?

6. The height of a solid cone is 22 centimeters and the radius of the base is 15 centimeters. A cut parallel to the circular base is made completely through the cone so that one of the two resulting solids is a smaller cone. If the radius of the base of the small cone is 5 centimeters, what is the height of the small cone, in centimeters?

LEVEL 4

7. A cylindrical container contains various kinds of beans. The container is filled to the top with a liquid broth. The height of the container is 10 inches and the base of the container has a diameter of 5 inches. If exactly 182 cubic inches of broth is needed to completely fill the container, which of the following is the closest to the total volume of beans in the container, in cubic inches?

   A) 7
   B) 14
   C) 30
   D) 50

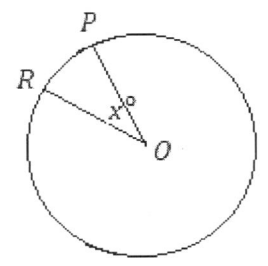

Note: Figure not drawn to scale.

8. In the figure above, O is the center of the circle, and the length of arc $\widehat{PR}$ is $\frac{2}{9}$ of the circumference of the circle. What is the value of x ?

214

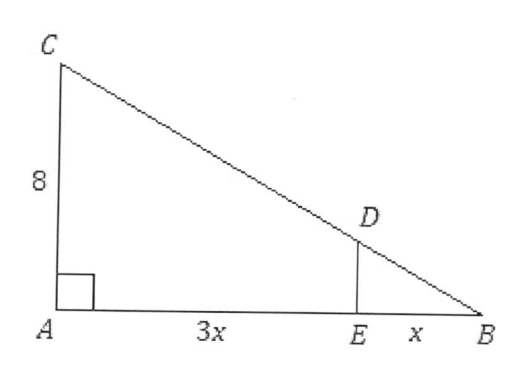

9. In the figure above, $\overline{AC} \parallel \overline{DE}$. What is the length of $\overline{DE}$?

10. If j and k are real numbers, $i = \sqrt{-1}$, and $(j - k) + 6i = 5 + ki$, what is jk ?

LEVEL 5

11. If a and b are real numbers, and $i = \sqrt{-1}$, which of the following must also be a real number?

    A) $(a + 2bi)^2$
    B) $(a - 2bi)(a + 2bi)$
    C) $ai^3 + 2bi^2$
    D) $\frac{a+2bi}{a-2bi}$

12. The lengths of the sides of a triangle are x, 3, and 5, where x is the shortest side. If the triangle is not isosceles, what is a possible value of x ?

Answers

1. A   2. C   3. 3   4. C   5. 70   6. 22/3, 7.33   7. B   8. 80   9. 2   10. 66   11. B   12. $2 < x < 3$

215

LESSON 33 – HEART OF ALGEBRA
SOLVING LINEAR SYSTEMS OF EQUATIONS

Two Linear Equations?! We Got This!

There are many different ways to solve linear systems of equations. In the solutions below, we will learn to solve linear systems using **substitution**, **elimination**, Gauss-Jordan Reduction, **graphical analysis**, and sometimes just **plugging in the answer choices** (see problem 4 below for all these).

LEVEL 1: HEART OF ALGEBRA – SOLVING LINEAR SYSTEMS OF EQUATIONS

$$y = 3 - x$$
$$2x = 6$$

1. Which of the following ordered pairs (x, y) satisfies the system of equations above?

   A) $(3, -1)$
   B) $(3, 0)$
   C) $(3, 1)$
   D) $(3, 2)$

LEVEL 2: HEART OF ALGEBRA – SOLVING LINEAR SYSTEMS OF EQUATIONS

2. If $x - y = 7$ and $\frac{x}{5} = 3$, what is the value of $x + y$?

   A) 18
   B) 20
   C) 21
   D) 23

LEVEL 3: HEART OF ALGEBRA – SOLVING LINEAR SYSTEMS OF EQUATIONS

$$\frac{2x}{3y} = 4$$
$$3(x - 2) = 6y$$

3. The system of equations above has solution (x, y). What is the value of x ?

   A) $\frac{1}{2}$
   B) 1
   C) 3
   D) 6

$$6x - 3y = -21$$
$$5y - x = -10$$

4. What is the solution (x, y) to the system of equations above?

    A) $(3, -5)$
    B) $(5, -3)$
    C) $(-5, -3)$
    D) $(-3, 5)$

5. An adoption center has puppies and kittens. The adoption fee for a puppy is $250 and the adoption fee for a kitten is $150. One Saturday, a total of 20 puppies and kittens were adopted for a total cost of $3700. How many kittens were adopted on this particular Saturday?

    A) 5
    B) 7
    C) 11
    D) 13

LEVEL 4: HEART OF ALGEBRA – SOLVING LINEAR SYSTEMS OF EQUATIONS

$$5x - 3y = 4$$
$$5x + 4y = 7$$

6. * For the solution (x, y) to the system of equations above, what is the value of xy, rounded to the nearest tenth?

$$s = 21.7 + 5p$$
$$d = 35.3 - 3p$$

7. In the equations above, s and d represent the supply (the quantity supplied) and demand (the quantity demanded), in units, of a product with a price of p dollars. What is the price when the supply is equal to the demand?

8. * A Mexican restaurant sells quesadillas for $8.25 each and tacos for $4.50 each. The restaurant's revenue from selling a total of 89 quesadillas and tacos in eight hours was $498. How many quesadillas were sold during that eight-hour period?

LEVEL 5: HEART OF ALGEBRA – SOLVING LINEAR SYSTEMS OF EQUATIONS

$$5x + 3 + c = 2x$$
$$5y + 3 + d = 2y$$

9. In the equations above, c and d are constants. If d is c minus $\frac{1}{4}$, which of the following is true?

   A) x is y minus $\frac{1}{4}$.
   B) x is y minus $\frac{1}{12}$.
   C) x is y plus $\frac{1}{4}$.
   D) x is y plus $\frac{1}{12}$.

10. If $2x = 7 - 3y$ and $5y = 5 - 3x$, what is the value of x?

Answers

1. B 2. D 3. C 4. C 5. D 6. 1/2, .5 7. 1.7 8. 26 9. B 10. 20

Full Solutions

1.
* Solution by plugging in: Since the ordered pairs in all the answer choices have $x = 3$, we can just substitute 3 for x into the first equation and solve for y. We get $y = 3 - x = 3 - 3 = 0$. So, the answer is $(3, 0)$, choice **B**.

Complete algebraic solution: We divide each side of the second equation by 2 to get $x = \frac{6}{2} = 3$. We then substitute $x = 3$ into the first equation to get $y = 3 - 3 = 0$. So, the answer is $(3, 0)$, choice **B**.

2.
Algebraic solution: We multiply each side of the second equation by 5 to get $x = 3 \cdot 5 = 15$. We now substitute $x = 15$ into the first equation to get $15 - y = 7$. Since $15 - 8 = 7$, we have $y = 8$. Finally, $x + y = 15 + 8 = 23$, choice **D**.

Note: In the solution above, we solved the equation $15 - y = 7$ informally. We can also solve this equation formally by first subtracting 15 from each side to get $-y = 7 - 15 = -8$, and then multiplying each side of this last equation by -1 to get $y = 8$.

3.
* Solution by starting with choice C: Let's start with choice C and guess that $x = 3$. Then the first equation becomes $\frac{2 \cdot 3}{3y} = 4$, or equivalently $\frac{2}{y} = 4$. Multiplying each side of this equation by y gives us $2 = 4y$. We divide each side of this equation by 4 to get $y = \frac{2}{4} = \frac{1}{2}$.

218

Now, we substitute $x = 3$ and $y = \frac{1}{2}$ into the second equation and we get $3(3-2) = 6 \cdot \frac{1}{2}$, or equivalently, $3 = 3$. Since this is true, the answer is choice **C**.

Algebraic solution: We multiply each side of the first equation by $3y$ to get $2x = 12y$. We distribute the left-hand side of the second equation to get $3x - 6 = 6y$. We can multiply each side of the equation $2x = 12y$ by $\frac{1}{2}$ to get $x = 6y$. So, we have $6y = x$ and $6y = 3x - 6$. So, $x = 3x - 6$. Thus, $2x = 6$, and therefore, $x = \frac{6}{2} = 3$, choice **C**.

4.
Solution by starting with choice C: Let's plug the point $(-5, -3)$ into the left-hand side of the second equation. We get $5(-3) - (-5) = -15 + 5 = -10$. This is correct. Let's check the first equation: $6(-5) - 3(-3) = -30 + 9 = -21$. This works too. So, the answer is choice **C**.

* **Solution using the elimination method:** Let's start by lining up the equations properly. We do this by rewriting $5y - x$ as $-x + 5y$ in the second equation.

$$6x - 3y = -21$$
$$-x + 5y = -10$$

We now multiply the second equation by 6 and add the two equations:

$$6x - 3y = -21$$
$$\underline{-6x + 30y = -60}$$
$$27y = -81$$

So, $y = \frac{-81}{27} = -3$.

We now substitute -3 for y into the second equation. We get $5(-3) - x = -10$. Therefore, $-15 - x = -10$. We add x and add 10 to each side of the equation to get $-5 = x$.

So, we have $x = -5$ and $y = -3$. The answer is therefore $(-5, -3)$, choice **C**.

Note: We chose to use 6 because multiplying by this number makes the x column "match up" so that when we add the two equations in the next step the x term vanishes.

Solution using Gauss-Jordan reduction (this solution requires a calculator): As in the previous solution, we first make sure the two equations are "lined up" properly.

$$6x - 3y = -21$$
$$-x + 5y = -10$$

Begin by pushing the MATRIX button (which is 2ND x^{-1}). Scroll over to EDIT and then select [A] (or press 1). We will be inputting a 2 × 3 matrix, so press 2 ENTER 3 ENTER. We then begin entering the numbers 6, −3, and −21 for the first row, and −1, 5, and −10 for the second row. To do this we can simply type 6 ENTER −3 ENTER −21 ENTER −1 ENTER 5 ENTER −10 ENTER.

Note: What we have just done was create the **augmented matrix** for the system of equations. This is simply an array of numbers which contains the coefficients of the variables together with the right-hand sides of the equations.

Now push the QUIT button (2ND MODE) to get a blank screen. Press MATRIX again. This time scroll over to MATH and select rref((or press B). Then press MATRIX again and select [A] (or press 1) and press ENTER.

Note: What we have just done is put the matrix into **reduced row echelon form**. In this form, we can read off the solution to the original system of equations.

Warning: Be careful to use the rref(button (2 r's), and not the ref(button (which has only one r).

The display will show the following.
$$[\,[1\ 0 - 5]$$
$$[0\ 1 - 3]\,]$$

The first line is interpreted as $x = -5$ and the second line as $y = -3$. So, the answer is choice **C**.

Note: We can solve the problem this way only if a calculator is allowed, of course.

Solution using substitution: We solve the second equation for x by adding x and adding 10 to each side of the equation to get $x = 5y + 10$. We then substitute this expression for x into the first equation: $6(5y + 10) - 3y = -21$. The left-hand side of this equation simplifies to $30y + 60 - 3y = 27y + 60$. So, we have $27y + 60 = -21$. Subtracting 60 from each side of this equation gives us $27y = -21 - 60 = -81$. We now divide by 27 to get $y = -\frac{81}{27} = -3$. Finally, we have $x = 5y + 10 = 5(-3) + 10 = -15 + 10 = -5$, so that the answer is $(-5, -3)$, choice **C**.

Graphical solution: We begin by solving each equation for y.

$$-3y = -21 - 6x \qquad\qquad 5y = -10 + x$$
$$y = 7 + 2x \qquad\qquad y = -2 + \frac{x}{5}$$

In your graphing calculator press the Y = button, and enter the following.
$$Y1 = 7 + 2X$$
$$Y2 = -2 + X/5$$

Now press ZOOM 6 to graph these two lines in a standard window. Then press 2nd TRACE (which is CALC) 5 (or select INTERSECT). Then press ENTER 3 times. You will see that the point of intersection of the two lines is $(-5, -3)$, choice **C**.

5.
* Solution using the elimination method: We let p be the number of puppies that were adopted and we let k be the number of kittens that were adopted. We are given the following system of equations.

$$p + k = 20$$
$$250p + 150k = 3700$$

We now multiply the first equation by -250 and add the two equations:

$$-250p - 250k = -5000$$
$$250p + 150k = 3700$$
$$-100k = -1300$$

So, $k = \frac{-1300}{-100} = 13$, choice **D**.

Note: The system of equations that we got here can also be solved by Gauss-Jordan reduction if a calculator is allowed for this problem.

Solution by starting with choice C: We start with choice C and guess that 11 kittens were adopted on Saturday. It follows that $20 - 11 = 9$ puppies were adopted on Saturday. The cost of all the puppies is $250 \cdot 9 = 2250$ dollars, and the cost of all the kittens is $150 \cdot 11 = 1650$ dollars. So, the total cost is $2250 + 1650 = 3900$ dollars. This is too big, and so there must have been more kittens (because kittens are less expensive). The answer is therefore choice **D**.

Note: For completeness, let's verify that choice D is correct. If 13 kittens were adopted, then the number of puppies adopted was $20 - 13 = 7$. The cost of all the puppies is $250 \cdot 7 = 1750$ dollars, and the cost of all the kittens is $150 \cdot 13 = 1950$, So, the total cost is $1750 + 1950 = 3700$ dollars. This is correct, and so the answer is choice D.

6.
Solution using the elimination method: We multiply the first equation by -1 and add the two equations.

$$-5x + 3y = -4$$
$$5x + 4y = 7$$
$$7y = 3$$

So, $y = \frac{3}{7}$. We substitute this value for y back into either of the original equations to find x. Let's use the first equation. We get $5x - 3 \cdot \frac{3}{7} = 4$. Multiplying each side of this equation by 7 gives us $35x - 9 = 28$. Adding 9 to each side of this equation yields $35x = 28 + 9 = 37$. We now divide each side of this last equation by 35 to get $x = \frac{37}{35}$.

Finally, we use our calculator to get $xy = \frac{37}{35} \cdot \frac{3}{7} \approx 0.45306$. To the nearest tenth, this is **.5**.

Notes: (1) We chose to multiply the first equation by -1 because this makes the x column "match up" so that when we add the two equations in the next step the x term vanishes. We could have multiplied the second equation by -1 instead.

(2) Instead of multiplying by -1 and adding, we could have saved a step by subtracting one of the equations from the other. Even though this is quicker, I prefer to multiply by -1 and add because you are less likely to make a computational error this way.

(3) Instead of plugging $y = \frac{3}{7}$ back into one of the equations, we could have started from the original two equations and used elimination again to find y. In this case, we could multiply the first equation by 4 and the second equation by 3, and then add the two equations.

* (4) Since we're allowed to use a calculator, and the final answer will be an approximation, Guass-Jordan reduction is probably the best method to use for this particular problem. I leave the details of this solution to the reader. Use the solution from problem 4 for guidance.

7.

* **Algebraic solution:** We set s equal to d to get $21.7 + 5p = 35.3 - 3p$. We now add $3p$ to each side of the equation and subtract 21.7 from each side of the equation to get $8p = 13.6$. We divide each side of this last equation by 8 to get $p = \frac{13.6}{8} = \mathbf{1.7}$.

8.

* **Solution using the elimination method:** Let's let x be the number of quesadillas sold, and y the number of tacos sold. Then we are given the following system of equations.

$$x + y = 89$$
$$8.25x + 4.50y = 498$$

We will now multiply each side of the first equation by -4.50.

$$-4.50(x + y) = (89)(-4.50)$$
$$8.25x + 4.50y = 498$$

Do not forget to distribute correctly on the left. Add the two equations.

$$-4.50x - 4.50y = -400.5$$
$$\underline{8.25x + 4.50y = 498}$$
$$3.75x = 97.5$$

We divide each side of this last equation by 3.75 to get $x = \frac{97.5}{3.75} = \mathbf{26}$.

Notes: (1) We chose to multiply the first equation by -4.50 because multiplying by this number makes the y column "match up" so that when we add the two equations in the next step the y term vanishes.

(2) If we wanted to find y instead of x we would multiply the first equation by -8.25. In general, if you are looking for only one variable, try to eliminate the one you are **not** looking for.

(3) We chose to multiply by a negative number so that we could add the equations instead of subtracting them. We could have also multiplied the first equation by 4.50, and subtracted (in either order).

(4) Gauss-Jordan reduction would also work very well to solve this problem.

9.

* **Solution using the elimination method:** We begin by replacing d by $c - \frac{1}{4}$, and interchanging the order of the two equations.

$$5y + 3 + c - \frac{1}{4} = 2y$$
$$5x + 3 + c \phantom{- \frac{1}{4}} = 2x$$

We then subtract the bottom equation from the top equation to get $5y - 5x - \frac{1}{4} = 2y - 2x$. We solve this last equation for x by adding $5x$ to and subtracting $2y$ from each side of the equation. This gives us $3y - \frac{1}{4} = 3x$. Finally, we multiply each side of this last equation by $\frac{1}{3}$ to get

$$x = \frac{1}{3}\left(3y - \frac{1}{4}\right) = \frac{1}{3} \cdot 3y - \frac{1}{3} \cdot \frac{1}{4} = y - \frac{1}{12}$$

So x is y minus $\frac{1}{12}$, choice **B**.

10.

* Solution using the elimination method: We begin by making sure that the two equations are "lined up" properly. We do this by adding $3y$ to each side of the first equation, and adding $3x$ to each side of the second equation.

$$2x + 3y = 7$$
$$3x + 5y = 5$$

We now multiply each side of the first equation by 5, and each side of the second equation by -3. And then we add the two equations.

$$\begin{aligned} 10x + 15y &= 35 \\ -9x - 15y &= -15 \\ \hline x &= 20 \end{aligned}$$

Note: We chose to use 5 and -3 because multiplying by these numbers makes the y column "match up" so that when we add the two equations in the next step the y term vanishes. We could have also used -5 and 3. And we could also have used 5 and 3, and then subtracted.

LESSON 34 – PASSPORT TO ADVANCED MATH
SOLVING QUADRATIC EQUATIONS

Let's Get Back to Our Square Roots

The **square root property** says that if $x^2 = a^2$, then $x = \pm a$.

For example, the equation $x^2 = 36$ has the two solutions $x = 6$ and $x = -6$.

Important note: Using the square root property is different from taking a square root. We apply the square root property to an equation of the form $x^2 = a^2$ to get two solutions, whereas when we take the positive square root of a number we get just one answer.

For example, when we take the positive square root of 36 we get 6, i.e., $\sqrt{36} = 6$. But when we apply the square root property to the equation $x^2 = 36$, we have seen that we get the two solutions $x = 6$ and $x = -6$.

Example: Solve the equation $(x-5)^2 = 3$ using the square root property.

Solution: When we apply the square root property we get $x - 5 = \pm\sqrt{3}$. We then add 5 to each side of this last equation to get the two solutions $x = 5 \pm \sqrt{3}$.

Completing the Square

Completing the square is a technique with many useful applications. We complete the square on an expression of the form $x^2 + bx$, where b is a constant.

To complete the square, we simply take half of b, and then square the result to get $\left(\frac{b}{2}\right)^2$.

The expression $x^2 + bx + \left(\frac{b}{2}\right)^2$ is always a perfect square. In fact,

$$x^2 + bx + \left(\frac{b}{2}\right)^2 = \left(x + \frac{b}{2}\right)^2$$

For example, let's complete the square in the expression $x^2 + 6x$.

Well half of 6 is 3, and when we square 3 we get 9. So, the new expression is $x^2 + 6x + 9$ which factors as $(x+3)^2$.

Important notes: (1) When we complete the square we usually get an expression that is NOT equal to the original expression. For example, $x^2 + 6x \neq x^2 + 6x + 9$.

(2) The coefficient of x^2 <u>must</u> be 1 before we complete the square. So, for example, we cannot complete the square on the expression $2x^2 + 32x$.

But we can first factor out the 2 to get $2(x^2 + 16x)$, and then complete the square on the expression $x^2 + 16x$ to get $2(x^2 + 16x + 64) = 2(x+8)^2$. Note that we increased the expression by $2 \cdot 64 = 128$.

Solving Quadratic Equations

A **quadratic equation** has the form $ax^2 + bx + c = 0$, where $a \neq 0$.

There are many different ways to solve quadratic equations, such as **factoring, the quadratic formula, completing the square, graphically,** and sometimes just by **guessing** or **plugging in answer choices**.

Let's use a simple example to illustrate the various methods for solving such an equation

LEVEL 3: PASSPORT TO ADVANCED MATH – SOLVING QUADRATIC EQUATIONS

$$x^2 - 2x = 15$$

1. In the quadratic equation above, find the positive solution for x.

Solution by guessing: We plug in guesses for x until we find the answer. For example, if we guess that $x = 3$, then $3^2 - 2 \cdot 3 = 9 - 6 = 3$. This is too small.

Let's try $x = 5$ next. We get $5^2 - 2 \cdot 5 = 25 - 10 = 15$. This is correct. So, the answer is **5**.

Solution by factoring: The given equation is equivalent to $x^2 - 2x - 15 = 0$. We then factor the left-hand side to get $(x-5)(x+3) = 0$. We now set each factor equal to zero and solve each of these equations for x. So, we have $x - 5 = 0$ or $x + 3 = 0$. It follows that $x = 5$ or $x = -3$. Since we want the positive solution for x, the answer is **5**.

Solution by using the quadratic formula: As in the last solution we bring everything to the left-hand side of the equation to get $\quad x^2 - 2x - 15 = 0$.

We identify $a = 1$, $b = -2$, and $c = -15$.

$$x = \frac{-b \pm \sqrt{b^2 - 4ac}}{2a} = \frac{2 \pm \sqrt{4 + 60}}{2} = \frac{2 \pm \sqrt{64}}{2} = \frac{2 \pm 8}{2} = \frac{2}{2} \pm \frac{8}{2} = 1 \pm 4$$

So, we get $x = 1 + 4 = 5$ or $x = 1 - 4 = -3$. Since we want the positive solution for x, the answer is **5**.

Solution by completing the square together with the square root property: For this solution, we leave the constant on the right-hand side: $x^2 - 2x = 15$.

We take half of -2, which is -1, and square this number to get 1. We then add 1 to each side of the equation to get $x^2 - 2x + 1 = 15 + 1$. This is equivalent to $(x-1)^2 = 16$. We now apply the square root property to get $x - 1 = \pm 4$. So, $x = 1 \pm 4$. This yields the two solutions $1 + 4 = 5$, and $1 - 4 = -3$. Since we want the positive solution for x, the answer is **5**.

Graphical solution: In your graphing calculator press the Y = button, and enter the following.

$$Y1 = X^2 - 2X - 15$$

Now press ZOOM 6 to graph the parabola in a standard window. Then press 2ND TRACE (which is CALC) 2 (or select ZERO), move the cursor just to the left of the second x-intercept and press ENTER. Now move the cursor just to the right of the second x-intercept and press ENTER again. Press ENTER once more, and you will see that the x-coordinate of the second x-intercept is **5**.

The Discriminant

Let's look at the quadratic formula one more time.
$$x = \frac{-b \pm \sqrt{b^2 - 4ac}}{2a}$$

The expression under the square root is called the discriminant of the quadratic equation. In other words, the **discriminant** of the quadratic equation $ax^2 + bx + c = 0$ is defined as
$$\Delta = b^2 - 4ac$$

Although computing the discriminant of a quadratic equation does not give the roots (solutions) of the equation, it does give us a lot of information about the nature of the roots.

If $\mathbf{\Delta = 0}$ (i.e., the discriminant is 0), then the quadratic formula simplifies to $x = -\frac{b}{2a}$, and we see that there is just one solution to the quadratic equation.

Additionally, if the coefficients a and b are integers, then the unique solution will be a rational number (a fraction where the numerator and denominator are both integers).

If $\mathbf{\Delta > 0}$ (i.e., the discriminant is positive), we wind up with a positive number under the square root in the quadratic formula. The square root of a positive number is a real number. We therefore wind up with the two real solutions
$$x = \frac{-b \pm \sqrt{b^2 - 4ac}}{2a}$$

If the discriminant also happens to be a perfect square (such as 1, 4, 9, 16, etc.), then both solutions will be rational numbers.

If $\mathbf{\Delta < 0}$ (i.e., the discriminant is negative), we wind up with a negative number under the square root in the quadratic formula. The square root of a negative number is an imaginary number. We therefore get two complex solutions.

Example: Find the discriminant of $x^2 + 6x + 9 = 0$. Then describe the nature of the roots of the equation.

Solution: In this question, we have $a = 1$, $b = 6$, and $c = 9$. So, the discriminant is
$$\Delta = b^2 - 4ac = 6^2 - 4(1)(9) = 36 - 36 = 0.$$

It follows that the roots of the quadratic equation are equal (in other words, there is really just one root) and rational (a fraction, where the numerator and denominator are both integers).

Time to Practice

LEVEL 1: PASSPORT TO ADVANCED MATH – SOLVING QUADRATIC EQUATIONS

2. If $x > 0$ and $x^2 - 9 = 0$, what is the value of x ?

LEVEL 2: PASSPORT TO ADVANCED MATH – SOLVING QUADRATIC EQUATIONS

3. If $j > 0$ and $9j^2 - 36 = 0$, what is the value of j ?

LEVEL 3: PASSPORT TO ADVANCED MATH – SOLVING QUADRATIC EQUATIONS

$$g(x) = (x + 7)^2 - 25$$

4. Which of the following is a value of x that satisfies $g(x) = 0$?

   A) -12
   B) -7
   C) 0
   D) 2

LEVEL 4: PASSPORT TO ADVANCED MATH – SOLVING QUADRATIC EQUATIONS

5. What are the solutions to $7x^2 - 56x + 35 = 0$?

   A) $x = -28 \pm 35\sqrt{11}$
   B) $x = -28 \pm \sqrt{11}$
   C) $x = 4 \pm 35\sqrt{11}$
   D) $x = 4 \pm \sqrt{11}$

$$f(x) = \frac{1}{(x-7)^2 - 12(x-7) + 36}$$

6. For what value of x is the function f above undefined?

LEVEL 5: PASSPORT TO ADVANCED MATH – SOLVING QUADRATIC EQUATIONS

$$x^2 + \frac{4h}{3}x = 4k$$

7. In the quadratic equation above, h and k are constants. What are the solutions for x ?

   A) $x = \frac{-2h \pm \sqrt{h^2 + 9k}}{3}$
   B) $x = \frac{-2h \pm 2\sqrt{h^2 + 9k}}{3}$
   C) $x = \frac{-2h \pm \sqrt{3h^2 + 9k}}{3}$
   D) $x = -2h \pm \sqrt{h^2 + 3k}$

8. What is the sum of all values of p that satisfy $2p^2 - 27p + 13 = 0$?

9. If $2t^{-2} + 3t^{-1} - 2 = 0$, which of the following could be the value of t ?

   A) $\frac{1}{3}$
   B) $\frac{1}{2}$
   C) 1
   D) 2

$$ax^2 - 3x = b$$

10. In the equation above, a and b are constants. If the equation has 2 distinct real solutions, which of the following could be the value of ab ?

    A) -4
    B) -3
    C) -2.25
    D) -1.75

Answers

1. 5   2. 3   3. 2   4. A   5. D   6. 13   7. B   8. 27/2, 13.5   9. D   10. D

Full Solutions

2.
Solution by guessing: Let's take a guess for x, say $x = 2$. Then $x^2 - 9 = 2^2 - 9 = 4 - 9 = -5$. This is too small.

Let's try $x = 3$ next. Then $x^2 - 9 = 3^2 - 9 = 9 - 9 = 0$. This is correct, and so the answer is 3.

* **Solution using the square root property:** We add 9 to each side of the given equation to get $x^2 = 9$. We now use the square root property to get $x = \pm 3$. Since we are given that $x > 0$, $x = \mathbf{3}$.

Note: Once we have $x^2 = 9$, instead of using the square root property we can just use informal reasoning to simply observe that $3^2 = 9$. This will save a little time.

Solution by factoring the difference of two squares: $x^2 - 9 = (x - 3)(x + 3)$. So, $x - 3 = 0$ or $x + 3 = 0$. Therefore, $x = 3$ or $x = -3$. Since we are given $x > 0$, we choose $x = \mathbf{3}$.

3.
* **Algebraic solution:** We add 36 to each side of the equation to get $9j^2 = 36$. We then divide each side of this last equation by 9 to get $j^2 = \frac{36}{9} = 4$. Since $2^2 = 4$ and $2 > 0$, the answer is **2**.

Notes: (1) We can also begin by factoring and dividing each side of the given equation by 9.

$$9(j^2 - 4) = 0$$
$$j^2 - 4 = 0$$

We can then add 4 to each side of the equation to get $j^2 = 4$, and then proceed as in the solution above to get $j = 2$.

(2) We can also solve this problem by guessing, using the square root property, or factoring. See the three solutions from problem 2 for details.

4.

* Solution by starting with choice C: Let's start with C. Then $g(0) = (0 + 7)^2 - 25 = 49 - 25 = 24$. Since $g(0) \neq 0$, we can eliminate choice C.

Let's try B: $g(-7) = (-7 + 7)^2 - 25 = 0 - 25 = -25$. So, $g(-7) \neq 0$, and we can eliminate B.

Let's try A: $g(-12) = (-12 + 7)^2 - 25 = (-5)^2 - 25 = 25 - 25 = 0$. Thus, the answer is choice **A**.

Note: $(-5)^2 = (-5)(-5) = 25$.

Algebraic solution: We solve the equation $g(x) = 0$.

$$(x + 7)^2 - 25 = 0$$
$$(x + 7)^2 = 25$$
$$x + 7 = \pm 5$$
$$x + 7 = -5 \quad \text{or} \quad x + 7 = 5$$
$$x = -5 - 7 = -12 \quad \text{or} \quad x = 5 - 7 = -2$$

So, $x = -12$ or $x = -2$. Since -12 is an answer choice, the answer is choice **A**.

5.

* Solution by completing the square: Let's divide through by 7 first to simplify the equation. We get $x^2 - 8x + 5 = 0$. Let's solve this equation by completing the square.

$$x^2 - 8x = -5$$
$$x^2 - 8x + 16 = -5 + 16$$
$$(x - 4)^2 = 11$$
$$x - 4 = \pm\sqrt{11}$$
$$x = 4 \pm \sqrt{11}$$

This is choice **D**.

Notes: (1) To get from the first equation to the second equation we completed the square on the expression $x^2 - 8x$. Half of -8 is -4. And when we square -4, we get 16. We added this last expression to each side of the equation.

(2) To get from the second equation to the third equation, we factored the left-hand side. Since we completed the square to get that expression, the expression factors as $(x - 4)^2$. Note that -4 is the number we got from taking half of -8.

(3) To get from the third equation to the fourth equation we used the square root property.

(4) To get from the fourth equation to the fifth equation we added 4 to each side of the equation.

(5) This problem can also be solved by using the quadratic formula or by picking numbers. I leave these solutions to the reader.

6.
* f will be undefined when the denominator is zero. So, we solve the equation $(x-7)^2 - 12(x-7) + 36 = 0$. The left-hand side of the equation factors as $(x-7-6)^2 = 0$, or equivalently $(x-13)^2 = 0$. So, $x - 13 = 0$, and therefore, $x = \mathbf{13}$.

Notes: (1) Many students might find it hard to see how to factor the expression $(x-7)^2 - 12(x-7) + 36$. To help see how to do this we can make a formal substitution of $u = x - 7$. The expression then becomes $u^2 - 12u + 36$ which factors as $(u-6)^2$. The equation $(u-6)^2 = 0$ has solution $u = 6$. But remember that $u = x - 7$. So, we have $x - 7 = 6$, and so $x = 6 + 7 = \mathbf{13}$.

(2) In note (1), we are regarding $x - 7$ as a **block**. See Lesson 25 for more information on blocks.

7.
* **Solution by completing the square:**

$$x^2 + \frac{4h}{3}x = 4k$$

$$x^2 + \frac{4h}{3}x + \left(\frac{2h}{3}\right)^2 = 4k + \left(\frac{2h}{3}\right)^2$$

$$\left(x + \frac{2h}{3}\right)^2 = 4k + \frac{4h^2}{9}$$

$$\left(x + \frac{2h}{3}\right)^2 = \frac{36k + 4h^2}{9}$$

$$\left(x + \frac{2h}{3}\right)^2 = \frac{4(9k + h^2)}{9}$$

$$x + \frac{2h}{3} = \pm \frac{2\sqrt{9k + h^2}}{3}$$

$$x = -\frac{2h}{3} \pm \frac{2\sqrt{9k + h^2}}{3}$$

$$x = \frac{-2h \pm 2\sqrt{h^2 + 9k}}{3}$$

This is choice **B**.

Notes: (1) To get from the first equation to the second equation we completed the square on the expression $x^2 + \frac{4h}{3}x$.

Half of $\frac{4h}{3}$ is $\frac{1}{2} \cdot \frac{4h}{3} = \frac{2h}{3}$. And when we square $\frac{2h}{3}$, we get $\left(\frac{2h}{3}\right)^2$.

We added this last expression to each side of the equation.

(2) To get from the second equation to the third equation, we factored the left-hand side. Since we completed the square to get that expression, the expression factors as $(x + b)^2$, where $b = \frac{2h}{3}$ (this is what we got when we took half of $\frac{4h}{3}$).

(3) To get from the third equation to the fourth equation we got a common denominator on the right-hand side. We have

$$4k = \frac{4k}{1} \cdot \frac{9}{9} = \frac{36k}{9}$$

So,

$$4k + \frac{4h^2}{9} = \frac{36k}{9} + \frac{4h^2}{9} = \frac{36k + 4h^2}{9}$$

(4) To get from the fourth equation to the fifth we factored the numerator of the right-hand side. Since the terms $36k$ and $4h^2$ have a common factor of 4, we have $36k + 4h^2 = 4(9k + h^2)$.

(5) To get from the fifth equation to the sixth equation we used the square root property.

(6) To get from the sixth equation to the seventh equation we subtracted $\frac{2h}{3}$ from each side of the equation.

(7) This problem can also be solved by using the quadratic formula or by picking numbers. I leave these solutions to the reader.

8.

QUADRATIC FACT: If r and s are the solutions of the quadratic equation $x^2 + bx + c = 0$, then $b = -(r + s)$ and $c = rs$. In words, b is the negative of the sum of the solutions and c is the product of the solutions.

* We divide each side of the equation by 2 to get $p^2 - \frac{27}{2}p + \frac{13}{2} = 0$. The sum we are looking for is the negative of the coefficient of p in the equation, i.e., the answer is **27/2** or **13.5**.

Notes: (1) Using the QUADRATIC FACT, we see that in this problem, the sum of the two solutions is $\frac{27}{2}$ and the product of the two solutions is $\frac{13}{2}$.

(2) Yes, you can also solve the equation $2p^2 - 27k + 13 = 0$ by completing the square or using the quadratic formula, but this is very time consuming. It is much better to simply use the QUADRATIC FACT mentioned above.

9.

Solution using a substitution: We make the substitution $u = t^{-1}$. It follows that $u^2 = (t^{-1})^2 = t^{-2}$. So, the given equation becomes $2u^2 + 3u - 2 = 0$.

We can solve this equation in several different ways. The quickest way in this case is by factoring.

$$(2u-1)(u+2) = 0$$
$$2u - 1 = 0 \quad \text{or} \quad u + 2 = 0$$
$$u = \tfrac{1}{2} \quad \text{or} \quad u = -2$$

We now replace u by t^{-1} and solve for t.

$$t^{-1} = \tfrac{1}{2} \quad \text{or} \quad t^{-1} = -2$$
$$t = 2 \quad \text{or} \quad t = -\tfrac{1}{2}$$

So, the answer is choice **D**.

Notes: (1) We can solve the quadratic equation $2u^2 + 3u - 2 = 0$ in several other ways. Here are two other methods:

Quadratic formula: We identify $a = 2$, $b = 3$, and $c = -2$.

$$\boldsymbol{u = \frac{-b \pm \sqrt{b^2 - 4ac}}{2a} = \frac{-3 \pm \sqrt{9+16}}{4} = \frac{-3 \pm \sqrt{25}}{4} = \frac{-3 \pm 5}{4}.}$$

So, we get $u = \frac{-3+5}{4} = \frac{2}{4} = \frac{1}{2}$ or $u = \frac{-3-5}{4} = -\frac{8}{4} = -2$.

Completing the square: For this solution, we move the constant to the right-hand side to get $2u^2 + 3u = 2$. We then divide each side of the equation by 2 to get $u^2 + \frac{3}{2}u = 1$

We take half of $\frac{3}{2}$, which is $\frac{3}{4}$, and square this number to get $\frac{9}{16}$. We then add $\frac{9}{16}$ to each side of the equation to get $u^2 + \frac{3}{2}u + \frac{9}{16} = 1 + \frac{9}{16} = \frac{16}{16} + \frac{9}{16} = \frac{25}{16}$. This is equivalent to $\left(u + \frac{3}{4}\right)^2 = \frac{25}{16}$. We now apply the square root property to get $u + \frac{3}{4} = \pm \frac{5}{4}$. So, $u = -\frac{3}{4} \pm \frac{5}{4}$. This yields the solutions $-\frac{3}{4} + \frac{5}{4} = \frac{2}{4} = \frac{1}{2}$, and $-\frac{3}{4} - \frac{5}{4} = -\frac{8}{4} = -2$.

(2) Once we find u, we need to remember to replace u by t^{-1}.

(3) Recall that $t^{-1} = \frac{1}{t^1} = \frac{1}{t}$. So, we can solve the equation $t^{-1} = \frac{1}{2}$ by taking the reciprocal of each side of this equation. We get $t = \frac{2}{1} = 2$.

Similarly, the equation $t^{-1} = -2$ has solution $t = \frac{1}{-2} = -\frac{1}{2}$.

* Solution without a formal substitution: We can factor the left-hand side of the given equation as $2t^{-2} + 3t^{-1} - 2 = (2t^{-1} - 1)(t^{-1} + 2)$.

We set each factor equal to 0 to get $2t^{-1} - 1 = 0$ or $t^{-1} + 2 = 0$.

So, $t^{-1} = \frac{1}{2}$ or $t^{-1} = -2$. Therefore, $t = 2$ or $t = -\frac{1}{2}$.

The answer is choice **D**.

10.
Solution using the quadratic formula: We bring everything to the left-hand side of the equation to get $ax^2 - 3x - b = 0$, and use the quadratic formula:

$$x = \frac{3 \pm \sqrt{9 + 4ab}}{2a}$$

In order to get 2 distinct real solutions, the expression under the square root needs to be positive. So, we need $9 + 4ab > 0$. Subtracting 9 from each side of this inequality gives us $4ab > -9$. Dividing by 4, we get $ab > -\frac{9}{4} = -2.25$. The only answer choice greater than -2.25 is -1.75, choice **D**.

* **Solution using the discriminant:** We bring everything to the left-hand side of the equation to get $ax^2 - 3x - b = 0$. The discriminant of this equation is $\Delta = (-3)^2 - 4a(-b) = 9 + 4ab$. Since we want the equation to have 2 distinct real solutions, we need the discriminant to be positive. So, we have $9 + 4ab > 0$. Subtracting 9 from each side of this inequality gives us $4ab > -9$. Dividing by 4, we get $ab > -\frac{9}{4} = -2.25$. The only answer choice greater than -2.25 is -1.75, choice **D**.

LESSON 35 – PROBLEM SOLVING
PERCENTS

1 Out of 100

The word **percent** means "out of 100." So, if you use the strategy of picking numbers (see Lesson 2) in a percent problem, the number 100 is usually a good choice.

Let's try an example.

LEVEL 4: PROBLEM SOLVING – PERCENTS

1. * Shelby bought a pair of jeans at a clothing store that gave a 40 percent discount off its original price. The total amount she paid to the cashier was x dollars, including a 7 percent sales tax on the discounted price. Which of the following represents the original price of the pair of jeans in terms of x ?

    A) $0.67x$
    B) $\frac{x}{0.67}$
    C) $(0.6)(1.07)x$
    D) $\frac{x}{(0.6)(1.07)}$

Solution by picking a number (calculator needed): Let's assume that the original price of the pair of jeans was **100** dollars. We can put a big dark circle around the number 100, because this is the original price, and that is what the question is asking for.

Now, when we take 40 percent off of 100 we get 60. And 7 percent of 60 is $0.07 \cdot 60 = 4.20$, and so the total amount Shelby paid was

$$x = 60 + 4.20 = 64.20 \text{ dollars.}$$

We now replace x by 64.20 in each answer choice and use our calculator.

　　A) $0.67 \cdot 64.20 = 43.014$
　　B) $\frac{64.20}{0.67} \approx 95.82$
　　C) $(0.6)(1.07)(64.20) = 41.2164$
　　D) $\frac{64.20}{(0.6)(1.07)} = 100$

Since choices A, B, and C came out incorrect we can eliminate them, and the answer is choice **D**.

Notes: (1) There are two ways to take 40 percent off of 100.

Method 1: We can take 40% of 100, and then subtract the result from 100:

$$0.40 \cdot 100 = 40 \text{ and } 100 - 40 = 60.$$

234

Method 2: Note that taking 40 percent off 100 is the same as taking 60% of 100:

$$0.60 \cdot 100 = 60.$$

(2) To see that Methods 1 and 2 lead to the same answer, note that

$$100 - 0.40 \cdot 100 = 100 - 40 = 60$$

(3) Instead of taking 7 percent of 60, and then adding this result to 60, we can simply multiply 60 by 1.07. Indeed, $1.07 \cdot 60 = 64.2$.

* Algebraic solution: Let's let z be the original price of the pair of jeans. When we discount this price by 40 percent, we get $0.6z$. We then add 7 percent of this last amount to get

$$x = 0.6z + (0.07)(0.6z) = (1 + 0.07)(0.6z) = (1.07)(0.6)z$$

Finally, we solve this last equation for z by dividing each side by $(1.07)(0.6)$ to get $z = \frac{x}{(1.07)(0.6)}$. This is equivalent to choice **D**.

Note: There are two ways to discount z by 40 percent.

Method 1: We can take 40% of z, and then subtract the result from z:

$$z - 0.40z = (1 - 0.40)z = 0.60z.$$

Method 2: Note that discounting z by 40 percent is the same as taking 60 percent of z to get $0.60z$.

Percent Change

Memorize the following simple formula for percent change problems.

$$\text{Percent Change} = \frac{\text{Change}}{\text{Original}} \times 100$$

Note that this is the same formula for both a percent increase and a percent decrease problem.

Let's try an example.

LEVEL 2: PROBLEM SOLVING – PERCENTS

2. In January, Jane was able to type 30 words per minute. In February, she was able to type 42 words per minute. By what percent did Jane's speed increase from January to February?

   A) 12%
   B) 18%
   C) 30%
   D) 40%

* This is a **percent increase** problem. So, we will use the formula for percent change. The **original** value is 30. The new value is 42, so that the **change** is 12. Using the percent change formula, we get that the percent increase is $\frac{12}{30} \cdot 100 = 40\%$, choice **D**.

Warning: Do not accidentally use the new value for "change" in the formula. The **change** is the positive difference between the original and new values.

Time to Practice

LEVEL 2: PROBLEM SOLVING – PERCENTS

3. * At Staten Island Middle School, approximately 5 percent of enrolled freshmen, 7 percent of enrolled sophomores, and 4 percent of enrolled juniors scored more than 80% on their State Exam in May 2016. If there were 276 freshmen, 365 sophomores, and 502 juniors at Staten Island Middle School in 2016, which of the following is closest to the total number of freshmen, sophomores, and juniors at Staten Island Middle School who scored more than 80% on their State Exam?

    A) 60
    B) 65
    C) 70
    D) 75

4. * Janice spent 22% of her 7-hour school day in her AP Calculus class. How many <u>minutes</u> of her school day were spent in AP Calculus?

    A) 1.54
    B) 24.3
    C) 46.97
    D) 92.4

5. * A geologist is studying igneous rock formations in two sections of a volcanic region. He observed that Section I had 26 percent more igneous rocks than Section II. Based on this observation, if Section I had 756 igneous rocks, then how many igneous rocks were in section II?

LEVEL 3: PROBLEM SOLVING – PERCENTS

6. A family with an adjustable mortgage had to make a payment of $3217.53 per month. The interest rate has adjusted so that the family's monthly payment is now $3259.36. To the nearest tenth of a percent, by what percent did the amount of the family's mortgage payment increase?

    A) 1.1%
    B) 1.3%
    C) 1.5%
    D) 1.7%

7. An author sells his book for 95% more than the cost of printing the book. The author decides to throw a sale, and during the sale, he charges 45% more than the cost of printing the book. If the price of the book during the sale is $6.35, what is the price of the book, in dollars, when the book is not on sale? Round your answer to the nearest cent.

LEVEL 4: PROBLEM SOLVING – PERCENTS

Questions 8 – 9 refer to the following information.

At the beginning of July, 58 percent of the animals in a shelter were dogs, and the rest were cats. By the end of July, 45 percent of the dogs and 63 percent of the cats were adopted.

8. * What percentage of the animals in the shelter were adopted? (Ignore the percent symbol when entering your answer.)

9. * What percentage of the animals that were adopted were cats? (Ignore the percent symbol when entering your answer.)

LEVEL 5: PROBLEM SOLVING – PERCENTS

10. *If Ted's weight increased by 36 percent and Jessica's weight decreased by 22 percent during a certain year, the ratio of Ted's weight to Jessica's weight at the end of the year was how many times the ratio at the beginning of the year?

Answers

1. D 2. D 3. A 4. D 5. 600 6. B 7. 8.54 8. 52.5, 52.6 9. 50.3 10. 1.74

Full Solutions

3.
* $(.05)(276) + (.07)(365) + (.04)(502) = 59.43$. So, the answer is choice **A**.

4.
* 7 hours is equal to $7 \cdot 60 = 420$ minutes, and 22% of 420 is $0.22 \cdot 420 = 92.4$, choice **D**.

5.
* **Algebraic solution:** Let x be the number of igneous rocks in Section II. Then the number of igneous rocks in Section I is $x + 0.26x = 1.26x$. So, we are given that $1.26x = 756$, and so, $x = \frac{756}{1.26} = \mathbf{600}$.

6.
* We use the formula for percent change. The **original** value is 3217.53. The new value is 3259.36, so that the **change** is $3259.36 - 3217.53 = 41.83$. Using the percent change formula, we get that the percent increase is $\frac{41.83}{3217.53} \cdot 100 \approx 1.3\%$, choice **B**.

7.
* The cost of printing the book is $\frac{6.35}{1.45} \approx 4.37931$. It follows that the regular price of the book is approximately $4.37931 \cdot 1.95 \approx 8.539655$. To the nearest cent, this is **8.54**.

Notes: (1) If we let C be the printing cost of the book and we let S be the sale price of the book, then we have $S = 1.45C$, so that $C = \frac{S}{1.45}$. We are given that $S = 6.35$, so that $C = \frac{6.35}{1.45}$.

(2) The regular price of the book is $1.95C$.

8.

Solution by picking a number: Let's assume that there were 100 animals in the shelter at the beginning of July. Then 58 of them were dogs and $100 - 58 = 42$ of them were cats. So, the total number adopted was $0.45 \cdot 58 + 0.63 \cdot 42 = 52.56$ Since we started with the number 100, we can grid in **52.5** or **52.6**.

Notes: (1) Recall that when picking numbers in percent problems it's usually best to choose the number 100. After all, the word percent means "out of 100."

(2) There cannot actually be 52.56 animals, of course (we cannot have decimal parts of animals), Nonetheless, as a percentage the number is correct.

(3) The exact answer to the question is 52.56 percent. The answer grid, however, has only four slots. So, we can either truncate this number to 52.5, or round it to 52.6.

Direct solution: As a decimal, the answer is $0.45 \cdot 0.58 + 0.63 \cdot 0.42 = 0.5256$. We change this to a percent by moving the decimal point two places to the right to get 52.56 percent.

So, we grid in **52.5** or **52.6**.

9.

Solution by picking a number: Let's assume that there were 100 animals in the shelter at the beginning of July. In the previous question we found that the total number of animals that were adopted was 52.56. The total number of cats that were adopted was $0.63 \cdot 42 = 26.46$

So, the percentage of the animals that were adopted that were cats was $\frac{26.46}{52.56} \cdot 100 \approx \mathbf{50.3}$

Note: To compute a percentage, use the simple formula
$$\text{Percentage} = \frac{\text{Part}}{\text{Whole}} \times 100$$
In this example, the "Part" is the number of cats that were adopted and the "Whole" is the total number of animals that were adopted.

10.

Solution by picking a number: Since this is a percent problem, let's choose 100 pounds for both Ted's weight and Jessica's weight at the beginning of the year. Ted's weight at the end of the year was then $100 + 36 = 136$ pounds and Jessica's weight at the end of the year was $100 - 22 = 78$ pounds. We then have that the ratio of Ted's weight to Jessica's weight at the beginning of the year was $\frac{100}{100} = 1$, and the ratio of Ted's weight to Jessica's weight at the end of the year was $\frac{136}{78} \approx 1.7435897$. Therefore, we grid in **1.74**.

Algebraic solution: Let Ted's and Jessica's weights at the beginning of the year be x and y, respectively. Then at the end of the year their weights are $1.36x$ and $0.78y$. The ratio of Ted's weight to Jessica's weight at the beginning of the year was $\frac{x}{y}$, and the ratio of Ted's weight to Jessica's weight at the end of the year was $\frac{1.36x}{0.78y} = \frac{68}{39} \cdot \frac{x}{y}$, which is $\frac{68}{39} \approx 1.74359$ times the ratio at the beginning of the year. We can therefore grid in **1.74**.

LESSON 36 – TRIGONOMETRY
RIGHT TRIANGLE TRIGONOMETRY

Sines and Cosines and Tangents, Oh My!

Let's consider the following right triangle, and let's focus our attention on angle A.

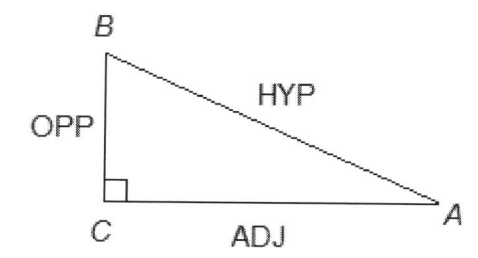

Note that the **hypotenuse** is ALWAYS the side opposite the right angle.

The other two sides of the right triangle, called the **legs**, depend on which angle is chosen. In this picture, we chose to focus on angle A. Therefore, the opposite side is BC, and the adjacent side is AC.

It's worth memorizing how to compute the six trig functions:

$$\sin A = \frac{\text{OPP}}{\text{HYP}} \qquad \csc A = \frac{\text{HYP}}{\text{OPP}}$$

$$\cos A = \frac{\text{ADJ}}{\text{HYP}} \qquad \sec A = \frac{\text{HYP}}{\text{ADJ}}$$

$$\tan A = \frac{\text{OPP}}{\text{ADJ}} \qquad \cot A = \frac{\text{ADJ}}{\text{OPP}}$$

Here are a couple of tips to help you remember these:

(1) Many students find it helpful to use the word SOHCAHTOA. You can think of the letters here as representing sin, opp, hyp, cos, adj, hyp, tan, opp, adj.

(2) The three trig functions on the right are the reciprocals of the three trig functions on the left. In other words, you get them by interchanging the numerator and denominator. It's pretty easy to remember that the reciprocal of tangent is cotangent. For the other two, just remember that the "s" goes with the "c" and the "c" goes with the "s." In other words, the reciprocal of sine is cosecant, and the reciprocal of cosine is secant.

Note: It is not clear if the SAT will ever ask about the reciprocal functions (csc, sec, and cot). Students that are trying to get an 800 in math may want to know them just in case.

Let's try an example.

LEVEL 2: TRIGONOMETRY – RIGHT TRIANGLE TRIGONOMETRY

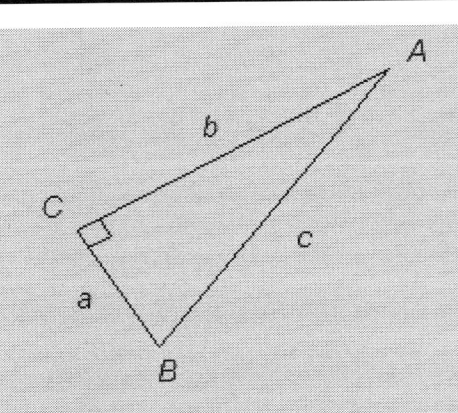

1. In the figure above, what is $\cos A$?

    A) $\frac{c}{b}$
    B) $\frac{a}{b}$
    C) $\frac{a}{c}$
    D) $\frac{b}{c}$

* $\cos A = \frac{\text{ADJ}}{\text{HYP}} = \frac{b}{c}$, choice **D**.

Note: For a little extra practice, let's evaluate the other five trig functions of angle A.

$$\sin A = \frac{\text{OPP}}{\text{HYP}} = \frac{a}{c}, \tan A = \frac{\text{OPP}}{\text{ADJ}} = \frac{a}{b}, \sec A = \frac{c}{b}, \csc A = \frac{c}{a}, \cot A = \frac{b}{a}$$

Trigonometric Identities

Here is a list of the **trigonometric identities** that are useful to know for the SAT. I have placed the cofunction identities in a box because they are so important for the SAT.

Quotient Identity:

$$\tan x = \frac{\sin x}{\cos x}$$

Negative Identities:

$$\cos(-x) = \cos x \qquad \sin(-x) = -\sin x \qquad \tan(-x) = -\tan x$$

Cofunction Identities:

$$\sin(90° - x) = \cos x \qquad \cos(90° - x) = \sin x$$

Pythagorean Identity:

$$\cos^2 x + \sin^2 x = 1$$

Time to Practice

LEVEL 2: TRIGONOMETRY – RIGHT TRIANGLE TRIGONOMETRY

2. Let $x = \cos t$ and $y = \sin t$ for any real value t. Then $x^2 + y^2 =$

   A) -1
   B) 0
   C) 1
   D) It cannot be determined from the information given.

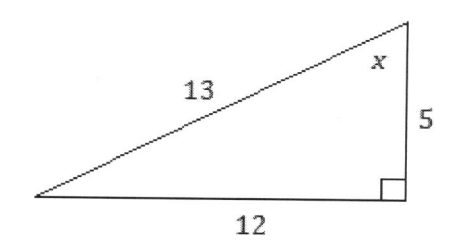

3. In the figure above, what is the value of $\tan x$?

LEVEL 3: TRIGONOMETRY – RIGHT TRIANGLE TRIGONOMETRY

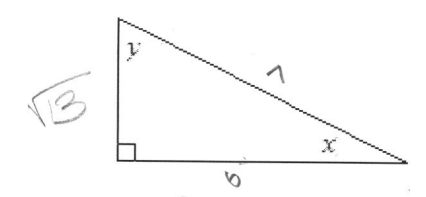

4. In the triangle above, the cosine of $x°$ is $\frac{6}{7}$. What is the tangent of $y°$?

   A) $\frac{\sqrt{13}}{7}$
   B) $\frac{\sqrt{13}}{6}$
   C) $\frac{6}{\sqrt{13}}$
   D) $\frac{7}{\sqrt{13}}$

5. In a right triangle, one angle measures $\theta°$, where $\cos \theta° = \frac{9}{11}$. What is $\sin((90 - \theta)°)$?

241

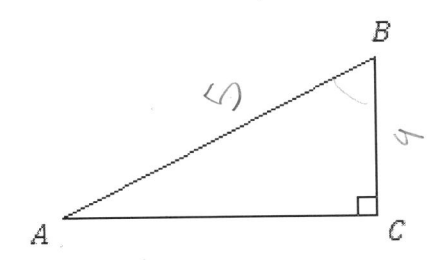

6. In the triangle above, the sine of A is 0.8. What is the cosine of B ?

LEVEL 4: TRIGONOMETRY – RIGHT TRIANGLE TRIGONOMETRY

7. In triangles CAT and DOG, the measures of angles A and O are 90°. Triangle DOG is similar to triangle CAT, with vertices D, O, and G corresponding to vertices C, A, and T, respectively. $CA = 20$, $CT = 25$, and each side of triangle DOG is $\frac{2}{5}$ the length of the corresponding side of triangle CAT. What is the value of $\tan G$?

LEVEL 5: TRIGONOMETRY – RIGHT TRIANGLE TRIGONOMETRY

8. Which of the following is equal to $\cos\left(\frac{\pi}{5}\right)$?

   A) $-\cos\left(-\frac{\pi}{5}\right)$
   B) $-\sin\left(\frac{\pi}{5}\right)$
   C) $\sin\left(\frac{3\pi}{10}\right)$
   D) $-\cos\left(\frac{3\pi}{10}\right)$

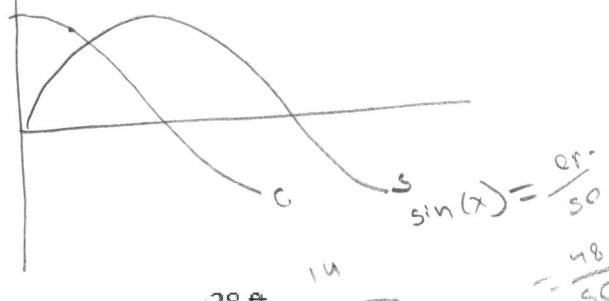

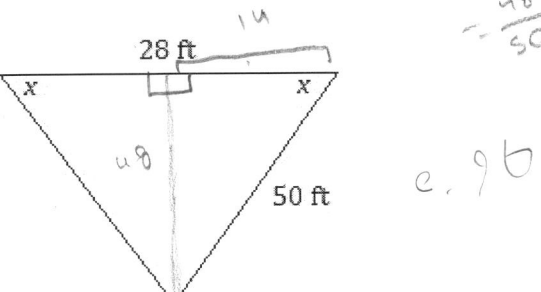

Note: Figure not drawn to scale.

9. * What is the value of $\sin x$ in the figure above?

10. The angle of elevation from the tip of the shadow of a 30 meter tall building to the top of the building has a cosine of $\frac{3}{7}$. What is the length of the shadow to the nearest meter?

Answers

1. D   2. C   3. 12/5, 2.4   4. C   5. 9/11, .818   6. 4/5, .8   7. 4/3, 1.33   8. C   9. .96   10. 14

242

Full Solutions

2.

* Solution using the Pythagorean identity:

$$x^2 + y^2 = (\cos t)^2 + (\sin t)^2 = \cos^2 t + \sin^2 t = 1$$

This is choice **C**.

Note: $(\cos t)^2$ is usually abbreviated as $\cos^2 t$. Similarly, $(\sin t)^2$ is usually abbreviated as $\sin^2 t$. In particular, $(\cos t)^2 + (\sin t)^2$ is usually written as $\cos^2 t + \sin^2 t$.

3.

* $\tan x = \frac{\text{OPP}}{\text{ADJ}} = $ **12/5 or 2.4**.

4.

* Basic trig solution: Since $\cos x = \frac{\text{ADJ}}{\text{HYP}}$, we label the side adjacent to x with a 6, and we label the hypotenuse with a 7.

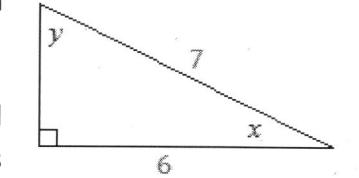

We now use the Pythagorean Theorem to get that the length of the third side of the triangle is $\sqrt{7^2 - 6^2} = \sqrt{49 - 36} = \sqrt{13}$. It follows that $\tan y° = \frac{\text{OPP}}{\text{ADJ}} = \frac{6}{\sqrt{13}}$, choice **C**.

Note: See Lesson 8 for more information on the Pythagorean Theorem.

5.

* Solution using a cofunction identity: $\sin((90 - \theta)°) = \cos \theta° = $ **9/11 or .818**.

Basic trig solution: Let's draw a picture:

Notice that I labeled one of the angles with θ, and used the fact that $\cos \theta = \frac{\text{ADJ}}{\text{HYP}}$ to label 2 sides of the triangle.

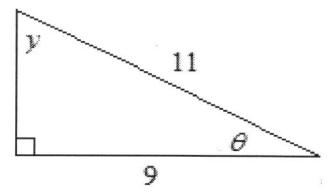

Now observe that $y° = (90 - \theta)°$, so that $\sin((90 - \theta)°) = \sin y° = \frac{\text{OPP}}{\text{HYP}} = $ **9/11 or .818**.

6.

* Solution using a cofunction identity: $\cos B = \sin A = $ **.8 or 4/5**. ANAL

Note: (1) The two cofunction identities are very popular on the SAT and very easy to use. If you know how to use them properly, you have a good chance of getting many SAT trigonometry questions correct.

(2) Geometrically the cofunction identities say that if ∠A and ∠B are the two nonright angles in a right triangle (just like in the figure for this problem), then $\cos A = \sin B$ and $\sin A = \cos B$.

243

(3) Algebraically, the cofunction identities say that if $x°$ and $y°$ add to $90°$, then $\cos x = \sin y$ and $\sin x = \cos y$.

(4) If you forget the cofunction identity, this can also be solved using basic trigonometry as was done in the second solution to problem 5. Since $\sin A = \frac{\text{OPP}}{\text{HYP}} = \frac{BC}{AB}$, we can label side BC with 0.8 and side AB with 1. It then follows that $\cos B = \frac{\text{ADJ}}{\text{HYP}} = \frac{BC}{AB} = \frac{0.8}{1} = 0.8$, and we can grid in $.8$.

Alternatively, we can write $0.8 = \frac{8}{10} = \frac{4}{5}$, and label side BC with 4 and side AB with 5, and once again evaluate $\cos B = \frac{\text{ADJ}}{\text{HYP}} = \frac{BC}{AB} = \frac{4}{5}$. So, we can grid in $4/5$.

7.
* Let's draw a picture. We start by drawing the two triangles next to each other so that congruent angles match up, and label the side lengths that we were given.

We can get AT by using the Pythagorean triple 3, 4, 5, and observing that $20 = 5 \cdot 4$, $25 = 5 \cdot 5$, and $15 = 5 \cdot 3$ (if you don't remember this Pythagorean triple, you can use the Pythagorean Theorem).

Now, $\tan G = \frac{\text{OPP}}{\text{ADJ}} = \frac{DO}{OG} = \frac{CA}{AT} = \frac{20}{15} = \mathbf{4/3}$ or $\mathbf{1.33}$.

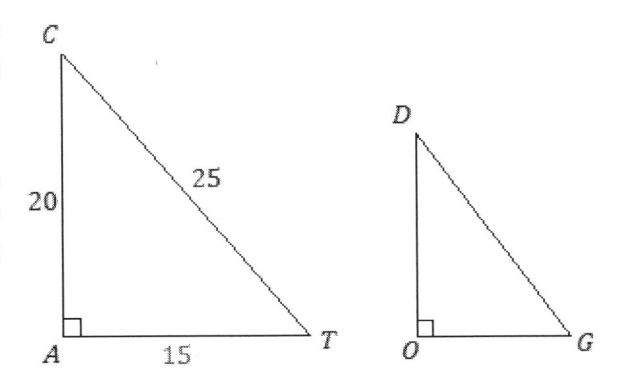

Notes: (1) See Lesson 8 for more information on the Pythagorean Theorem and Pythagorean triples.

(2) See Lesson 24 for more information on similarity.

(3) The specific value $\frac{2}{5}$ is not important here. The only thing this number is needed for is to tell us that the two triangles are similar. Once we have that, we get $\frac{DO}{OG} = \frac{CA}{AT}$.

(4) Trigonometric functions behave the same on the corresponding angles of similar triangles. For example, $\tan G = \tan T = \frac{20}{15}$.

8.
* **Solution using a cofunction identity:** $\cos\left(\frac{\pi}{5}\right) = \sin\left(\frac{\pi}{2} - \frac{\pi}{5}\right) = \sin\left(\frac{3\pi}{10}\right)$, choice **C**.

Notes: (1) Recall that a function f with the property that $f(-x) = f(x)$ for all x in the domain of f is called an **even** function (see Lesson 6). $\cos x$ is an even function. It follows that $\cos(-A) = \cos A$. In particular, $\cos\left(-\frac{\pi}{5}\right) = \cos\left(\frac{\pi}{5}\right)$, and so $-\cos\left(-\frac{\pi}{5}\right) = -\cos\left(\frac{\pi}{5}\right) \neq \cos\left(\frac{\pi}{5}\right)$. This eliminates A.

(2) $\cos A$ and $\sin A$ are *not* negatives of each other in general. If $\cos A = -\sin A$, then $\frac{\cos A}{\sin A} = -1$. Taking reciprocals, $\frac{\sin A}{\cos A} = -1$, so that $\tan A = -1$. This happens only when $A = \pm\frac{3\pi}{4}, \pm\frac{7\pi}{4}, \pm\frac{11\pi}{4}, \ldots$ This eliminates choice B.

(3) Since we know that choice C is the answer, we can use the same reasoning as in note (2) to show that $\cos\left(\frac{\pi}{5}\right)$ cannot be equal to $-\cos\left(\frac{3\pi}{10}\right)$.

(4) If a calculator were allowed for this problem, we could put our calculator in radian mode and then approximate the given expression and all the answer choices in our calculator to get the answer.

9.
* Since two of the angles of the triangle have equal measure, the triangle is isosceles. It follows that the median and altitude from the vertex of the triangle are the same.

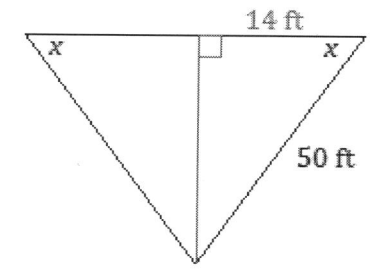

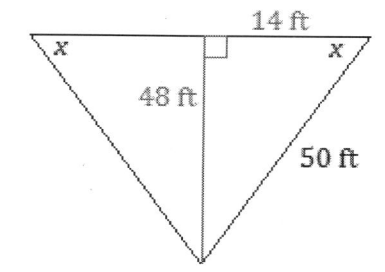

In the figure on the left we drew the altitude from the vertex angle. Since this is also the median, we get a right triangle with leg $\frac{28}{2} = 14$ ft. long.

We can now find the length of the other leg by using the Pythagorean Theorem, or better yet, by noticing that we have a multiple of the Pythagorean triple 7, 24, 25. Since $14 = 7 \cdot 2$ and $50 = 25 \cdot 2$, it follows that the length of the other leg is $24 \cdot 2 = 48$ ft.

Finally, we have $\sin x = \frac{\text{OPP}}{\text{HYP}} = \frac{48}{50} = .96$.

Note: See Lesson 8 for more information on the Pythagorean Theorem, Pythagorean triples, and altitudes and medians in isosceles triangles.

10.
* Let's draw a picture of the situation.

In the triangle on the left, θ is the angle of elevation, the vertical segment represents the building with a height of 30 meters, and the horizontal segment represents the unknown shadow length.

In the triangle on the right, we used $\cos\theta = \frac{\text{ADJ}}{\text{HYP}} = \frac{3}{7}$ to label two sides of the triangle. By the Pythagorean Theorem, we see that the third side is $\sqrt{7^2 - 3^2} = \sqrt{49 - 9} = \sqrt{40}$.

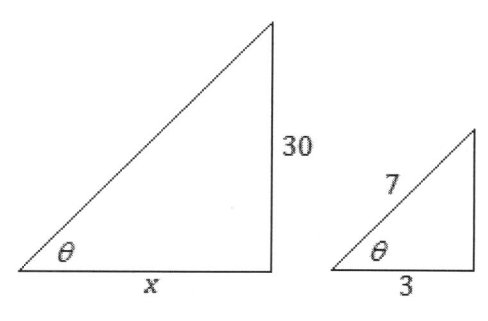

Since the two triangles are similar, we can find x by using the fact that the sides are in proportion.

$$\frac{x}{30} = \frac{3}{\sqrt{40}} \Rightarrow x = \frac{3 \cdot 30}{\sqrt{40}} \approx 14.23$$

To the nearest meter, this is **14**.

LESSON 37 – HEART OF ALGEBRA
SETTING UP LINEAR SYSTEMS

Words, Words, Words...

Let's jump right into some problems.

LEVEL 3: HEART OF ALGEBRA – SETTING UP LINEAR SYSTEMS

1. A geologist has a collection of 55 rocks weighing a total of 15.34 pounds. Each of his igneous rocks weighs 0.12 pounds and each of his sedimentary rocks weighs 0.35 pounds. If the geologist has g igneous rocks and s sedimentary rocks, which of the following systems of equations can be used to find the number of igneous rocks in the geologist's collection?

   A) $g + s = 15.34$
   $0.12g + 0.35s = 55$

   B) $g + s = 15.34$
   $0.35g + 0.12s = 55$

   C) $g + s = 55$
   $0.12g + 0.35s = 15.34$

   D) $g + s = 55$
   $0.35g + 0.12s = 15.34$

2. A grocery store sells whole milk and low-fat milk in half-gallon containers. A half-gallon of whole milk costs $3.75 and a half-gallon of low-fat milk costs $4.25. During a typical week, 128 half-gallon cartons of milk were sold bringing in total revenue of $516 to the grocery store. Which of the following systems of equations could be used to find the number of half-gallon cartons of whole milk, W, and the number of half-gallon cartons of low-fat milk, L, that were sold at the grocery store?

   A) $W + L = 128$
   $3.75W + 4.25L = 516$

   B) $W + L = 516$
   $3.75W + 4.25L = 128$

   C) $W + L = 128$
   $4.25W + 3.75L = 516$

   D) $W + L = 128$
   $(3.75W)(4.25L) = 516$

246

LEVEL 4: HEART OF ALGEBRA – SETTING UP LINEAR SYSTEMS

3. A high school has a budget of $740 for math text books. Each geometry book costs $35 and each algebra book costs $40. The school needs to order at least 18 books. Which of the following systems of inequalities represents this situation in terms of x and y, where x is the number of geometry books ordered and y is the number of algebra books ordered?

   A) $x + y \geq 18$
      $35x + 40y \geq 740$

   B) $x + y \geq 18$
      $35x + 40y \leq 740$

   C) $x + y \leq 18$
      $35x + 40y \geq 740$

   D) $x + y \leq 18$
      $35x + 40y \leq 740$

4. A grocer plans to order a maximum of 200 cans of beans. Black beans cost the grocer $0.35 per can and kidney beans cost the grocer $0.42 per can. If the grocer can spend no more than $75 in total and the grocer orders b cans of black beans and k cans of kidney beans, which of the following systems best represents the constraints on b and k ?

   A) $b + k \leq 0.77$
      $0.35b + 0.42k \leq 200$

   B) $b + k \leq 200$
      $0.35b + 0.42k \leq 75$

   C) $b + k \leq 0.77$
      $0.35b + 0.42k > 200$

   D) $b + k \leq 200$
      $0.35b + 0.42k \geq 75$

5. Containers of two different weights are loaded into a storage facility. Each of the lighter containers weighs 32 pounds, and each of the heavier containers weighs 61 pounds. Let x be the number of lighter containers in the storage facility and let y be the number of heavier containers in the storage facility. The storage facility has a maximum weight limit of 2000 pounds and it has enough space for a total of 42 containers. Which of the following systems of inequalities represents this relationship?

   A) $\begin{cases} x + y \leq 2000 \\ 32x + 61y \leq 42 \end{cases}$

   B) $\begin{cases} x + y \leq 42 \\ 32x + 61y \leq 2000 \end{cases}$

   C) $\begin{cases} \frac{x}{32} + \frac{y}{61} \leq 2000 \\ x + y \leq 42 \end{cases}$

   D) $\begin{cases} x + y \leq 2000 \\ 32x + 61y \leq 2000 \end{cases}$

6. John is planning to spend his Sunday playing video games at an arcade. Each classic arcade game costs $0.75 per game, and each new arcade game costs $2.25 per game. John would like to play at least 60 games and he can spend at most $75. If c represents the number of classic video games played and n represents the number of new video games played, which of the following systems of inequalities represents the situation?

A) $\begin{cases} c + n \leq 60 \\ 0.75c + 2.25n \geq 75 \end{cases}$

B) $\begin{cases} c + n \leq 60 \\ 2.25c + 0.75n \geq 75 \end{cases}$

C) $\begin{cases} c + n \geq 60 \\ 0.75c + 2.25n \leq 75 \end{cases}$

D) $\begin{cases} c + n \geq 60 \\ 2.25c + 0.75n \leq 75 \end{cases}$

LEVEL 5: HEART OF ALGEBRA – SETTING UP LINEAR SYSTEMS

7. A movie is available on DVD and Blue-ray. The box for the DVD has a volume of 260 cubic centimeters and the box for the Blu-ray has a volume of 230 cubic centimeters. An order of DVDs and Blue-rays was shipped to a warehouse. The total volume shipped was 12,010 cubic centimeters, and the shipment contained 50 copies of the movie. Which of the following systems of equations can be used to determine the number of DVDs, d, and the number of Blue-rays, b, that were shipped to the warehouse?

A) $d - b = 50$
$245(d + b) = 12,010$

B) $d - b = 50$
$260d + 230b = 12,010$

C) $50 - d = b$
$230d + 260b = 12,010$

D) $50 - b = d$
$260d + 230b = 12,010$

8. A real estate agent was selling all the houses on a block. The basic house was being sold for $800,000 and the house with upgrades was being sold for $925,000. Her goal was to sell at least 15 of the homes within 6 months. She didn't meet her goal, but she did sell houses that totaled over $10,000,000. Which of the following systems of inequalities describes x, the possible number of standard houses and y, the possible number of upgraded houses?

A) $x + y > 15$
$800,000x + 925,000y > 10,00,0000$

B) $x + y > 15$
$800,000x + 925,000y < 10,00,0000$

C) $x + y < 15$
$800,000x + 925,000y > 10,00,0000$

D) $x + y < 15$
$800,000x + 925,000y < 10,00,0000$

9. A film producer needs to hire at least 20 crew members for a project. The crew will be made up of electricians, who must be paid $200 per day, and assistants, who must be paid $120 per day. The project's budget for paying the crew members is $3200 per day. At least 2 electricians and 3 assistants are needed. Which of the following systems of inequalities represents the given conditions if x is the number of electricians and y is the number of assistants?

A) $200x + 120y \leq 3200$
$x + y \geq 20$
$x \leq 2$
$y \leq 3$

B) $200x + 120y \geq 3200$
$x + y \leq 20$
$x \geq 2$
$y \geq 3$

C) $200x + 120y \leq 3200$
$x + y \geq 20$
$x \geq 2$
$y \geq 3$

D) $200x + 120y \leq 3200$
$x + y \leq 20$
$x \leq 2$
$y \leq 3$

10. A printer is purchasing paper and ink from its supplier. The supplier will deliver at most 250 pounds per shipment. Each ream of paper weighs 20 pounds and each ink cartridge weighs $\frac{1}{3}$ of a pound. The printer wants to purchase at least twice as many ink cartridges as reams of paper. Let r represent the number of reams of paper, and let c represent the number of ink cartridges, where r and c are positive integers. Which of the following systems of inequalities best represents this situation?

A) $20r + \frac{1}{3}c \leq 250$
$2r \leq c$
$r > 0$
$c > 0$

B) $20r + \frac{1}{3}c \leq 250$
$2r \geq c$
$r > 0$
$c > 0$

C) $\frac{1}{3}r + 20c \geq 250$
$2r \leq c$
$r > 0$
$c > 0$

D) $\frac{1}{3}r + 20c \geq 250$
$2r \geq c$
$r > 0$
$c > 0$

Answers

1. C   2. A   3. B   4. B   5. B   6. C   7. D   8. C   9. C   10. A

Full Solutions

1.
* Since g is the number of igneous rocks the geologist has and s is the number of sedimentary rocks the geologist has, it follows that the geologist has $g + s$ rocks in total. We are told that the geologist has 55 rocks, and so $g + s = 55$. This narrows down the possible answers to choices C and D.

Now, $0.12g$ is the weight of the igneous rocks, in pounds, and $0.35s$ is the weight of the sedimentary rocks, in pounds. So, the total weight of the rocks is $0.12g + 0.35s$. We are told that the total weight of the rocks is 15.34 pounds, and so $0.12g + 0.35s = 15.34$. So, the answer is choice **C**.

2.

* Since W is the number of half-gallon cartons of whole milk that were sold, L is the number of half-gallon cartons of low-fat milk that were sold, and 128 half-gallon cartons of milk were sold in total, we have $W + L = 128$. This eliminates choice B.

Now, $3.75W$ is the revenue brought in from whole milk sold, in dollars, and $4.25L$ is the revenue brought in from low-fat milk sold, in dollars. It follows that total revenue brought in from milk sold, in dollars, is $3.75W + 4.25L$. We are given that this quantity is equal to 516. Therefore, we have $3.75W + 4.25L = 516$, and the answer is choice **A**.

3.

* Since x is the number of geometry books ordered and y is the number of algebra books ordered, it follows that the total number of math text books ordered is $x + y$. We are told that the school needs to order *at least* 18 books, and so $x + y \geq 18$. This narrows down the possible choices to A and B.

Now, $35x$ is the cost for geometry books, in dollars, and $40y$ is the cost for algebra books, in dollars. So, the total cost for math text books, in dollars, is $35x + 40y$. We are told that the school has a budget of \$740, and so we must have $35x + 40y \leq 740$. So, the answer is choice **B**.

4.

* The total number of beans is $b + k$, and so we must have $b + k \leq 200$. This narrows down our answer to either choice B or D. The total cost of the black beans, in dollars, is $0.35b$ and the total cost of the kidney beans, in dollars, is $0.42k$. It follows that the total cost of all the beans is $0.35b + 0.42k$. Therefore, we must have $0.35b + 0.42k \leq 75$. The answer is choice **B**.

5.

* The total number of containers is $x + y$, and so we must have $x + y \leq 42$. This narrows down our answer to either choice B or C. The total weight of the lighter containers is $32x$ and the total weight of the heavier containers is $61y$. It follows that the total weight of all the containers is $32x + 61y$. So, we must have $32x + 61y \leq 2000$. Therefore, the answer is choice **B**.

6.

* The total number of games played is $c + n$, and so we want to have $c + n \geq 60$. This narrows down our answer to either choice C or D. The total cost of playing the classic games, in dollars, is $0.75c$ and the total cost of playing the new games, in dollars, is $2.25n$. It follows that the total cost of playing all the games is $0.75c + 2.25n$. Therefore, we must have $0.75c + 2.25n \leq 75$. The answer is choice **C**.

7.

* Since d was the number of DVDs shipped to the warehouse and b was the number of Blue-rays shipped to the warehouse, it follows that the total number of movies shipped to the warehouse was $d + b$. We are told that 50 copies of the movie were shipped to the warehouse, and so we have $d + b = 50$. From this information, we can eliminate choices A and B (the first equations in choices C and D are both equivalent to $d + b = 50$).

Now, $260d$ is the total volume of the DVD boxes, in cubic centimeters, and $230b$ is the total volume of the Blue-ray boxes, in cubic centimeters. So, the total volume of the boxes, in cubic centimeters, is $260d + 230b$ We are told that the total volume shipped was 12,010 cubic inches, and so we have $260d + 230b = 12,010$. So, the answer is choice **D**.

Note: If we subtract b from each side of the equation $d + b = 50$, we get $d = 50 - b$, which is equivalent to the first equation in choice D.

8.

* The total number of houses sold was $x + y$. If the real estate agent had met her goal, then we would have $x + y \geq 15$. However, she did NOT meet her goal, and so we have $x + y < 15$. This narrows down the answer to either choice C or D.

The total value of the basic houses sold, in dollars, is $800,000x$ and the total value of the upgraded houses sold, in dollars, is $925,000y$. So, the total value, in dollars, of all houses sold was $800,000x + 925,000y$. We are told that this value is over $10,000,000. Therefore, we have $800,000x + 925,000y > 10,000,000$, and the answer is choice **C**.

9.

* The total number of crew members being hired is $x + y$, and so we want to have $x + y \geq 20$. This narrows down our answer to either choice A or C.

The total cost of paying electricians, in dollars per day, is $200x$ and the total cost of paying assistants, in dollars per day, is $120y$. It follows that the total cost of paying all the crew members is $200x + 120y$. Therefore, we must have $200x + 120y \leq 3200$. Choices A and C still work.

Since we need at least 2 electricians, we must have $x \geq 2$. This eliminates choice A, and so the answer is choice **C**.

Note: For completeness, observe that since we need at least 3 assistants, we must have $y \geq 3$.

10.

* Since we want at least twice as many ink cartridges as reams of paper, we must have $c \geq 2r$. This is equivalent to $2r \leq c$. The weight of the reams of paper, in pounds, is $20r$ and the weight of the ink cartridges, in pounds, is $\frac{1}{3}c$, making the total weight $20r + \frac{1}{3}c$. Since the supplier will deliver at most 250 pounds per shipment, we must have $20r + \frac{1}{3}c \leq 250$. The answer is choice **A**.

Note: The sentence "at least twice as many ink cartridges as reams of paper" is a tricky one to translate into an inequality. I suggest "taking a guess" for the correct inequality and then plugging in numbers to make sure your guess is correct. For example, suppose we were to guess (incorrectly) that the inequality should be $2r \geq c$. Let's let there be 5 reams of paper and 11 ink cartridges. Notice that twice as many reams of paper would be 10. So, with 11 ink cartridges, there are at least twice as many ink cartridges as reams of paper. We have $c = 11$ and $r = 5$. Let's plug these numbers into the inequality $2r \geq c$. We get $2 \cdot 5 \geq 11$, or equivalently, $10 \geq 11$. This is false, and so we chose the wrong inequality. Therefore, the correct inequality must be $2r \leq c$.

LESSON 38 – PASSPORT TO ADVANCED MATH
NONLINEAR SYSTEMS OF EQUATIONS

What Do You Get When You Cross a Linear Equation with a Nonlinear Equation?

The SAT likes to give systems of equations where one of the equations is linear and the other one is quadratic. The elimination method and Gauss-Jordan reduction from the previous section no longer work for these problems, but we can still use **substitution, graphical analysis**, and sometimes just **plugging in the answer choices**.

LEVEL 1: PASSPORT TO ADVANCED MATH – NONLINEAR SYSTEMS OF EQUATIONS

$$y = x^2$$
$$y = x$$

1. Which value is an x-coordinate of a solution to the system of equations above?

   A) -2
   B) -1
   C) 1
   D) 2

LEVEL 2: PASSPORT TO ADVANCED MATH – NONLINEAR SYSTEMS OF EQUATIONS

$$x = \frac{y-4}{2}$$
$$y = x^2 + 4x - 11$$

2. Which of the following ordered pairs (x, y) satisfies both of the above equations?

   A) $(-2, 0)$
   B) $(-5, 6)$
   C) $(3, 10)$
   D) $(2, 1)$

LEVEL 3: PASSPORT TO ADVANCED MATH – NONLINEAR SYSTEMS OF EQUATIONS

3. In the xy-plane, the graph of $y = 5x^2 - 9x$ intersects the graph of $y = 2x$ at the points $(0, 0)$ and $(c, 2c)$, where $c \neq 0$. What is the value of c?

LEVEL 4: PASSPORT TO ADVANCED MATH – NONLINEAR SYSTEMS OF EQUATIONS

$$x = y^2$$
$$5x + 12 = 2(y + 6)$$

4. If (x, y) is a solution of the system of equations above and $y > 0$, what is the value of $\frac{y}{x}$?

    A) 1.5
    B) 2
    C) 2.5
    D) 3

$$x + y^2 = 3$$
$$3y - x = 7$$

5. Which value is an x-coordinate of a solution to the system of equations above?

    A) -1
    B) 0
    C) 1
    D) 22

$$y = ax^2 - b$$
$$y = 8$$

6. In the system of equations above, a and b are nonzero constants. For which of the following values of a and b does the system of equations have exactly one real solution?

    A) $a = -2, b = -8$
    B) $a = 2, b = -6$
    C) $a = 2, b = -4$
    D) $a = 2, b = 4$

LEVEL 5: PASSPORT TO ADVANCED MATH – NONLINEAR SYSTEMS OF EQUATIONS

$$y = x^2 + 5x + 6$$
$$7x + 4 - y = 0$$

7. How many solutions are there to the system of equations above of the form (x, y), with x a real number?

    A) 0
    B) 1
    C) 2
    D) More than 2

$$y = x^2 + x + 12$$
$$y = 7x + 3$$

8. What is the y-coordinate of the point of intersection of the graphs of the equations above?

$$y = 3 - 2x$$
$$y = x^2 - 9x + 3$$

9. If the ordered pair (x, y) satisfies the system of equations above, and $x \neq 0$, what is one possible value of $|xy|$?

$$y = (2 - x)(3x - 1)$$
$$x = 2y + 5$$

10. * How many ordered pairs (x, y) satisfy the system of equations shown above?

Answers

1. C   2. C   3. 11/5, 2.2   4. C   5. A   6. A   7. A   8. 24   9. 77   10. 2

Full Solutions

1.
* Solution by starting with choice C: Let's start with choice C and guess that $x = 1$. Then the first equation gives us $y = x^2 = 1^2 = 1$, and the second equation gives us $y = x = 1$. Since these two equations agree, the answer is choice **C**.

Complete algebraic solution: From the second equation, $y = x$. So, we can replace y by x in the first equation giving us $x = x^2$. We subtract x from each side of this equation to get $x^2 - x = 0$. We factor the left-hand side of this equation to get $x(x - 1) = 0$. So, $x = 0$ or $x - 1 = 0$, and we get the solutions $x = 0$ and $x = 1$. Only 1 is an answer choice. This is choice **C**.

2.
* Solution by starting with choice C: Let's start with choice C and guess that $(3, 10)$ is a solution of the system. Substituting into the first equation gives us $3 = \frac{10-4}{2} \Leftrightarrow 3 = \frac{6}{2} \Leftrightarrow 3 = 3$. This works.

Substituting into the second equation gives $10 = 3^2 + 4 \cdot 3 - 11 \Leftrightarrow 10 = 9 + 12 - 11 \Leftrightarrow 10 = 10$. This also works, and so the answer is choice **C**.

Complete algebraic solution: Let's solve the first equation for y. Multiplying each side of the equation by 2 gives us $2x = y - 4$. Adding 4 to each side of this last equation gives $2x + 4 = y$. So, we have $y = 2x + 4$ and $y = x^2 + 4x - 11$. It follows that $x^2 + 4x - 11 = 2x + 4$. Subtracting $2x$ and 4 from each side of the equation yields $x^2 + 2x - 15 = 0$. Factoring on the left gives us $(x + 5)(x - 3) = 0$. So, $x = -5$ or $x = 3$. When $x = 3$, $y = 2 \cdot 3 + 4 = 6 + 4 = 10$. So, $(3, 10)$ satisfies both equations, choice **C**.

Note: When $x = -5$, $y = 2(-5) + 4 = -10 + 4 = -6$. But $(-5, -6)$ is not an answer choice. If you overlook the minus sign in front of the 6, you could accidentally pick choice B.

3.

* Algebraic solution: We are given that the point $(c, 2c)$ lies on both graphs. In particular, it lies on the graph of the first equation. So, we have $2c = 5c^2 - 9c$. Subtracting $2c$ from each side of this equation yields $5c^2 - 11c = 0$. We factor on the left to get $c(5c - 11) = 0$. Therefore, $c = 0$ or $5c - 11 = 0$. Solving the second equation for c gives us $c =$ **11/5** or **2.2**.

Notes: (1) When we substitute $c = \frac{11}{5}$ for x into each of the two given equations, we get $y = \frac{22}{5} = 2 \cdot \frac{11}{5}$. For example, $5\left(\frac{11}{5}\right)^2 - 9 \cdot \frac{11}{5} = 5 \cdot \frac{121}{25} - \frac{99}{5} = \frac{121}{5} - \frac{99}{5} = \frac{121-99}{5} = \frac{22}{5} = 2 \cdot \frac{11}{5}$.

(2) The question is simply asking us to find the x-coordinate of the solution to the system of equations consisting of $y = 5x^2 - 9x$ and $y = 2x$. The question gives an extra hint by letting us know that the solution we are looking for has the form $(c, 2c)$. This is actually already evident from the second equation: if $x = c$, then $y = 2x = 2c$.

4.

* Algebraic solution: Since $x = y^2$ (from the first equation), we can replace x by y^2 in the second equation and solve for y.

$$5y^2 + 12 = 2(y + 6)$$
$$5y^2 + 12 = 2y + 12$$
$$5y^2 = 2y$$
$$5y^2 - 2y = 0$$
$$y(5y - 2) = 0$$
$$y = 0 \text{ or } 5y - 2 = 0$$

Since we are given that $y > 0$, we must have $5y - 2 = 0$. So, $5y = 2$, and therefore, $y = \frac{2}{5}$. It follows that $x = y^2 = \left(\frac{2}{5}\right)^2 = \frac{4}{25}$. Finally, $\frac{y}{x} = \frac{2}{5} \div \frac{4}{25} = \frac{2}{5} \cdot \frac{25}{4} = \frac{2}{4} \cdot \frac{25}{5} = \frac{1}{2} \cdot 5 = \frac{5}{2} = 2.5$, choice **C**.

5.

* Algebraic solution: We add the two equations to get $y^2 + 3y = 10$. Subtracting 10 from each side of this equation gives us $y^2 + 3y - 10 = 0$. We factor on the left to get $(y + 5)(y - 2) = 0$. So, $y + 5 = 0$ or $y - 2 = 0$. Therefore, $y = -5$ or $y = 2$.

We solve the second equation for x by adding x to each side and subtracting 7 from each side. We get $x = 3y - 7$. When $y = 2$, this gives us $x = 3 \cdot 2 - 7 = 6 - 7 = -1$, choice **A**.

Note: When $y = -5$, we have $x = 3(-5) - 7 = -15 - 7 = -22$. So, -22 is also an x-coordinate of a solution to the system of equations. However, this number is not one of the choices.

6.

*Solution using the square root property: Replacing y with 8 in the first equation yields $8 = ax^2 - b$. Adding b to each side of this equation give us $8 + b = ax^2$. We now divide by a (assuming $a \neq 0$) to get $x^2 = \frac{8+b}{a}$. We use the square root property to get $x = \pm\sqrt{\frac{8+b}{a}}$.

This will yield exactly one real solution if the expression under the square root is zero. So, we need $8 + b = 0$, or equivalently $b = -8$, choice **A**.

Note: We can also find the discriminant of the quadratic equation $ax^2 - b - 8 = 0$, and set it equal to 0. The discriminant is $\Delta = 0^2 - 4a(-b - 8) = 4ab + 32a = 4a(b + 8)$. This is 0 when $a = 0$ or $b = -8$. Since we are given that a is nonzero, we must have $b = -8$, choice A.

See the end of Lesson 34 for more information on the discriminant.

7.
* **Solution by substitution:** We solve the second equation for y by adding y to each side of the equation: $7x + 4 = y$

We now replace y by $7x + 4$ in the first equation to get $7x + 4 = x^2 + 5x + 6$.

We now add $-7x - 4$ to each side of the equation to get $0 = x^2 - 2x + 2$.

The equation $x^2 - 2x + 2 = 0$ has discriminant $b^2 - 4ac = (-2)^2 - 4 \cdot 1 \cdot 2 = 4 - 8 = -4$.

Since the discriminant is negative, there are no real values of x that satisfy the equation. So, the answer is choice **A**.

Notes: (1) We can also begin this problem by adding the two equations. When we do this, we get $7x + 4 = x^2 + 5x + 6$. We would then proceed as in the solution above.

(2) See the end of Lesson 34 for more information on the discriminant.

8.
* **Algebraic solution:** Since each equation has y by itself, we have $x^2 + x + 12 = 7x + 3$. We subtract $7x$ and 3 from each side of this equation to get $x^2 - 6x + 9 = 0$. Factoring the left-hand side of this equation gives us $(x - 3)^2 = 0$, and so $x = 3$. It follows from the second equation that $y = 7x + 3 = 7 \cdot 3 + 3 = 21 + 3 = \mathbf{24}$.

9.
* **Algebraic solution:** Since each equation has y by itself, we have $x^2 - 9x + 3 = 3 - 2x$. We subtract 3 from each side of this equation and add $2x$ to each side of this equation to get $x^2 - 7x = 0$. Factoring the left-hand side of this equation gives us $x(x - 7) = 0$, and so $x = 0$ or $x = 7$. We are given that $x \neq 0$, and so we must have $x = 7$. So, $y = 3 - 2 \cdot 7 = 3 - 14 = -11$. Therefore, $|xy| = |7(-11)| = |-77| = \mathbf{77}$.

10.
Solution by substitution: We replace x by $2y + 5$ twice in the right-hand side of the first equation to get

$$y = (2 - (2y + 5))(3(2y + 5) - 1) = (2 - 2y - 5)(6y + 15 - 1) = (-2y - 3)(6y + 14)$$
$$= -12y^2 - 28y - 18y - 42 = -12y^2 - 46y - 42$$

Bringing everything over to the left-hand side of the equation yields

$$12y^2 + 47y + 42 = 0$$

This is a quadratic equation with $a = 12$, $b = 47$, and $c = 42$. We compute the discriminant of this equation to get $b^2 - 4ac = 47^2 - 4(12)(42) = 2209 - 2016 > 0$. Since the discriminant is positive, the quadratic equation has 2 real solutions. The answer is **2**.

Notes: (1) See the end of Lesson 34 for more information on the discriminant.

(2) It was not necessary to finish computing the discriminant in this problem. We needed only to find out if it was positive, zero, or negative.

* **Quick graphical solution:** We can get a quick rough sketch of the parabola by plotting the two x-intercepts $(2,0)$ and $(\frac{1}{3}, 0)$ and noting that the parabola opens downwards. We can then plot the x-intercept of the line, $(5, 0)$ and note that the slope of the line is $m = \frac{1}{2}$. A quick sketch will show that the line must hit the parabola twice. So, the answer is **2**.

Notes: (1) To see that the slope of the line is $\frac{1}{2}$, we need to solve the second equation for y to get $y = \frac{1}{2}x - \frac{5}{2}$.

(2) If a calculator were allowed for this problem, we could also solve by graphing the two equations in our calculator, finding an appropriate window, and counting the points of intersection. Note that we would first have to solve the second equation for y. I leave the details of this solution to the reader.

(3) See Lesson 42 for more information on graphing parabolas.

LESSON 39 – PROBLEM SOLVING
PROBABILITY

Simple Principle

Simple Probability Principle: To compute a simple probability where all outcomes are equally likely, divide the number of "successes" by the total number of outcomes. Let's try an example.

LEVEL 1: PROBLEM SOLVING – PROBABILITY

Instruments Played by Children in a Community

Instrument	Piano	Guitar	Drums	Violin	Trumpet
Number of children who play instrument	3	7	15	1	4

1. * The instruments that each of 30 children in a community can play is shown in the chart above. Assume that each child plays exactly one instrument. If a child is chosen at random, which of the following is closest to the probability that the child can play the trumpet?

   A) 0.03
   B) 0.13
   C) 0.23
   D) 0.5

* Solution using the simple probability principle: The total number of outcomes is 30 and the number of successes is 4. So, the desired probability is $\frac{4}{30} \approx 0.133$. The closest answer in the choices is 0.13, choice **B**.

Under One Condition!

A **conditional probability** measures the probability of an event given that another event has occurred. Let's use an example to illustrate conditional probability.

LEVEL 3: PROBLEM SOLVING – PROBABILITY

	Less than 2.5	Between 2.5 and 3.5	Greater than 3.5	Total
School A	272	117	36	425
School B	146	308	121	575
Total	418	425	157	1000

2. * The data in the table above categorizes the GPAs of the students from two high schools. If a student with a GPA between 2.5 and 3.5 is chosen at random, what is the probability that the student goes to school B?

* This is a conditional probability. We want the probability the student goes to school B *given* the student has a GPA between 2.5 and 3.5. This is $\frac{308}{425} \approx .724$ or $.725$.

Notes: (1) In this question we are being asked to use the table to compute a conditional probability. Let's name the events as follows: X will stand for "the student selected has a GPA between 2.5 and 3.5" and B will stand for "the student selected goes to school B."

The requested probability is $P(B|X)$. This is read as "the probability that the student goes to school B given that the student has a GPA between 2.5 and 3.5" (in particular, the vertical line is read "given"). We can say this more simply as "the probability that a student with a GPA between 2.5 and 3.5 goes to school B."

(2) For the total, we use the Total row and the "Between 2.5 and 3.5" column. So, the total is 425. For the successes, we use the "School B" row and the "Between 2.5 and 3.5" column. This is 308.

(3) The technical formula for the conditional probability we are computing here is $P(B|X) = \frac{P(B \cap X)}{P(X)}$. $B \cap X$, read "B intersect X" or "B and X," is the event consisting of all outcomes common to both B and X. These are students that go to school B and have a GPA between 2.5 and 3.5.

Time to Practice

LEVEL 3: PROBLEM SOLVING – PROBABILITY

Questions 3 - 5 refer to the following information.

A survey was conducted among a randomly chosen sample of 100 males and 100 females to gather data on pet ownership. The data are shown in the table below.

	Has pets	Does not have pets	Total
Men	75	25	100
Women	63	37	100
Total	138	62	200

3. According to the table, what is the probability that a randomly selected person has pets?

   A) $\frac{3}{8}$

   B) $\frac{25}{46}$

   C) $\frac{69}{100}$

   D) $\frac{3}{4}$

4. According to the table, what is the probability that a randomly selected man does not have pets?

5. * According to the table, what is the probability that a randomly selected person with pets is female?

Questions 6 - 7 refer to the following information.

Number of Students by Quiz and Grade						
1990	0%	25%	50%	75%	100%	Total
Quiz 1	2	4	6	10	8	30
Quiz 2	2	8	9	6	5	30
Quiz 3	1	3	5	9	12	30
Total	5	15	20	25	25	90

30 students in a math class took 3 short quizzes during the school year. Each quiz consisted of 4 questions, each question contributing to 25% of the quiz grade. The number of students receiving each of the 5 possible grades on each quiz is shown in the table above.

6. What was the mean grade of the students on the second quiz? (Disregard the percent symbol when gridding your answer.)

LEVEL 4: PROBLEM SOLVING – PROBABILITY

7. Assume that no student received the same grade on two different quizzes. If a student is selected at random, what is the probability that that student received a score of 100% on the first or third quiz, assuming that the student received a grade of 100% on one of the three quizzes?

LEVEL 5: PROBLEM SOLVING – PROBABILITY

Questions 8 - 10 refer to the following information.

Average Number of Meals Per Day

	Less than 3	3 to 5	More than 5	Total
Active	21	56	123	200
Inactive	56	96	48	200
Total	77	152	171	400

The table above was created by a health and fitness researcher studying the number of meals active and inactive people eat per day.

8. If a person is chosen at random from those who eat at least 3 meals per day, what is the probability that the person is active?

   A) $\frac{7}{19}$

   B) $\frac{179}{400}$

   C) $\frac{179}{323}$

   D) $\frac{179}{200}$

9. What is the probability that a randomly selected inactive person eats exactly 2 meals per day?

   A) $\frac{7}{75}$

   B) $\frac{7}{25}$

   C) $\frac{56}{77}$

   D) Cannot be determined from the given information

10. What is the probability that a randomly selected person is inactive or eats no more than 5 meals per day?

Answers

1. B   2. .724, .725   3. C   4. 1/4, .25   5. .456, .457   6. 53.3   7. 4/5, .8   8. C   9. D   10. .692, .693

Full Solutions

3.
* There is a total of 200 people, and of these people 138 have pets. So, the desired probability is $\frac{138}{200} = \frac{69}{100}$, choice **C**.

Notes: (1) The denominator of the fraction is 200, the total number of people. To find this number we look in the column labeled "Total" and the row labeled "Total."

(2) The numerator of the fraction is 138, the number of people who have pets. To find this number we look in the column labeled "Has pets" and the row labeled "Total."

4.
* There is a total of 100 men, and of these men 25 do not have pets. So, the desired probability is $\frac{25}{100} = 1/4$ or $.25$.

Notes: (1) The denominator of the fraction is 100, the total number of men. To find this number we look in the column labeled "Total" and the row labeled "Men."

(2) The numerator of the fraction is 25, the number of men who do not have pets. To find this number we look in the column labeled "Does not have pets" and the row labeled "Men."

5.
* There are 138 people who have pets, and of these 63 are women. So, the desired probability is $\frac{63}{138} \approx 0.4565217$. Therefore, we can grid in $.456$ or $.457$.

6.
* $\frac{2 \cdot 0 + 8 \cdot 25 + 9 \cdot 50 + 6 \cdot 75 + 5 \cdot 100}{30} = \frac{200 + 450 + 450 + 500}{30} = \frac{1600}{30} \approx 53.33$. So, we grid in 53.3.

7.
* The number of students that received a grade of 100% on one of the three quizzes is 25. The number of students that scored 100% on the first or third quiz is $8 + 12 = 20$. So, the desired probability is $\frac{20}{25} = 4/5$ or $.8$.

8.
* The number of people who eat at least 3 meals per day is $152 + 171 = 323$ and of these, the number that are active is $56 + 123 = 179$. So, the desired probability is $\frac{179}{323}$, choice **C**.

9.
* The table does not give any information about people who eat EXACTLY 2 meals per day. So, this probability cannot be determined, choice **D**.

10.
* The total is 400. Let's highlight all the "successes" in the table.

Average Number of Meals Per Day

	Less than 3	3 to 5	More than 5	Total
Active	21	56	123	200
Inactive	56	96	48	200
Total	77	152	171	400

We see that the number of successes is $21 + 56 + 56 + 96 + 48 = 277$. Therefore, the desired probability is $\frac{277}{400} = 0.6925$. So, we can grid in $.692$ or $.693$.

LESSON 40 – GEOMETRY
POLYGONS

Quadrilaterals

A **quadrilateral** is a two-dimensional geometric figure with four sides and four angles. The sum of the degree measures of all four interior angles of a quadrilateral is 360.

A **rectangle** is a quadrilateral in which each angle is a right angle. That is, each angle has a measure of 90 degrees. The **perimeter** of a rectangle is $P = 2l + 2w$, and the area of a rectangle is $A = lw$.

A **square** is a rectangle with four equal sides. The perimeter of a square is $P = 4s$ and the area of a square is $A = s^2$.

Example:

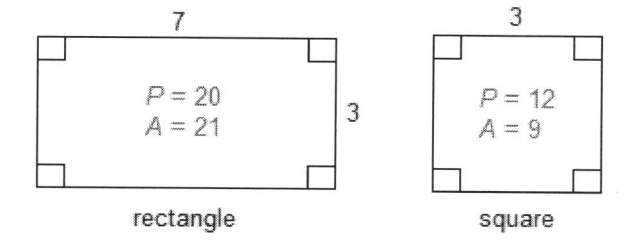

rectangle: 7 by 3, $P = 20$, $A = 21$

square: 3 by 3, $P = 12$, $A = 9$

Let's try an SAT problem.

LEVEL 1: GEOMETRY – POLYGONS

1. What is the area of a rectangle, in square centimeters, that has a perimeter of 100 centimeters and a length of 20 centimeters?

We have
$$P = 2l + 2w$$
$$100 = 2(20) + 2w$$
$$100 = 40 + 2w$$
$$60 = 2w$$
$$30 = w$$

So, $A = lw = (20)(30) = \mathbf{600}$.

* **Quick solution:** $w = \frac{100-2(20)}{2} = \frac{100-40}{2} = \frac{60}{2} = 30$, and therefore, $A = (20)(30) = \mathbf{600}$.

A **parallelogram** is a quadrilateral whose opposite sides are parallel.

Facts about parallelograms:
(1) Opposite sides are congruent.
(2) Opposite angles are congruent.
(3) Adjacent angles are supplementary.
(4) The diagonals bisect each other.

263

Note that rectangles are parallelograms, and therefore, squares are also parallelograms.

The **area** of a parallelogram is $A = bh$.

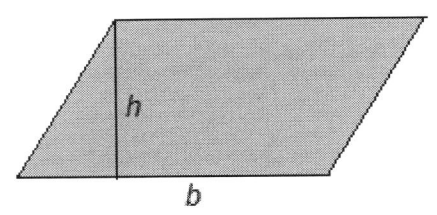

A **rhombus** is a parallelogram with four equal sides.

Facts about rhombuses:
(1) The diagonals are perpendicular.
(2) The diagonals bisect the angles.

Note that squares are rhombuses.

A **trapezoid** is a quadrilateral with two parallel sides (and two nonparallel sides). The two parallel sides are called **bases**, and the nonparallel sides are called **legs**.

A trapezoid is **isosceles** if the nonparallel sides are congruent. Note that isosceles trapezoids have two pairs of congruent angles, and noncongruent angles are supplementary.

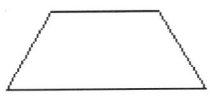

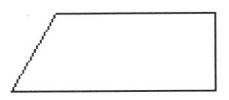

isosceles trapezoid   nonisosceles trapezoid

The **area** of a trapezoid is $A = \frac{(b_1+b_2)}{2} h$. In other words, to compute the area of a trapezoid we take the average of the two bases and multiply by the height.

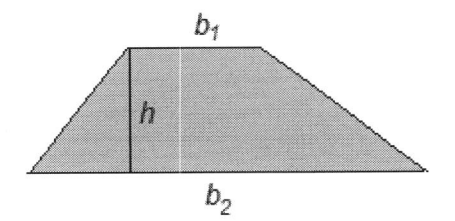

Just Another Regular Polygon

A **regular** polygon is a polygon with all sides equal in length, and all angles equal in measure.

The total number of degrees in the interior of an n-sided polygon is $(n-2) \cdot 180$.

For example, a six-sided polygon (or hexagon) has $(6-2) \cdot 180 = 4 \cdot 180 = 720$ degrees in its interior. Therefore, each angle of a **regular** hexagon measures $\frac{720}{6} = 120$ degrees.

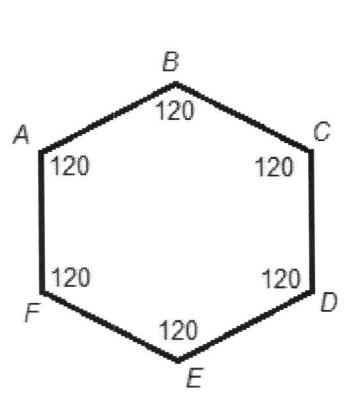

For those of us that do not like to memorize formulas, there is a quick visual way to determine the total number of degrees in the interior of an n-sided polygon. Simply split the polygon up into triangles and quadrilaterals by drawing nonintersecting line segments between vertices. Then add 180 degrees for each triangle and 360 degrees for each quadrilateral. For example, here is one way to do it for a hexagon.

Since the hexagon has been split up into 2 triangles and 1 quadrilateral, the hexagon has $2(180) + 360 = \mathbf{720}$ degrees. This is the same number we got from the formula.

To avoid potential errors, let me give a picture that would be incorrect.

The figure to the right **cannot** be used to compute the number of interior angles in the hexagon because segment $\overline{AD}$ is "crossing through" segment $\overline{BF}$.

Now let's draw a segment from the center of a regular hexagon to each vertex of the hexagon.

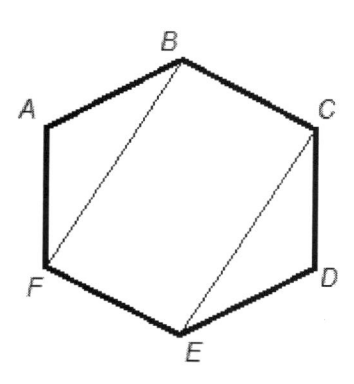

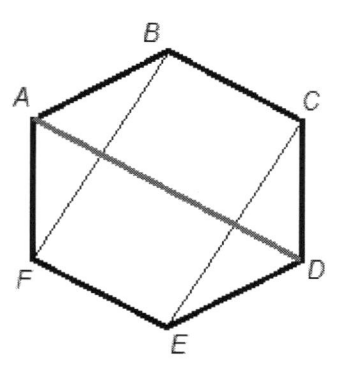

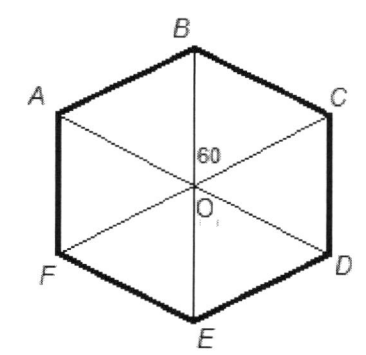

We see that the central angles formed must add up to 360 degrees. Therefore, each central angle measures 60 degrees as shown in the figure above.

In general, the number of degrees in a central angle of a regular n-sided polygon is $\dfrac{360}{n}$.

It is worth looking at a regular hexagon in a bit more detail.

Each of the segments just drawn in the previous figure is a radius of the circumscribed circle of this hexagon, and therefore they are all congruent. This means that each triangle is isosceles, and so the measure of each of the other two angles of any of these triangles is $\dfrac{180-60}{2} = 60$. Therefore, each of these triangles is equilateral. This fact is worth committing to memory.

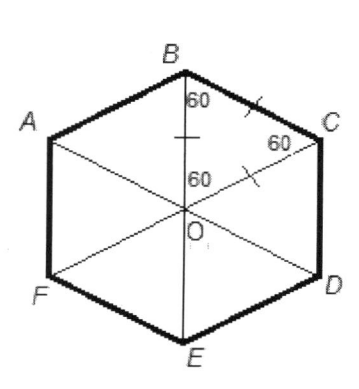

Time to Practice

LEVEL 2: GEOMETRY – POLYGONS

2. The perimeter of a rectangle with side lengths a and b is $P = 2a + 2b$. Each side of Rectangle I has a length that is 3 times the length of Rectangle II. The perimeter of Rectangle II is what fraction of the perimeter of Rectangle I?

LEVEL 3: GEOMETRY – POLYGONS

3. A rectangle has a perimeter of 100 feet. What is the area of the rectangle, in square feet?

    A) 200
    B) 400
    C) 600
    D) Cannot be determined from the given information

4. In the figure to the right, what is the value of x ?

    A) 100
    B) 105
    C) 108
    D) 110

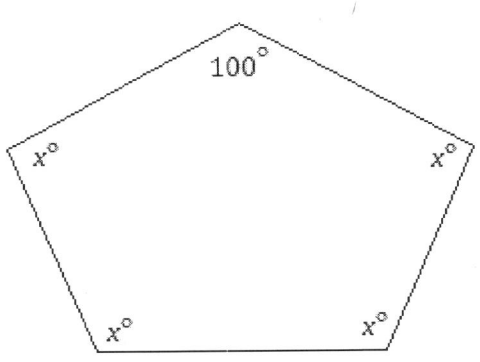

    Note: Figure not drawn to scale.

5. The measure x, in degrees, of an exterior angle of a regular polygon is related to the number of sides, n, of the polygon by the formula $nx = 360$. If the measure of an exterior angle of a regular polygon is less than 50°, what is the least number of sides it can have?

LEVEL 4: GEOMETRY – POLYGONS

6. A line segment is drawn from the center of a 12-sided regular polygon to each vertex of the polygon forming 12 isosceles triangles. What is the measure of a base angle of one of these triangles? (Disregard the degree symbol when gridding your answer.)

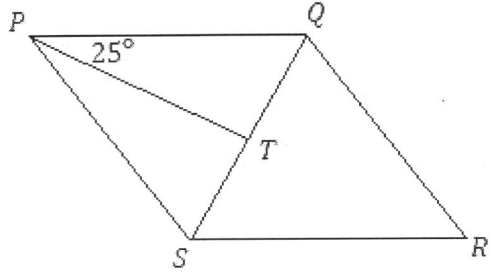

7. In the rhombus shown above, $m\angle QPT = 25°$ and T splits $\overline{QS}$ into two equal pieces. What is $m\angle QSR$? (Disregard the degree symbol when gridding your answer.)

266

LEVEL 5: GEOMETRY – POLYGONS

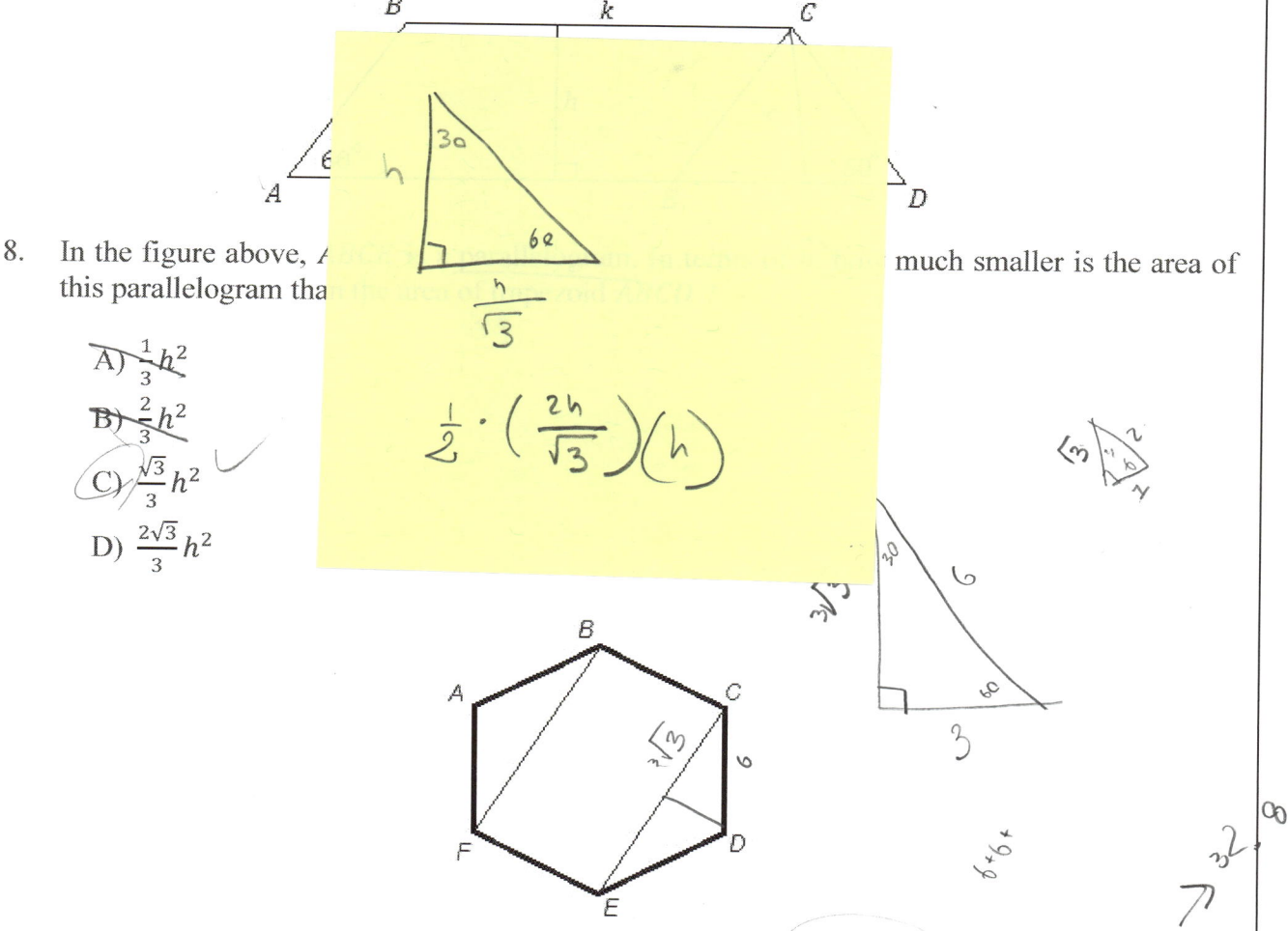

8. In the figure above, ABCD is a parallelogram. In terms of h, how much smaller is the area of this parallelogram than the area of trapezoid ABCD?

   A) $\frac{1}{3}h^2$
   B) $\frac{2}{3}h^2$
   C) $\frac{\sqrt{3}}{3}h^2$
   D) $\frac{2\sqrt{3}}{3}h^2$

9. * In the figure above, ABCDEF is a regular hexagon and $CD = 6$. What is the perimeter of rectangle BCEF to the nearest tenth?

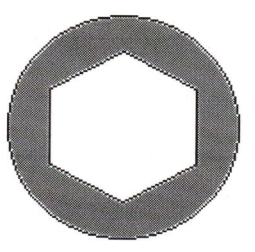

10. * The head of a copper "hexagon head screw bolt" (one cross section of which is shown above) has the shape of a cylinder with a hole shaped like a regular hexagon. The cylindrical head is 2 cm thick with a base diameter of 3 cm. The hexagonal hole is only half the thickness of the entire head, and each side of a hexagonal cross section has a length of 1 cm. Given that the density of copper is 8.96 grams per cubic cm, and density is mass divided by volume, find the mass of the head to the nearest gram.

267

Answers

1. 600   2. 1/3, .333   3. D   4. D   5. 8   6. 75   7. 65   8. C   9. 32.8   10. 103

Full Solutions

2.

* Quick solution: Let the sides of Rectangle II have lengths a and b. It follows that the sides of Rectangle I have lengths $3a$ and $3b$. The perimeter of Rectangle I is then $6a + 6b$, and the perimeter of Rectangle II is $2a + 2b = \frac{1}{3}(6a + 6b)$. So, the fraction we are looking for is **1/3** or **.333**.

Note: We can also pick numbers to solve this problem. I leave this solution to the reader.

3.

* In problem 1 above we saw that if $l = 20$, then $A = 600$. If we instead let $l = 10$, then we have $w = \frac{100-2(10)}{2} = \frac{100-20}{2} = \frac{80}{2} = 40$, and therefore, $A = (10)(40) = 400$. Therefore, the answer cannot be determined from the given information, choice **D**.

4.

* Since the figure is a 5-sided polygon, the total number of degrees in the figure's interior is $(5 - 2) \cdot 180 = 3 \cdot 180 = 540$. So, we have $4x + 100 = 540$. We subtract 100 from each side of this equation to get $4x = 440$. Dividing by 4 yields $x = \frac{440}{4} = 110$, choice **D**.

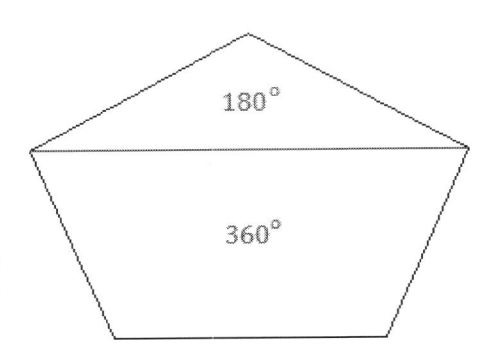

Note: We can also find the total number of degrees in the figure's interior by splitting the polygon up into a triangle and a quadrilateral as shown in the figure to the right. We then have that the total number of degrees is $180 + 360 = 540°$.

5.

* We are given $x < 50$, so that $\frac{1}{x} > \frac{1}{50}$. It follows that

$$n = \frac{360}{x} = 360\left(\frac{1}{x}\right) > 360\left(\frac{1}{50}\right) = 7.2.$$

So, the least possible value for n is **8.**

6.

* The measure of the vertex angle of one of these triangles is $\frac{360}{12} = 30°$. If we let x be the measure of one of the base angles of the triangle, in degrees, then we have $2x = 180 - 30 = 150$, and therefore, $x = \frac{150}{2} = \textbf{75}$.

7.

* Since the diagonals of a rhombus are perpendicular, it follows that $m\angle PTQ = 90°$. Since the angle measures inside a triangle sum to $180°$, we have $m\angle PQT = 180 - 25 - 90 = 65°$. $\overline{PQ} \parallel \overline{SR}$, and $\overline{QS}$ is a transversal. It follows that $m\angle QSR = m\angle PQS = 65°$. So, we grid in **65**.

268

Note: The figure to the right shows the rhombus with all the angles we found in the solution above.

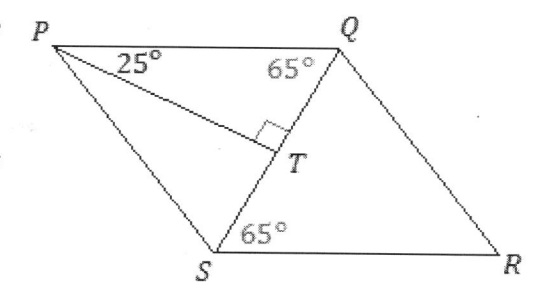

8.
* The difference between the two areas is the area of triangle CED. This triangle is equilateral with height h. If we draw altitude $\overline{CF}$, we form the 30, 60, 90 triangle CFD. Since the side opposite the 60° angle has length h, the side opposite the 30° angle has length $\frac{h}{\sqrt{3}}$. So, $ED = \frac{2h}{\sqrt{3}}$, and it follows that the area of the triangle is $\frac{1}{2}\left(\frac{2h}{\sqrt{3}}\right)h = \frac{h^2}{\sqrt{3}} = \frac{h^2}{\sqrt{3}} \cdot \frac{\sqrt{3}}{\sqrt{3}} = \frac{\sqrt{3}}{3}h^2$, choice **C**.

Note: In the figure to the right, we see altitude $\overline{CF}$ drawn to base $\overline{ED}$ forming the 30, 60, 90 triangle CFD. We have also labeled the three angles of the triangle, the height h, and the length of $\overline{FD}$ as x. Using the special 30, 60, 90 triangle given on the SAT, we see that $h = \sqrt{3}x$, so that $x = \frac{h}{\sqrt{3}}$.

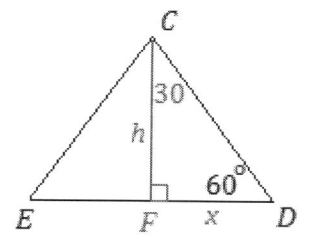

9.
* Since the hexagon is regular, $BC = EF = CD = 6$. Now let's add a bit to the picture (see the picture to the right).

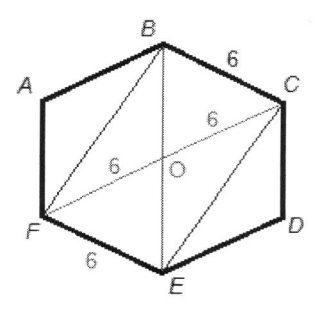

Again, note that the hexagon is regular. So, each angle of triangle BOC measures 60 degrees. Thus, triangle BOC is equilateral. So, $OF = OC = BC = 6$. Since $EF = 6$ and $FC = 12$, triangle CEF is a 30, 60, 90 triangle. It follows that $CE = 6\sqrt{3}$. Since $BCEF$ is a rectangle, $BF = 6\sqrt{3}$ as well. Therefore, the perimeter of rectangle $BCEF$ is $6 + 6 + 6\sqrt{3} + 6\sqrt{3} = 12 + 12\sqrt{3} \approx 32.78$. To the nearest tenth the answer is **32.8**.

10.
* We first compute the volume of the head. There are two parts to the volume.

The bottom half of the head is a cylinder with height $\frac{2}{2} = 1$ cm and base radius $\frac{3}{2}$ cm. It follows that the volume is $V = \pi r^2 h = \pi \left(\frac{3}{2}\right)^2 (1) = \frac{9\pi}{4}$ cm³.

The top half of the head consists of the same cylinder as the bottom half, but this time we have to subtract off the volume of a hexagonal prism. The regular hexagonal face can be divided into 6 equilateral triangles, each with area $A = \frac{s^2\sqrt{3}}{4} = \frac{1^2\sqrt{3}}{4} = \frac{\sqrt{3}}{4}$. So, the volume of the hexagonal prism is $V = Bh = \left(\frac{6\sqrt{3}}{4}\right)(1) = \frac{3\sqrt{3}}{2}$ cm³ and the volume of the top half of the head is $\frac{9\pi}{4} - \frac{3\sqrt{3}}{2}$ cm³.

It follows that the total volume of the head is $\frac{9\pi}{4} + \left(\frac{9\pi}{4} - \frac{3\sqrt{3}}{2}\right) = \frac{18\pi}{4} - \frac{3\sqrt{3}}{2} = \frac{9\pi - 3\sqrt{3}}{2}$ cm³.

Finally, $D = \frac{M}{V} \Rightarrow 8.96 = \frac{M}{\frac{9\pi - 3\sqrt{3}}{2}} \Rightarrow M = 8.96 \cdot \frac{9\pi - 3\sqrt{3}}{2} \approx 103.39$ grams.

To the nearest gram, the answer is **103**.

Notes: (1) The radius of a circle is $\frac{1}{2}$ the diameter, or $r = \frac{1}{2}d$.

In this problem, the base diameter of the cylinder is 3 cm. It follows that the base radius of the cylinder is $\frac{3}{2}$ cm or 1.5 cm.

(2) The volume of a cylinder is $\boldsymbol{V = \pi r^2 h}$, where r is the base radius of the cylinder and h is the height of the cylinder.

For example, the bottom half of the screw is a cylinder with base radius $\frac{3}{2}$ cm and height 1 cm. So, the volume is $V = \pi \left(\frac{3}{2}\right)^2 (1) = \frac{9\pi}{4}$ cm^3.

(3) The area of an equilateral triangle with side length s is $A = \frac{\sqrt{3}}{4}s^2$ (see note (4) below).

It follows that the area of an equilateral triangle with side length 1 is $\frac{\sqrt{3}}{4}(1)^2 = \frac{\sqrt{3}}{4}$.

(4) Most students do not know the formula for the area of an equilateral triangle, so here is a quick derivation.

Let's start by drawing a picture of an equilateral triangle with side length s, and draw an **altitude** from a vertex to the opposite base. Note that an altitude of an equilateral triangle is the same as the **median** and **angle bisector** (this is in fact true for any isosceles triangle – see problem 9 from Lesson 8).

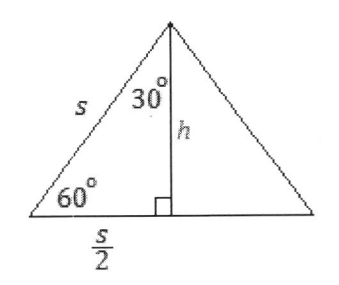

So, we get two $30, 60, 90$ right triangles, each with a leg of length $\frac{s}{2}$ and hypotenuse of length s.

We can find h by recalling that the side opposite the 60-degree angle has length $\sqrt{3}$ times the length of the side opposite the 30-degree angle. So, $h = \frac{\sqrt{3}s}{2}$.

Alternatively, we can use the Pythagorean Theorem to find h:

$$h^2 = s^2 - \left(\frac{s}{2}\right)^2 = s^2 - \frac{s^2}{4} = \frac{4s^2}{4} - \frac{s^2}{4} = \frac{3s^2}{4}. \text{ So, } h = \frac{\sqrt{3}s}{2}.$$

It follows that the area of the triangle is

$$A = \frac{1}{2}\left(\frac{s}{2} + \frac{s}{2}\right)\left(\frac{\sqrt{3}s}{2}\right) = \frac{1}{2}s\left(\frac{\sqrt{3}s}{2}\right) = \frac{\sqrt{3}}{4}s^2.$$

(5) The volume of a prism is $\boldsymbol{V = Bh}$ where B is the area of the base of the prism and h is the height of the prism. In this problem, we have a hexagonal prism with $B = \frac{6\sqrt{3}}{4} = \frac{3\sqrt{3}}{2}$ and $h = 1$. It follows that the volume of this prism is $V = \left(\frac{3\sqrt{3}}{2}\right)(1) = \frac{3\sqrt{3}}{2}$.

LESSON 41 – HEART OF ALGEBRA
ADVANCED LINEAR SYSTEMS

The None, The One, The Infinitely Many

The **general form of an equation of a line** is $ax + by = c$, where a, b, and c are real numbers. If $b \neq 0$, then the slope of this line is $m = -\frac{a}{b}$. If $b = 0$, then the line is vertical and has no slope.

Let us consider 2 such equations.

$$ax + by = c$$
$$dx + ey = f$$

(1) If there is a number r such that $ra = d$, $rb = e$, and $rc = f$, then the two equations represent the **same line**. Equivalently, the two equations represent the same line if $\frac{a}{d} = \frac{b}{e} = \frac{c}{f}$. In this case, the system of equations has **infinitely many solutions**.

(2) If there is a number r such that $ra = d$, $rb = e$, but $rc \neq f$, then the two equations represent **parallel** but distinct lines. Equivalently, the two equations represent parallel but distinct lines if $\frac{a}{d} = \frac{b}{e} \neq \frac{c}{f}$. In this case the system of equations has **no solution**.

(3) Otherwise the two lines intersect in a single point. In this case $\frac{a}{d} \neq \frac{b}{e}$, and the system of equations has a **unique solution**.

These three cases are illustrated in the figure below.

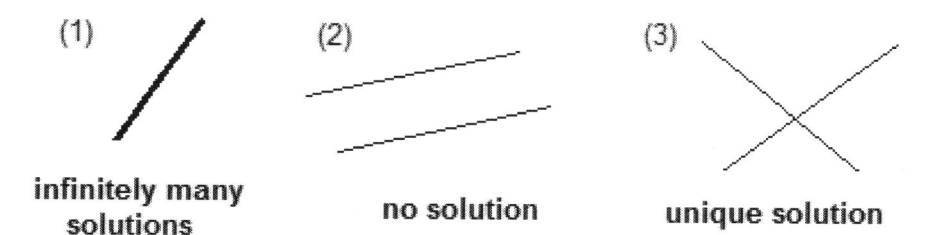

(1) infinitely many solutions
(2) no solution
(3) unique solution

Let's try an example.

LEVEL 4: HEART OF ALGEBRA – ADVANCED LINEAR SYSTEMS

$$2x + 8y = 6$$
$$3x + 12y = 9$$

1. Which of the following statements is true about the system of equations shown above?

   A) The two equations represent parallel but distinct lines.
   B) The two equations represent the same line.
   C) The graphs of the two equations intersect at a single point.
   D) The graphs of the two equations intersect at 2 points.

* Quick solution: Observe that $\frac{2}{3} = \frac{8}{12} = \frac{6}{9}$. It follows that the two equations represent the same line, choice **B**.

Alternate solution: Let $r = \frac{3}{2}$ and note that $\left(\frac{3}{2}\right)(2) = 3$, $\left(\frac{3}{2}\right)(8) = 12$, and $\left(\frac{3}{2}\right)(6) = 9$. It follows that the two equations represent the same line, choice **B**.

Note: Here is how we find r: we are looking for a number so that when we multiply 2 by that number, we get 3. So, we solve the equation $2r = 3$. It follows that $r = \frac{3}{2}$. We then check if multiplying 8 by $\frac{3}{2}$ produces 12, and if multiplying 6 by $\frac{3}{2}$ produces 9.

We could have also solved either the equation $8r = 12$ or $6r = 9$ to find r.

Since all three of these equations produce the same r-value, the system of equations has infinitely many solutions, or equivalently, the two equations represent the same line.

Two Linear Inequalities Are Better Than One

Let's use an example to see how to solve a **system of linear inequalities**.

LEVEL 5: HEART OF ALGEBRA – ADVANCED LINEAR SYSTEMS

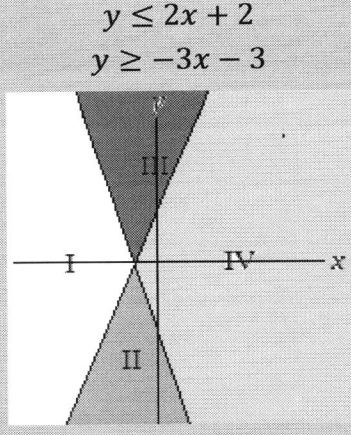

$$y \leq 2x + 2$$
$$y \geq -3x - 3$$

2. A system of inequalities and a graph are shown above. Which section or sections of the graph could represent all the solutions to the system?

   A) Section I
   B) Section IV
   C) Sections II and III
   D) Sections I, II, and IV

* Quick solution: The line $y = 2x + 2$ has a slope of $2 > 0$, and therefore the graph is the line that moves upwards as it is drawn from left to right.

The point $(0, 0)$ satisfies the inequality $y \leq 2x + 2$ since $0 \leq 2(0) + 2$, or equivalently, $0 \leq 2$ is true.

It follows that the graph of $y \leq 2x + 2$ consists of sections II and IV.

The line $y = -3x - 3$ has a slope of $-3 < 0$, and therefore the graph is the line that moves downwards as it is drawn from left to right.

$(0, 0)$ satisfies the inequality $y \geq -3x - 3$ since $0 \geq -3(0) - 3$, or equivalently $0 \geq -3$ is true.

It follows that the graph of $y \geq -3x - 3$ consists of sections III and IV.

The intersection of the two solution graphs is section IV, choice **B**.

Complete algebraic solution: Let's sketch each inequality, one at a time, starting with $y \leq 2x + 2$. We first sketch the line $y = 2x + 2$. There are several ways to do this. A quick way is to plot the two intercepts. We get the y-intercept by setting $x = 0$. In this case we get $y = 2 \cdot 0 + 2 = 2$. So, the point $(0, 2)$ is on the line. We get the x-intercept by setting $y = 0$. In this case we get $0 = 2x + 2$, so that $-2 = 2x$, and $x = -\frac{2}{2} = -1$. So, the point $(-1, 0)$ is on the line. This line is shown in the figure on the left below.

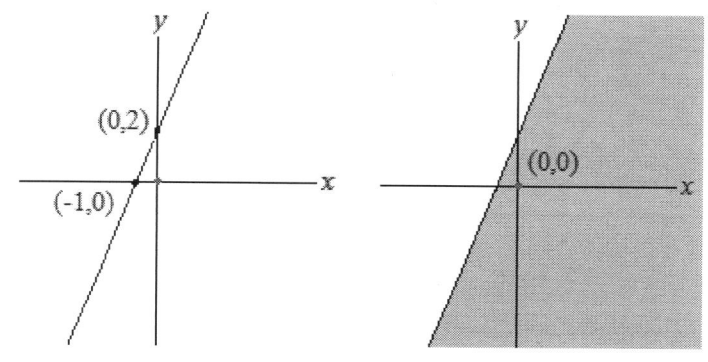

Now we need to figure out which direction to shade. To do this we plug any point *not on the line* into the inequality. For example, we can use $(0, 0)$. Substituting this point into $y \leq 2x + 2$ gives $0 \leq 2$. Since this expression is true, we shade the region that includes $(0, 0)$ as shown above in the figure on the right.

We now do the same thing for the second inequality. The intercepts of $y = -3x - 3$ are $(0, -3)$ and $(-1, 0)$. When we test $(0, 0)$ we get the true statement $0 \geq -3$.

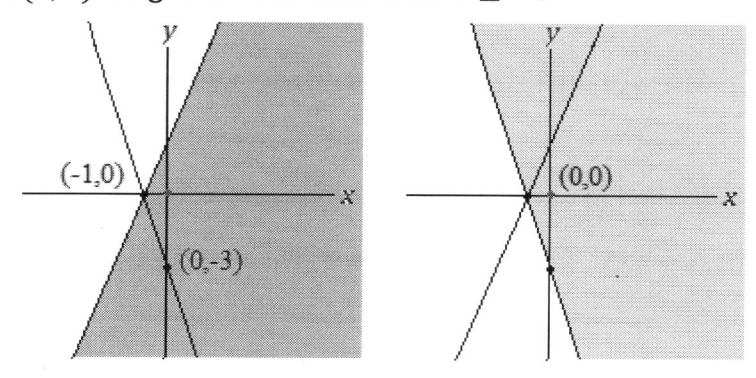

The figure on the above left shows the graph of $y = -3x - 3$ with the intercepts plotted, and the graph on the right shows the solution set of $y \geq -3x - 3$ (the shaded part).

The intersection of the two shaded regions in both figures above is the solution of the system of inequalities. This is region IV, choice **B**.

273

Time to Practice

LEVEL 2: HEART OF ALGEBRA – ADVANCED LINEAR SYSTEMS

$$y > 5x + 2$$
$$y - x \leq 3$$

3. Which of the following ordered pairs (x, y) satisfies the system of inequalities above?

   A) $(5, 2)$
   B) $(0, 4)$
   C) $(-1, 1)$
   D) $(1, -1)$

LEVEL 3: HEART OF ALGEBRA – ADVANCED LINEAR SYSTEMS

$$y < x + k$$
$$y > m - x$$

4. In the xy-plane, $(0,0)$ is a solution to the system of inequalities above. Which of the following relationships between k and m must be true?

   A) $k = -m$
   B) $k > m$
   C) $k < m$
   D) $|k| < |m|$

$$x + y < 1$$
$$3y > 2$$

5. Which of the following consists of the x-coordinates of all the points that satisfy the system of inequalities above?

   A) $x < \frac{1}{3}$
   B) $x < 1$
   C) $x > \frac{1}{3}$
   D) $x > 1$

LEVEL 4: HEART OF ALGEBRA – ADVANCED LINEAR SYSTEMS

$$16x - ky = 8$$
$$kx + 4y = 3$$

6. In the system of equations above, k is a constant and x and y are variables. For what real value of k will the system of equations have no real solution?

   A) -8
   B) 0
   C) 8
   D) There is no such value of k.

$$y + 15x = 2$$
$$5y + 3y = 10$$

7. How many solutions (x, y) are there to the system of equations above?

   A) None
   B) One
   C) Two
   D) More than two

LEVEL 5: HEART OF ALGEBRA – ADVANCED LINEAR SYSTEMS

$$5x + 15y = 23$$
$$cx + dy = 49$$

8. In the system of equations above, c and d are constants. If the system has infinitely many solutions, what is the value of $\frac{c}{d}$?

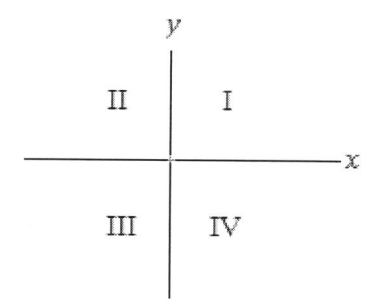

9. If the system of inequalities $y > 4x + 1$ and $y \leq -\frac{1}{2}x - 2$ is graphed in the xy-plane above, which quadrants contain no solutions to the system?

   A) Quadrant II
   B) Quadrant III
   C) Quadrants I and IV
   D) There are solutions in all four quadrants.

$$y \geq -7x + 1045$$
$$y \geq 4x$$

10. In the xy-plane, if a point with coordinates (a, b) lies in the solution set of the system of inequalities above, what is the minimum possible value of b?

Answers

1. B   2. B   3. C   4. B   5. A   6. D   7. B   8. 1/3, .333   9. C   10. 380

Full Solutions

3.

* Solution by starting with choice C: We start with choice C, letting $x = -1$ and $y = 1$. We substitute these values into the first inequality giving us $1 > 5(-1) + 2$, or equivalently, $1 > -3$. This is true, and so the point $(-1, 1)$ satisfies the first inequality. Let's substitute the same values into the second inequality. We get $1 - (-1) \leq 3$, or equivalently, $2 \leq 3$. This is also true, so that the answer is **C**.

4.

* Solution by plugging in the point: We replace x and y by 0 in the first equation to get $0 < 0 + k$, or equivalently, $k > 0$.

We then replace x and y by 0 in the second equation to get $0 > m - 0$, or equivalently, $0 > m$.

So, we have $k > 0 > m$, so that $k > m$, choice **B**.

5.

* Algebraic solution: Let's begin by solving the first inequality for x by subtracting y from each side. We get $x < 1 - y$. We now multiply each side of the second inequality by $-\frac{1}{3}$ to get $-y < -\frac{2}{3}$. Adding 1 to each side of this last inequality gives us $1 - y < 1 - \frac{2}{3}$, or equivalently, $1 - y < \frac{1}{3}$. So, we have $x < 1 - y$ and $1 - y < \frac{1}{3}$. It follows that we have $x < \frac{1}{3}$. This is choice **A**.

* Solution by picking a number: We can choose values for x to try to eliminate answer choices. For example, if we let $x = 0$, then the two inequalities become $0 + y < 1$ and $3y > 2$, or equivalently, $y < 1$ and $y > \frac{2}{3}$. We can rewrite this as $\frac{2}{3} < y < 1$. Since there are numbers between $\frac{2}{3}$ and 1, $x = 0$ produces solutions to the system of inequalities. We can therefore eliminate choices C and D.

Let's now use the value $x = \frac{2}{3}$ to eliminate one of the remaining choices. In this case, the two inequalities become $\frac{2}{3} + y < 1$ and $3y > 2$, or equivalently, $y < \frac{1}{3}$ and $y > \frac{2}{3}$. Since there is no y-value that is simultaneously less than $\frac{1}{3}$ and greater than $\frac{2}{3}$, $x = \frac{2}{3}$ does NOT produce any solutions to the system of inequalities. We can therefore eliminate choice B, and the answer is choice **A**.

Notes: (1) Since $x = 0$ is a solution to the system of inequalities, but NOT a solution to the inequalities in choices C and D, we can eliminate choices C and D.

(2) Since $x = \frac{2}{3}$ is NOT a solution to the system of inequalities, but is a solution to the inequality in choice B, we can eliminate choice B.

6.

* The given system of equations has no solution if $\frac{16}{k} = \frac{-k}{4} \neq \frac{8}{3}$. In particular, we must have $\frac{16}{k} = \frac{-k}{4}$, or equivalently $-k^2 = 64$. Since the right-hand side of this equation is positive and the left-hand side CANNOT be positive, the answer is choice **D**.

Note: The equation $-k^2 = 64$ is equivalent to the equation $k^2 = -64$. The solutions to this equation are $k = \pm 8i$.

Since the solutions are imaginary, we see that there are no real solutions to this equation.

7.

* Since $\frac{1}{5} \neq \frac{15}{3}$, the system of equations has a unique solution. So the answer is One, choice **B**.

8.

* The given system of equations has infinitely many solutions if $\frac{5}{c} = \frac{15}{d} = \frac{23}{49}$. In particular, we must have $\frac{5}{c} = \frac{15}{d}$, or equivalently $\frac{c}{d} = \frac{5}{15} = $ **1/3** or **.333**.

Notes: (1) In this problem we did not need to find c and d themselves.

(2) If we did need to find c we could solve the equation $\frac{5}{c} = \frac{23}{49}$ to get $23c = 5 \cdot 49 = 245$, and so, $c = \frac{245}{23}$.

(3) Similarly, we can find d by solving $\frac{15}{d} = \frac{23}{49}$ to get $23d = 15 \cdot 49 = 735$, and so, $d = \frac{735}{23}$.

9.

* **Complete algebraic solution:** Let's sketch each inequality, one at a time, starting with $y > 4x + 1$. We first sketch the line $y = 4x + 1$ by plotting the two intercepts. We get the y-intercept by setting $x = 0$. In this case, we get $y = 4 \cdot 0 + 1 = 1$. So, the point $(0,1)$ is on the line. We get the x-intercept by setting $y = 0$. In this case, we get $0 = 4x + 1$, so that $-1 = 4x$, and $x = -\frac{1}{4}$. Therefore, the point $(-\frac{1}{4}, 0)$ is on the line. This line is shown in the figure on the left below. Note that we draw a dotted line because the strict inequality $<$ tells us that points on this line are not actually solutions to the inequality $y > 4x + 1$.

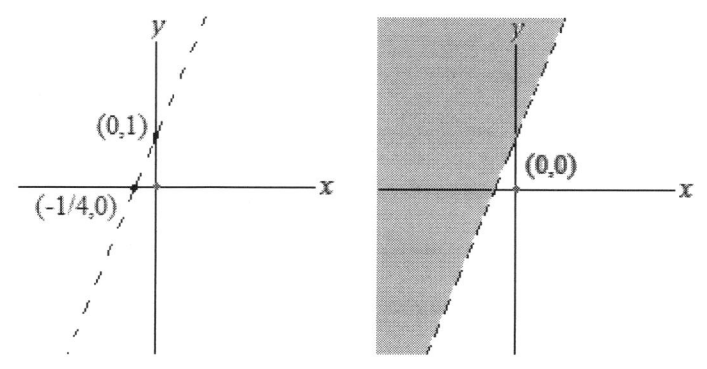

Now we need to figure out which direction to shade. To do this we plug any point *not on the line* into the inequality. For example, we can use $(0,0)$. Substituting this point into $y > 4x + 1$ gives $0 > 1$. Since this expression is false, we shade the region that does NOT include $(0,0)$ as shown above in the figure on the right.

We now do the same thing for the second inequality. The intercepts of $y = -\frac{1}{2}x - 2$ are $(0, -2)$ and $(-4, 0)$. When we test $(0, 0)$ we get the false statement $0 \leq -2$.

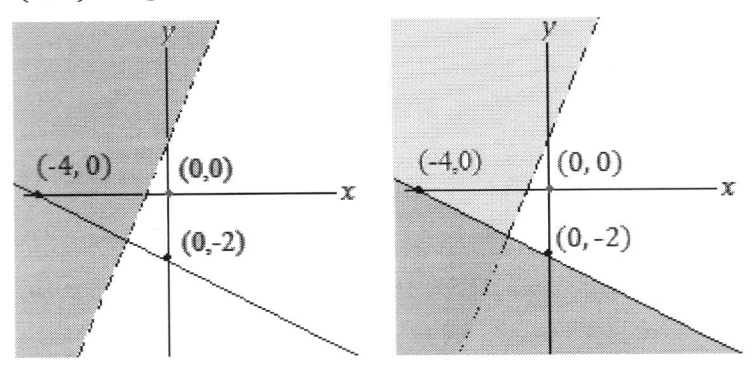

The figure on the above left shows the graph of $y = -\frac{1}{2}x - 2$ with the intercepts plotted, and the graph on the right shows three different shadings. The lower left shading is the solution set of the given system.

Note that there are solutions in quadrants II and III, and there are no solutions in quadrants I and IV, choice **C**.

10.

* Solution by solving the corresponding system of equations: We solve the system of equations

$$b = -7a + 1045$$
$$b = 4a$$

I will do it here by substitution. We have $4a = -7a + 1045$, so that $11a = 1045$. Therefore, we have $a = \frac{1045}{11} = 95$. It follows that $b = 4 \cdot 95 = \mathbf{380}$.

Notes: (1) It's probably not obvious to you that 380 is actually the answer to the question. But it would certainly be a good guess that if a minimum value for b exists, then it would be given by the y-coordinate of the point of intersection of the two lines.

(2) Although a minimum does not necessarily have to exist, since this is a grid in question, we are expected to give an answer. It follows that a minimum must exist, and note (1) gives us a quick way to find it.

(3) To be certain that 380 is actually the minimum possible value of b, we should sketch the system of inequalities. I leave this as an exercise for the reader (see problems 2 and 9).

LESSON 42 – PASSPORT TO ADVANCED MATH
GRAPHS OF PARABOLAS

Parabolas Deserve Equations Too

The **standard form for a quadratic function** is

$$y - k = a(x - h)^2 \quad \text{or} \quad y = a(x - h)^2 + k$$

The graph is a parabola with **vertex** at (h, k). The parabola opens upwards if $a > 0$ and downwards if $a < 0$.

Let's try an example.

LEVEL 3: PASSPORT TO ADVANCED MATH – GRAPHS OF PARABOLAS

1. Let the function f be defined by $f(x) = 3(x - 2)^2 + 1$. For what value of x will the function f have its minimum value?

    A) -3
    B) -2
    C) 2
    D) 3

* The graph of this function is an upward facing parabola with vertex $(2, 1)$. Therefore, the answer is $x = 2$, choice **C**.

Notes: (1) In this example, $k = 1$ and k is on the right-hand side of the equation.

(2) A sketch of the parabola is shown to the right. Observe that the parabola opens upwards and the vertex is the point $(2, 1)$. Also, note that the y-intercept of the graph is the point $(0, 13)$. We can find this value by computing $f(0) = 3(0 - 2)^2 + 1 = 3(-2)^2 + 1 = 3 \cdot 4 + 1 = 13$.

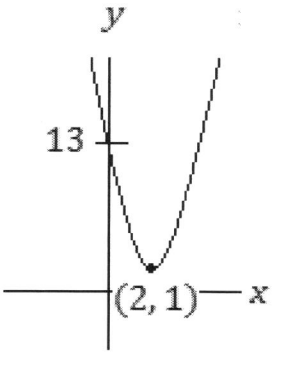

There Can Be Only One (Equation for a Parabola in General Form)

The **general form for a quadratic function** is

$$y = ax^2 + bx + c$$

The graph of this function is a parabola whose vertex has x-coordinate

$$-\frac{b}{2a}$$

The parabola opens upwards if $a > 0$ and downwards if $a < 0$.

Let's try an example.

279

LEVEL 4: PASSPORT TO ADVANCED MATH – GRAPHS OF PARABOLAS

2. Let the function f be defined by $f(x) = -7x^2 + 3x + 1$. For what value of x will the function f have its maximum value?

* The graph of this function is a downward facing parabola, and we see that $a = -7$ and $b = 3$. Therefore, the x-coordinate of the vertex is $x = \frac{-3}{-14} = 3/14$ or $.214$.

Time to Practice

LEVEL 3: PASSPORT TO ADVANCED MATH – GRAPHS OF PARABOLAS

$$y = x^2 - 12x + 27$$

3. The equation above represents a parabola in the xy-plane. Which of the following equivalent forms of the equation displays the x-intercept(s) of the parabola as constants or coefficients?

   A) $y - 27 = x^2 - 12x$
   B) $y + 9 = (x - 6)^2$
   C) $y = x(x - 12) + 27$
   D) $y = (x - 3)(x - 9)$

4. In the xy-plane, the parabola with equation $y = (x + 7)^2$ intersects the line with equation $y = 9$ at two points, P and Q. What is the length of $\overline{PQ}$?

LEVEL 4: PASSPORT TO ADVANCED MATH – GRAPHS OF PARABOLAS

5. The graph of the function h defined by $h(x) = (x + 5)(x + 6)$ in the xy-plane is a parabola. Which of the following intervals contains the x-coordinate of the vertex of the graph of h?

   A) $-7 < x < -5$
   B) $-5 < x < -2$
   C) $-2 < x < 2$
   D) $2 < x < 6$

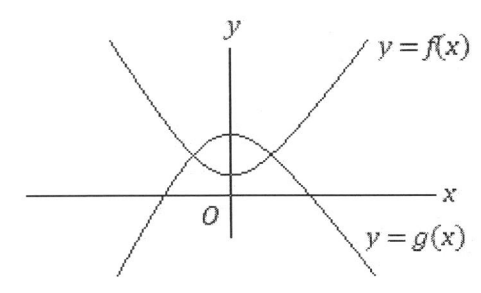

6. The functions f and g, whose graphs are shown above, are defined by $f(x) = 4x^2 + 1$ and $g(x) = -4x^2 + 3$. The graphs of f and g intersect at the points $(a, 2)$ and $(-a, 2)$. Given that $a > 0$, what is the value of a?

LEVEL 5: PASSPORT TO ADVANCED MATH – GRAPHS OF PARABOLAS

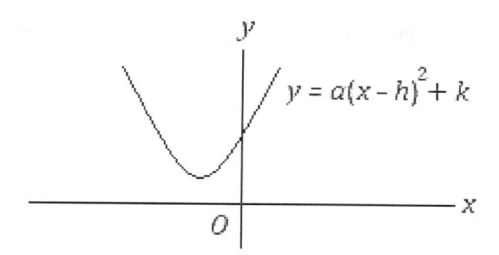

7. The vertex of the parabola in the xy-plane above is (h, k). Which of the following is true about the parabola with the equation $y = -ax^2 + k$?

    A) The parabola opens upward and the vertex is $(0, k)$.
    B) The parabola opens downward and the vertex is $(0, k)$.
    C) The parabola opens upward and the vertex is $(0, -k)$.
    D) The parabola opens downward and the vertex is $(0, -k)$.

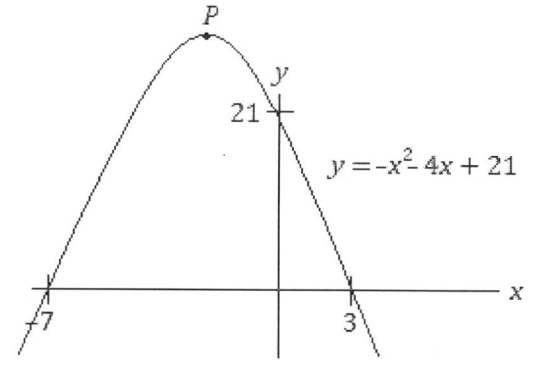

8. Which of the following is an equivalent form of the function f whose graph is shown above in the xy-plane, from which the coordinates of vertex P can be identified as constants in the equation?

    A) $f(x) = -(x - (-2))^2 + 25$
    B) $f(x) = -x(x + 2) + 21$
    C) $f(x) = (x + 7)(x - 3)$
    D) $f(x) = (x + 7)(3 - x)$

$$y = p(x - 3)(x + 7)$$

9. In the quadratic equation above, p is a nonzero constant. The graph of the equation in the xy-plane is a parabola with vertex (h, k). What is the value of $\sqrt{-\frac{k}{p}}$?

10. * An arrow is launched upward with an initial speed of 30 m/s (meters per second). The equation $v^2 = v_0^2 - 2gh$ describes the motion of the arrow, where v_0 is the initial speed of the arrow, v is the speed of the arrow as it is moving up in the air, h is the height of the arrow above the ground, t is the time elapsed since the arrow was projected upward, and g is the acceleration due to gravity (approximately 9.8 m/s²). What is the maximum height from the ground the arrow will rise to the nearest meter?

281

Answers

1. C   2. 3/14, .214   3. D   4. 6   5. A   6. 1/2, .5   7. B   8. A   9. 5   10. 46

Full Solutions

3.
* Solution by factoring:

$$x^2 - 12x + 27 = (x-3)(x-9)$$

This is choice **D**.

Notes: (1) $(x-3)(x-9)$ is in a form where the x-intercepts 3 and 9 of the parabola are displayed as constants.

(2) Every answer choice gives an equivalent way of writing the given equation. But choices A, B, and C are **wrong** because the x-intercepts 3 and 9 do not appear as constants or coefficients in those equations!

4.
* Solution using the square root property: Replacing y with 9 in the first equation yields $(x+7)^2 = 9$. We use the square root property to get $x + 7 = \pm 3$. So, $x = -7 \pm 3$. So, the two solutions are $x = -7 + 3 = -4$ and $x = -7 - 3 = -10$. So, $P = (-4, 9)$ and $Q = (-10, 9)$. The distance between these two points is $|-10 - (-4)| = |-10 + 4| = |-6| = $ **6**.

Notes: (1) To find the points of intersection of the parabola and the line, we solve the given system of equations. We chose to use the **substitution method** here.

(2) Instead of formally applying the square root property to solve $(x+7)^2 = 9$, we can simply "guess" the solutions, or solve the equation informally. It's not too hard to see that $x = -4$ and $x = -10$ will make the equation true.

(3) It's not necessary to write down the points P and Q. Since the y-coordinates of the two points are the same, we can simply subtract one x-coordinate from the other (disregarding the minus sign if it appears) to get the desired distance.

(4) We can also plot the two points and observe that the distance between them is 6.

5.
*Quick solution: The x-intercepts of the parabola are -6 and -5. The x-coordinate of the vertex of a parabola lies midway between the two x-intercepts. If we let x be the x-coordinate of the vertex, then $-6 < x < -5$. This interval is contained in the interval given in choice A, and so, the answer is **A**.

Note: The x-coordinate of the vertex of a parabola is always exactly midway between the two x-intercepts of the parabola (if the parabola has two x-intercepts). In this problem, the x-coordinate of the vertex is $\frac{-6+(-5)}{2} = -\frac{11}{2} = -5.5$. This value is between -7 and -5, confirming that choice A is the answer.

Solution using the general form of a quadratic function: We put the quadratic function into general form by expanding the function: $h(x) = (x+5)(x+6) = x^2 + 6x + 5x + 30 = x^2 + 11x + 30$. So, the x-coordinate of the vertex of the parabola is $x = -\frac{11}{2} = -5.5$. Since $-7 < -5.5 < -5$, the answer is choice **A**.

Solution using the standard form of a quadratic function: From the previous solution, we have $h(x) = x^2 + 11x + 30$. We now put the equation in standard form by completing the square. We get $h(x) = \left(x + \frac{11}{2}\right)^2 - \frac{1}{4}$. So, the x-coordinate of the vertex of the parabola is $x = -\frac{11}{2} = -5.5$. Since $-7 < -5.5 < -5$, the answer is choice **A**.

Notes: (1) To change an equation of a parabola from general form to standard form, we **complete the square**. See Lesson 34 for more information on completing the square.

Recall that to complete the square on the expression $x^2 + bx$, we take half of the number b to get $\frac{b}{2}$, and square this result to get $\left(\frac{b}{2}\right)^2$.

For example, to complete the square on $x^2 + 11x$, we take half of 11 to get $\frac{11}{2}$, and then square $\frac{11}{2}$ to get $\left(\frac{11}{2}\right)^2 = \frac{121}{4}$.

We then add this to the original expression to get $x^2 + 11x + \frac{121}{4}$. This new expression is a perfect square. In fact, it factors as follows:

$$x^2 + 11x + \frac{121}{4} = \left(x + \frac{11}{2}\right)\left(x + \frac{11}{2}\right) = \left(x + \frac{11}{2}\right)^2$$

Note that the number $\frac{11}{2}$ is the same as the number we got from taking half of 11. This is not a coincidence. It always happens.

(2) Completing the square *does not* produce an expression that is equivalent to the original expression. For example, the expression $\left(x + \frac{11}{2}\right)^2 = x^2 + 11x + \frac{121}{4}$ is $\frac{121}{4}$ more than the original expression $x^2 + 11x$. We can fix this problem by subtracting $\frac{121}{4}$ from the expression. So, we have

$$x^2 + 11x = x^2 + 11x + \frac{121}{4} - \frac{121}{4} = \left(x + \frac{11}{2}\right)^2 - \frac{121}{4}$$

(3) Now, we have

$$x^2 + 11x + 30 = \left(x + \frac{11}{2}\right)^2 - \frac{121}{4} + 30 = \left(x + \frac{11}{2}\right)^2 - \frac{121}{4} + \frac{120}{4} = \left(x + \frac{11}{2}\right)^2 - \frac{1}{4}$$

(4) Once the equation is in the standard form $h(x) = \left(x + \frac{11}{2}\right)^2 - \frac{1}{4}$, we can easily pick out the vertex by matching the equation up with the standard form $y = a(x - h)^2 + k$. Observe that $h = -\frac{11}{2}$ and $k = -\frac{1}{4}$.

(5) It is very common for students to make sign errors here. Note that the expression $\left(x + \frac{11}{2}\right)^2$ indicates that $h = -\frac{11}{2}$, whereas the $-\frac{1}{4}$ on the right-hand side of the equation indicates $k = -\frac{1}{4}$.

6.
* We can use either point and either function. Let's use the point $(a, 2)$ and the function f.

We are given that $(a, 2)$ is on the graph of f. This is equivalent to $f(a) = 2$. So, $2 = f(a) = 4a^2 + 1$. Subtracting 1 from each side of this equation gives us $1 = 4a^2$. We now divide by 4 to get $\frac{1}{4} = a^2$. We now use the square root property to get $a = \pm \frac{1}{2}$. Since we are given $a > 0$, $a = \mathbf{1/2}$ or **.5**.

7.
* From the picture, we see that the graph of the given equation is an upward facing parabola. It follows that $a > 0$. Therefore, $-a < 0$, and the graph of $y = -ax^2 + k$ is a downward facing parabola. So, we can eliminate choices A and C.

Now, the equation $y = -ax^2 + k$ can be written as $y = -a(x - 0)^2 + k$. This is in standard form, and the graph of this equation is a parabola with vertex $(0, k)$. So, the answer is choice **B**.

Notes: (1) Here is a graph of both parabolas drawn on the same set of axes.

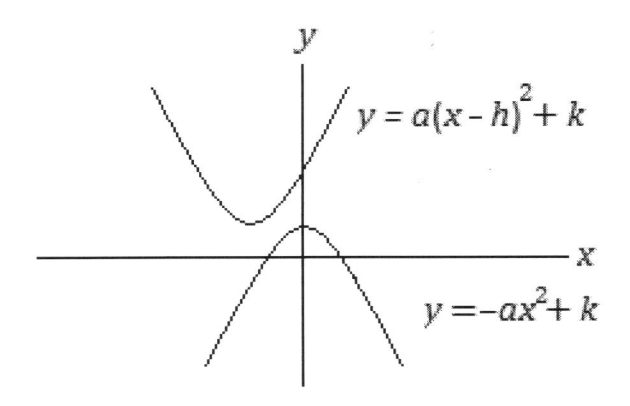

(2) We can get the new graph from the old by a sequence of transformations. In this case, it's a little tricky, and I would advise against thinking of it this way. For completeness, however, I'll include one possible sequence of transformations that would take you from the given parabola to the new one.

Step 0: We start with the equation $y = a(x - h)^2 + k$ whose graph is given in the problem. Note that the graph is shifted to the left, indicating that h must actually be negative.

Step 1: We reflect the graph in the x-axis by negating the right-hand side of the equation to get $y = -[a(x - h)^2 + k] = -a(x - h)^2 - k$.

Step 2: We shift the new graph h units to the right by replacing x by $(x + h)$. This gives us $y = -a\big((x + h) - h\big)^2 - k = -ax^2 - k$.

Step 3: We shift the last graph up $2k$ units by adding $2k$ to the right-hand side of the equation. This gives us $y = -ax^2 - k + 2k = -ax^2 + k$.

8.

*Quick solution: The question is asking us to write the equation of the parabola in standard form. The only answer choice that is in standard form is choice **A**.

Note: Recall that the standard form for a quadratic function is $y = a(x - h)^2 + k$.

The graph is a parabola with **vertex** at (h, k). The parabola opens upward if $a > 0$ and downward if $a < 0$.

For example, the function f defined by $f(x) = -(x - (-2))^2 + 25$ is in standard form (this is choice A). The graph of this function is a downward facing parabola with vertex $(-2, 25)$. Here we have $h = -2$ and $k = 25$. Observe that the point $(-2, 25)$ seems to be the vertex of the parabola shown in the graph.

Algebraic solution: $y = -x^2 - 4x + 21 = -(x^2 + 4x) + 21$
$$= -(x^2 + 4x + 4) + 4 + 21 = -(x + 2)^2 + 25 = -(x - (-2))^2 + 25$$

This is choice **A**.

Notes: (1) Recall that the **general form** for the equation of a parabola is $y = ax^2 + bx + c$.

The equation we are given in this problem is in general form.

This form, however, is not that useful for identifying specific information about the parabola such as the vertex.

For this purpose, one of the following standard forms is better.

$$y = a(x - h)^2 + k, \text{ or equivalently, } y - k = a(x - h)^2$$

In either of these forms, we can identify the vertex of the parabola as (h, k).

(2) To change an equation of a parabola from general form to standard form, we **complete the square**. See problem 5 above for a more straightforward example of completing the square.

Recall that to complete the square on the expression $x^2 + bx$, we take half of the number b to get $\frac{b}{2}$, and square this result to get $\left(\frac{b}{2}\right)^2$.

For example, to complete the square on $x^2 + 4x$, we take half of 4 to get 2, and then square 2 to get $2^2 = 4$.

We then add this to the original expression to get $x^2 + 4x + 4$. This new expression is a perfect square. In fact, it factors as $x^2 + 4x + 4 = (x + 2)(x + 2) = (x + 2)^2$.

Note that the number 2 is the same as the number we got from taking half of 4. This is not a coincidence. It always happens.

(3) We must have an expression of the form $x^2 + bx$ before completing the square. In other words, there *cannot* be a number in front of x^2 (in technical terms, the coefficient of x^2 must be 1).

In the given problem, there is a coefficient of -1 in front of x^2 (note that $-x^2 = -1x^2$). We can deal with this by factoring -1 from the expression:

$$f(x) = -x^2 - 4x + 21 = -(x^2 + 4x - 21)$$

(4) Completing the square *does not* produce an expression that is equivalent to the original expression. For example, the expression $(x + 2)^2 = x^2 + 4x + 4$ is 4 more than the original expression $x^2 + 4x$.

We can fix this problem in two different ways:

Method 1: Add and subtract what we need inside the parentheses

Using this method, we write $f(x) = -(x^2 + 4x + 4 - 4 - 21)$.

Notice how we added and subtracted 4 inside the parentheses.

We can now simplify this expression to

$$f(x) = -(x^2 + 4x + 4 - 25) = -(x^2 + 4x + 4) + 25 = -(x + 2)^2 + 25$$

Note how we distributed the -1 to $(x^2 + 4x + 4)$ and (-25), a slightly unconventional use of the distributive property.

Method 2: Add what we need inside the parentheses and adjust the other constant accordingly.

Using this method, we write $f(x) = -(x^2 + 4x + 4 - 25)$.

Since we added 4, we adjusted the -21 by subtracting 4, i.e,. we have $-21 - 4 = -25$.

Now proceed as in Method 1 to put the equation in standard form.

(5) If you don't like dealing with the -1 on the right-hand side of the equation, it can temporarily be moved to the left before completing the square as follows:

We rewrite $f(x) = -(x^2 + 4x - 21)$ as $-f(x) = x^2 + 4x - 21$.

Now complete the square on $x^2 + 4x$ to get $x^2 + 4x + 4$. So, we need to add 4 to the right-hand side of the equation. We can undo this by either (i) subtracting 4 from the same side (as in Method 1 above), (ii) adjusting the -21 to -25 (as in Method 2 above), or (iii) adding 4 to the left-hand side to balance the equation.

Let's use (iii) this time and write $-f(x) = x^2 + 4x - 21$ as

$$-f(x) + 4 = x^2 + 4x + 4 - 21$$

We then have $-f(x) + 4 = (x + 2)^2 - 21$.

Subtracting 4 gives $-f(x) = (x + 2)^2 - 25$.

Finally, multiplying by -1 yields $f(x) = -(x + 2)^2 + 25$.

(6) Once the equation is in the standard form

$$f(x) = -(x+2)^2 + 25 \quad \text{or} \quad f(x) - 25 = -(x+2)^2$$

we can easily pick out the vertex by matching the equation up with the standard form

$$y = a(x-h)^2 + k \quad \text{or} \quad y - k = a(x-h)^2$$

Observe that $h = -2$ and $k = 25$.

(7) It is very common for students to make sign errors here. Note that the expression $(x+2)^2$ indicates that $h = -2$, while the expression $f(x) - 25$ indicates that $k = 25$.

9.
* Solution by completing the square: Let's put the equation into standard form. We first multiply $(x-3)(x+7)$ to get the equation in general form:

$$y = p(x^2 + 4x - 21)$$

We now complete the square as follows:

$$y = p(x^2 + 4x + 4 - 4 - 21) = p(x^2 + 4x + 4) - 25p = p(x+2)^2 - 25p$$

So, $h = -2$, $k = -25p$, and $\sqrt{-\frac{k}{p}} = \sqrt{-\frac{-25p}{p}} = \sqrt{25} = \mathbf{5}$.

10.
* We are given that $v_0 = 30$ and $g \approx 9.8$ so that $v^2 = 900 - 19.6h$. The maximum height occurs when $v = 0$. It follows that $900 - 19.6h = 0^2 = 0$, and so $900 = 19.6h$.

We divide each side of this last equation by 19.6 to get

$$h = \frac{900}{19.6} \approx 45.9$$

To the nearest meter, this is **46**.

LESSON 43 – PROBLEM SOLVING
GROWTH

Grow Up or Go Down

A general **exponential function** has the form $f(t) = a(1+r)^{ct}$, where $a = f(0)$ is the *initial amount* and r is the *growth rate*. If $r > 0$, then we have **exponential growth** and if $r < 0$, we have **exponential decay**.

Examples: (1) The exponential function $f(t) = 300(2)^t$ can be used to model a population with a growth rate of $1 = 100\%$ each year that begins with 300 specimens. The growth rate of 100% tells us that the population doubles each year.

(2) The exponential function $f(t) = 50(3)^{2t}$ can be used to model a population with a growth rate of $2 = 200\%$ every 6 months that begins with 50 specimens. The growth rate of 200% tells us that the population triples. Since $c = 2$, the tripling occurs every $\frac{1}{2}$ year or 6 months.

(3) The exponential function $f(t) = 120(0.75)^{\frac{t}{3}}$ can be used to model a substance which is decaying at a rate of $1 - 0.75 = 0.25 = 25\%$ every 3 years. The initial amount of the substance might be 120 grams. Since $c = \frac{1}{3}$, the 25% decay occurs every 3 years.

(4) A quantity that continually doubles over a fixed time period can be modeled by the exponential function $f(t) = a(2)^{\frac{t}{d}}$ where a is the quantity at time $t = 0$, and d is the doubling time in years.

Time to Practice

LEVEL 3: PROBLEM SOLVING – GROWTH

Questions 1 - 2 refer to the following information.

Grant invests in a bond that earns 4.2 percent interest compounded annually. His initial deposit was $700, and he uses the expression $\$700(1+r)^t$ to find the value of the bond after t years.

1. What is the value of r in the expression?

2. * Grant's cousin Tana opened a savings account that earns 3.3 percent interest compounded annually. Tana also made an initial investment of $700 at the same time that Grant made his initial investment of $700. After 5 years, how much more money will Grant's investment have earned than Tana's initial investment? (Round your answer to the nearest cent and ignore the dollar sign when gridding your response.)

LEVEL 4: PROBLEM SOLVING – GROWTH

3. The value of an amethyst is expected to increase by 3.5 percent from one year to the next beginning in the year 2018. What type of relationship should be expected between the age of the amethyst and the amethyst's value?

   A) Linear relationship
   B) Quadratic relationship
   C) Cubic relationship
   D) Exponential relationship

4. 100 bullfrogs were introduced into a small pond. The population of the bullfrogs in the pond, starting with the time they were introduced, is estimated over the course of 5 years as shown in the following table.

Time (years)	Bullfrog Population
0	100
1	150
2	224
3	334
4	500
5	747

   Which of the following best describes the relationship between time and the estimated population of bullfrogs during the 5 years?

   A) Decreasing Linear
   B) Increasing Linear
   C) Exponential Decay
   D) Exponential Growth

5. The 60 plus population in New York City has grown at an average rate of approximately 3.2% per year from 2000 to 2010 with about 1.4 million people aged 60 and above living in New York City in 2000. Which of the following functions represents the 60 plus population in New York City, P, in millions of people, t years after 2000, with $0 \le t \le 10$?

   A) $P(t) = 1.032t + 1.4$
   B) $P(t) = 1.32t + 1.4$
   C) $P(t) = 1.4(1.032)^t$
   D) $P(t) = 1.4(1.32)^t$

6. * A rare gem is worth $1500 today. A jeweler believes that the gem will increase in value by 8% each month for the next eight months. The jeweler uses the equation $A = 1500(r)^t$ to model the value, A, of the gem after t months. To the nearest dollar, what does the jeweler believe the gem will be worth at the end of eight months?

LEVEL 5: PROBLEM SOLVING – GROWTH

7. * Sarah made an investment of D dollars on January 1, 2010. The amount of money in the account tripled each year until the investment was worth 1000 dollars on January 1, 2013. What is the value of D, to the nearest dollar?

8. * Satellites can be powered by the nuclear energy derived from radioactive isotopes. The table below shows the approximate output, in watts, of the radioactive power supply for a satellite at 10 day intervals following the activation of the power supply.

Days after activation	Output (watts)
0	30
10	29.11
20	28.25
30	27.42
40	26.6

The output, in watts, of the radioactive power supply t days after activation is modeled by the function $W = 30k^{-0.003t}$. If W approximates the values in the table to within 0.1 watts, what is the value of k, rounded to the nearest tenth?

Questions 9 - 10 refer to the following information.

An environmentalist is monitoring the mosquito population in an environment which currently contains 200 million mosquitos. The number of mosquitos, in millions, that the environmentalist expects each month, x_{next}, can be estimated from the number of mosquitos, in millions, the previous month, $x_{previous}$, by the following equation.

$$x_{next} = x_{previous} + 0.3 x_{previous}\left(1 - \frac{x_{previous}}{E}\right)$$

The constant E in the formula is the number of mosquitos, in millions, that can be supported by the environment.

9. * If the environment can support 700 million mosquitos, what will be the number of mosquitos, in millions, three months from now? (Round your answer to the nearest whole number.)

10. The environmentalist suggests restricting the environment so that the mosquito population does not increase so rapidly. What is the number of mosquitos that can be supported in the restricted environment if the population only increases from 200 million to 225 million from this year to next year?

Answers

1. .042   2. 36.5   3. D   4. D   5. C   6. 2276   7. 37   8. 2.7   9. 341   10. 400

Full Solutions

1.

Solution by picking a number: Let's let $t = 1$. After 1 year, the interest earned on \$700 is $0.042 \cdot 700 = \$29.40$. Therefore, the amount in the account after 1 year is $700 + 29.40 = 729.40$.

So, we have $729.40 = 700(1 + r)^1$. We divide each side of this last equation by 700 to get $1 + r = 729.40/700 = 1.042$. So, $r = 1.042 - 1 = .042$.

* **Quick solution:** We have exponential growth with a growth rate of $4.2\% = .042$.

2.

* $700(1.042)^5 - 700(1.033)^5 \approx 36.4988613$. When we round this to the nearest cent (and ignore the dollar sign), we get 36.50. So, we grid in **36.5**.

Notes: (1) In the last problem we found that if the interest rate is 4.2, then $r = 0.042$, and so, the formula becomes $700(1 + 0.042)^t = 700(1.042)^t$

(2) A similar computation shows that if the interest rate is 3.3, then $r = 0.033$, and the formula becomes $700(1 + 0.033)^t = 700(1.033)^t$

(3) The question is asking for the difference between these two expressions when $t = 5$ (after 5 years). So, we replace t by 5 in each expression, and then subtract.

3.

* **Direct solution:** The value of the amethyst is modeled by $V = k(1.035)^t$, where k is the initial value of the amethyst and t is the number of years after 2018. This is an exponential relationship, choice **D**.

Notes: (1) A linear relationship has the form $y = ax + b$.

(2) A quadratic relationship has the form $y = ax^2 + bx + c$.

(3) A cubic relationship has the form $y = ax^3 + bx^2 + cx + d$.

(4) An exponential relationship has the form $y = a(1 + r)^{ct}$.

(5) Let's suppose that the value of the amethyst at the beginning of 2018 (the initial value) is k. There are two ways we can increase k by 3.5 percent.

<u>Method 1</u>: We can take 3.5% of k, and then add the result to k:

$$k + 0.035k = 1k + 0.035k = (1 + 0.035)k = 1.035k$$

<u>Method 2</u>: Note that increasing k by 3.5% is the same as taking 103.5% of k: $1.035k$

So, when $t = 1$, the value of the amethyst will be $V = k(1.035)$.

(6) In note (5), we saw that at the beginning of 2018 ($t = 1$), the value of the amethyst will be $V = k(1.035)$. In another year, the value of the amethyst will increase another 3.5%. Using Method 2 in note (5), we see that we need to once again multiply by 1.035. When we do this, we get $V = k(1.035)(1.035) = k(1.035)^2$.

Notice that the number of years ($t = 2$) matches the exponent.

(7) Continuing as in notes (5) and (6), we see that after t years, the value of the amethyst is $V = k(1.035)^t$. This defines an exponential relationship where $a = k, r = 0.035$, and $c = 1$ (see note (4)).

(8) In this problem, we have exponential growth (as opposed to exponential decay) because $r = 0.035 > 0$.

4.

* **Solution by process of elimination:** A relationship is linear if equal "jumps" in the independent variable lead to equal "jumps" in the dependent variable. In the table, the Time values are increasing 1 at a time (so, the jumps in Time are equal). However, the jumps in Bullfrog Population are NOT equal. For example, the first jump is $150 - 100 = 50$ and the second jump is $224 - 150 = 74$. Therefore, the relationship is NOT linear, and we can eliminate choices A and B.

Now, since the Bullfrog Population increases as Time increases, the population is growing and NOT decaying. So, we can eliminate choice C, leaving us with answer choice **D**.

Note: As Time increases, the jumps in Bullfrog Population are getting bigger and bigger. This is evidence that the relationship might be exponential. In any case, it is certainly not linear, as linear relationships require constant jumps.

5.

* The situation being described is an exponential relationship $P(t) = a(1 + r)^{ct}$ between the number of years, t, after 2000 ($0 \leq t \leq 10$) and the 60 plus population, P, in millions of people in New York City. We are given that $a = 1.4, c = 1$, and $r = 0.032$. So, $P(t) = 1.4(1.032)^t$, choice **C**.

6.

* $r = 1 + 0.08 = 1.08$. It follows that $A = 1500(1.08)^8 \approx 2776.395315$. To the nearest dollar this is **2776**.

Notes: (1) We can also find the value of r by picking a number as follows: After 1 month, the gem should increase its value by 8%. So, if we let $t = 1$, then $A = 1620$. So, we have $1620 = 1500(r)^1$. So, $r = \frac{1620}{1500} = \mathbf{1.08}$.

(2) We can increase 1500 by 8% by multiplying 1500 by 1.08 to get $1.08 \cdot 1500 = 1620$

Alternatively, we can take 8% of 1500 and then add the result to 1500:

$$1500 + 0.08 \cdot 1500 = 1500 + 120 = 1620$$

7.

* If we let A be the amount of money in the account, then we have $A = D(r)^t$ with $A = 1000, r = 3$, and $t = 2013 - 2010 = 3$. So, we have $1000 = D \cdot 3^3 = 27D$. Therefore, $D = \frac{1000}{27} \approx 37.037$. To the nearest dollar, this is **37**.

8.

* **Solution by plugging in a point:** We can use any row of the table except the first one. Let's use the second row. We are given that $W = 29.11$ when $t = 10$. So, we substitute these values into the given equation to get $29.11 = 30k^{-0.003 \cdot 10} = 30k^{-0.03}$.

Dividing each side of the equation by 30 gives us $k^{-0.03} = \frac{29.11}{30} \approx 0.970333$. We now raise each side of the equation to $-\frac{1}{0.03}$ to get $k \approx 0.970333^{-\frac{1}{0.03}} \approx 2.728778$. To the nearest tenth, this is **2.7**.

Note: Any row in the table will give the same result. For example, if we were to use the third row, we would have $28.25 = 30k^{-0.003 \cdot 20} = 30k^{-0.06}$. Therefore, $k^{-0.06} = \frac{28.25}{30} \approx 0.941667$. Finally, we would have $k \approx 0.941667^{-\frac{1}{0.06}} \approx 2.72$. To the nearest tenth, this is also 2.7.

9.
* We substitute $E = 700$ and $x_{\text{previous}} = 200$ into the formula to get

$$x_{\text{next}} = 200 + 0.3 \cdot 200 \left(1 - \frac{200}{700}\right) \approx 242.8571429$$

This is the approximate number of mosquitos there will be, in millions, 1 month from now.

We now substitute $E = 700$ and $x_{\text{previous}} = 242.8571429$ into the formula (use the ANS button) to get $x_{\text{next}} = \text{ANS} + 0.3 \cdot \text{ANS} \left(1 - \frac{\text{ANS}}{700}\right) \approx 290.4373178$.

This is the approximate number of mosquitos there will be, in millions, 2 months from now.

We repeat this computation one more time: $x_{\text{next}} = \text{ANS} + 0.3 \cdot \text{ANS} \left(1 - \frac{\text{ANS}}{700}\right) \approx 341.4168693$.

We round to the nearest whole number to get **341**.

10.
* We substitute $x_{\text{previous}} = 200$ and $x_{\text{next}} = 230$ into the formula and solve for E.

$$230 = 200 + 0.3 \cdot 200 \left(1 - \frac{200}{E}\right) \Leftrightarrow 30 = 0.3 \cdot 200 \left(1 - \frac{200}{E}\right) \Leftrightarrow 30 = 60 \left(1 - \frac{200}{E}\right)$$

$$\Leftrightarrow \frac{1}{2} = 1 - \frac{200}{E} \Leftrightarrow -\frac{1}{2} = -\frac{200}{E} \Leftrightarrow \frac{1}{2} = \frac{200}{E} \Leftrightarrow E = \mathbf{400}$$

Notes: (1) To get from the first to the second equation, we subtracted 200 from each side.

(2) To get from the second to the third equation, we just multiplied $0.3 \cdot 200 = 60$.

(3) To get from the third to the fourth equation, we divided each side by 60. Note that $\frac{30}{60} = \frac{1}{2}$.

(4) To get from the fourth to the fifth equation, we subtracted 1 from each side. Note that $\frac{1}{2} - 1 = \frac{1}{2} - \frac{2}{2} = \frac{1-2}{2} = -\frac{1}{2}$.

(5) To get from the fifth equation to the sixth equation, we multiplied each side by -1. Equivalently, we just dropped the minus sign from each side.

(6) To get from the sixth equation to the seventh equation, we cross multiplied to get $1E = 2 \cdot 200$.

LESSON 44 – COORDINATE GEOMETRY
GRAPHS OF CIRCLES

Standard Form for the Equation of a Circle

The **standard form** for the equation of a circle with center (h, k) and radius r is

$$(x - h)^2 + (y - k)^2 = r^2$$

Let's look at an example.

LEVEL 3: COORDINATE GEOMETRY – GRAPHS OF CIRCLES

1. In the standard (x, y) coordinate plane, let C be the center and let r be the radius of the circle with equation $(x - 3)^2 + (y + 5)^2 = 7$. Which of the following gives the correct values for C and r?

   A) $C = (3, -5); r = \sqrt{7}$
   B) $C = (3, -5); r = 7$
   C) $C = (-3, 5); r = \sqrt{7}$
   D) $C = (-3, 5); r = 7$

* The equation of the circle is in standard form. We have $h = 3$, $k = -5$, and $r^2 = 7$ So, the center of the circle is $C = (3, -5)$ and the radius of the circle is $r = \sqrt{7}$, choice **A**.

Note: In this problem, $(y + 5) = (y - (-5))$. This is why $k = -5$ instead of 5.

General Form for the Equation of a Circle

The **general form** for the equation of a circle is

$$x^2 + y^2 + ax + by + c = 0.$$

This form for the equation is not very useful since we cannot easily determine the center or radius of the circle. We will want to apply the method of completing the square twice in order to change the equation into standard form. Let's use an example to illustrate this procedure.

LEVEL 5: COORDINATE GEOMETRY – GRAPHS OF CIRCLES

2. In the standard (x, y) coordinate plane, let C be the center and r the radius of the circle with equation $x^2 - 8x + y^2 + 10y + 15 = 0$. Which of the following gives the correct values for C and r?

   A) $C = (4, 5); r = \sqrt{15}$
   B) $C = (4, -5); r = \sqrt{26}$
   C) $C = (-4, 5); r = 15$
   D) $C = (-5, -4); r = 26$

294

* Solution by completing the square: $x^2 - 8x = x^2 - 8x + 16 - 16 = (x-4)^2 - 16$

$$y^2 + 10y = y^2 + 10y + 25 - 25 = (y+5)^2 - 25$$

So, $x^2 - 8x + y^2 + 10y + 15 = (x-4)^2 - 16 + (y+5)^2 - 25 + 15 = (x-4)^2 + (y+5)^2 - 26$.

So, the given equation is equivalent to $(x-4)^2 + (y+5)^2 - 26 = 0$. We add 26 to each side of this last equation to put the equation of the circle in the standard form $(x-4)^2 + (y+5)^2 = 26$.

It follows that the center of the circle is $C = (4, -5)$, and the radius of the circle is $r = \sqrt{26}$, choice **B**.

Notes: (1) To complete the square in the expression $x^2 - 8x$, we first take half of -8 to get -4. We then square this result to get 16. Note that $x^2 - 8x + 16 = (x-4)(x-4) = (x-4)^2$.

But be aware that it is not really okay to add 16 here – this changes the expression. So, we have to undo the damage we just did. We undo this damage by subtracting 16.

(2) To complete the square in the expression $y^2 + 10y$, we first take half of 10 to get 5. We then square this result to get 25. Note that we have $y^2 + 10y + 25 = (y+5)(y+5) = (y+5)^2$.

But be aware that it is not really okay to add 25 here – this changes the expression. So, we have to undo the damage we just did. We undo this damage by subtracting 25.

Time to Practice

LEVEL 2: COORDINATE GEOMETRY – GRAPHS OF CIRCLES

3. Which of the following is an equation of the circle in the xy-plane that has center $(0,0)$ and radius 3 ?

   A) $x^2 + y^2 = 3$
   B) $x^2 + y^2 = 6$
   C) $x^2 + y^2 = 9$
   D) $x^2 + y^2 = 27$

LEVEL 3: COORDINATE GEOMETRY – GRAPHS OF CIRCLES

$$(x+3)^2 + (y-1)^2 = 25$$

4. The graph of the equation above in the xy-plane is a circle. Point A with coordinates $(-3, 6)$ is on the circle. Given that $\overline{AB}$ is a diameter of the circle, what are the coordinates of point B ?

   A) $(-3, -4)$
   B) $(1, 2)$
   C) $(1, -3)$
   D) $(1, -8)$

5. In the xy-plane, which of the following is an equation of a circle with center $(5,0)$ and a radius with endpoint $(3,\frac{1}{2})$?

   A) $(x+5)^2 + y^2 = \frac{17}{4}$
   B) $(x-5)^2 + y^2 = \frac{17}{4}$
   C) $(x+5)^2 + y^2 = \frac{\sqrt{17}}{2}$
   D) $(x-5)^2 + y^2 = \frac{\sqrt{17}}{2}$

LEVEL 4: COORDINATE GEOMETRY – GRAPHS OF CIRCLES

6. A circle in the xy-plane has equation $(x-2)^2 + (y+4)^2 = 36$. Which of the following points does NOT lie in the interior of the circle?

   A) $(2,-4)$
   B) $(1,-9)$
   C) $(-2,1)$
   D) $(0,0)$

LEVEL 5: COORDINATE GEOMETRY – GRAPHS OF CIRCLES

$$x^2 + 14x + y^2 - 10y = -65$$

7. The equation above defines a circle in the xy-plane. What are the coordinates of the center of the circle?

   A) $(14,-10)$
   B) $(7,-5)$
   C) $(-7,5)$
   D) $(-14,10)$

8. In the xy-plane, the graph of $3x^2 - 12x + 3y^2 + 30y + 71 = 0$ is a circle. What is the radius of the circle?

   A) $\frac{4\sqrt{3}}{3}$
   B) 2.31
   C) $\sqrt{23}$
   D) 23

9. Which of the following equations describes a circle with radius 6 whose graph in the xy-plane passes through the origin?

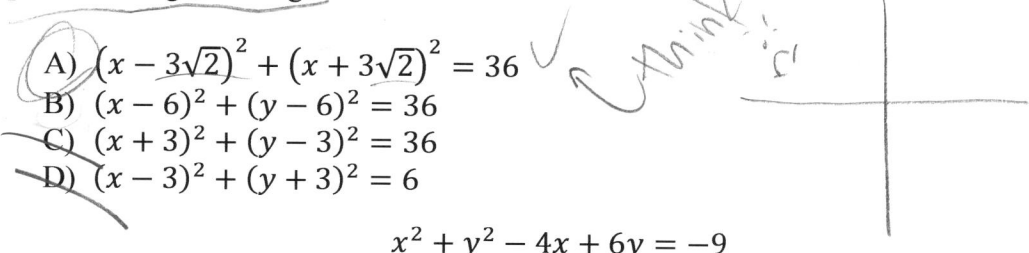

A) $(x - 3\sqrt{2})^2 + (x + 3\sqrt{2})^2 = 36$
B) $(x - 6)^2 + (y - 6)^2 = 36$
C) $(x + 3)^2 + (y - 3)^2 = 36$
D) $(x - 3)^2 + (y + 3)^2 = 6$

$$x^2 + y^2 - 4x + 6y = -9$$

10. The equation of a circle in the xy-plane is shown above. What is the radius of the circle?

Answers

1. A 2. B 3. C 4. A 5. B 6. C 7. C 8. A 9. A 10. 2

Full Solutions

3.
* Recall that the equation of a circle with center (h, k) and radius r is $(x - h)^2 + (y - k)^2 = r^2$. In this question, we have $h = 0$, $k = 0$, and $r^2 = 9$. So, an equation of the circle in standard form is $(x - 0)^2 + (y - 0)^2 = 9$. This is equivalent to $x^2 + y^2 = 9$, choice **C**.

4.
* The center of the circle is $C(-3, 1)$. Note that the center of the circle is the midpoint of diameter $\overline{AB}$.

To get from point A to point C, we need to move down 5 units. So, to get from point C to point B, we must also move down 5 units. So, the coordinates of point B are $(-3, -4)$, choice **A**.

Note: Instead of counting, we can also use the midpoint formula (see also problem 1 from Lesson 32). If point A has coordinates (x_1, y_1) and point B has coordinates (x_2, y_2), then the midpoint C has coordinates $(\frac{x_1+x_2}{2}, \frac{y_1+y_2}{2})$. In this case, we have $x_1 = -3$, $y_1 = 6$, $\frac{x_1+x_2}{2} = -3$, and $\frac{y_1+y_2}{2} = 1$.

Substituting $x_1 = -3$ into the third equation gives $\frac{-3+x_2}{2} = -3$. We multiply by 2 to get $-3 + x_2 = -6$. We add 3 to get $x_2 = -3$. Substituting $y_1 = 6$ into the fourth equation we have $\frac{6+y_2}{2} = 1$. We multiply by 2 to get $6 + y_2 = 2$. We subtract 6 to get $y_2 = -4$. So, point B has coordinates $(-3, -4)$, choice A.

5.
* Recall that the equation of a circle with center (h, k) and radius r is $(x - h)^2 + (y - k)^2 = r^2$.

In this problem, $h = 5$ and $k = 0$. So, the equation is

$$(x - 5)^2 + (y - 0)^2 = r^2$$

or equivalently,

$$(x - 5)^2 + y^2 = r^2$$

297

This eliminates choices A and C.

Since the point $(3,\frac{1}{2})$ lies on the circle, we can plug this point in to find r^2.

$$(3-5)^2 + \left(\frac{1}{2}\right)^2 = (-2)^2 + \frac{1}{4} = 4 + \frac{1}{4} = \frac{16}{4} + \frac{1}{4} = \frac{17}{4}$$

So, $r^2 = \frac{17}{4}$, and the answer is choice **B**.

Note: Be careful here. The radius of the circle is $r = \sqrt{\frac{17}{4}} = \frac{\sqrt{17}}{2}$, but the right-hand side of the standard form of an equation of a circle is r^2.

6.

Solution by starting with choice C: Let's plug the point $(-2, 1)$ into the left-hand side of the equation of the circle. We get $(-2-2)^2 + (1+4)^2 = (-4)^2 + 5^2 = 16 + 25 = 41$. Since $41 > 36$, the point $(-2, 1)$ lies outside of the circle, and the answer is choice **C**.

Notes: (1) Let's check the other points. For choice A, we have $(2-2)^2 + (-4+4)^2 = 0$. Since $0 < 36$, this point lies inside the circle.

For choice B, we have $(1-2)^2 + (-9+4)^2 = (-1)^2 + (-5)^2 = 1 + 25 = 26$. Since $26 < 36$, this point also lies inside the circle.

For choice D, we have $(0-2)^2 + (0+4)^2 = (-2)^2 + 4^2 = 4 + 16 = 20$. Since $20 < 36$, this point lies inside the circle as well.

(2) In general, if $(x-h)^2 + (y-k)^2 = r^2$, then the point (x, y) lies on the circle centered at (h, k) with radius r.

If $(x-h)^2 + (y-k)^2 < r^2$, then the point (x, y) lies in the interior of the circle centered at (h, k) with radius r.

And if $(x-h)^2 + (y-k)^2 > r^2$, then the point (x, y) lies in the exterior of the circle centered at (h, k) with radius r.

7.

Solution by completing the square: We complete the square twice on the left-hand side.

$$x^2 + 14x + y^2 - 10y = -65$$
$$x^2 + 14x + 49 + y^2 - 10y + 25 = -65 + 49 + 25$$
$$(x+7)^2 + (y-5)^2 = 9$$

It follows that the center of the circle is $C = (-7, 5)$, choice **C**.

Notes: (1) To complete the square in the expression $x^2 + 14x$, we first take half of 14 to get 7. We then square this result to get 49. We can then either (i) add and subtract 49 to the left-hand side of the equation (as was done in problem 2), or (ii) add 49 to both sides of the equation (as was done in the solution above).

Note that $x^2 + 14x + 49 = (x+7)(x+7) = (x+7)^2$.

(2) To complete the square in the expression $y^2 - 10y$, we first take half of -10 to get -5. We then square this result to get 25. As in note (1), we chose to add 25 to each side of the equation.

Note that we have $y^2 - 10y + 25 = (y-5)(y-5) = (y-5)^2$.

(3) We also found that the radius was $r = \sqrt{9} = 3$.

(4) It was not necessary to find r to answer this question. We could have saved a little time by disregarding the right-hand side of the equation, and just focusing our attention on the left-hand side. In other words, we could have simply done this:

$$x^2 + 14x + y^2 - 10y = x^2 + 14x + 49 + y^2 - 10y + 25 = (x+7)^2 + (y-5)^2$$

8.

* **Solution by completing the square:** Before we can complete the square, we must make sure that the coefficients of x^2 and y^2 are 1. To do this, we divide each side of the given equation by 3 to get

$$x^2 - 4x + y^2 + 10y + \frac{71}{3} = 0$$

Let's also bring $\frac{71}{3}$ over to the right-hand side by subtracting it.

$$x^2 - 4x + y^2 + 10y = -\frac{71}{3}$$

We complete the square twice on the left-hand side.

$$x^2 - 4x + 4 + y^2 + 10y + 25 = -\frac{71}{3} + 4 + 25$$

$$(x-2)^2 + (y+5)^2 = \frac{16}{3}$$

It follows that the radius of the circle is $r = \sqrt{\frac{16}{3}} = \frac{\sqrt{16}}{\sqrt{3}} = \frac{4}{\sqrt{3}} = \frac{4\sqrt{3}}{3}$, choice **A**.

Notes: (1) Remember that you can complete the square only on an expression of the form $x^2 + bx$. In this problem, we must divide the equation through by 3 first to get the given equation into a form where we can complete the square.

(2) If a calculator is allowed for this problem, we can simply type $\sqrt{(-71/3 + 4 + 25)}$ ENTER into our calculator to get approximately 2.309. We could then enter the answer choices into our calculator to see which choice matches up. In this case, that will be choice A.

(3) If a calculator is not allowed, then first we need to add on the right to get

$$r^2 = -\frac{71}{3} + 4 + 25 = -\frac{71}{3} + 29 = -\frac{71}{3} + \frac{29}{1} \cdot \frac{3}{3} = \frac{-71 + 87}{3} = \frac{16}{3}$$

We then have $r = \sqrt{\frac{16}{3}} = \frac{\sqrt{16}}{\sqrt{3}} = \frac{4}{\sqrt{3}} = \frac{4}{\sqrt{3}} \cdot \frac{\sqrt{3}}{\sqrt{3}} = \frac{4\sqrt{3}}{3}$.

Notice how we *rationalized the denominator* at the end by multiplying both the numerator and denominator of the fraction by the denominator.

9.
* Solution by starting with choice C: Let's start with choice C and substitute $(0, 0)$ (the origin) into the left-hand side of the equation. We get $(0 + 3)^2 + (0 - 3)^2 = 3^2 + (-3)^2 = 9 + 9 = 18$. Since $18 \neq 36$, we can eliminate choice C. It's also easy to see that essentially the same computation eliminates choice D (also, the equation in choice D is of a circle with radius $\sqrt{6}$ and not 6).

For choice B, we have $(0 - 6)^2 + (0 - 6)^2 = (-6)^2 + (-6)^2 = 36 + 36 = 72$. Since $72 \neq 36$, we can eliminate choice B, and therefore the answer is choice **A**.

Note: For completeness, let's substitute $(0, 0)$ into the left-hand side of the equation in choice A:
$$(0 - 3\sqrt{2})^2 + (0 + 3\sqrt{2})^2 = (-3\sqrt{2})^2 + (3\sqrt{2})^2 = (-3)^2(\sqrt{2})^2 + 3^2(\sqrt{2})^2 = 9 \cdot 2 + 9 \cdot 2 = 18 + 18 = 36$$

10.
* Solution by completing the square: We complete the square twice on the left-hand side.
$$x^2 - 4x + 4 + y^2 + 6y + 9 = -9 + 4 + 9$$
$$(x - 2)^2 + (y + 3)^2 = 4$$

So, the radius of the circle is **2**.

LESSON 45 – HEART OF ALGEBRA
ADDITIONAL PRACTICE 3

Full solutions to these problems are available for free download here:
www.SATPrepGet800.com/48SATy5

LEVEL 1

$$a - \frac{1}{3}b + \frac{1}{6}c = 7$$

1. If $a = 1$ and $b = 3$ in the equation above, what is the value of c ?

$$C = 49.99 + 0.25t$$

3. The equation above models the total cost C, in dollars, to purchase a prepaid cell phone and send t texts. The total cost consists of a flat fee to buy the phone plus a charge for each text. When the equation is graphed in the xy-plane, what does the y-intercept of the graph represent in the model?

   A) A charge per text of $0.25
   B) A charge per text of $49.99
   C) A $0.25 fee to purchase the phone
   D) A $49.99 fee to purchase the phone

LEVEL 2

2. A line in the xy-plane passes through the origin and has a slope of $\frac{1}{5}$. Which of the following points lies on the line?

   A) $(10, 2)$
   B) $(5, 5)$
   C) $(1, 5)$
   D) $(0, 5)$

LEVEL 3

$$y = 3x + 5$$
$$x + 3y = 11$$

4. The system of equations above consists of two equations, and the graph of each equation in the xy-plane is a line. Which of the following statements is true about these two lines?

   A) The lines are the same.
   B) The lines are parallel, but distinct.
   C) The lines are perpendicular.
   D) The lines have the same y-intercept.

5. Tickets for a concert cost $4.50 for children and $12.00 for adults. 4460 concert tickets were sold for a total cost of $29,220. Solving which of the following systems of equations yields the number of children, c, and number of adults, a, that purchased concert tickets?

A) $c + a = 4460$
$4.50c + 12a = 58,440$

B) $c + a = 4460$
$4.50c + 12a = 29,220$

C) $c + a = 4460$
$4.50c + 12a = 14,610$

D) $c + a = 29,220$
$4.50c + 12a = 4460$

6. If $45 - 6x$ is 8 less than 13, what is the value of $4x$?

$$3(x - 2) = y$$
$$\frac{y}{x} = 5$$

7. If (x, y) is the solution to the system of equations above, what is the value of xy?

LEVEL 4

8. Jonathon purchases a car worth $28,800. The car depreciates at a constant rate for 16 years, after which the car is worth $2200. How much is the car worth 6 years after Jonathon makes the purchase?

A) $15,500
B) $18,825
C) $22,150
D) $25,475

302

9. Line k is the graph of the equation $y = -\frac{1}{3}x + 1$, and line m intersects line k at the point $(-1, \frac{4}{3})$. Which of the following could be an equation of line m?

A) $y = 3x - 5$
B) $y + 3x = 7$
C) $x = 7 - 6y$
D) $2y = x + 3$

10. A retailer ships phones and tablets. Each phone weighs 2 pounds, and each tablet weighs 7 pounds. A shipment of 83 units weighing a total of 301 pounds is sent out to a university. How many phones are in the shipment?

11. In the xy-plane, the equations $10x - 6y = k$ and $5x - 3y = 7$ represent the same line for some constant k. What is the value of k?

LEVEL 5

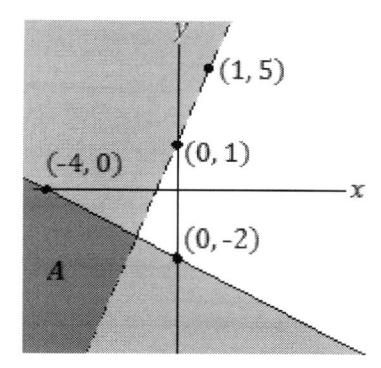

12. The shaded region labeled A in the xy-plane above is the solution to a system of inequalities. Which of the following ordered pairs satisfies the system of inequalities?

A) $(0, 1)$
B) $(-2, -7)$
C) $(-3, -4)$
D) $(-5, 1)$

Answers

1. 42 2. A 3. D 4. C 5. B 6. 80/3, 26.6, 26.7 7. 45 8. B 9. C 10. 56 11. 14 12. C

LESSON 46 – PASSPORT TO ADVANCED MATH
ADDITIONAL PRACTICE 3

Full solutions to these problems are available for free download here:
www.SATPrepGet800.com/48SATy5

LEVEL 1

1. For the function $f(x) = 3x^2 - 2x + 1$, what is the value of $f(-7)$?

LEVEL 2

$$5x^2 - 6x - 4$$
$$8x^2 - 2x + 11$$

2. If the sum of the two polynomials given above is written in the form $ax^2 + bx + c$, then $a + b + c =$

$$|7 - x| = 3$$

3. The value of one solution to the above equation is 4. What is the value of the other solution?

LEVEL 3

x	$p(x)$
-5	2
-2	-3
1	1
5	0

4. The function p is defined by a polynomial. Some values of x and $p(x)$ are shown in the table above. Which of the following must be a factor of $p(x)$?

   A) $x - 5$
   B) $x - 2$
   C) $x - 1$
   D) $x + 5$

5. What are the solutions to the equation $7x^2 - 567 = 0$?

   A) $-\sqrt{567}$ and $\sqrt{567}$
   B) $-\frac{\sqrt{567}}{5}$ and $\frac{\sqrt{567}}{7}$
   C) -81 and 81
   D) -9 and 9

LEVEL 4

6. In the xy-plane, the graph of the function f has x-intercepts at $-5, -3, 0, 1,$ and 2. Which of the following could define f ?

   A) $x(x-5)(x-3)(x+1)(x+2)$
   B) $x(x-1)(x-2)(x-3)(x-5)$
   C) $x^2(x+5)(x+3)(x+1)^2(x+2)$
   D) $x(x-1)^2(x-2)(x+3)^3(x+5)$

$$abc + bcd = ab + ad$$

7. In the equation above, $a \neq bc$. Which of the following is equivalent to d ?

   A) 1
   B) $\frac{1-c}{c}$
   C) $-1 + \frac{1}{c}$
   D) $\frac{ab(1-c)}{bc-a}$

8. Which of the following is equivalent to $\frac{(x^{10}+x^9+x^8)(y^5+y^4)}{y^4(x^2+x+1)}$?

   A) $x^8 y$
   B) $x^8(y+1)$
   C) $x^{24} y^5$
   D) $(x^8 + x^7 + x^6)(y+1)$

LEVEL 5

9. If $x - 4$ is a factor of $ax^2 - a^2 x - 12$, where a is a positive constant, what are the possible values of a ?

   A) 1 only
   B) 3 only
   C) 1 and 3 only
   D) 1, 3, and 4

10. The function g is defined by the equation $g(x) = 3^x + 2$. Which of the following could be the graph of $y = g(-x)$ in the xy-plane?

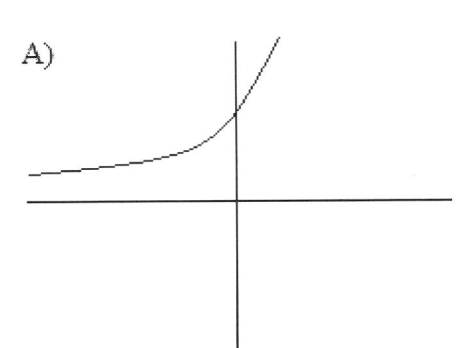

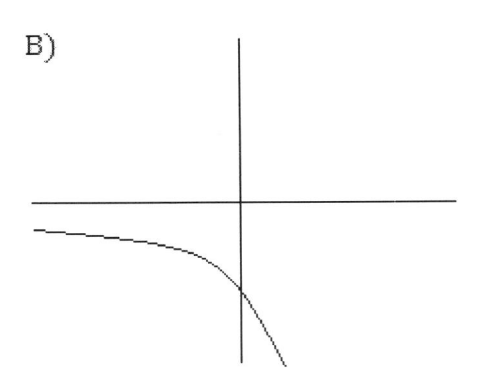

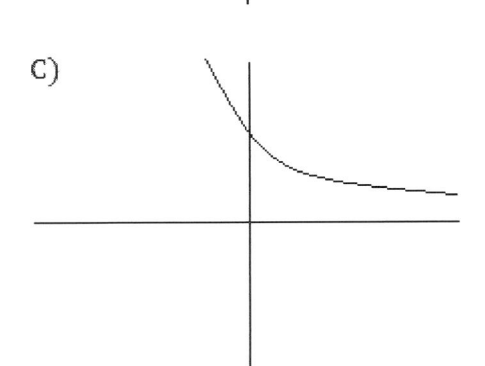

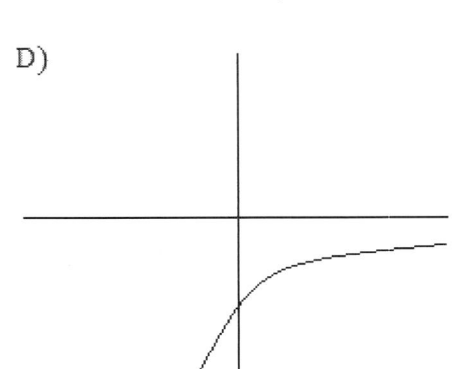

A)

B)

C)

D)

$$3x^2 + 2y^2 = 550$$
$$2x + 12y = 0$$

11. If (x, y) is a solution to the system of equations above, what is the value of y^2?

$$y = p(x - 4)(x + 2)$$

12. In the quadratic equation above, p is a nonzero constant. The graph of the equation in the xy-plane is a parabola with vertex (h, k). What is the value of $h - \frac{k}{p}$?

Answers

1. 162 2. 12 3. 10 4. A 5. D 6. D 7. D 8. B 9. C 10. C 11. 5 12. 10

LESSON 47 – PROBLEM SOLVING
ADDITIONAL PRACTICE 3

Full solutions to these problems are available for free download here:
www.SATPrepGet800.com/48SATy5

LEVEL 1

1. * An air pump is used to fill at least 60 tires per hour and at most 85 tires per hour. What is a possible amount of time, in hours, that it could have taken to fill 427 tires?

LEVEL 2

2. A tree is growing at a rate of approximately 1.6 feet every six months. According to this estimate, how long will it take, in <u>years</u>, for the tree's height to increase by 8 feet?

LEVEL 3

Questions 3 - 4 refer to the following information.

	Salary Range				Total
	Less than $80,000	$80,000 –$199,999	$200,000 –$460,000	Greater than $460,000	
Male	5	82	57	15	159
Female	3	76	74	18	171
Total	8	158	131	33	330

A group of lawyers responded to a survey that asked what their annual salary was. The survey data were broken down as shown in the table above.

3. *According to the table, which of the following categories accounts for approximately 17 percent of all the survey respondents?

   A) Females making less than $80,000
   B) Females making between $80,000 and $199,999
   C) Females making greater than $460,000
   D) Males making between $200,000 and $460,000

4. * If a lawyer is selected at random, which of the following is the probability that this lawyer will be a male making between $80,000 and $199,999 to the nearest tenth?

   A) 0.2
   B) 0.3
   C) 0.4
   D) 0.5

Questions 5 – 6 refer to the following information.

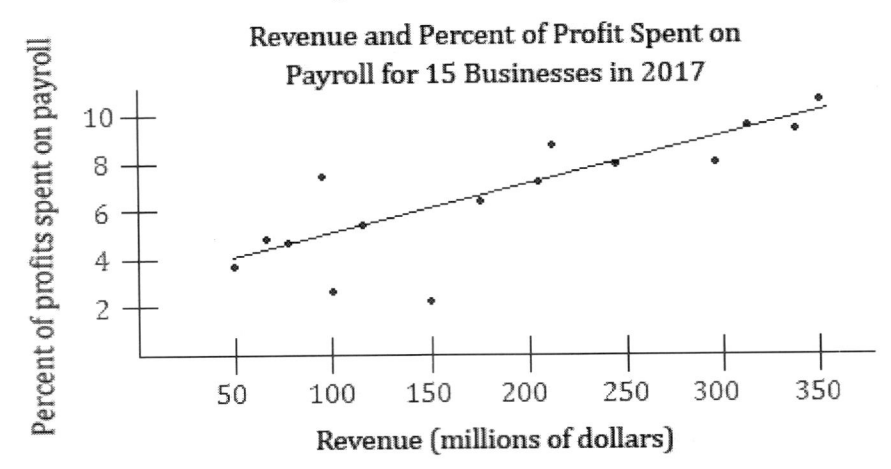

Revenue and Percent of Profit Spent on Payroll for 15 Businesses in 2017

The scatterplot above shows data for fifteen businesses along with the line of best fit.

5. For the business with the lowest percent of profit spent on payroll, which of the following is closest to the difference between the actual percent and the percent predicted by the line of best fit?

   A) 0.5%
   B) 2%
   C) 4%
   D) 8%

6. According to the line of best fit, which of the following is closest to the predicted increase in the percent of profits spent on payroll, for each million dollar increase in revenue?

   A) 0.01
   B) 0.02
   C) 1
   D) 2

LEVEL 4

Percent of Students at Six Universities Who Plan to Apply to a PhD Program

University	Percent of students
University 1	37.2%
University 2	24.6%
University 3	11.1%
University 4	15.6%
University 5	33.4%
University 6	28.6%

7. Students from 30 universities were asked if they planned to apply to a PhD program. The results from 6 of the universities are shown in the table above. The median percent of students planning to apply to a PhD program for all 30 universities was 23.9%. What is the positive difference between the median percent of students planning to apply to a PhD program for all 30 universities and the median percent of students planning to apply to a PhD program for the 6 universities shown in the table?

   A) 0.7%
   B) 2.7%
   C) 4.7%
   D) 10.55%

8. For a school project, a student questioned 300 people at random from a group of cat owners. The 300 people were asked if they liked dogs. Of those questioned, 98% said they liked dogs. Which of the following inferences can appropriately be drawn from this result?

   A) At least 98% of people who have pets like dogs.
   B) At least 98% of people who like cats also like dogs.
   C) Most people who do not have cats dislike dogs.
   D) Most people who have cats like dogs.

9. A radioactive substance decays at an annual rate of 11 percent. If the initial amount of the substance is 416 grams, which of the following functions h models the remaining amount of the substance, in grams, t years later?

   A) $h(t) = 0.89(416)^t$
   B) $h(t) = 0.92(416)^t$
   C) $h(t) = 416(0.11)^t$
   D) $h(t) = 416(0.89)^t$

LEVEL 5

Year	Paperbacks sold
2012	1349
2013	4370

10. * The publisher *Get 800* reported paperback book sales as shown in the table above. The percent increase in sales from 2012 to 2013 was approximately triple the percent increase in sales from 2013 to 2014. Which of the following most closely estimates the number of paperback books sold by *Get 800* in 2014?

    A) 6880
    B) 7100
    C) 7420
    D) 7630

$$E = 12(1.01)^t$$

11. The equation above models the number of employees, E, working at a company t years from when the company began hiring. Of the following, which equation most closely models the number of employees at the company m months after the company began hiring?

    A) $E = 12(1.01)^{12m}$
    B) $E = 12(1.01)^{\frac{m}{12}}$
    C) $E = 12(1.003)^m$
    D) $E = 12(1.0008)^{12m}$

12. How many quarts of a 40% saline solution must be added to 5 quarts of a 25% saline solution to arrive at a 30% saline solution?

Answers

1. $5.03 \leq t \leq 7.11$ 2. 2.5, 5/2 3. D 4. A 5. C 6. B 7. B 8. D 9. D 10. D 11. B
12. 2.5, 5/2

LESSON 48 – GEOMETRY AND COMPLEX NUMBERS
ADDITIONAL PRACTICE 3

Full solutions to these problems are available for free download here:
www.SATPrepGet800.com/48SATy5

LEVEL 1

1. What is the sum of the complex numbers $1 + 2i$ and $3 + 4i$, where $i = \sqrt{-1}$?

   A) 10
   B) $10i$
   C) $3 + 8i$
   D) $4 + 6i$

2. A square has an area of 49 square inches. Which of the following is equal to the perimeter of the square, in inches?

   A) 28
   B) 21
   C) 14
   D) 7

LEVEL 2

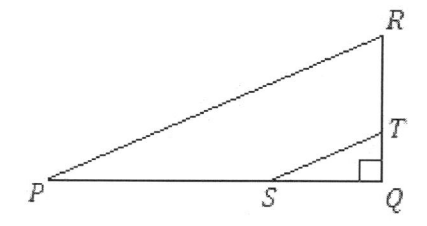

3. In the figure above, $\overline{ST} \parallel \overline{PR}$, $PQ = 8$, and $PR = 10$. What is the ratio of the length of segment SQ to the length of segment ST?

   A) 1:3
   B) 2:3
   C) 2:5
   D) 4:5

LEVEL 3

4. A circle with radius $\sqrt{3}$ and center at $(2, -8)$ is graphed in the xy-plane. Which of the following could be an equation of the circle?

   A) $(x + 2)^2 + (y - 8)^2 = \sqrt{3}$
   B) $(x + 2)^2 - (y - 8)^2 = \sqrt{3}$
   C) $(x - 2)^2 + (y + 8)^2 = 3$
   D) $(x - 2)^2 + (y + 8)^2 = 9$

5. In right triangle ABC, $m\angle B = 90°$ and $\sin C = \frac{4}{7}$. What is $\cos A$?

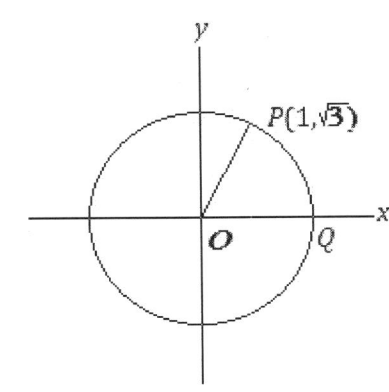

LEVEL 4

6. An ice cube with a side of length 2 centimeters has a density of approximately 0.92 grams per cubic centimeter. Given that density is defined as mass per unit volume, what is the mass of the ice cube, to the nearest tenth of a gram?

   A) 0.7
   B) 5.5
   C) 7.4
   D) 55

7. In the xy-plane above, O is the center of the circle, and the measure of $\angle POQ$ is $\frac{3\pi}{2a}$ radians. What is the value of a?

$$\frac{7-i}{6-2i}$$

8. If the expression above is written in the form $a + bi$, where a and b are real numbers, and $i = \sqrt{-1}$, what is the value of b?

LEVEL 5

9. * In right triangle ABC, $m\angle B = 30°$ and hypotenuse BC has length 10. What is the perimeter of the triangle to the nearest tenth?

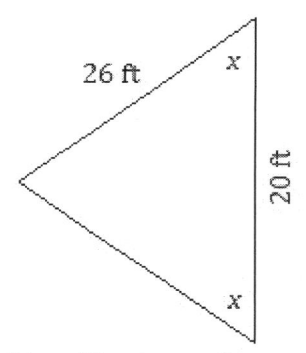

10. * A homeowner drew a sketch of their triangle-shaped garden as shown above. Although the sketch was not drawn accurately to scale, the triangle was labeled with the proper dimensions. What is the value of $\tan x$?

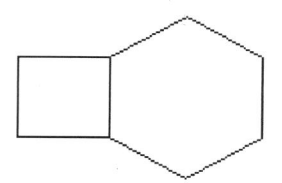

Note: Figure not drawn to scale.

11. The figure above shows a regular hexagon and a square sharing a common side. If the area of the hexagon is $54\sqrt{3}$ square centimeters, what is the perimeter, in square centimeters, of the square?

$$x^2 + y^2 - x + 3y - 5 = 0$$

12. * The equation of a circle in the xy-plane is shown above. What is the <u>diameter</u> of the circle, to the nearest tenth?

Answers

1. D 2. A 3. D 4. C 5. 4/7, .571 6. C 7. 9/2, 4.5 8. 1/5, .2 9. 23.7 10. 12/5, 2.4
11. 24 12. 5.5

313

ACTIONS TO COMPLETE AFTER YOU HAVE READ THIS BOOK

1. Take another practice SAT
You should see a substantial improvement in your score.

2. Continue to practice SAT math problems for 10 to 20 minutes each day
You may want to purchase *500 SAT Math Problems arranged by Topic and Difficulty Level* for additional practice problems.

3. 'Like' my Facebook page
This page is updated regularly with SAT prep advice, tips, tricks, strategies, and practice problems. Visit the following webpage and click the 'like' button.

www.facebook.com/SATPrepGet800

4. Review this book
If this book helped you, please post your positive feedback on the site you purchased it from; e.g. Amazon, Barnes and Noble, etc.

5. Claim your FREE bonuses
If you have not done so yet, visit the following webpage and enter your email address to receive solutions to all the supplemental problems in this book and other materials.

www.SATPrepGet800.com/48SATy5

About the Author

Dr. Steve Warner, a New York native, earned his Ph.D. at Rutgers University in Pure Mathematics in May 2001. While a graduate student, Dr. Warner won the TA Teaching Excellence Award.

After Rutgers, Dr. Warner joined the Penn State Mathematics Department as an Assistant Professor. In September 2002, Dr. Warner returned to New York to accept an Assistant Professor position at Hofstra University. By September 2007, Dr. Warner had received tenure and was promoted to Associate Professor. He has taught undergraduate and graduate courses in Precalculus, Calculus, Linear Algebra, Differential Equations, Mathematical Logic, Set Theory and Abstract Algebra.

Over that time, Dr. Warner participated in a five-year NSF grant, "The MSTP Project," to study and improve mathematics and science curriculum in poorly performing junior high schools. He also published several articles in scholarly journals, specifically on Mathematical Logic.

Dr. Warner has more than 15 years of experience in general math tutoring and tutoring for standardized tests such as the SAT, ACT and AP Calculus exams. He has tutored students both individually and in group settings.

In February 2010 Dr. Warner released his first SAT prep book "The 32 Most Effective SAT Math Strategies," and in 2012 founded Get 800 Test Prep. Since then Dr. Warner has written books for the SAT, ACT, SAT Math Subject Tests, AP Calculus exams, and GRE.

Dr. Steve Warner can be reached at

steve@SATPrepGet800.com

BOOKS BY DR. STEVE WARNER

www.Get800TestPrep.com

CONNECT WITH DR. STEVE WARNER

Made in the USA
Middletown, DE
28 July 2018